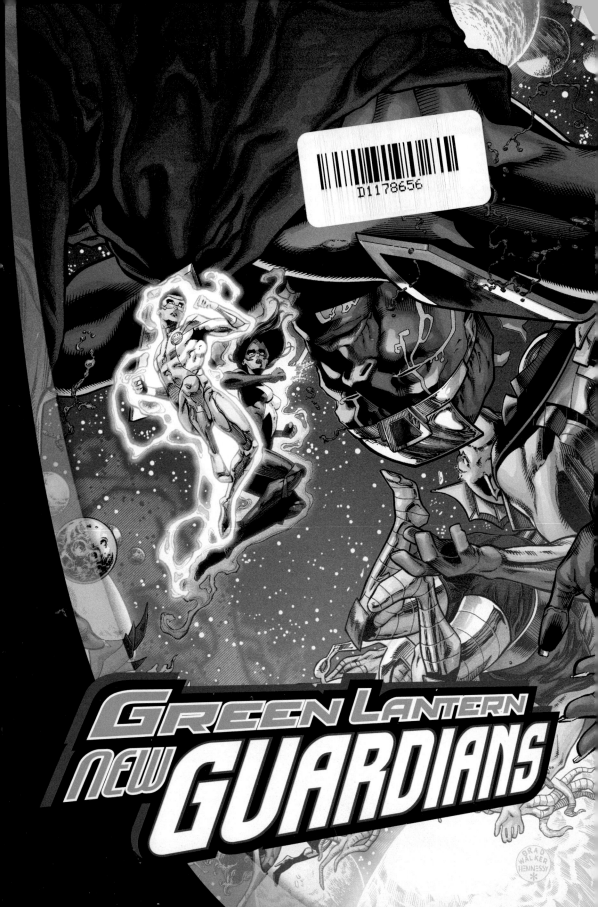

Green Lantern
NEW GUARDIANS

VOLUME 5   THE GODKILLERS

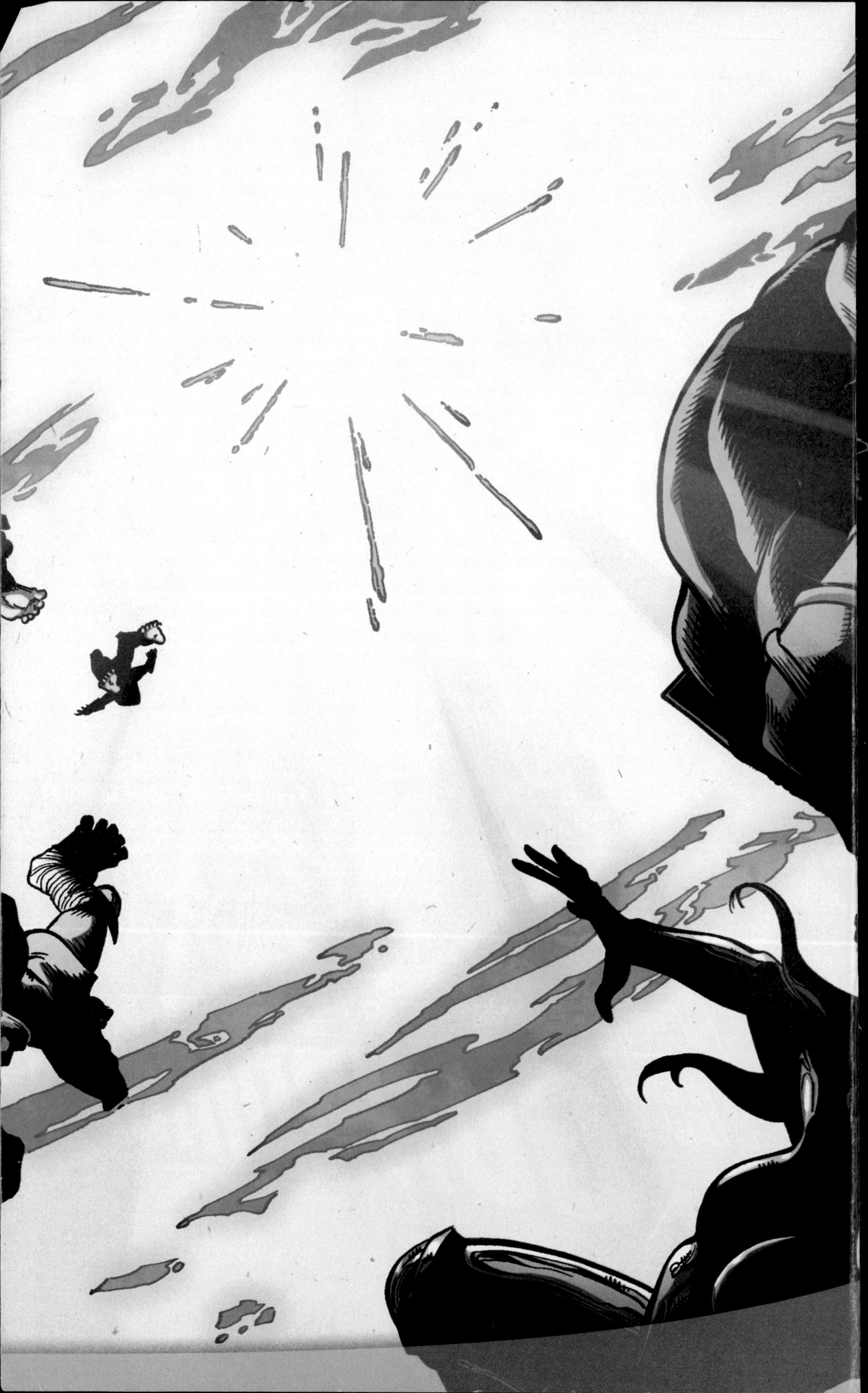

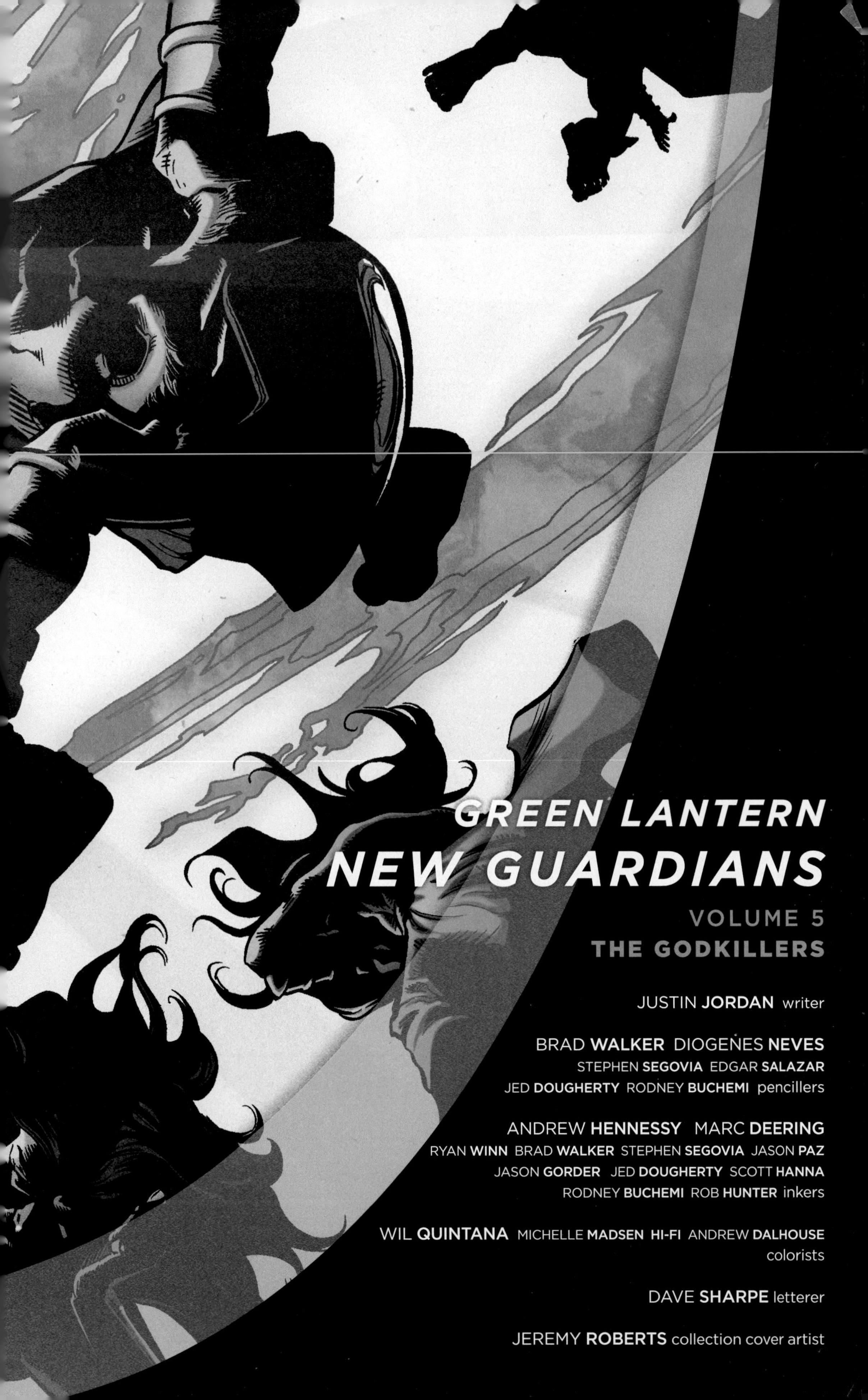

GREEN LANTERN NEW GUARDIANS

VOLUME 5

THE GODKILLERS

JUSTIN **JORDAN** writer

BRAD **WALKER** DIOGENES **NEVES**
STEPHEN **SEGOVIA** EDGAR **SALAZAR**
JED **DOUGHERTY** RODNEY **BUCHEMI** pencillers

ANDREW **HENNESSY** MARC **DEERING**
RYAN **WINN** BRAD **WALKER** STEPHEN **SEGOVIA** JASON **PAZ**
JASON **GORDER** JED **DOUGHERTY** SCOTT **HANNA**
RODNEY **BUCHEMI** ROB **HUNTER** inkers

WIL **QUINTANA** MICHELLE **MADSEN** **HI-FI** ANDREW **DALHOUSE**
colorists

DAVE **SHARPE** letterer

JEREMY **ROBERTS** collection cover artist

CHRIS CONROY DARREN SHAN Editors – Original Series LIZ ERICKSON Editor
ROBBIN BROSTERMAN Design Director – Books ROBBIE BIEDERMAN Publication Design

BOB HARRAS Senior VP – Editor-in-Chief, DC Comics

DIANE NELSON President DAN DIDIO and JIM LEE Co-Publishers GEOFF JOHNS Chief Creative Officer
AMIT DESAI Senior VP – Marketing and Franchise Management
AMY GENKINS Senior VP – Business and Legal Affairs NAIRI GARDINER Senior VP – Finance
JEFF BOISON VP – Publishing Planning MARK CHIARELLO VP – Art Direction and Design
JOHN CUNNINGHAM VP – Marketing TERRI CUNNINGHAM VP – Editorial Administration
LARRY GANEM VP – Talent Relations and Services ALISON GILL Senior VP – Manufacturing and Operations
HANK KANALZ Senior VP – Vertigo and Integrated Publishing JAY KOGAN VP – Business and Legal Affairs, Publishing
JACK MAHAN VP – Business Affairs, Talent NICK NAPOLITANO VP – Manufacturing Administration SUE POHJA VP – Book Sales
FRED RUIZ VP – Manufacturing Operations COURTNEY SIMMONS Senior VP – Publicity BOB WAYNE Senior VP – Sales

GREEN LANTERN – NEW GUARDIANS VOLUME 5: THE GODKILLERS

DC Comics, 1700 Broadway, New York, NY 10019
A Warner Bros. Entertainment Company.
Printed by RR Donnelley, Owensville, MO, USA. 1/16/15. First Printing.

ISBN: 978-1-4012-5088-1

SUSTAINABLE
FORESTRY
INITIATIVE

Certified Chain of Custody
20% Certified Forest Content,
80% Certified Sourcing
www.sfiprogram.org
SFI-01042
APPLIES TO TEXT STOCK ONLY

Library of Congress Cataloging-in-Publication Data

Jordan, Justin, author.
Green Lantern: New Guardians. Volume 5, Godkillers / Justin Jordan, Brad Walker.
pages cm — (The New 52!)
ISBN 978-1-4012-5088-1 (paperback)
1. Graphic novels. I. Walker, Brad (Comic book artist) illustrator. II. Title. III. Title: Gods and Monsters.
PN6728.G74J69 2014
741.5'973 — dc23
2014011631

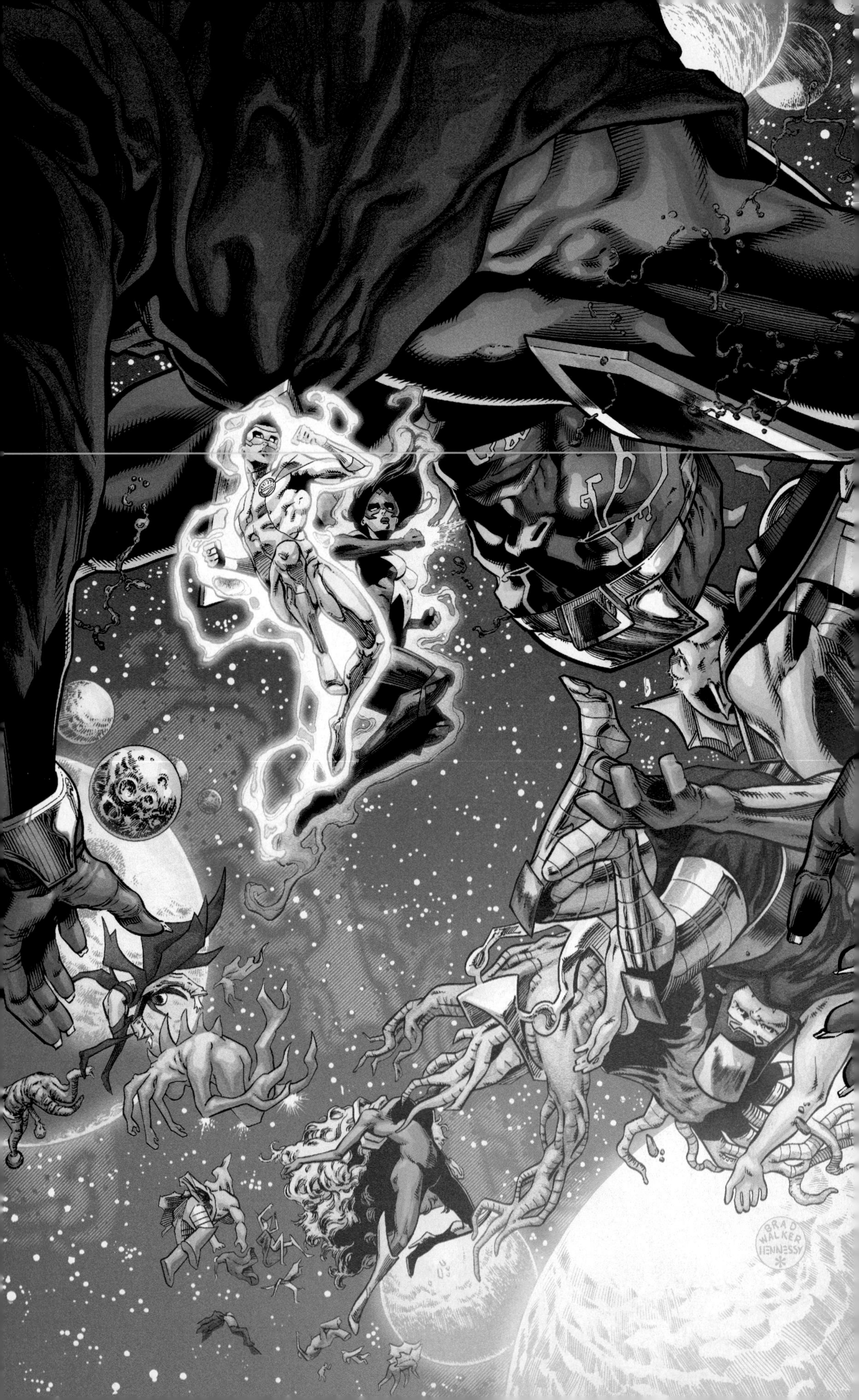
BRAD
WALKER
HENNESSY

LIGHT AND FIRE: THE GODKILLERS PART I

JUSTIN JORDAN writer **BRAD WALKER** penciller **ANDREW HENNESSY** with **RYAN WINN** inkers **WIL QUINTANA** colorist
DAVE SHARPE letterer cover art by **WALKER, HENNESSY** and **HI-FI** variant cover by **KLAUS JANSON** with **JOSE VILLARRUBIA**

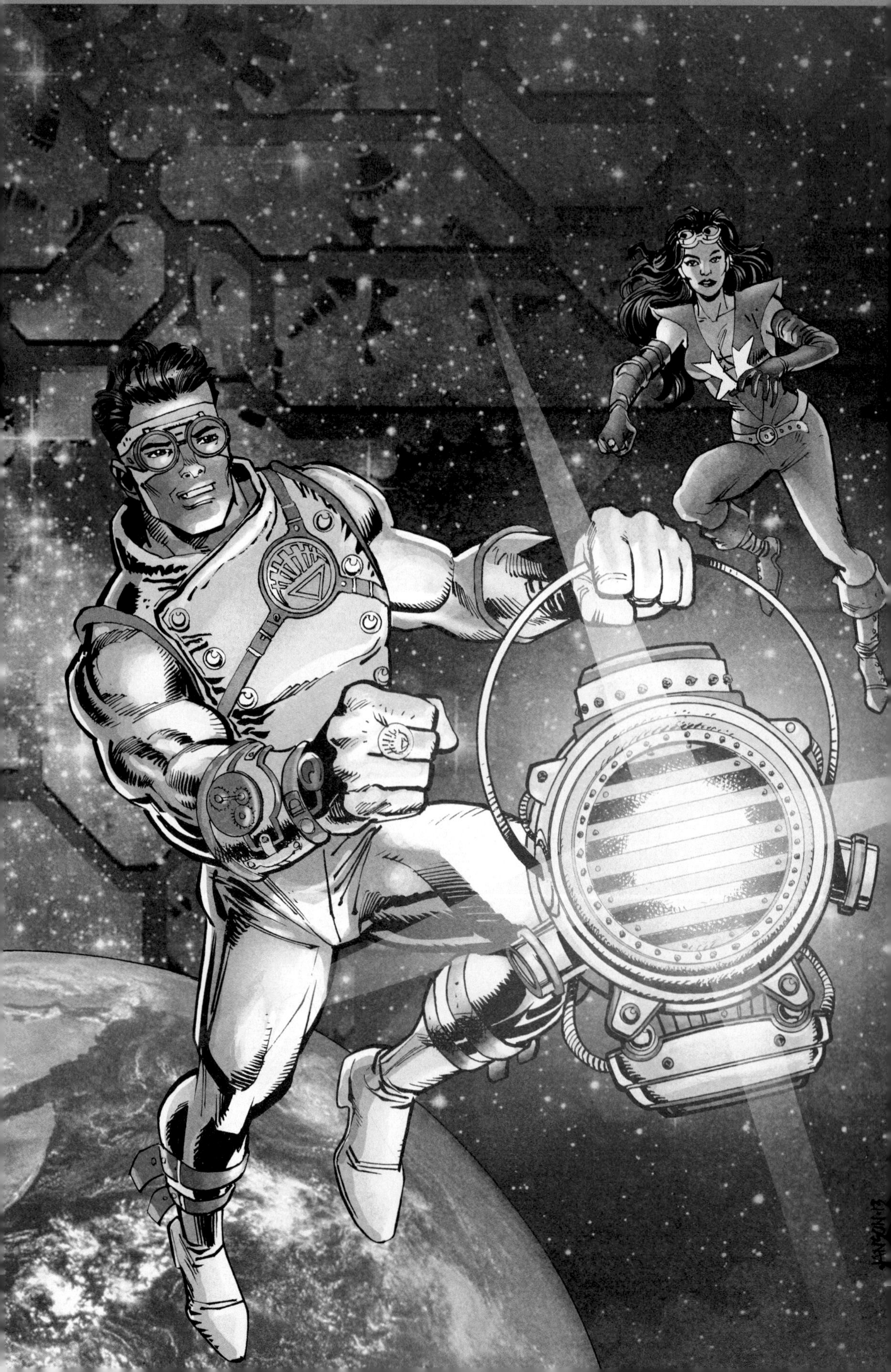

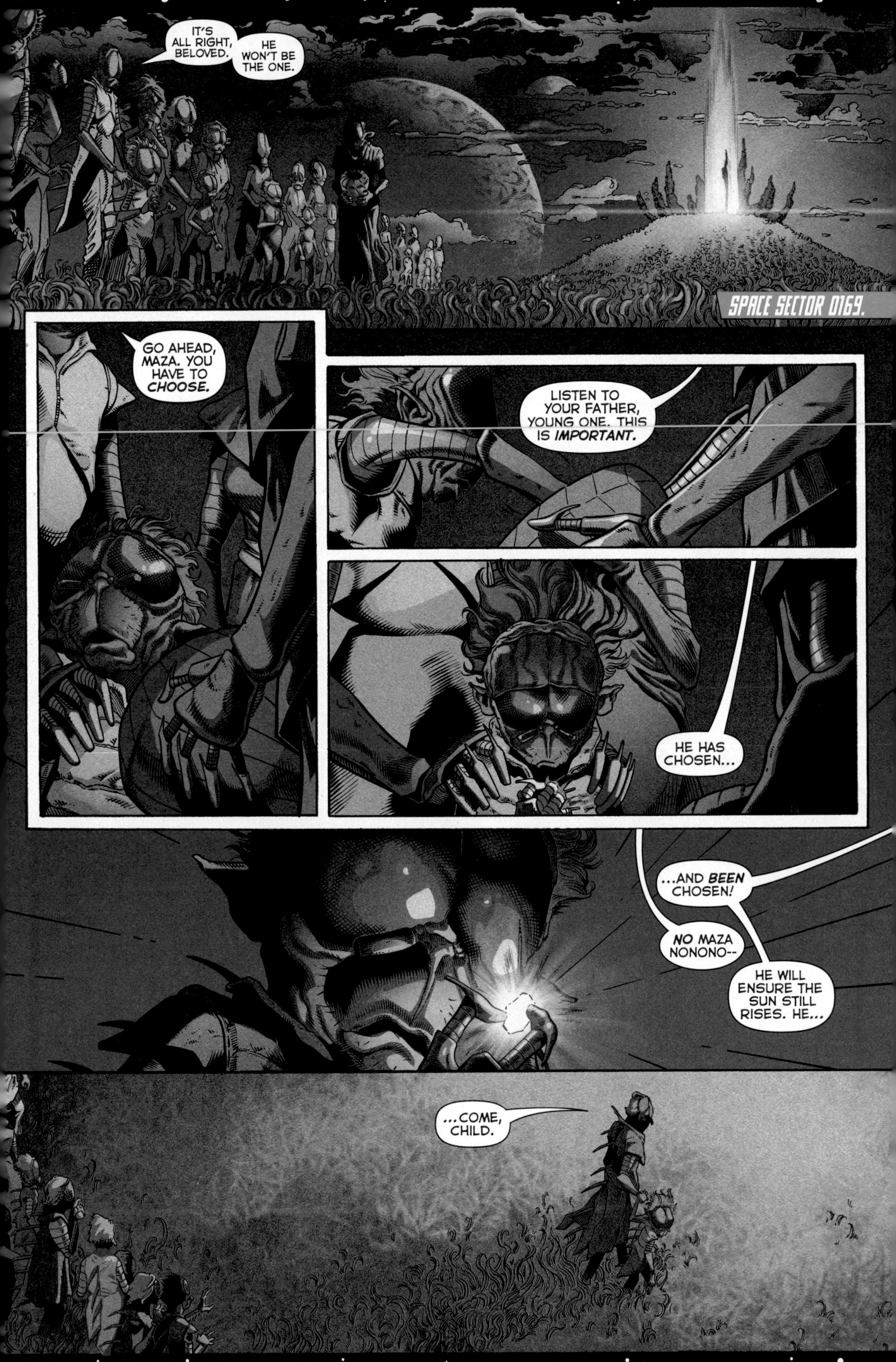
IT'S ALL RIGHT, BELOVED.
HE WON'T BE THE ONE.
SPACE SECTOR 0169.
GO AHEAD, MAZA. YOU HAVE TO CHOOSE.
LISTEN TO YOUR FATHER, YOUNG ONE. THIS IS IMPORTANT.
HE HAS CHOSEN...
...AND BEEN CHOSEN!
NO MAZA NONONO--
HE WILL ENSURE THE SUN STILL RISES. HE...
...COME, CHILD.

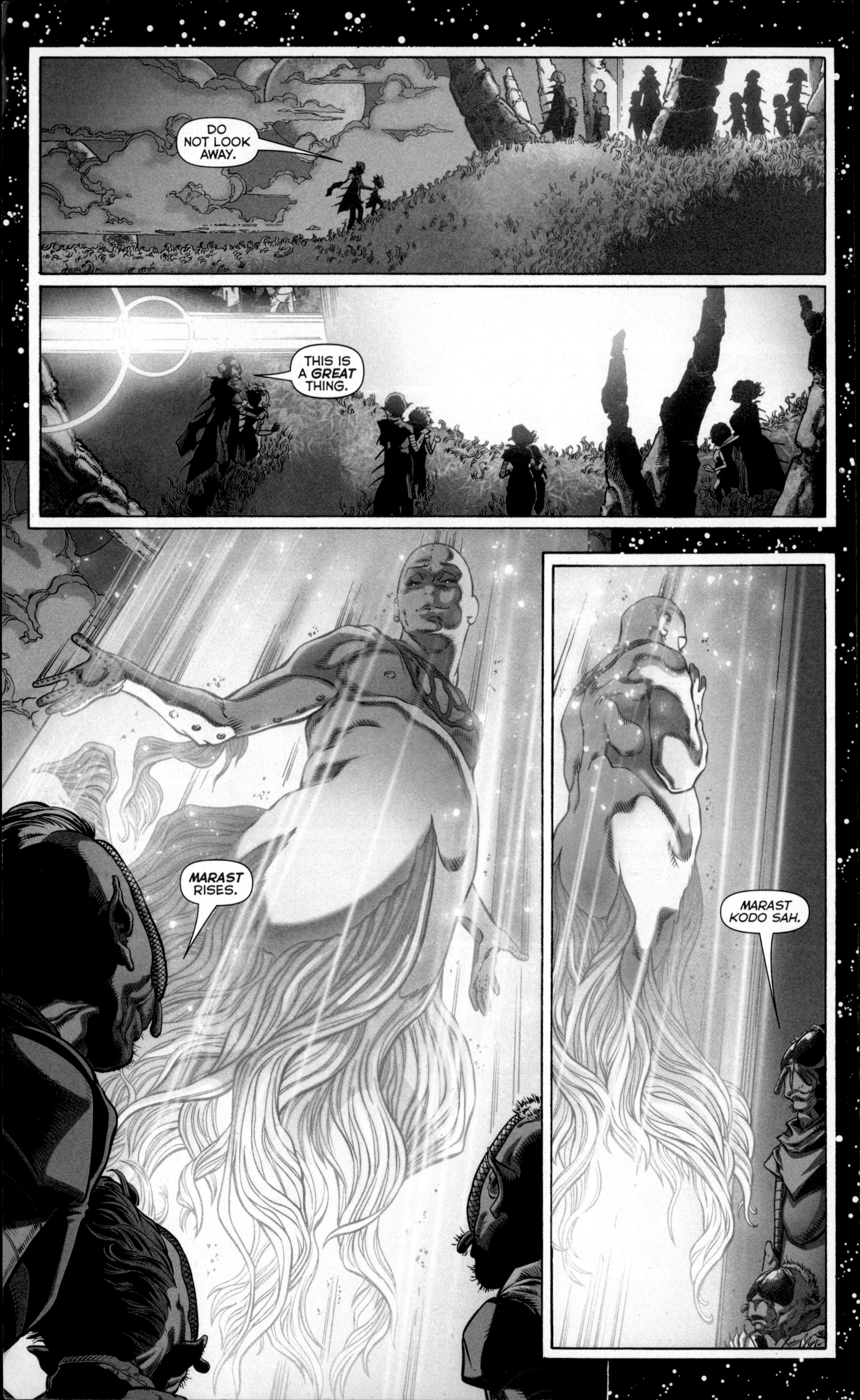
DO NOT LOOK AWAY.
THIS IS A *GREAT* THING.
MARAST RISES.
MARAST KODO SAH.

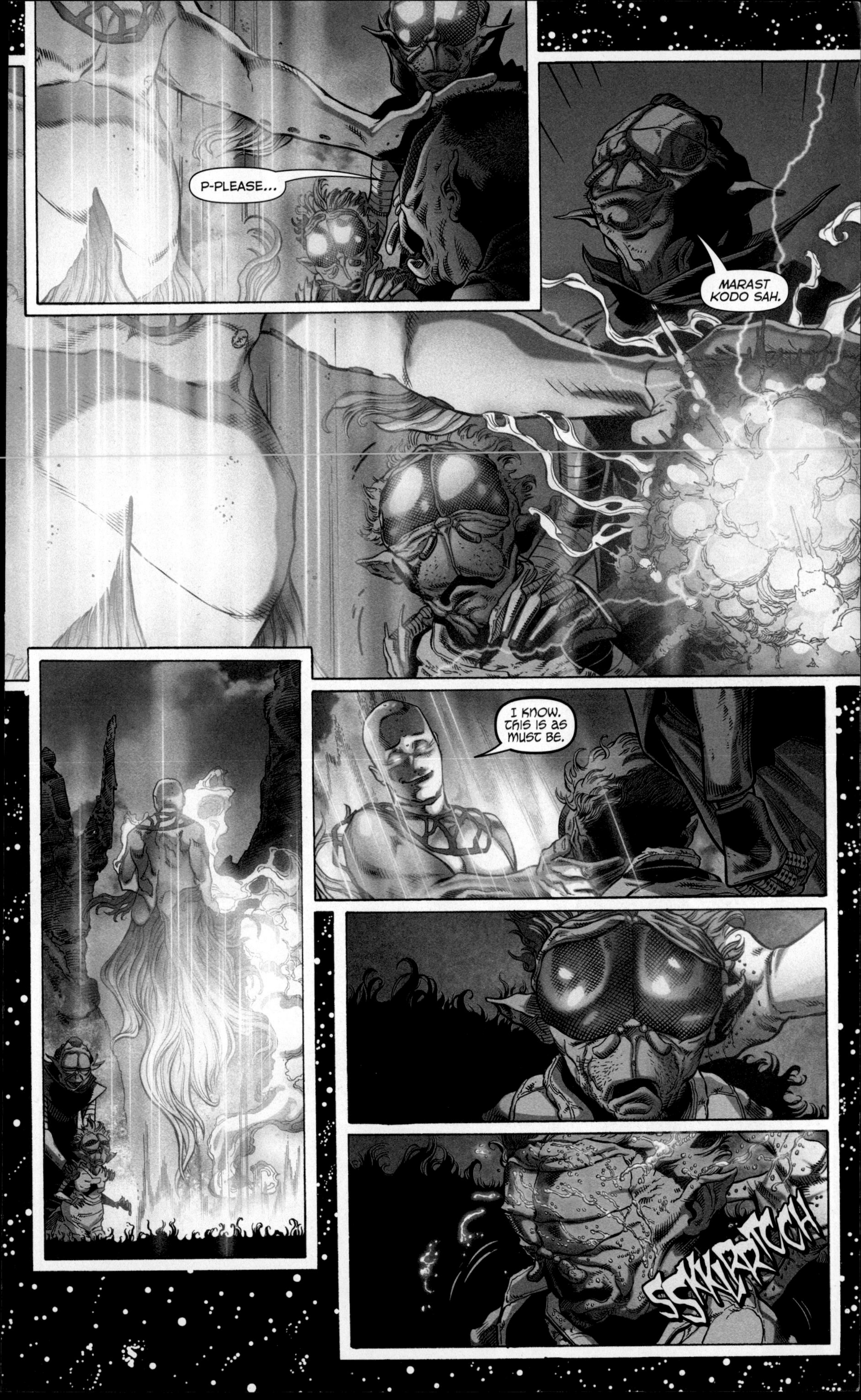
P-PLEASE...
MARAST KODO SAH.
I KNOW. THIS IS AS MUST BE.
SSKKRRTCH

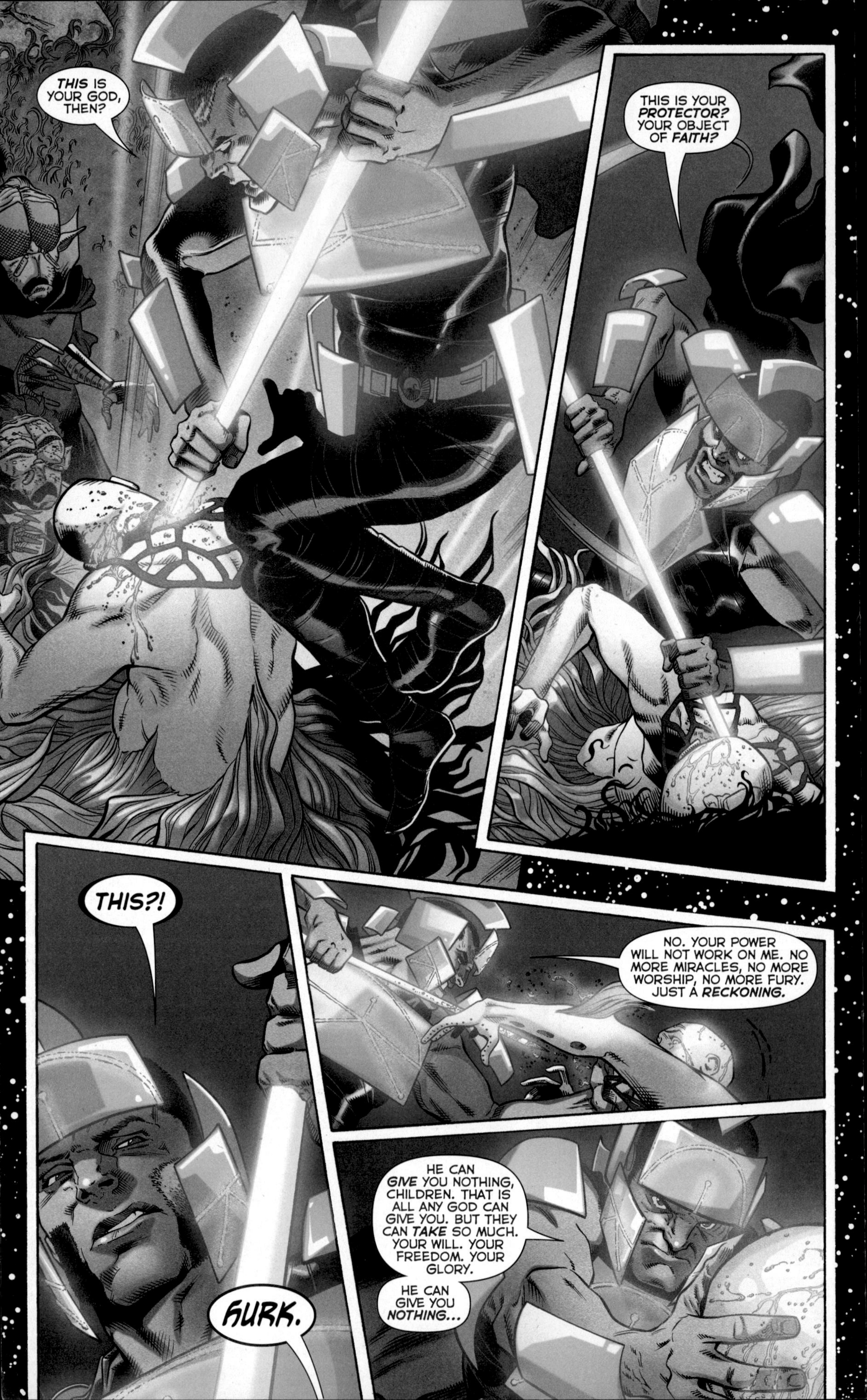
THIS IS YOUR GOD, THEN?
THIS IS YOUR PROTECTOR? YOUR OBJECT OF FAITH?
THIS?!
NO. YOUR POWER WILL NOT WORK ON ME. NO MORE MIRACLES, NO MORE WORSHIP, NO MORE FURY. JUST A RECKONING.
HE CAN GIVE YOU NOTHING, CHILDREN. THAT IS ALL ANY GOD CAN GIVE YOU. BUT THEY CAN TAKE SO MUCH. YOUR WILL. YOUR FREEDOM. YOUR GLORY.
HE CAN GIVE YOU NOTHING...
HURK.

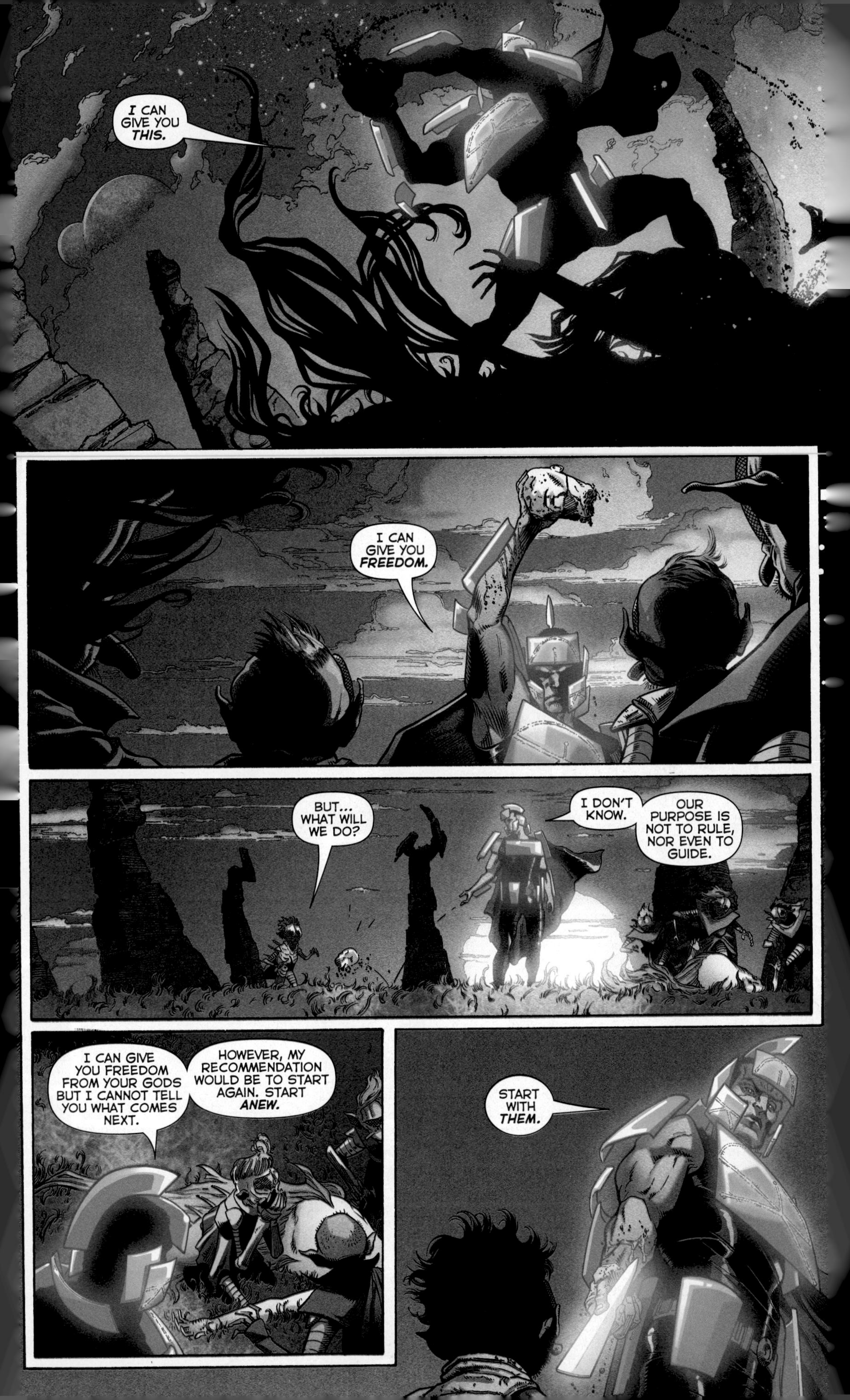
I CAN GIVE YOU *THIS.*
I CAN GIVE YOU *FREEDOM.*
BUT... WHAT WILL WE DO?
I DON'T KNOW.
OUR PURPOSE IS NOT TO RULE, NOR EVEN TO GUIDE.
I CAN GIVE YOU FREEDOM FROM YOUR GODS BUT I CANNOT TELL YOU WHAT COMES NEXT.
HOWEVER, MY RECOMMENDATION WOULD BE TO START AGAIN. START *ANEW.*
START WITH *THEM.*

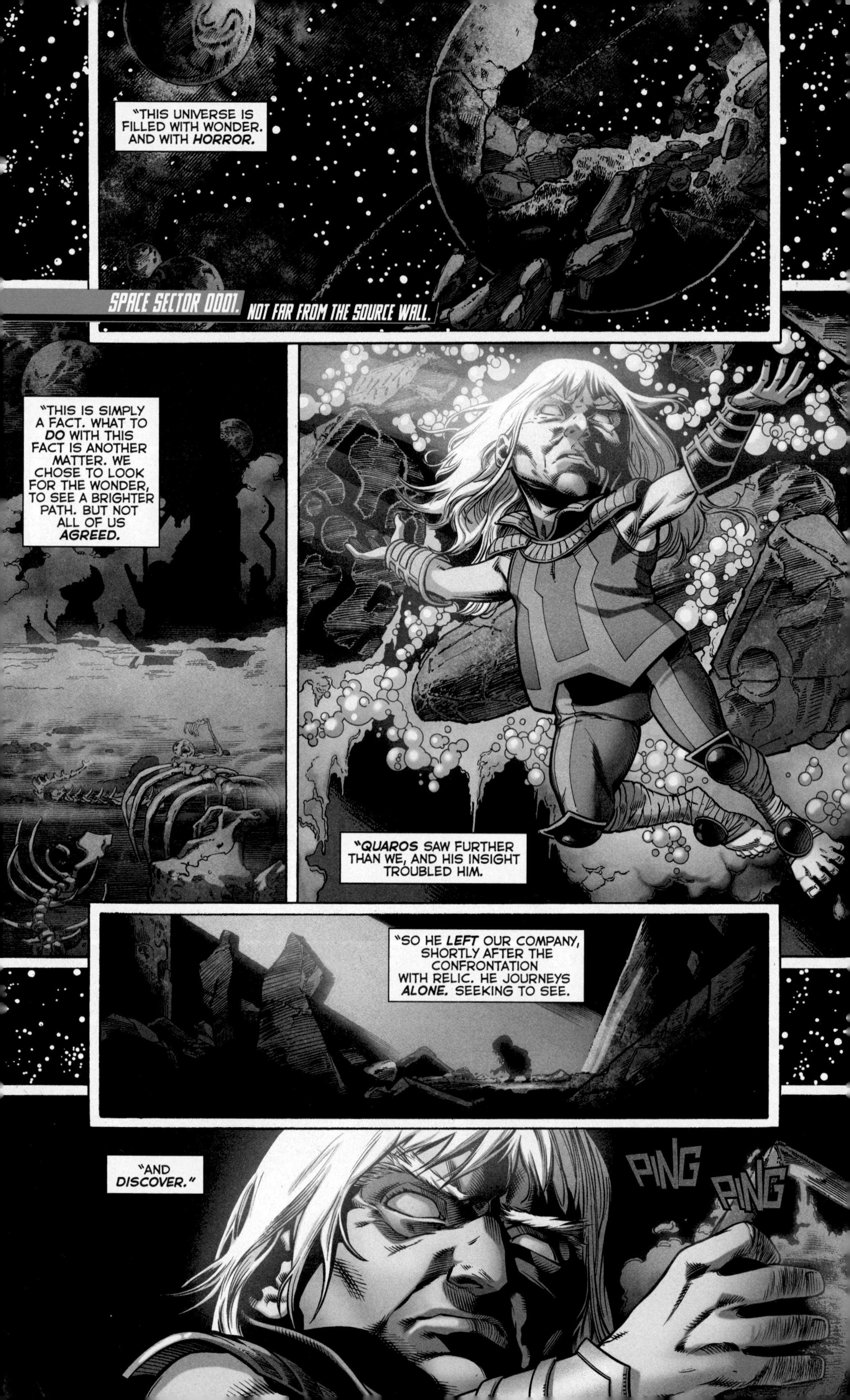
"THIS UNIVERSE IS FILLED WITH WONDER. AND WITH HORROR.
SPACE SECTOR 0001.
NOT FAR FROM THE SOURCE WALL.
"THIS IS SIMPLY A FACT. WHAT TO DO WITH THIS FACT IS ANOTHER MATTER. WE CHOSE TO LOOK FOR THE WONDER, TO SEE A BRIGHTER PATH. BUT NOT ALL OF US AGREED.
"QUAROS SAW FURTHER THAN WE, AND HIS INSIGHT TROUBLED HIM.
"SO HE LEFT OUR COMPANY, SHORTLY AFTER THE CONFRONTATION WITH RELIC. HE JOURNEYS ALONE. SEEKING TO SEE.
"AND DISCOVER."
PING
PING

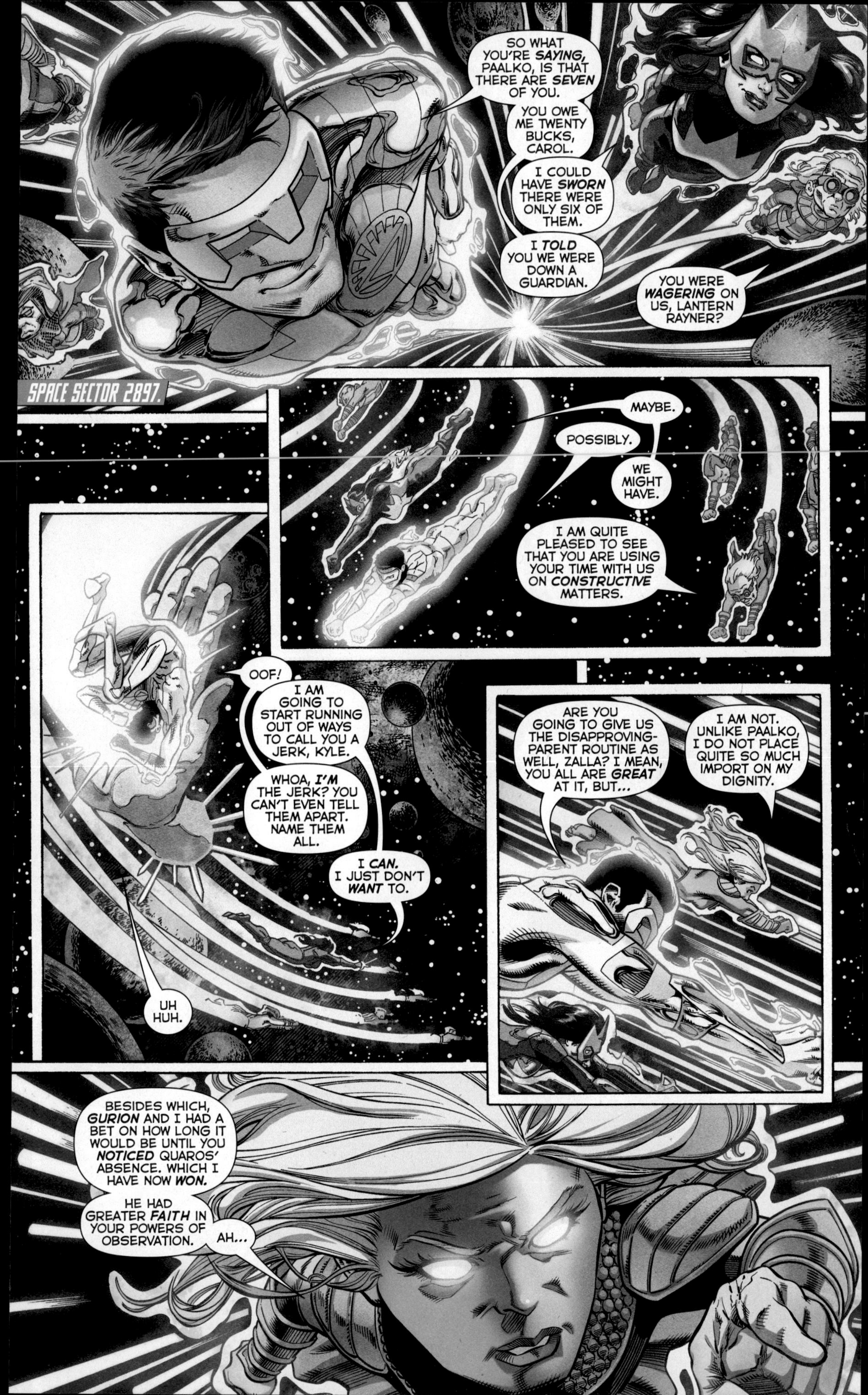
SO WHAT YOU'RE SAYING, PAALKO, IS THAT THERE ARE SEVEN OF YOU.
YOU OWE ME TWENTY BUCKS, CAROL.
I COULD HAVE SWORN THERE WERE ONLY SIX OF THEM.
I TOLD YOU WE WERE DOWN A GUARDIAN.
YOU WERE WAGERING ON US, LANTERN RAYNER?
SPACE SECTOR 2897.
MAYBE.
POSSIBLY.
WE MIGHT HAVE.
I AM QUITE PLEASED TO SEE THAT YOU ARE USING YOUR TIME WITH US ON CONSTRUCTIVE MATTERS.
OOF!
I AM GOING TO START RUNNING OUT OF WAYS TO CALL YOU A JERK, KYLE.
WHOA, I'M THE JERK? YOU CAN'T EVEN TELL THEM APART. NAME THEM ALL.
I CAN. I JUST DON'T WANT TO.
UH HUH.
ARE YOU GOING TO GIVE US THE DISAPPROVING-PARENT ROUTINE AS WELL, ZALLA? I MEAN, YOU ALL ARE GREAT AT IT, BUT...
I AM NOT. UNLIKE PAALKO, I DO NOT PLACE QUITE SO MUCH IMPORT ON MY DIGNITY.
BESIDES WHICH, GURION AND I HAD A BET ON HOW LONG IT WOULD BE UNTIL YOU NOTICED QUAROS' ABSENCE. WHICH I HAVE NOW WON.
HE HAD GREATER FAITH IN YOUR POWERS OF OBSERVATION.
AH...

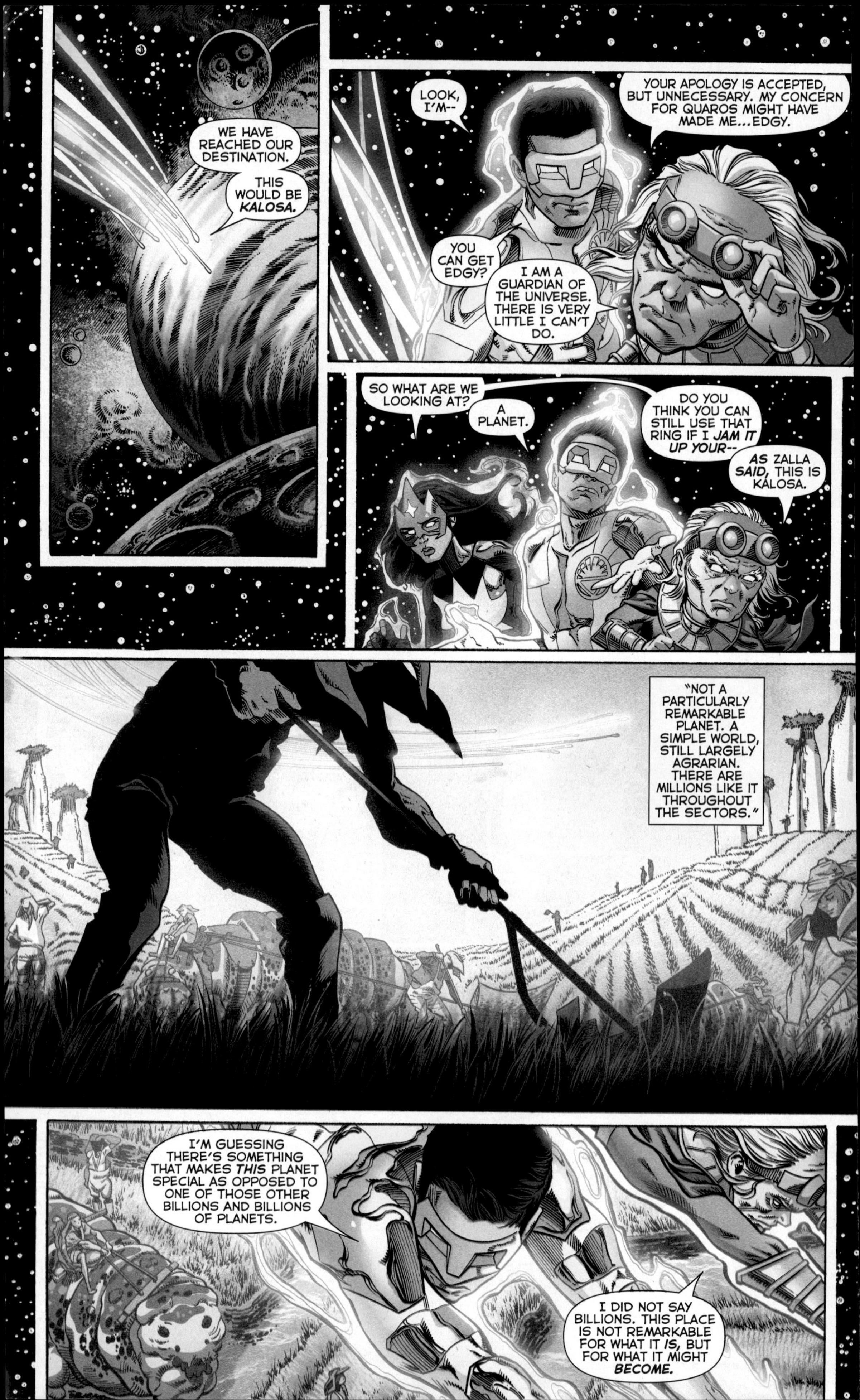

WE HAVE REACHED OUR DESTINATION.
THIS WOULD BE *KALOSA.*
LOOK, I'M--
YOUR APOLOGY IS ACCEPTED, BUT UNNECESSARY. MY CONCERN FOR QUAROS MIGHT HAVE MADE ME...EDGY.
YOU CAN GET EDGY?
I AM A GUARDIAN OF THE UNIVERSE. THERE IS VERY LITTLE I CAN'T DO.
SO WHAT ARE WE LOOKING AT?
A PLANET.
DO YOU THINK YOU CAN STILL USE THAT RING IF I *JAM IT UP YOUR--*
AS ZALLA *SAID,* THIS IS KALOSA.
"NOT A PARTICULARLY REMARKABLE PLANET. A SIMPLE WORLD, STILL LARGELY AGRARIAN. THERE ARE MILLIONS LIKE IT THROUGHOUT THE SECTORS."
I'M GUESSING THERE'S SOMETHING THAT MAKES *THIS* PLANET SPECIAL AS OPPOSED TO ONE OF THOSE OTHER BILLIONS AND BILLIONS OF PLANETS.
I DID NOT SAY BILLIONS. THIS PLACE IS NOT REMARKABLE FOR WHAT IT *IS,* BUT FOR WHAT IT MIGHT *BECOME.*

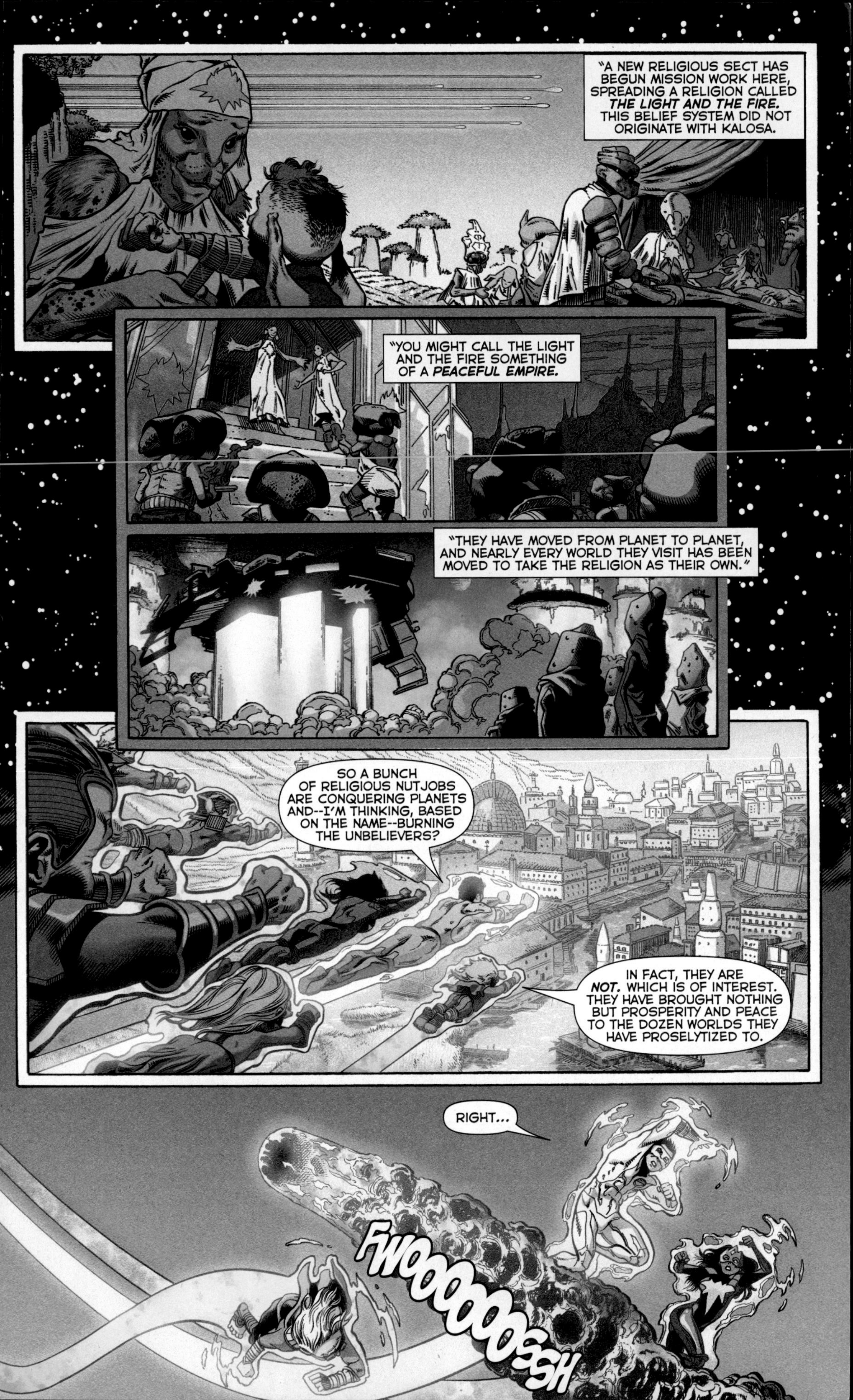
"A NEW RELIGIOUS SECT HAS BEGUN MISSION WORK HERE, SPREADING A RELIGION CALLED *THE LIGHT AND THE FIRE.* THIS BELIEF SYSTEM DID NOT ORIGINATE WITH KALOSA.
"YOU MIGHT CALL THE LIGHT AND THE FIRE SOMETHING OF A *PEACEFUL EMPIRE.*
"THEY HAVE MOVED FROM PLANET TO PLANET, AND NEARLY EVERY WORLD THEY VISIT HAS BEEN MOVED TO TAKE THE RELIGION AS THEIR OWN."
SO A BUNCH OF RELIGIOUS NUTJOBS ARE CONQUERING PLANETS AND--I'M THINKING, BASED ON THE NAME--BURNING THE UNBELIEVERS?
IN FACT, THEY ARE *NOT.* WHICH IS OF INTEREST. THEY HAVE BROUGHT NOTHING BUT PROSPERITY AND PEACE TO THE DOZEN WORLDS THEY HAVE PROSELYTIZED TO.
RIGHT...
FWOOOOOOOSSH

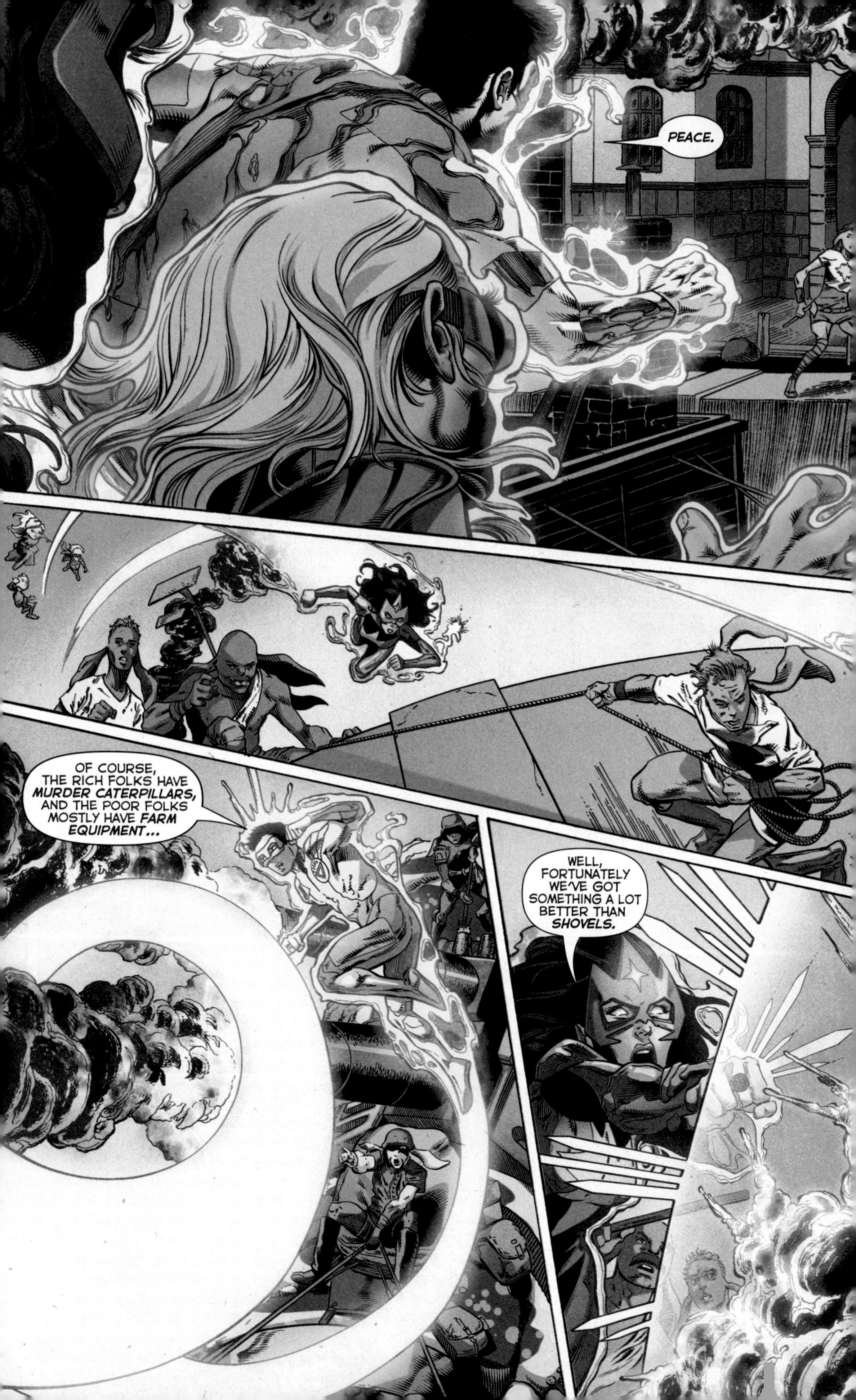
PEACE.
OF COURSE, THE RICH FOLKS HAVE MURDER CATERPILLARS, AND THE POOR FOLKS MOSTLY HAVE FARM EQUIPMENT...
WELL, FORTUNATELY WE'VE GOT SOMETHING A LOT BETTER THAN SHOVELS.

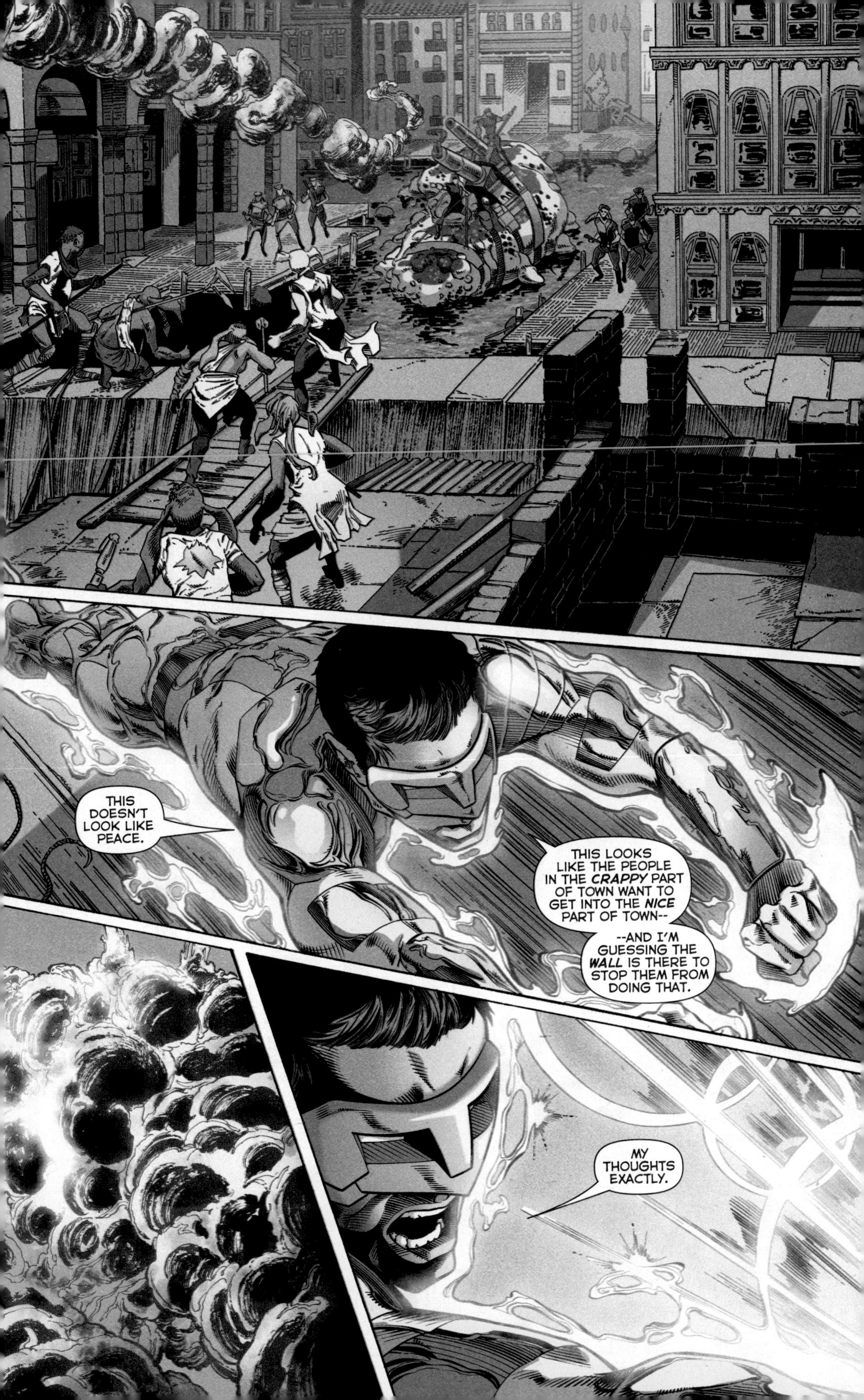
THIS DOESN'T LOOK LIKE PEACE.
THIS LOOKS LIKE THE PEOPLE IN THE CRAPPY PART OF TOWN WANT TO GET INTO THE NICE PART OF TOWN--
--AND I'M GUESSING THE WALL IS THERE TO STOP THEM FROM DOING THAT.
MY THOUGHTS EXACTLY.

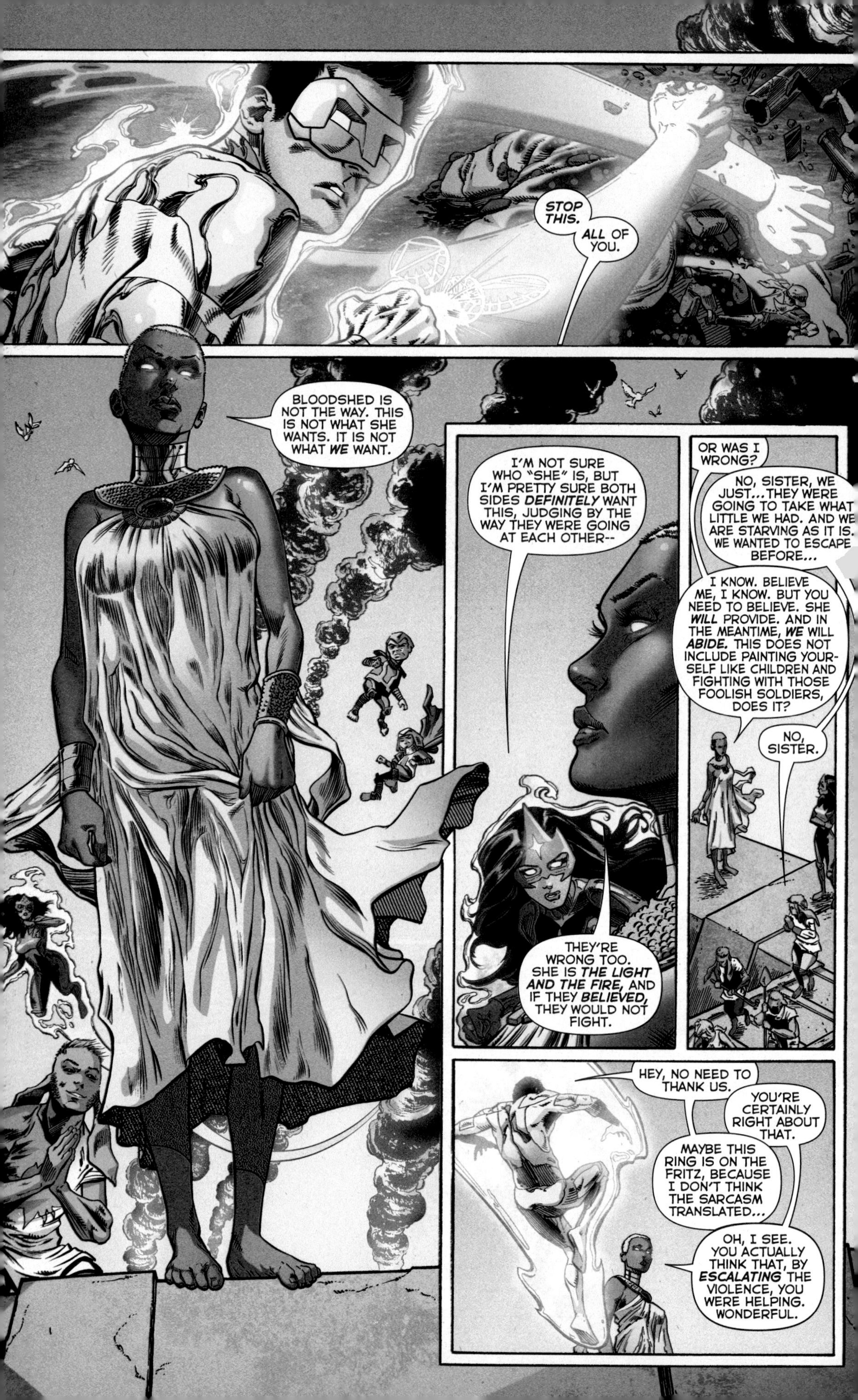
STOP THIS.
ALL OF YOU.
BLOODSHED IS NOT THE WAY. THIS IS NOT WHAT SHE WANTS. IT IS NOT WHAT WE WANT.
I'M NOT SURE WHO "SHE" IS, BUT I'M PRETTY SURE BOTH SIDES DEFINITELY WANT THIS, JUDGING BY THE WAY THEY WERE GOING AT EACH OTHER--
THEY'RE WRONG TOO. SHE IS THE LIGHT AND THE FIRE, AND IF THEY BELIEVED, THEY WOULD NOT FIGHT.
OR WAS I WRONG?
NO, SISTER, WE JUST...THEY WERE GOING TO TAKE WHAT LITTLE WE HAD. AND WE ARE STARVING AS IT IS. WE WANTED TO ESCAPE BEFORE...
I KNOW. BELIEVE ME, I KNOW. BUT YOU NEED TO BELIEVE. SHE WILL PROVIDE. AND IN THE MEANTIME, WE WILL ABIDE. THIS DOES NOT INCLUDE PAINTING YOURSELF LIKE CHILDREN AND FIGHTING WITH THOSE FOOLISH SOLDIERS, DOES IT?
NO, SISTER.
HEY, NO NEED TO THANK US.
YOU'RE CERTAINLY RIGHT ABOUT THAT.
MAYBE THIS RING IS ON THE FRITZ, BECAUSE I DON'T THINK THE SARCASM TRANSLATED...
OH, I SEE. YOU ACTUALLY THINK THAT, BY ESCALATING THE VIOLENCE, YOU WERE HELPING. WONDERFUL.

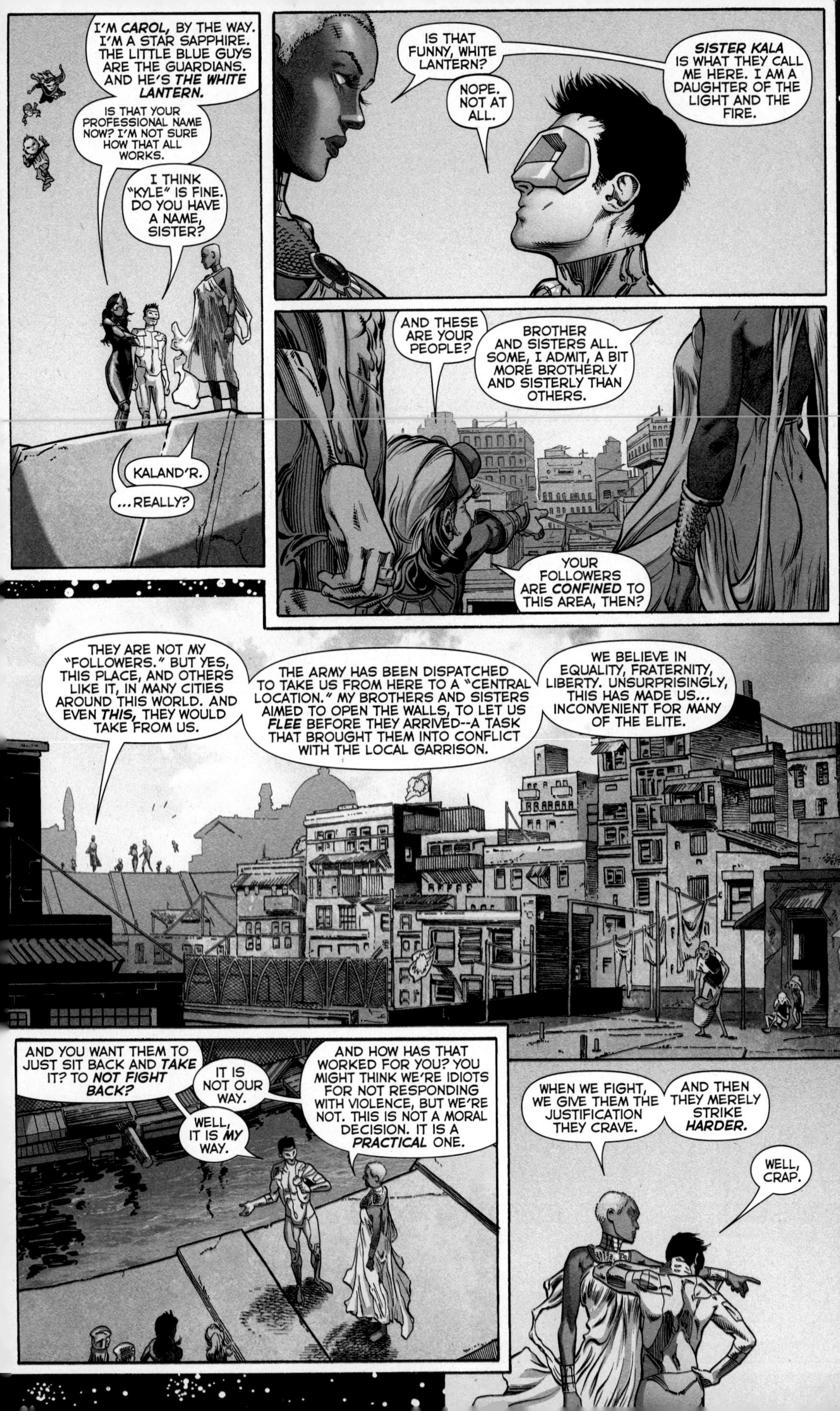
I'M CAROL, BY THE WAY. I'M A STAR SAPPHIRE. THE LITTLE BLUE GUYS ARE THE GUARDIANS. AND HE'S THE WHITE LANTERN.
IS THAT YOUR PROFESSIONAL NAME NOW? I'M NOT SURE HOW THAT ALL WORKS.
I THINK "KYLE" IS FINE. DO YOU HAVE A NAME, SISTER?
KALAND'R.
...REALLY?
IS THAT FUNNY, WHITE LANTERN?
NOPE. NOT AT ALL.
SISTER KALA IS WHAT THEY CALL ME HERE. I AM A DAUGHTER OF THE LIGHT AND THE FIRE.
AND THESE ARE YOUR PEOPLE?
BROTHER AND SISTERS ALL. SOME, I ADMIT, A BIT MORE BROTHERLY AND SISTERLY THAN OTHERS.
YOUR FOLLOWERS ARE CONFINED TO THIS AREA, THEN?
THEY ARE NOT MY "FOLLOWERS." BUT YES, THIS PLACE, AND OTHERS LIKE IT, IN MANY CITIES AROUND THIS WORLD. AND EVEN THIS, THEY WOULD TAKE FROM US.
THE ARMY HAS BEEN DISPATCHED TO TAKE US FROM HERE TO A "CENTRAL LOCATION." MY BROTHERS AND SISTERS AIMED TO OPEN THE WALLS, TO LET US FLEE BEFORE THEY ARRIVED--A TASK THAT BROUGHT THEM INTO CONFLICT WITH THE LOCAL GARRISON.
WE BELIEVE IN EQUALITY, FRATERNITY, LIBERTY. UNSURPRISINGLY, THIS HAS MADE US... INCONVENIENT FOR MANY OF THE ELITE.
AND YOU WANT THEM TO JUST SIT BACK AND TAKE IT? TO NOT FIGHT BACK?
IT IS NOT OUR WAY.
WELL, IT IS MY WAY.
AND HOW HAS THAT WORKED FOR YOU? YOU MIGHT THINK WE'RE IDIOTS FOR NOT RESPONDING WITH VIOLENCE, BUT WE'RE NOT. THIS IS NOT A MORAL DECISION. IT IS A PRACTICAL ONE.
WHEN WE FIGHT, WE GIVE THEM THE JUSTIFICATION THEY CRAVE.
AND THEN THEY MERELY STRIKE HARDER.
WELL, CRAP.

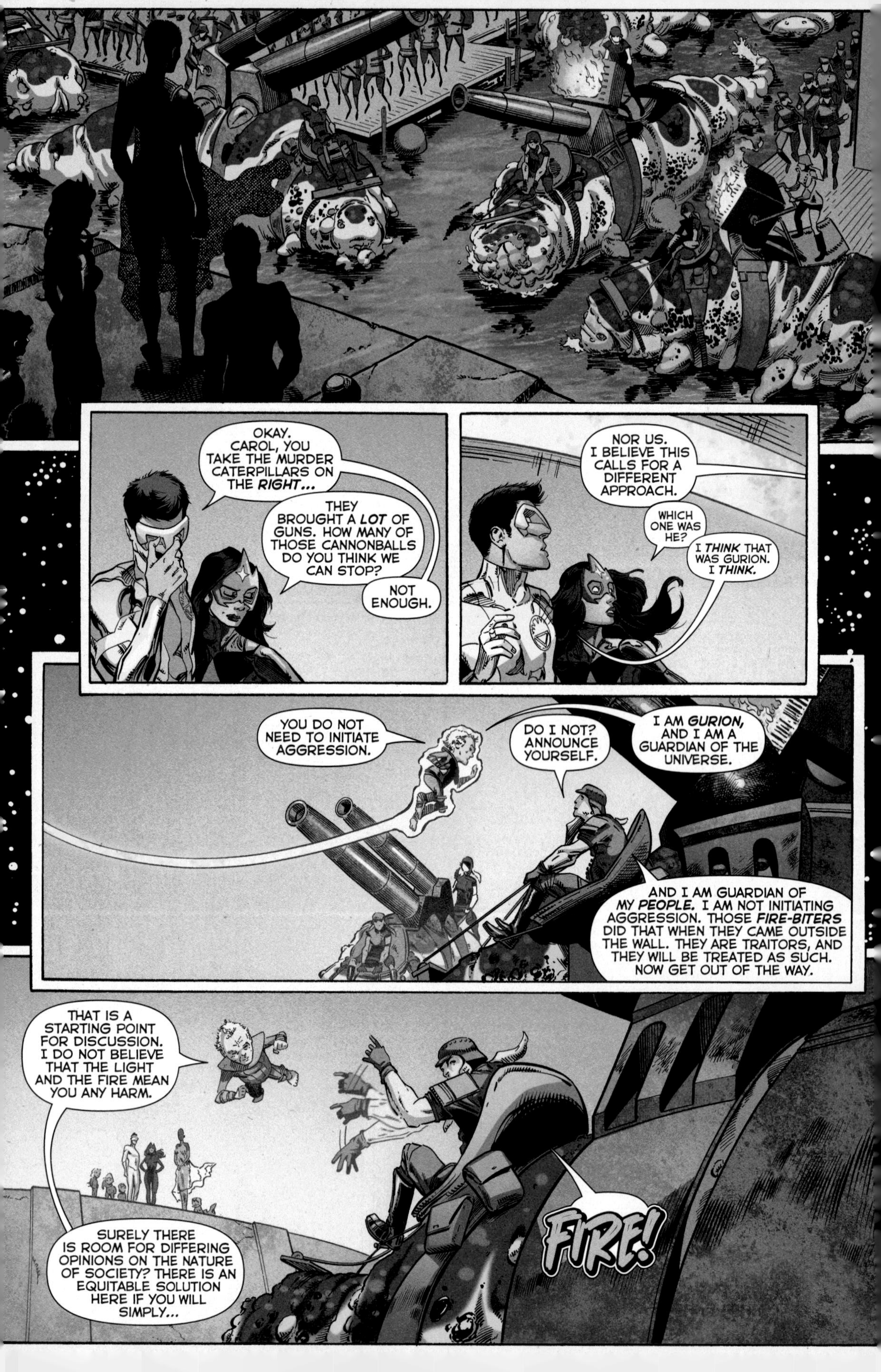
OKAY. CAROL, YOU TAKE THE MURDER CATERPILLARS ON THE RIGHT...
THEY BROUGHT A LOT OF GUNS. HOW MANY OF THOSE CANNONBALLS DO YOU THINK WE CAN STOP?
NOT ENOUGH.
NOR US. I BELIEVE THIS CALLS FOR A DIFFERENT APPROACH.
WHICH ONE WAS HE?
I THINK THAT WAS GURION. I THINK.
YOU DO NOT NEED TO INITIATE AGGRESSION.
DO I NOT? ANNOUNCE YOURSELF.
I AM GURION, AND I AM A GUARDIAN OF THE UNIVERSE.
AND I AM GUARDIAN OF MY PEOPLE. I AM NOT INITIATING AGGRESSION. THOSE FIRE-BITERS DID THAT WHEN THEY CAME OUTSIDE THE WALL. THEY ARE TRAITORS, AND THEY WILL BE TREATED AS SUCH. NOW GET OUT OF THE WAY.
THAT IS A STARTING POINT FOR DISCUSSION. I DO NOT BELIEVE THAT THE LIGHT AND THE FIRE MEAN YOU ANY HARM.
SURELY THERE IS ROOM FOR DIFFERING OPINIONS ON THE NATURE OF SOCIETY? THERE IS AN EQUITABLE SOLUTION HERE IF YOU WILL SIMPLY...
FIRE!

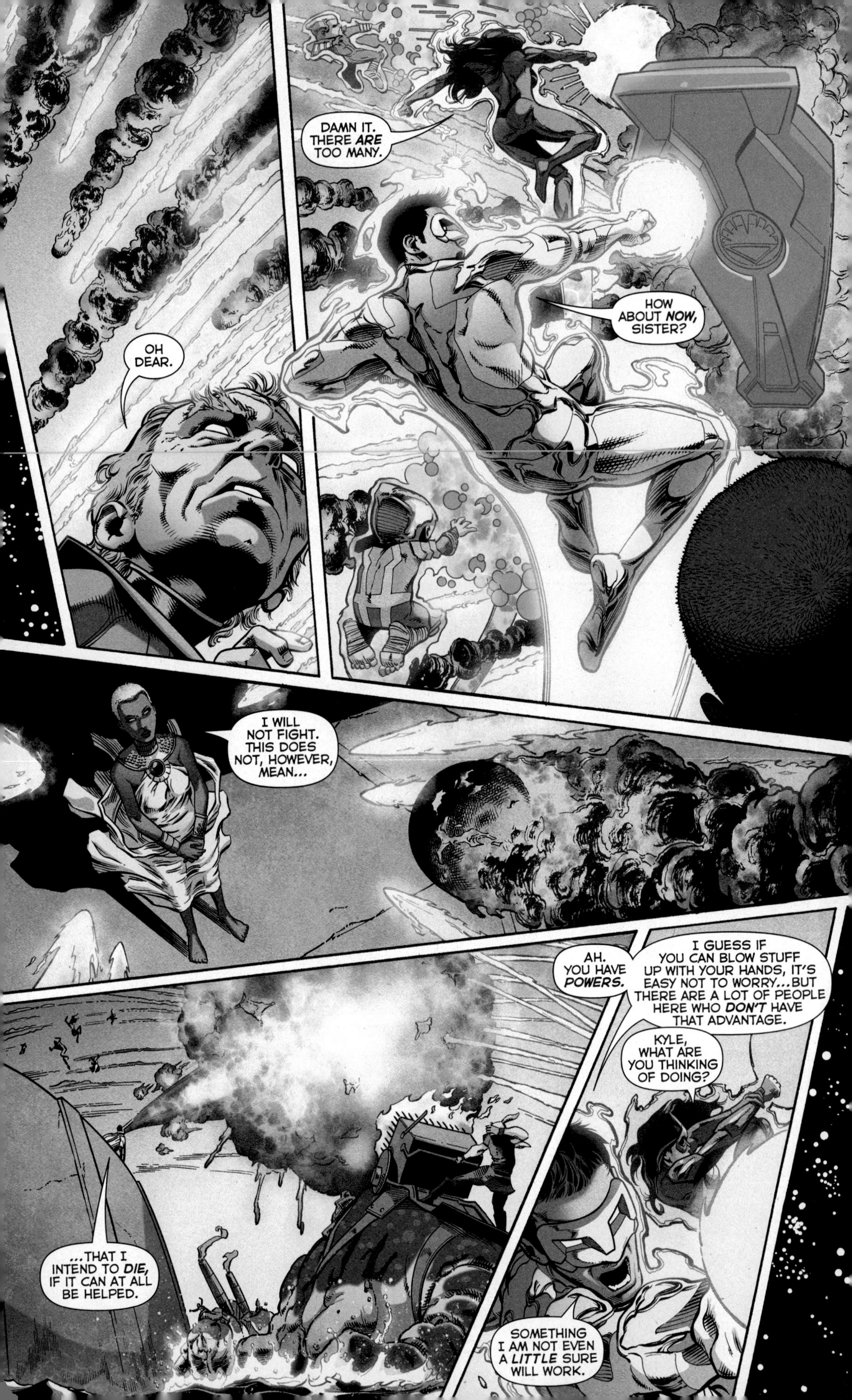
DAMN IT. THERE ARE TOO MANY.
OH DEAR.
HOW ABOUT NOW, SISTER?
I WILL NOT FIGHT. THIS DOES NOT, HOWEVER, MEAN...
...THAT I INTEND TO DIE, IF IT CAN AT ALL BE HELPED.
AH. YOU HAVE POWERS.
I GUESS IF YOU CAN BLOW STUFF UP WITH YOUR HANDS, IT'S EASY NOT TO WORRY...BUT THERE ARE A LOT OF PEOPLE HERE WHO DON'T HAVE THAT ADVANTAGE.
KYLE, WHAT ARE YOU THINKING OF DOING?
SOMETHING I AM NOT EVEN A LITTLE SURE WILL WORK.

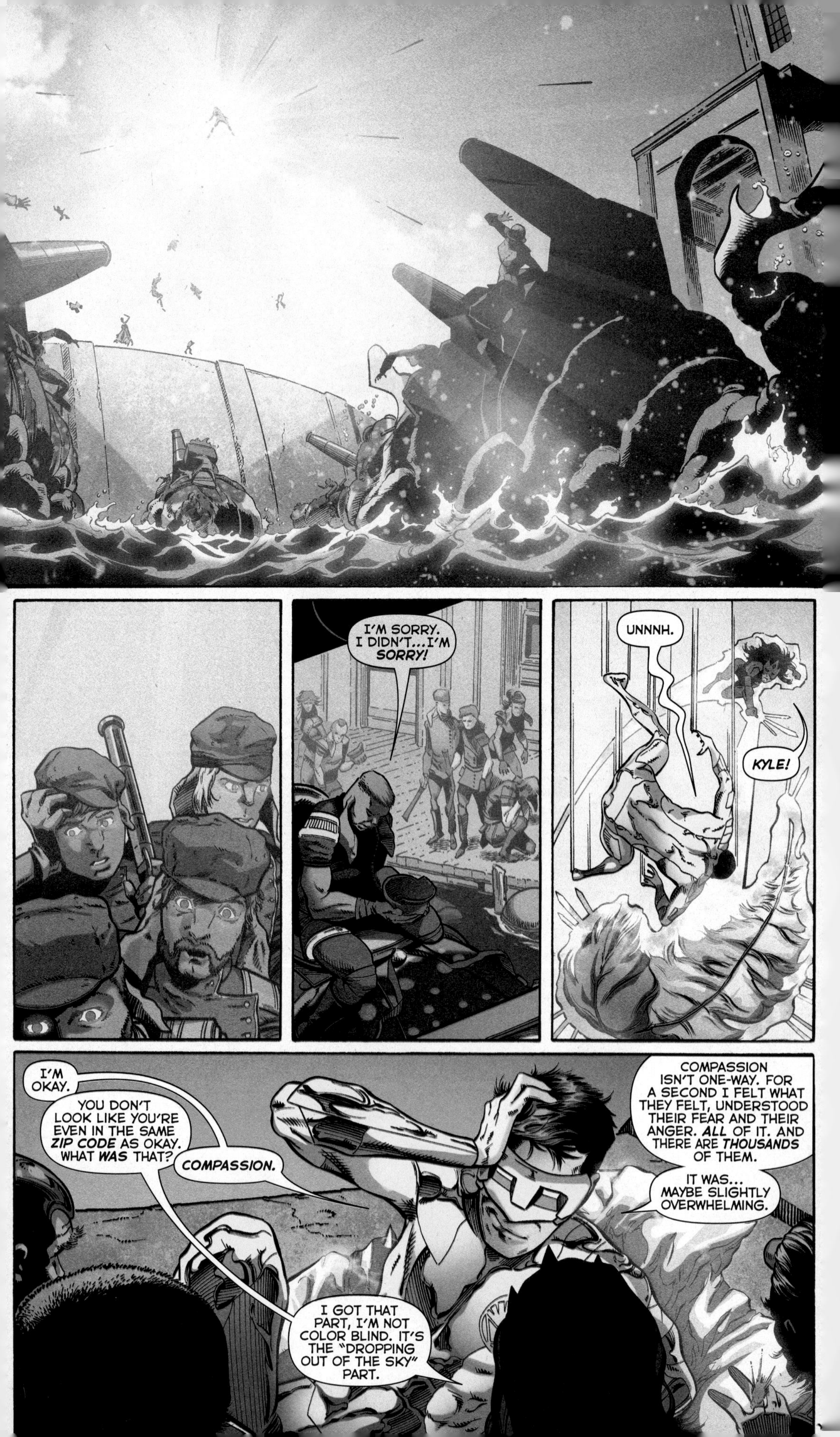
I'M SORRY. I DIDN'T...I'M SORRY!
UNNNH.
KYLE!
I'M OKAY.
YOU DON'T LOOK LIKE YOU'RE EVEN IN THE SAME ZIP CODE AS OKAY. WHAT WAS THAT?
COMPASSION.
COMPASSION ISN'T ONE-WAY. FOR A SECOND I FELT WHAT THEY FELT, UNDERSTOOD THEIR FEAR AND THEIR ANGER. ALL OF IT. AND THERE ARE THOUSANDS OF THEM.
IT WAS... MAYBE SLIGHTLY OVERWHELMING.
I GOT THAT PART, I'M NOT COLOR BLIND. IT'S THE "DROPPING OUT OF THE SKY" PART.

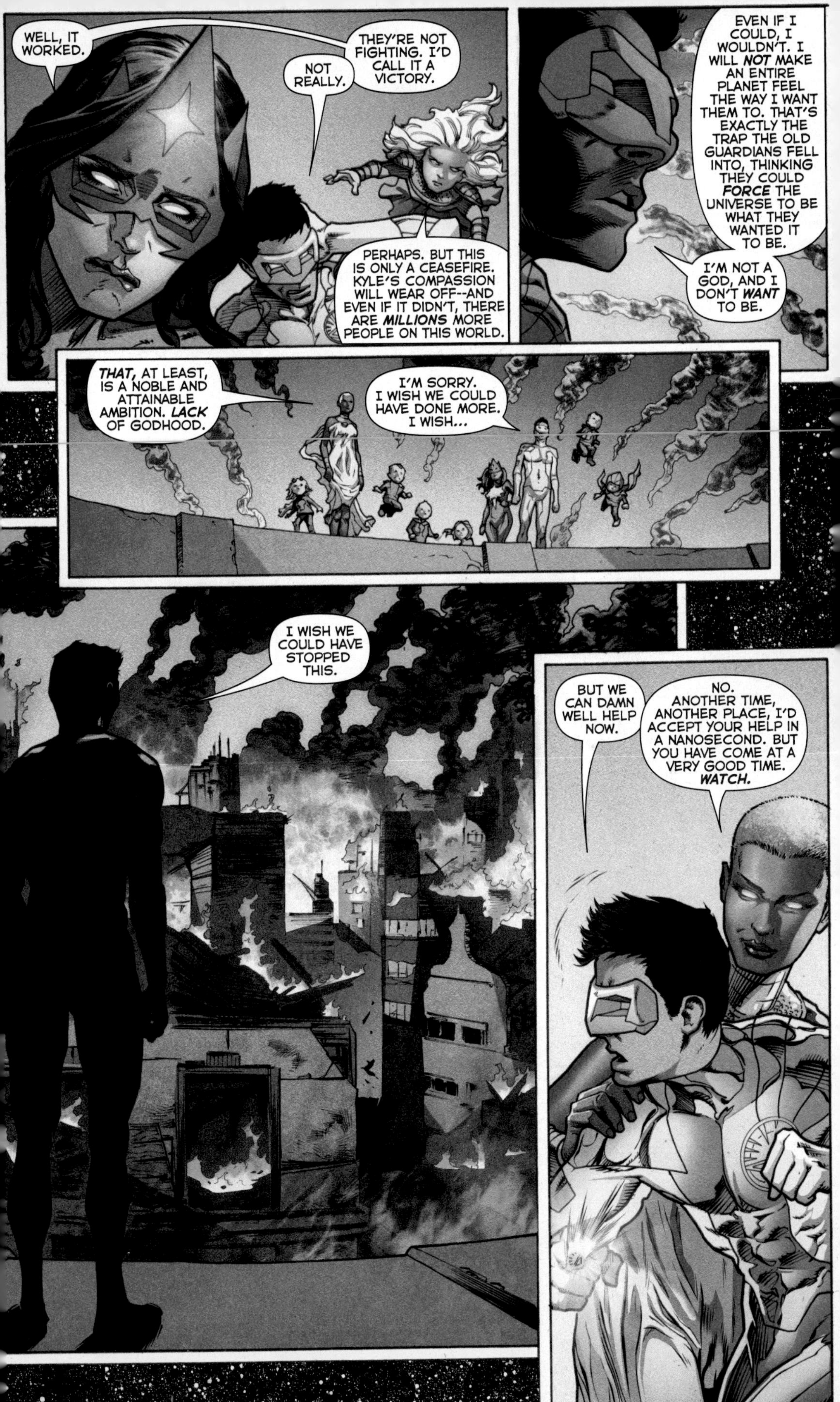
WELL, IT WORKED.
THEY'RE NOT FIGHTING. I'D CALL IT A VICTORY.
NOT REALLY.
PERHAPS. BUT THIS IS ONLY A CEASEFIRE. KYLE'S COMPASSION WILL WEAR OFF--AND EVEN IF IT DIDN'T, THERE ARE MILLIONS MORE PEOPLE ON THIS WORLD.
EVEN IF I COULD, I WOULDN'T. I WILL NOT MAKE AN ENTIRE PLANET FEEL THE WAY I WANT THEM TO. THAT'S EXACTLY THE TRAP THE OLD GUARDIANS FELL INTO, THINKING THEY COULD FORCE THE UNIVERSE TO BE WHAT THEY WANTED IT TO BE.
I'M NOT A GOD, AND I DON'T WANT TO BE.
THAT, AT LEAST, IS A NOBLE AND ATTAINABLE AMBITION. LACK OF GODHOOD.
I'M SORRY. I WISH WE COULD HAVE DONE MORE. I WISH...
I WISH WE COULD HAVE STOPPED THIS.
BUT WE CAN DAMN WELL HELP NOW.
NO. ANOTHER TIME, ANOTHER PLACE, I'D ACCEPT YOUR HELP IN A NANOSECOND. BUT YOU HAVE COME AT A VERY GOOD TIME. WATCH.

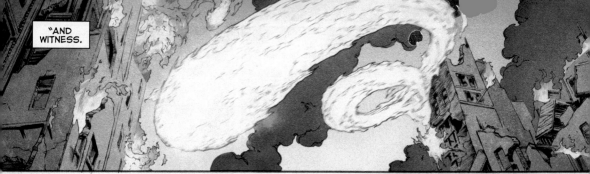

"AND WITNESS.

"AS THE LIGHT AND FIRE *RENEWS* AND *REBUILDS*...

"AS *SHE* RESTORES."

SO...THIS DEFINITELY ISN'T YET ANOTHER NEW KYLE TRICK YOU HAVEN'T TOLD ME ABOUT, RIGHT?

NO.

RIGHT. JUST CHECKING.

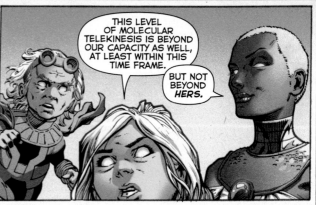

THIS LEVEL OF MOLECULAR TELEKINESIS IS BEYOND OUR CAPACITY AS WELL, AT LEAST WITHIN THIS TIME FRAME.

BUT NOT BEYOND *HERS.*

I KNOW WHAT YOU CAME HERE THINKING. THAT OUR BELIEF WAS AN *EMPTY* THING, A SUPERSTITION TO HELP US IN DEALING WITH AN UNCARING UNIVERSE.

BUT YOU ARE WRONG.

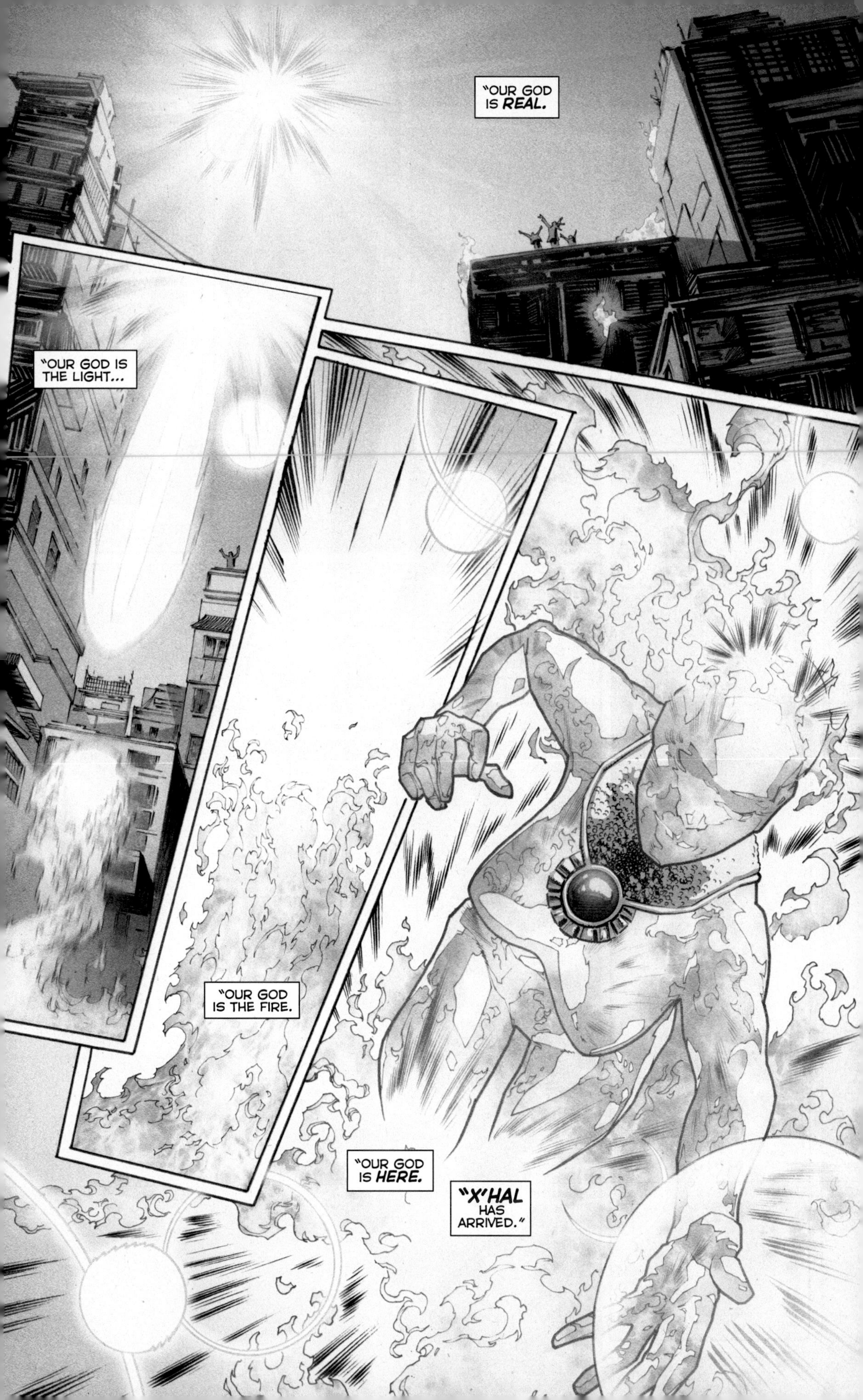
"OUR GOD IS REAL.
"OUR GOD IS THE LIGHT...
"OUR GOD IS THE FIRE.
"OUR GOD IS HERE.
"X'HAL HAS ARRIVED."

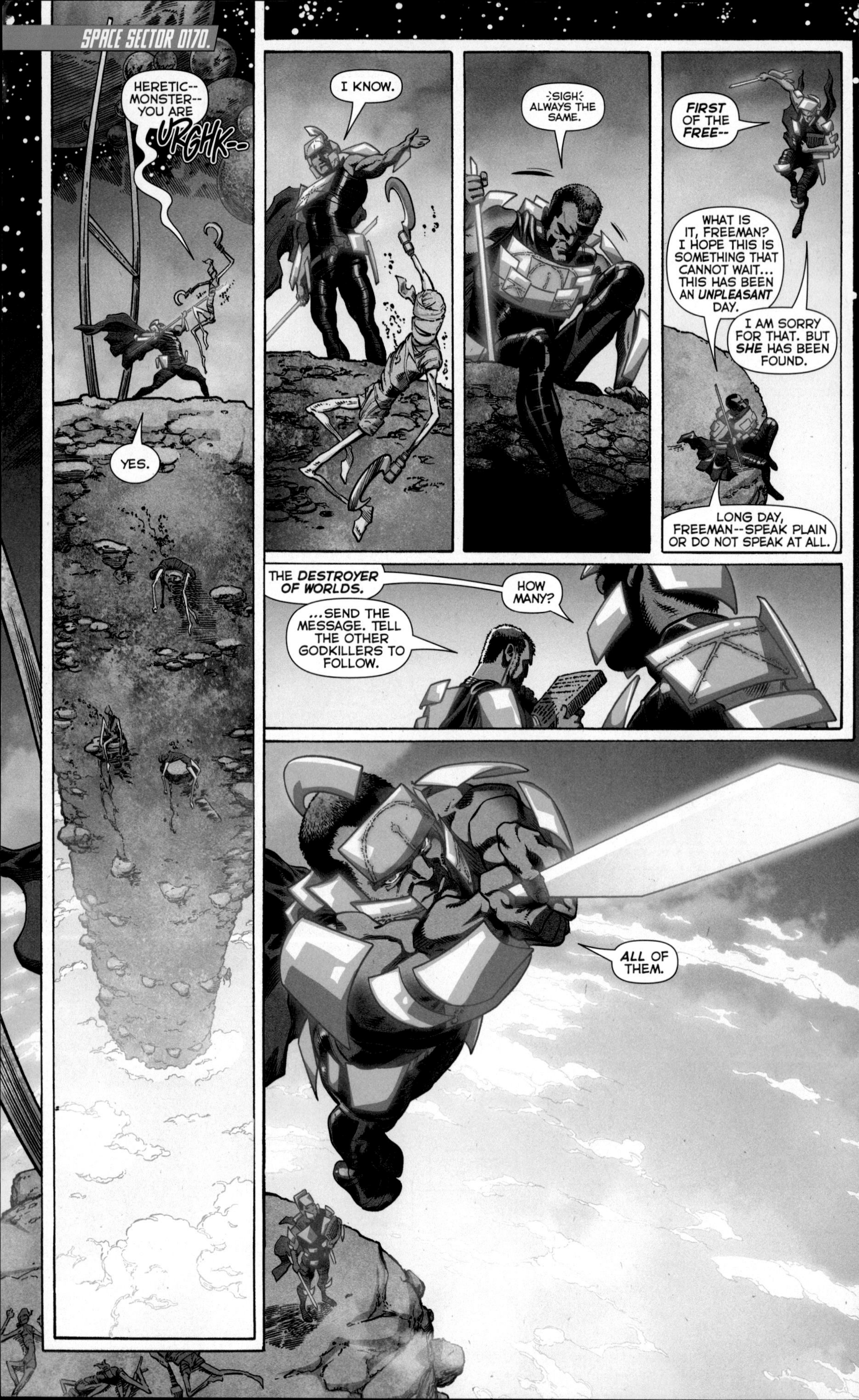
SPACE SECTOR 0170.
HERETIC--
MONSTER--
YOU ARE
URGHK--
YES.
I KNOW.
-SIGH-
ALWAYS THE
SAME.
FIRST
OF THE
FREE--
WHAT IS
IT, FREEMAN?
I HOPE THIS IS
SOMETHING THAT
CANNOT WAIT...
THIS HAS BEEN
AN UNPLEASANT
DAY.
I AM SORRY
FOR THAT. BUT
SHE HAS BEEN
FOUND.
LONG DAY,
FREEMAN--SPEAK PLAIN
OR DO NOT SPEAK AT ALL.
THE DESTROYER
OF WORLDS.
HOW
MANY?
...SEND THE
MESSAGE. TELL
THE OTHER
GODKILLERS TO
FOLLOW.
ALL OF
THEM.

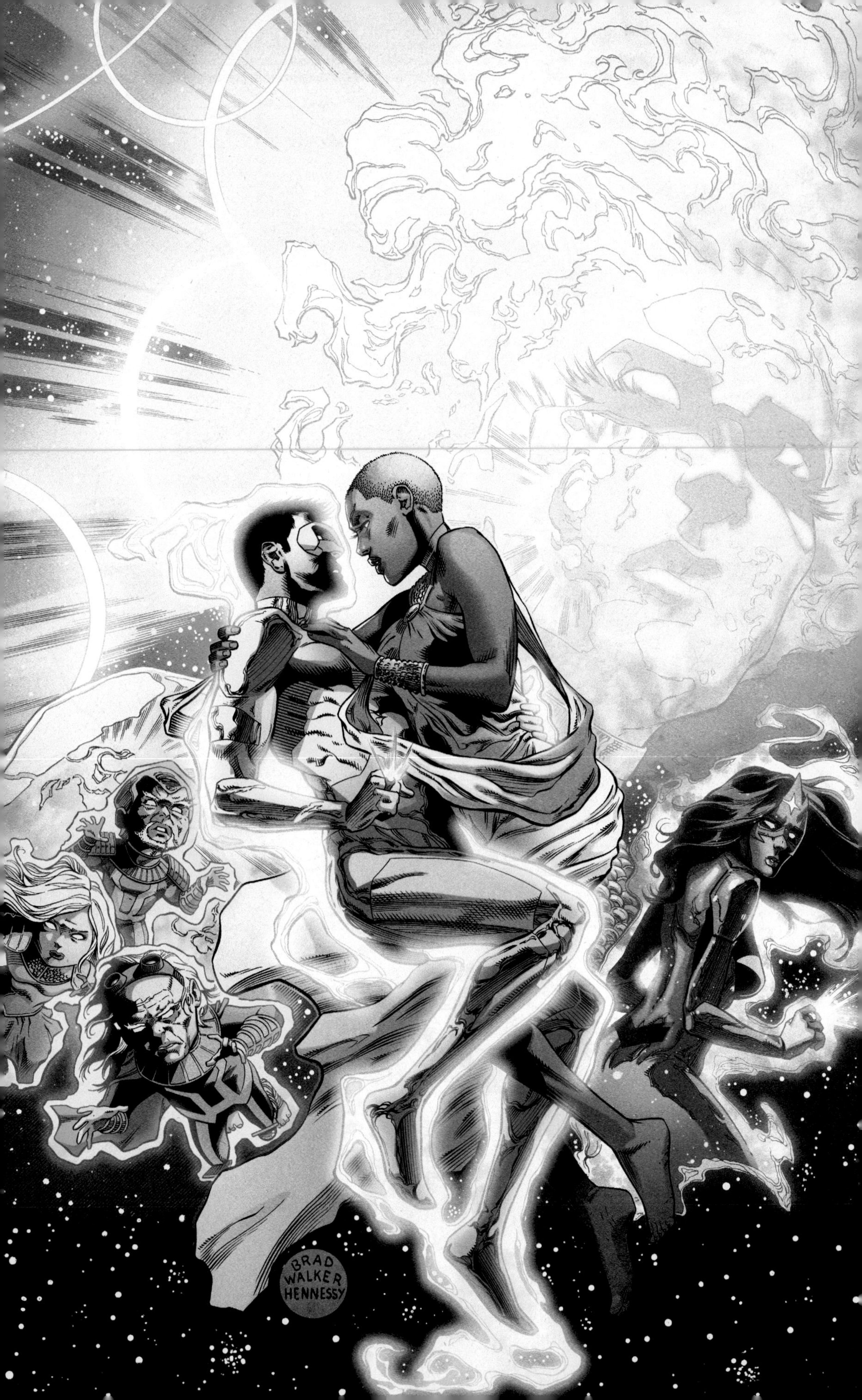
BRAD
WALKER
HENNESSY

CATHEDRALS: THE GODKILLERS PART II

JUSTIN JORDAN writer BRAD WALKER penciller ANDREW HENNESSY with BRAD WALKER (pgs 29-32) inkers
WIL QUINTANA with HI-FI (pgs 29-32, 44-45) colorists DAVE SHARPE letterer cover art by BRAD WALKER, ANDREW HENNESSY and WIL QUINTANA

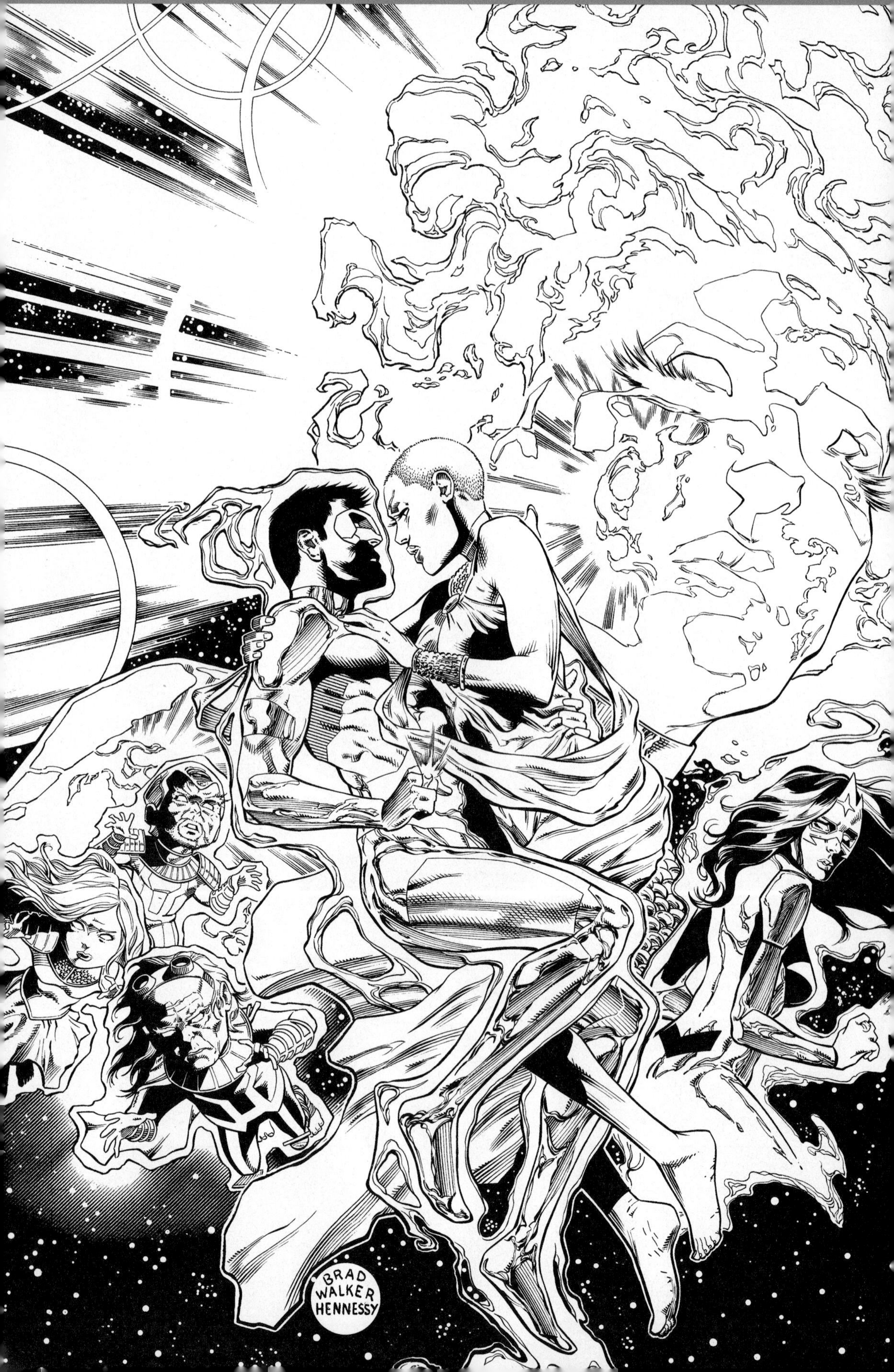
BRAD WALKER HENNESSY

THIS WAS *TAMARAN.* LONG AGO.

THIS WAS *X'HAL.* SHE WHO FREED US FROM OUR ENEMIES, AND BROUGHT PEACE TO OUR WORLD.

THIS WAS X'HAL, AND SHE WAS OUR GODDESS...

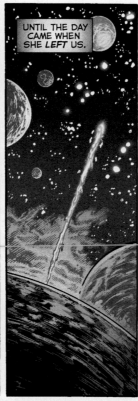

UNTIL THE DAY CAME WHEN SHE *LEFT* US.

MOST OF HER PEOPLE *STAYED* ON TAMARAN.

BUT SOME FOLLOWED HER TO THE STARS.

THEY PURSUED THEIR GOD UNTIL THEY COULD NO LONGER...

...AND LANDED ON THE FIRST PLACE THAT COULD SUSTAIN THEM. EVEN IF IT WAS ONLY BARELY ABLE TO.

AND ON THAT DESOLATE WORLD, THEY WAITED FOR CENTURIES. THIS WAS THE WORLD, AND FAITH, I WAS BORN INTO.

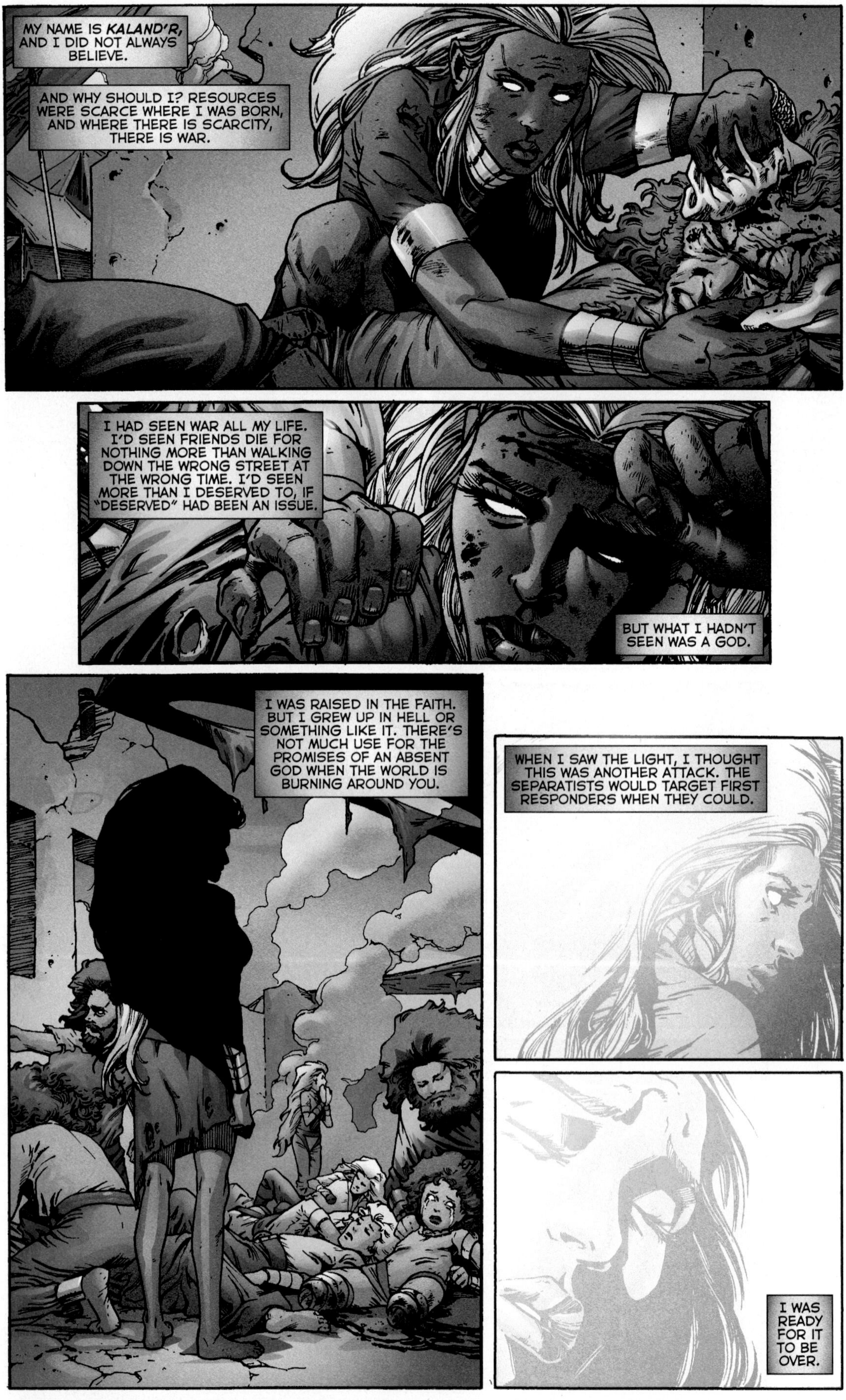
MY NAME IS *KALAND'R,* AND I DID NOT ALWAYS BELIEVE.
AND WHY SHOULD I? RESOURCES WERE SCARCE WHERE I WAS BORN, AND WHERE THERE IS SCARCITY, THERE IS WAR.
I HAD SEEN WAR ALL MY LIFE. I'D SEEN FRIENDS DIE FOR NOTHING MORE THAN WALKING DOWN THE WRONG STREET AT THE WRONG TIME. I'D SEEN MORE THAN I DESERVED TO, IF "DESERVED" HAD BEEN AN ISSUE.
BUT WHAT I HADN'T SEEN WAS A GOD.
I WAS RAISED IN THE FAITH. BUT I GREW UP IN HELL OR SOMETHING LIKE IT. THERE'S NOT MUCH USE FOR THE PROMISES OF AN ABSENT GOD WHEN THE WORLD IS BURNING AROUND YOU.
WHEN I SAW THE LIGHT, I THOUGHT THIS WAS ANOTHER ATTACK. THE SEPARATISTS WOULD TARGET FIRST RESPONDERS WHEN THEY COULD.
I WAS READY FOR IT TO BE OVER.

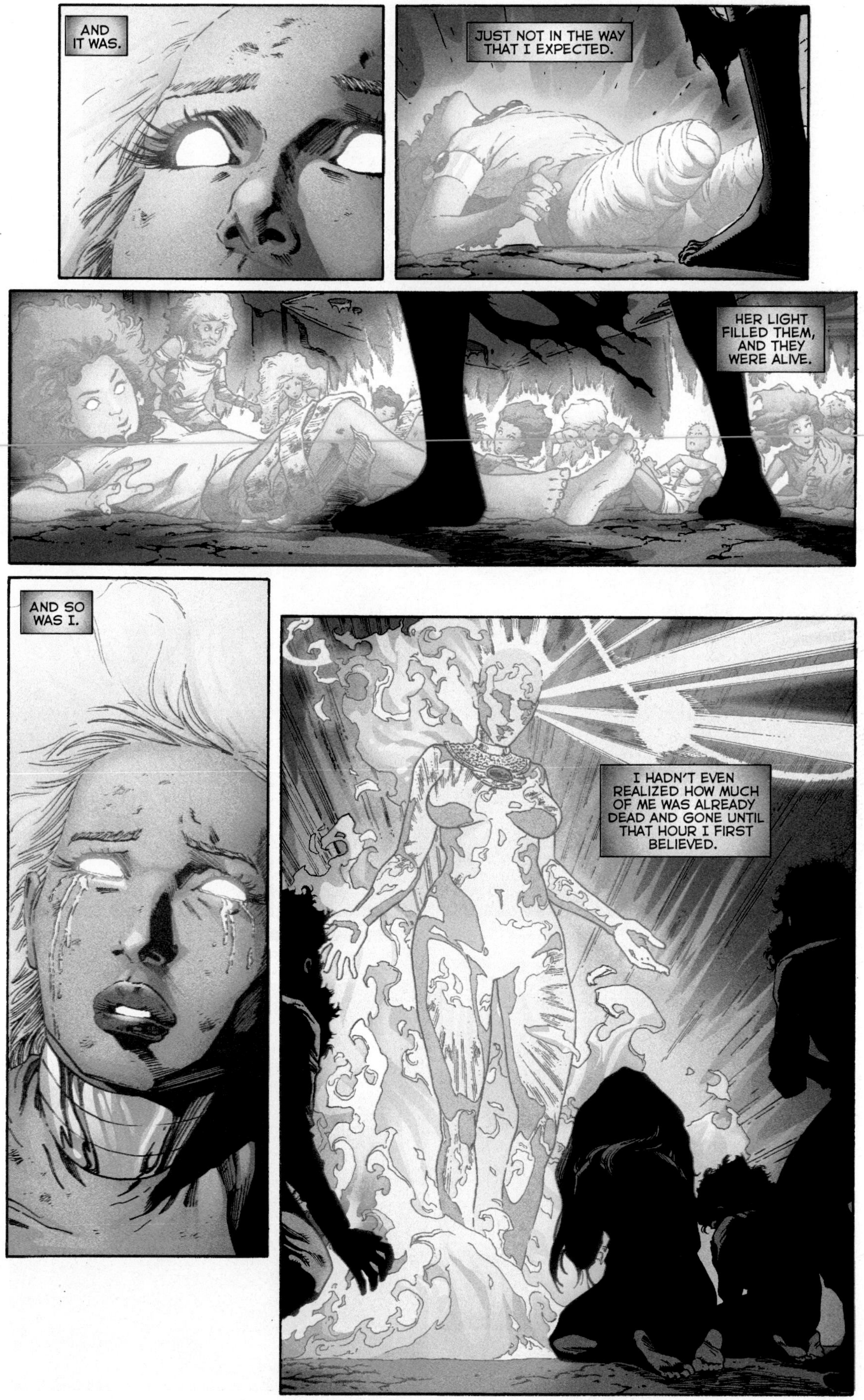
AND IT WAS.
JUST NOT IN THE WAY THAT I EXPECTED.
HER LIGHT FILLED THEM, AND THEY WERE ALIVE.
AND SO WAS I.
I HADN'T EVEN REALIZED HOW MUCH OF ME WAS ALREADY DEAD AND GONE UNTIL THAT HOUR I FIRST BELIEVED.

X'HAL HAD RETURNED. AND WITH HER ARRIVAL, THE PEACE AND PROSPERITY THE DEVOTED ALWAYS BELIEVED WOULD FOLLOW BECAME REAL.

BUT X'HAL WAS NOT DONE. SHE HAD GIVEN US MUCH, SO MUCH WAS EXPECTED. WE WOULD *TRAVEL*, WE WOULD SPREAD THE WORD OF HER BLESSINGS.

WE WOULD BE *THE LIGHT AND THE FIRE.*

SHE GAVE *ME* A PART OF HER POWER, AS PROOF OF THINGS UNSEEN. SO THAT THOSE WE SPOKE TO WOULDN'T HAVE TO BE LIKE ME, FAITHLESS AND UNBELIEVING.

BUT EVEN WITH HER BEHIND US, IT WAS NOT EASY. AS YOU HAVE SEEN ON THIS WORLD, THOSE THAT RECEIVED THE WORD WERE CAST OUT, CONFINED, AND PERSECUTED...

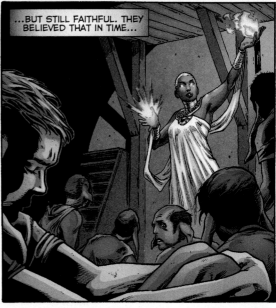

...BUT STILL FAITHFUL. THEY BELIEVED THAT IN TIME...

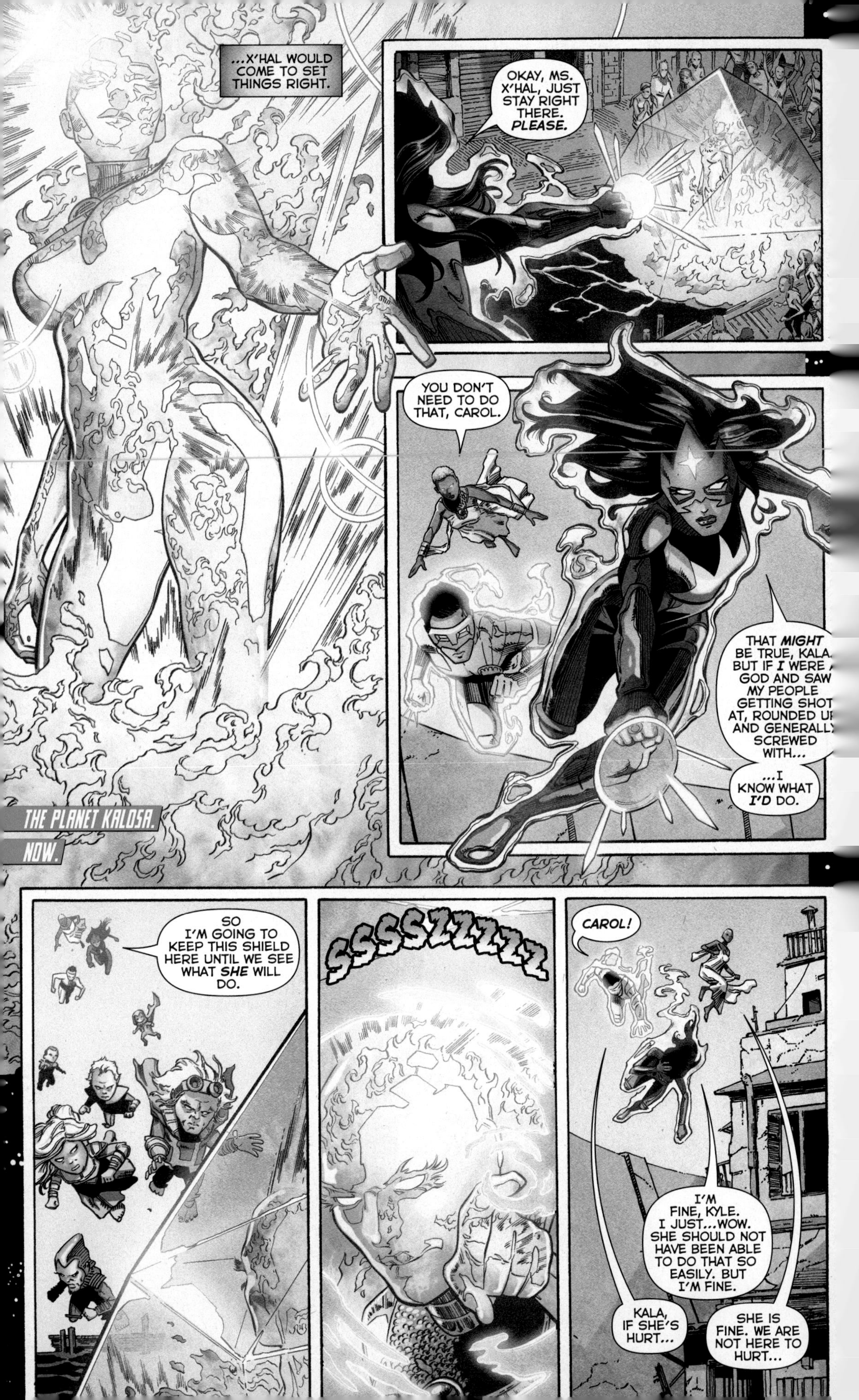
...X'HAL WOULD COME TO SET THINGS RIGHT.
OKAY, MS. X'HAL, JUST STAY RIGHT THERE. PLEASE.
YOU DON'T NEED TO DO THAT, CAROL.
THAT MIGHT BE TRUE, KALA. BUT IF I WERE A GOD AND SAW MY PEOPLE GETTING SHOT AT, ROUNDED UP AND GENERALLY SCREWED WITH...
...I KNOW WHAT I'D DO.
THE PLANET KALOSA.
NOW.
SO I'M GOING TO KEEP THIS SHIELD HERE UNTIL WE SEE WHAT SHE WILL DO.
SSSSZZZZZZ
CAROL!
I'M FINE, KYLE. I JUST...WOW. SHE SHOULD NOT HAVE BEEN ABLE TO DO THAT SO EASILY. BUT I'M FINE.
KALA, IF SHE'S HURT...
SHE IS FINE. WE ARE NOT HERE TO HURT...

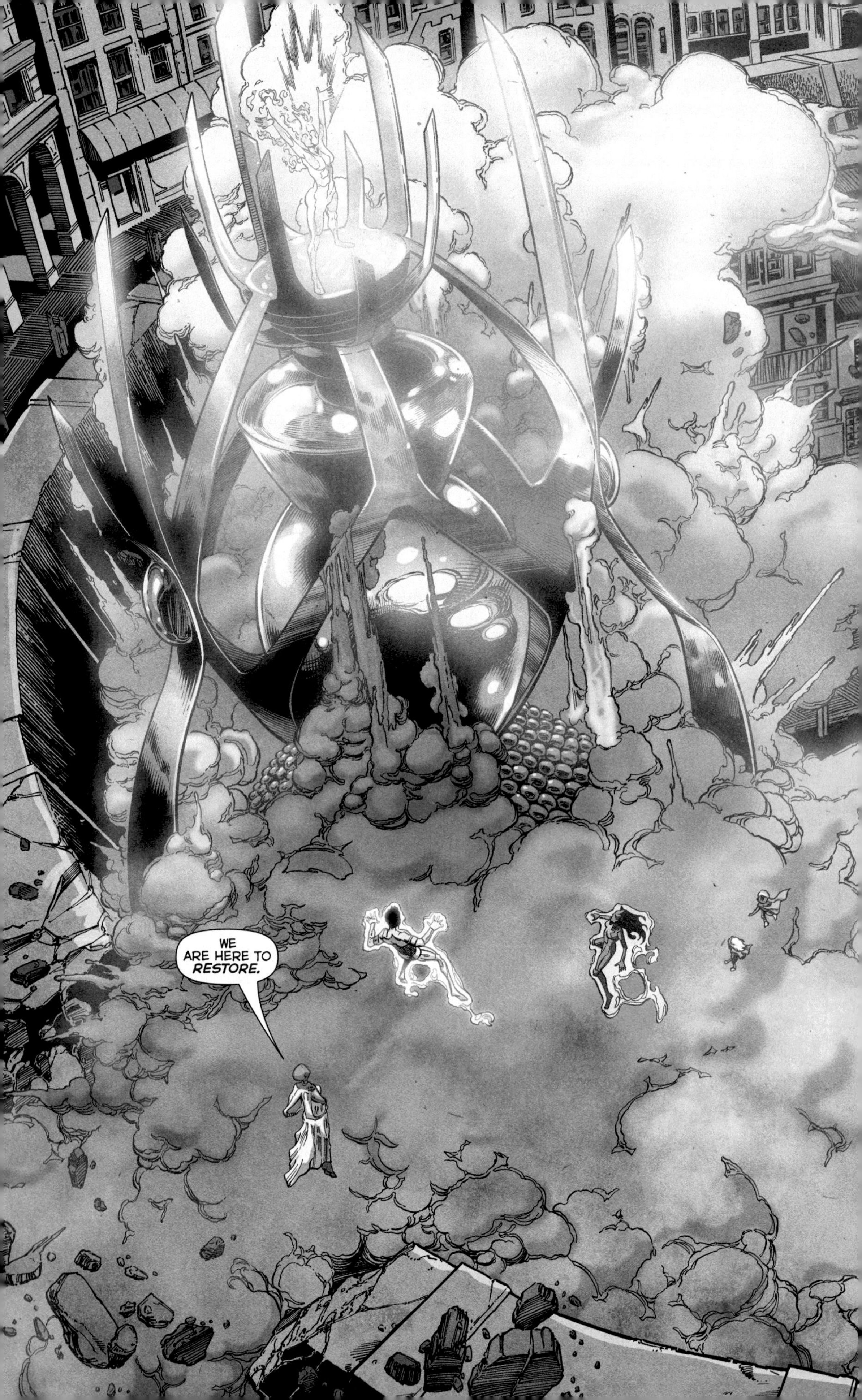
WE ARE HERE TO *RESTORE.*

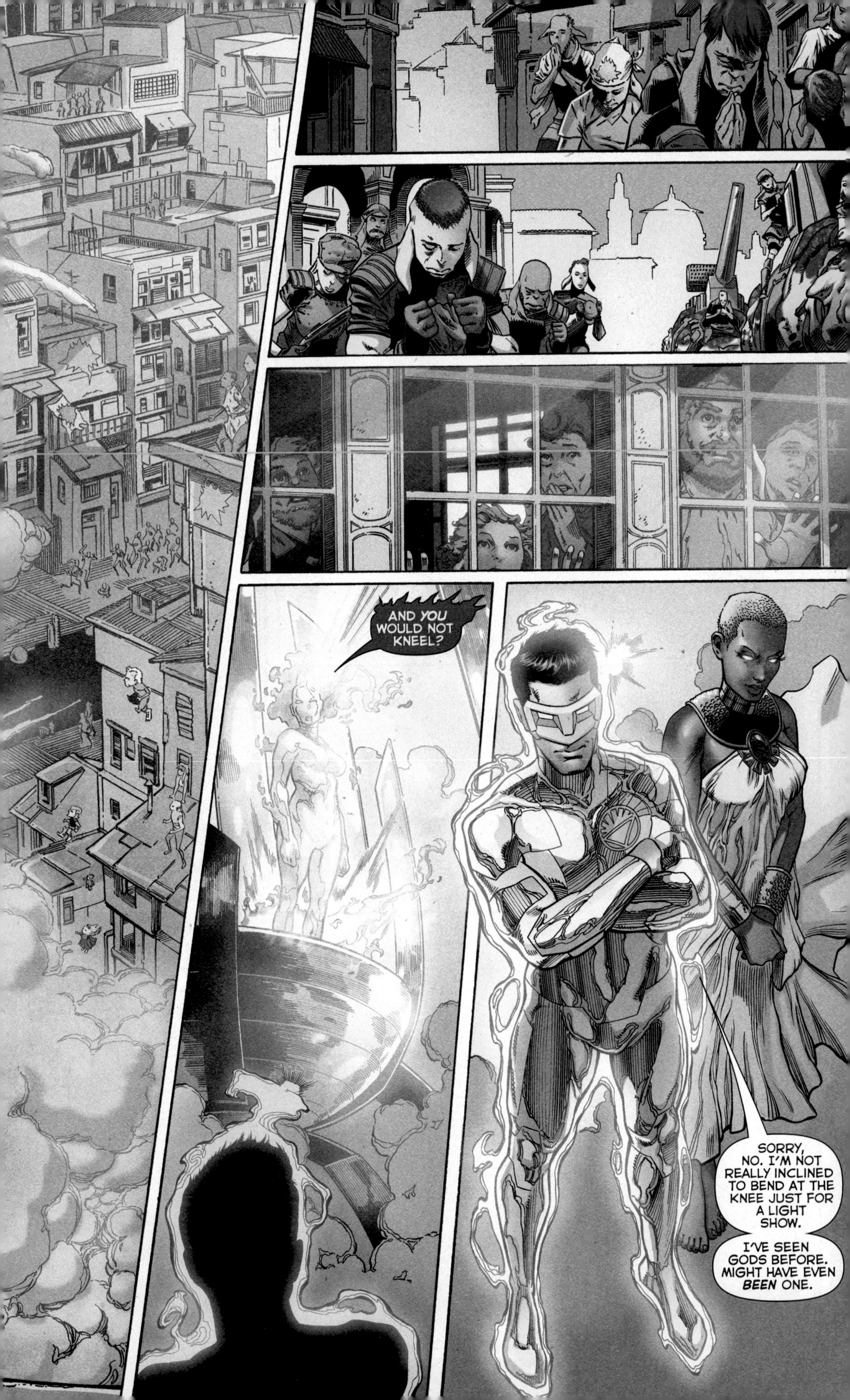
AND YOU WOULD NOT KNEEL?
SORRY, NO. I'M NOT REALLY INCLINED TO BEND AT THE KNEE JUST FOR A LIGHT SHOW.
I'VE SEEN GODS BEFORE. MIGHT HAVE EVEN BEEN ONE.

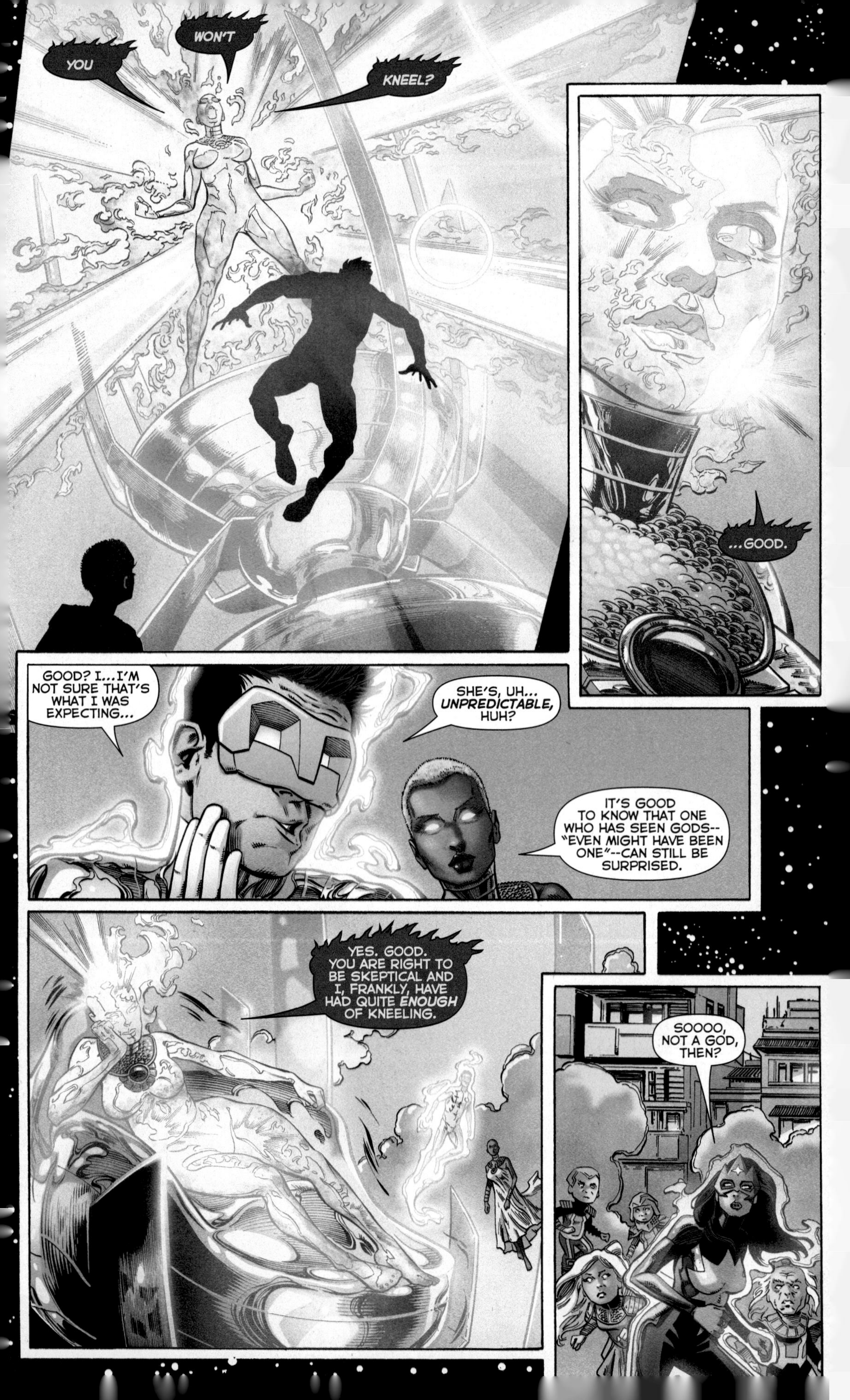
YOU
WON'T
KNEEL?
...GOOD.
GOOD? I...I'M NOT SURE THAT'S WHAT I WAS EXPECTING...
SHE'S, UH... *UNPREDICTABLE,* HUH?
IT'S GOOD TO KNOW THAT ONE WHO HAS SEEN GODS-- "EVEN MIGHT HAVE BEEN ONE"--CAN STILL BE SURPRISED.
YES. GOOD. YOU ARE RIGHT TO BE SKEPTICAL AND I, FRANKLY, HAVE HAD QUITE *ENOUGH* OF KNEELING.
SOOOO, NOT A GOD, THEN?

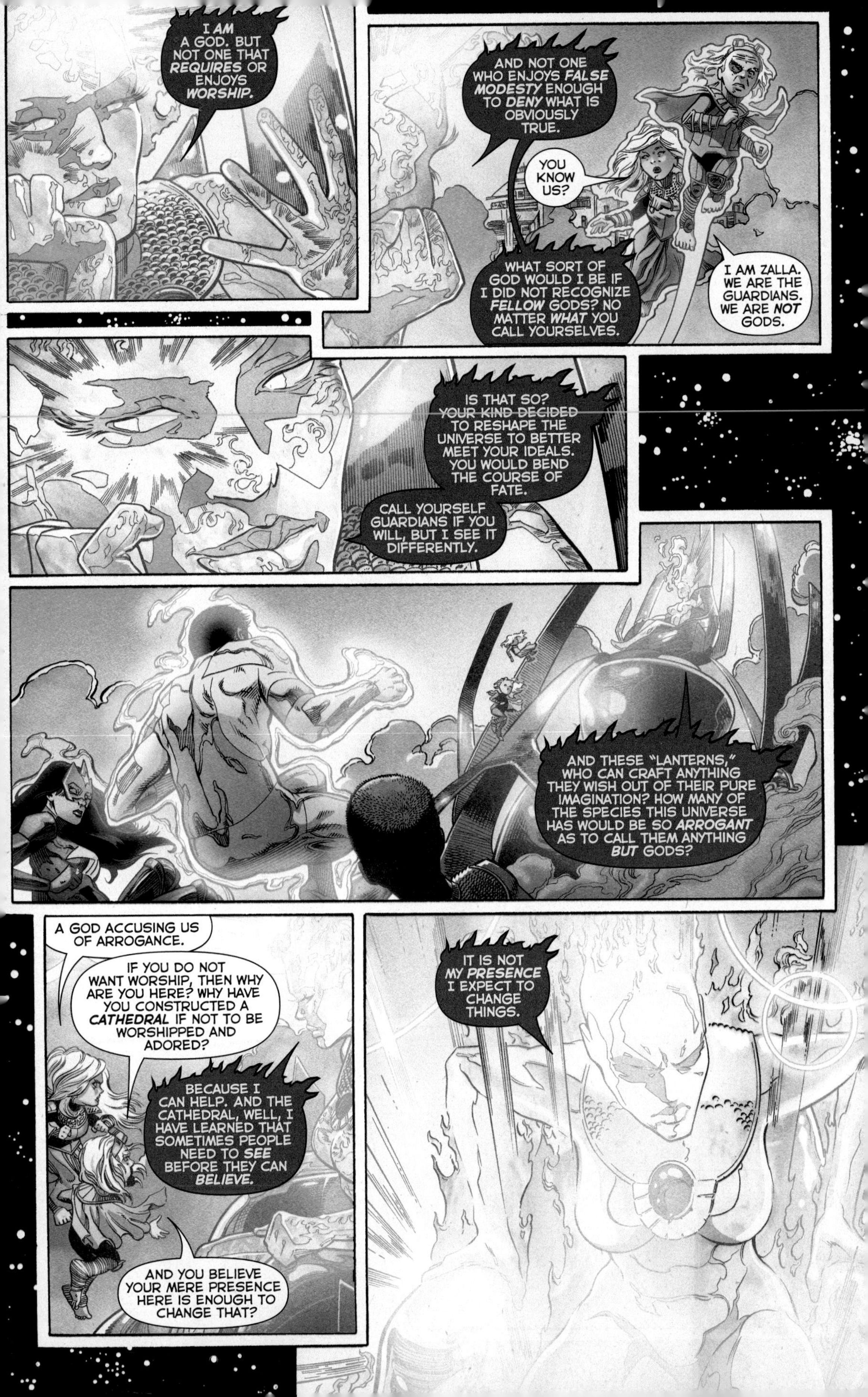
I AM A GOD. BUT NOT ONE THAT REQUIRES OR ENJOYS WORSHIP.
AND NOT ONE WHO ENJOYS FALSE MODESTY ENOUGH TO DENY WHAT IS OBVIOUSLY TRUE.
YOU KNOW US?
WHAT SORT OF GOD WOULD I BE IF I DID NOT RECOGNIZE FELLOW GODS? NO MATTER WHAT YOU CALL YOURSELVES.
I AM ZALLA. WE ARE THE GUARDIANS. WE ARE NOT GODS.
IS THAT SO? YOUR KIND DECIDED TO RESHAPE THE UNIVERSE TO BETTER MEET YOUR IDEALS. YOU WOULD BEND THE COURSE OF FATE.
CALL YOURSELF GUARDIANS IF YOU WILL, BUT I SEE IT DIFFERENTLY.
AND THESE "LANTERNS," WHO CAN CRAFT ANYTHING THEY WISH OUT OF THEIR PURE IMAGINATION? HOW MANY OF THE SPECIES THIS UNIVERSE HAS WOULD BE SO ARROGANT AS TO CALL THEM ANYTHING BUT GODS?
A GOD ACCUSING US OF ARROGANCE.
IF YOU DO NOT WANT WORSHIP, THEN WHY ARE YOU HERE? WHY HAVE YOU CONSTRUCTED A CATHEDRAL IF NOT TO BE WORSHIPPED AND ADORED?
BECAUSE I CAN HELP. AND THE CATHEDRAL, WELL, I HAVE LEARNED THAT SOMETIMES PEOPLE NEED TO SEE BEFORE THEY CAN BELIEVE.
AND YOU BELIEVE YOUR MERE PRESENCE HERE IS ENOUGH TO CHANGE THAT?
IT IS NOT MY PRESENCE I EXPECT TO CHANGE THINGS.

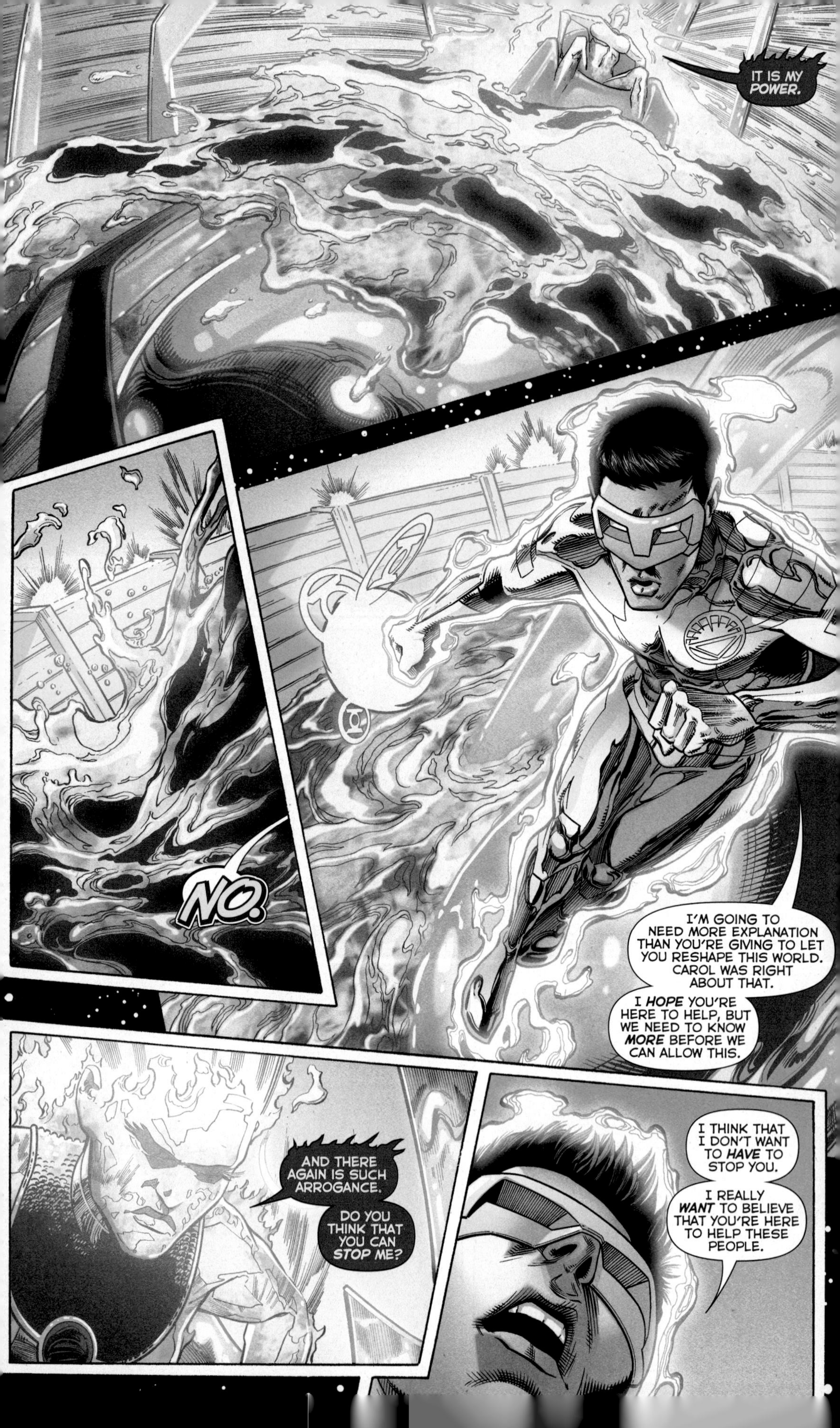
IT IS MY POWER.
NO.
I'M GOING TO NEED MORE EXPLANATION THAN YOU'RE GIVING TO LET YOU RESHAPE THIS WORLD. CAROL WAS RIGHT ABOUT THAT.
I HOPE YOU'RE HERE TO HELP, BUT WE NEED TO KNOW MORE BEFORE WE CAN ALLOW THIS.
AND THERE AGAIN IS SUCH ARROGANCE.
DO YOU THINK THAT YOU CAN STOP ME?
I THINK THAT I DON'T WANT TO HAVE TO STOP YOU.
I REALLY WANT TO BELIEVE THAT YOU'RE HERE TO HELP THESE PEOPLE.

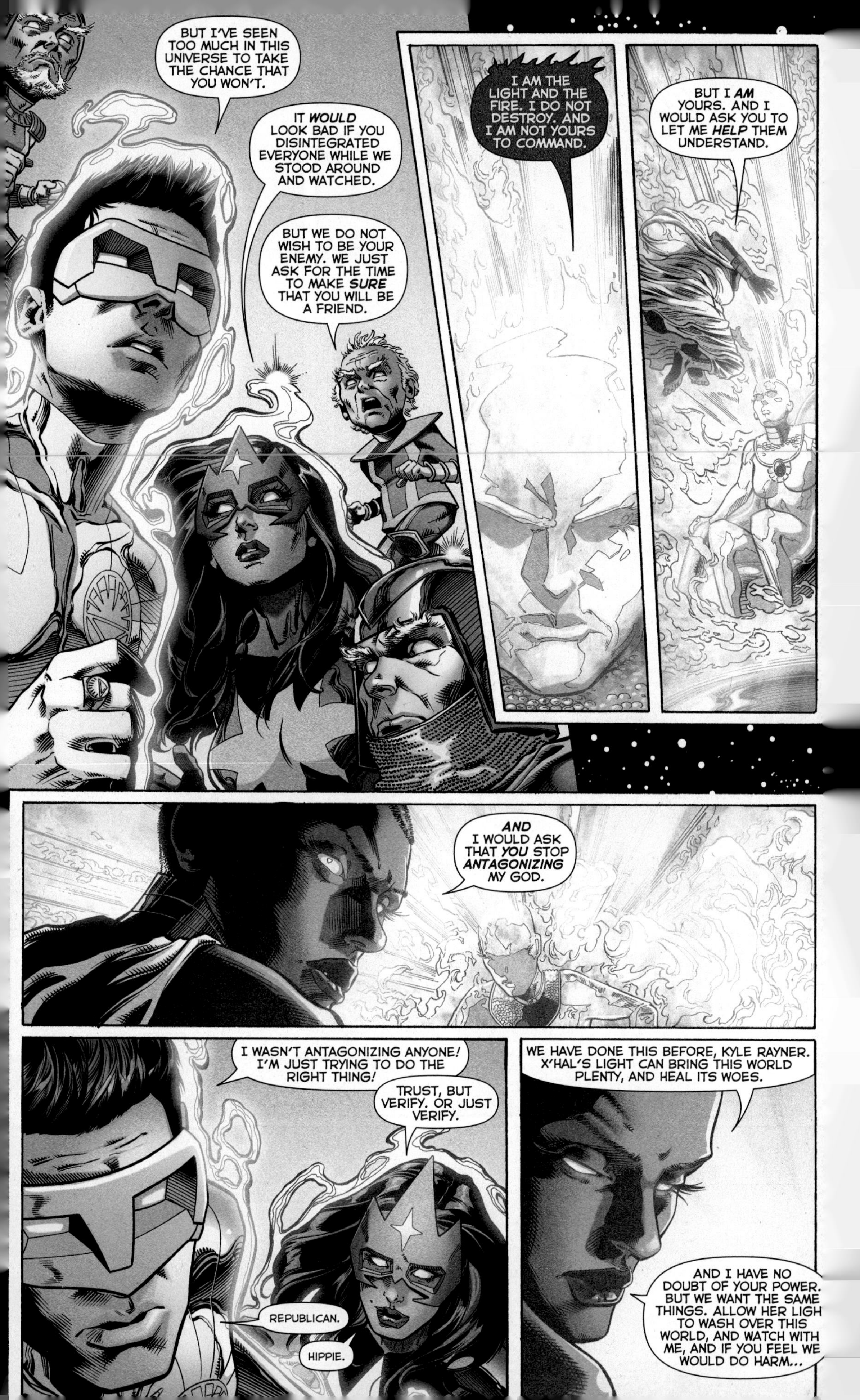

BUT I'VE SEEN TOO MUCH IN THIS UNIVERSE TO TAKE THE CHANCE THAT YOU WON'T.
IT *WOULD* LOOK BAD IF YOU DISINTEGRATED EVERYONE WHILE WE STOOD AROUND AND WATCHED.
BUT WE DO NOT WISH TO BE YOUR ENEMY. WE JUST ASK FOR THE TIME TO MAKE *SURE* THAT YOU WILL BE A FRIEND.
I AM THE LIGHT AND THE FIRE. I DO NOT DESTROY. AND I AM NOT YOURS TO COMMAND.
BUT I *AM* YOURS. AND I WOULD ASK YOU TO LET ME *HELP* THEM UNDERSTAND.
AND I WOULD ASK THAT *YOU* STOP *ANTAGONIZING* MY GOD.
I WASN'T ANTAGONIZING ANYONE! I'M JUST TRYING TO DO THE RIGHT THING!
TRUST, BUT VERIFY. OR JUST VERIFY.
REPUBLICAN.
HIPPIE.
WE HAVE DONE THIS BEFORE, KYLE RAYNER. X'HAL'S LIGHT CAN BRING THIS WORLD PLENTY, AND HEAL ITS WOES.
AND I HAVE NO DOUBT OF YOUR POWER. BUT WE WANT THE SAME THINGS. ALLOW HER LIGH TO WASH OVER THIS WORLD, AND WATCH WITH ME, AND IF YOU FEEL WE WOULD DO HARM...

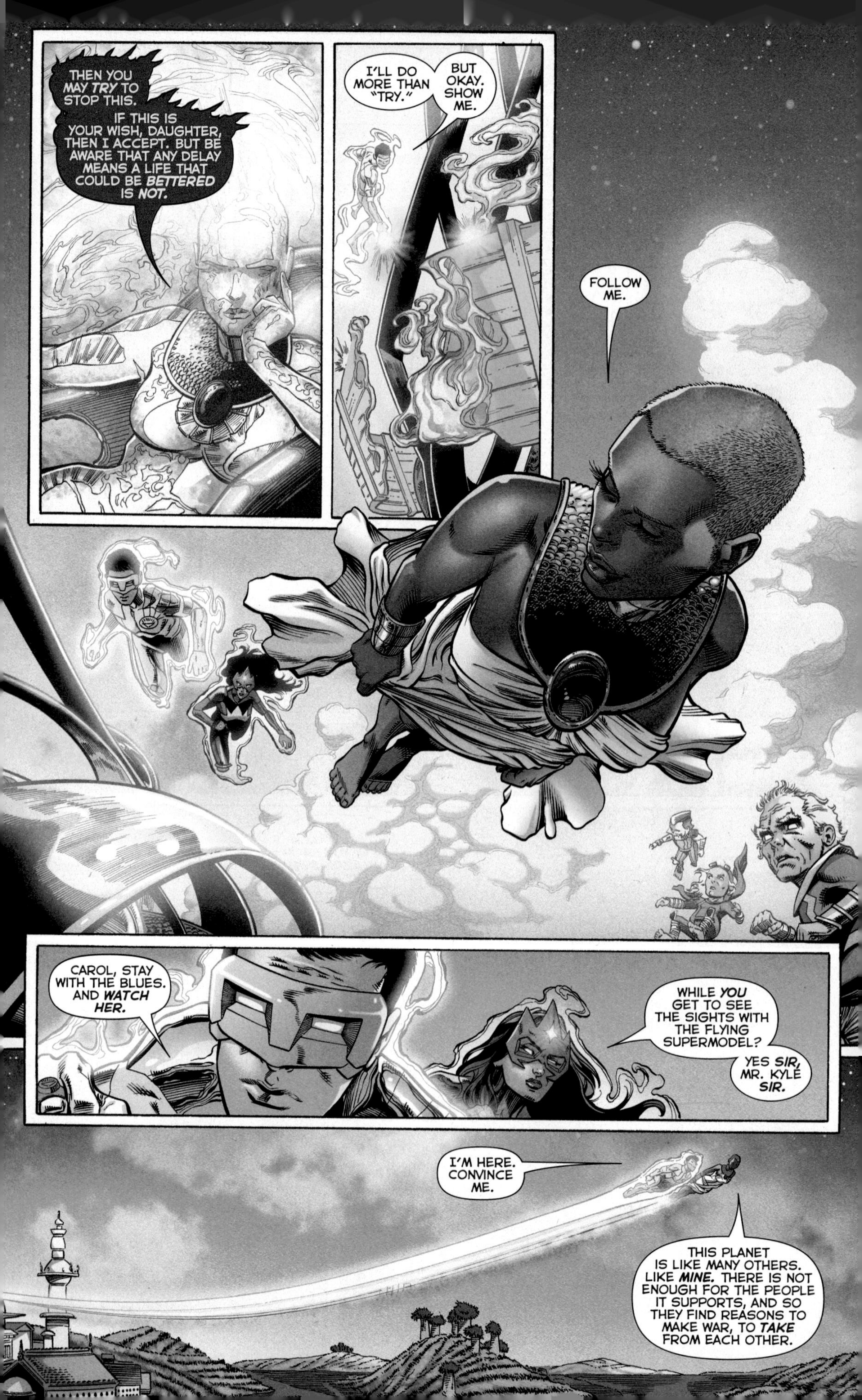
THEN YOU MAY *TRY* TO STOP THIS.
IF THIS IS YOUR WISH, DAUGHTER, THEN I ACCEPT. BUT BE AWARE THAT ANY DELAY MEANS A LIFE THAT COULD BE *BETTERED* IS *NOT.*
I'LL DO MORE THAN "TRY."
BUT OKAY. SHOW ME.
FOLLOW ME.
CAROL, STAY WITH THE BLUES. AND *WATCH HER.*
WHILE *YOU* GET TO SEE THE SIGHTS WITH THE FLYING SUPERMODEL?
YES *SIR,* MR. KYLE *SIR.*
I'M HERE. CONVINCE ME.
THIS PLANET IS LIKE MANY OTHERS. LIKE *MINE.* THERE IS NOT ENOUGH FOR THE PEOPLE IT SUPPORTS, AND SO THEY FIND REASONS TO MAKE WAR, TO *TAKE* FROM EACH OTHER.

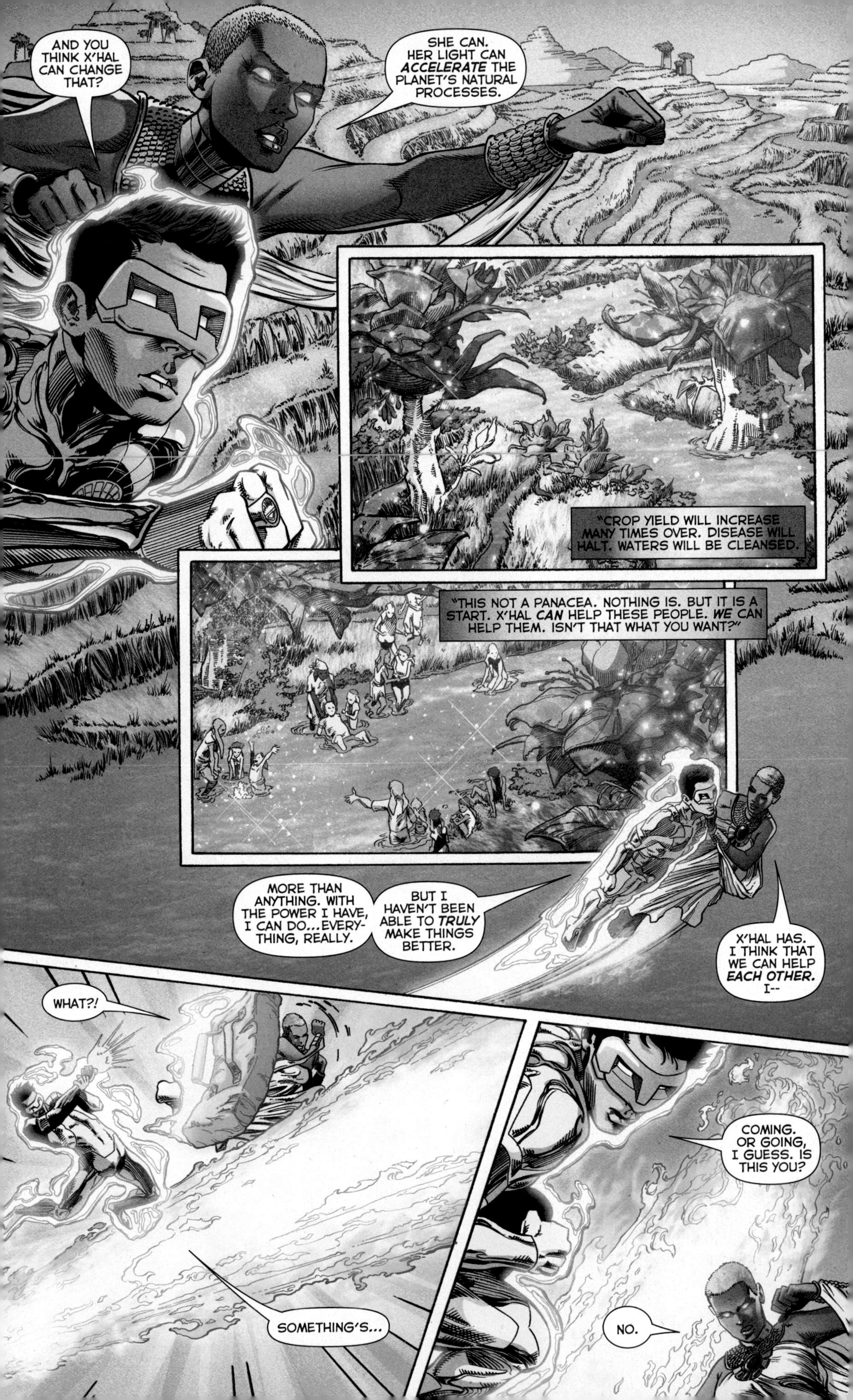
AND YOU THINK X'HAL CAN CHANGE THAT?
SHE CAN. HER LIGHT CAN *ACCELERATE* THE PLANET'S NATURAL PROCESSES.
"CROP YIELD WILL INCREASE MANY TIMES OVER. DISEASE WILL HALT. WATERS WILL BE CLEANSED.
"THIS NOT A PANACEA. NOTHING IS. BUT IT IS A START. X'HAL *CAN* HELP THESE PEOPLE. *WE* CAN HELP THEM. ISN'T THAT WHAT YOU WANT?"
MORE THAN ANYTHING. WITH THE POWER I HAVE, I CAN DO...EVERY-THING, REALLY.
BUT I HAVEN'T BEEN ABLE TO *TRULY* MAKE THINGS BETTER.
X'HAL HAS. I THINK THAT WE CAN HELP *EACH OTHER.* I--
WHAT?!
SOMETHING'S...
COMING. OR GOING, I GUESS. IS THIS YOU?
NO.

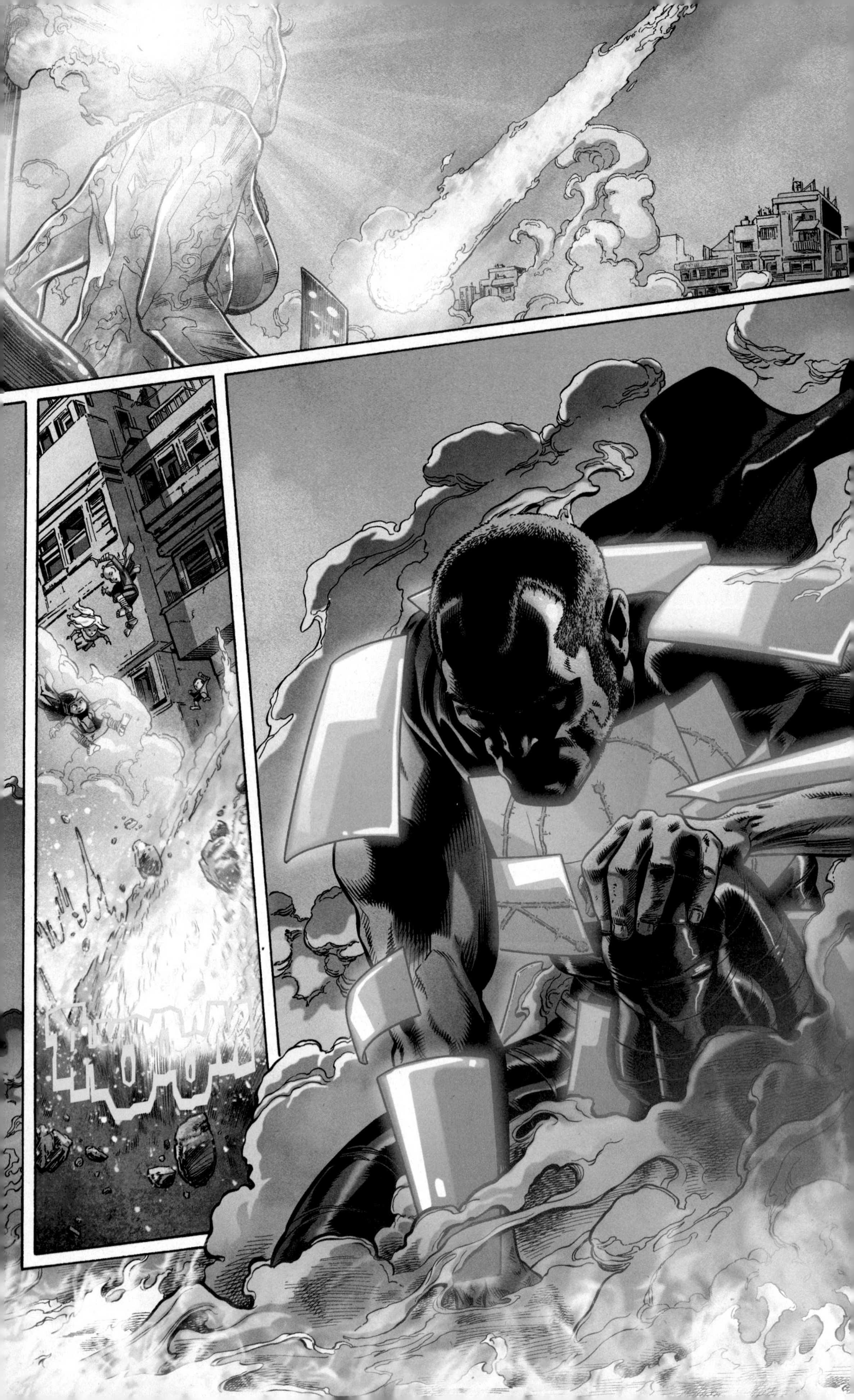
THOOM

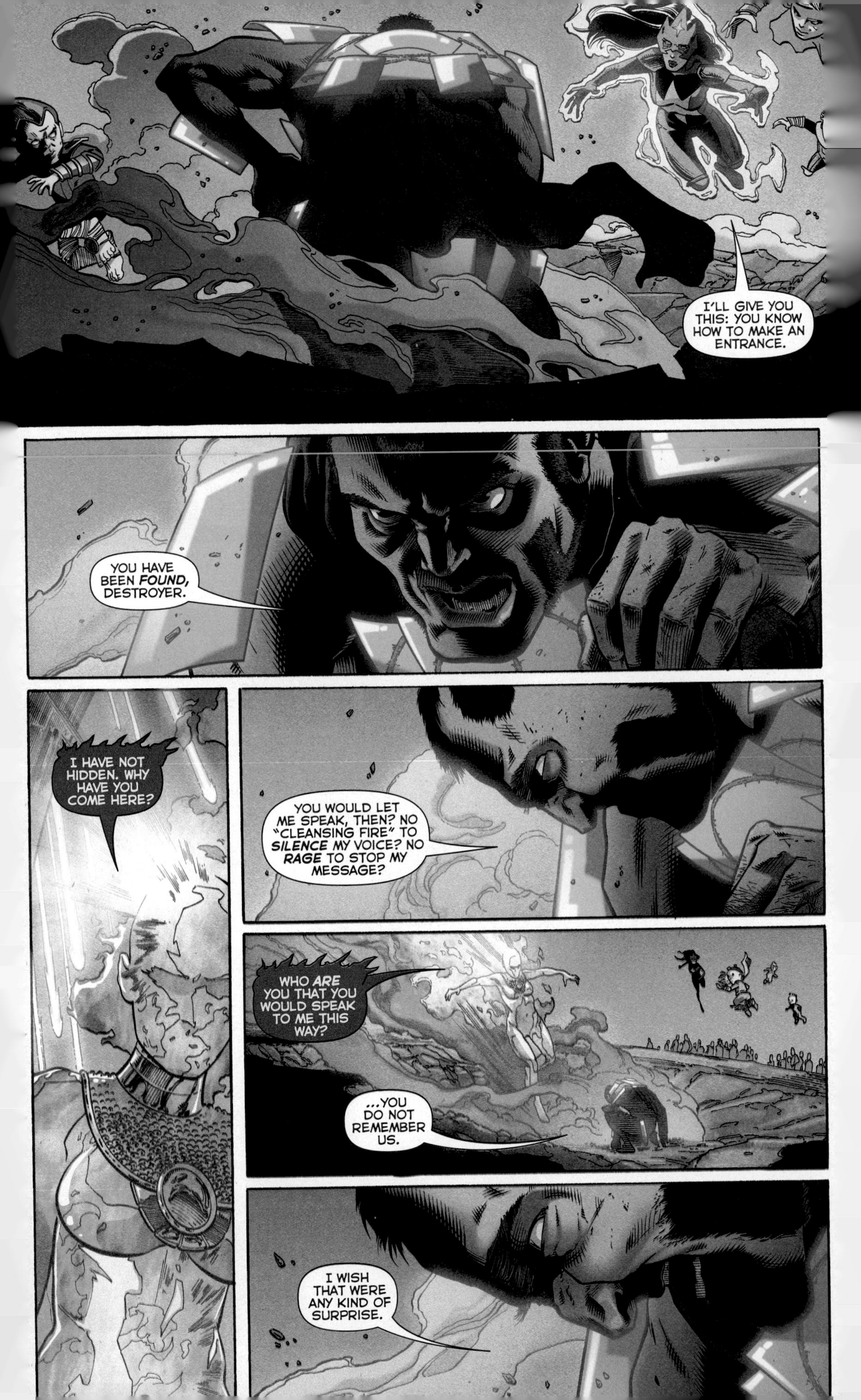
I'LL GIVE YOU THIS: YOU KNOW HOW TO MAKE AN ENTRANCE.
YOU HAVE BEEN FOUND, DESTROYER.
I HAVE NOT HIDDEN. WHY HAVE YOU COME HERE?
YOU WOULD LET ME SPEAK, THEN? NO "CLEANSING FIRE" TO SILENCE MY VOICE? NO RAGE TO STOP MY MESSAGE?
WHO ARE YOU THAT YOU WOULD SPEAK TO ME THIS WAY?
...YOU DO NOT REMEMBER US.
I WISH THAT WERE ANY KIND OF SURPRISE.

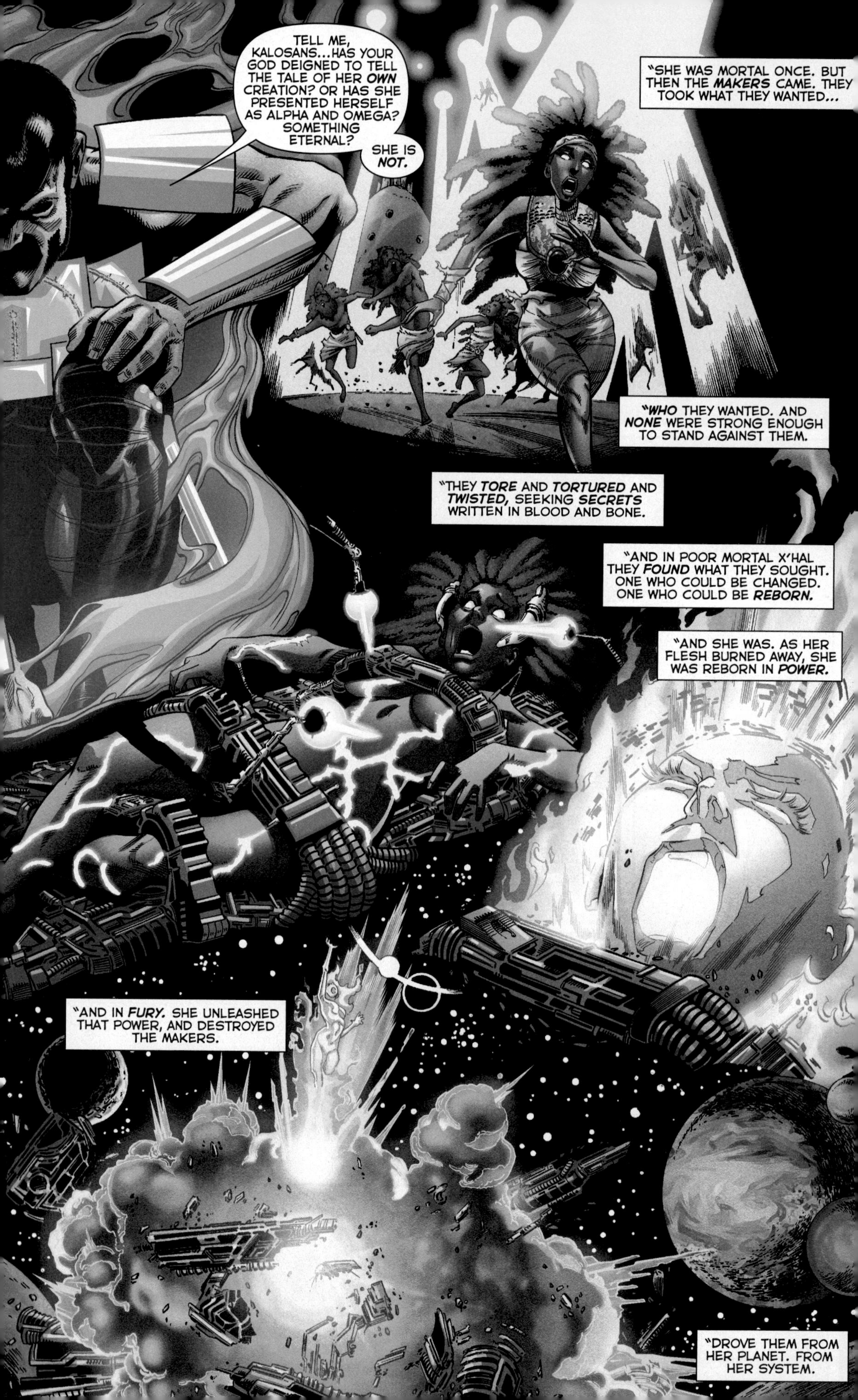
TELL ME, KALOSANS...HAS YOUR GOD DEIGNED TO TELL THE TALE OF HER OWN CREATION? OR HAS SHE PRESENTED HERSELF AS ALPHA AND OMEGA? SOMETHING ETERNAL?
SHE IS NOT.
"SHE WAS MORTAL ONCE. BUT THEN THE MAKERS CAME. THEY TOOK WHAT THEY WANTED...
"WHO THEY WANTED. AND NONE WERE STRONG ENOUGH TO STAND AGAINST THEM.
"THEY TORE AND TORTURED AND TWISTED, SEEKING SECRETS WRITTEN IN BLOOD AND BONE.
"AND IN POOR MORTAL X'HAL THEY FOUND WHAT THEY SOUGHT. ONE WHO COULD BE CHANGED. ONE WHO COULD BE REBORN.
"AND SHE WAS. AS HER FLESH BURNED AWAY, SHE WAS REBORN IN POWER.
"AND IN FURY. SHE UNLEASHED THAT POWER, AND DESTROYED THE MAKERS.
"DROVE THEM FROM HER PLANET. FROM HER SYSTEM.

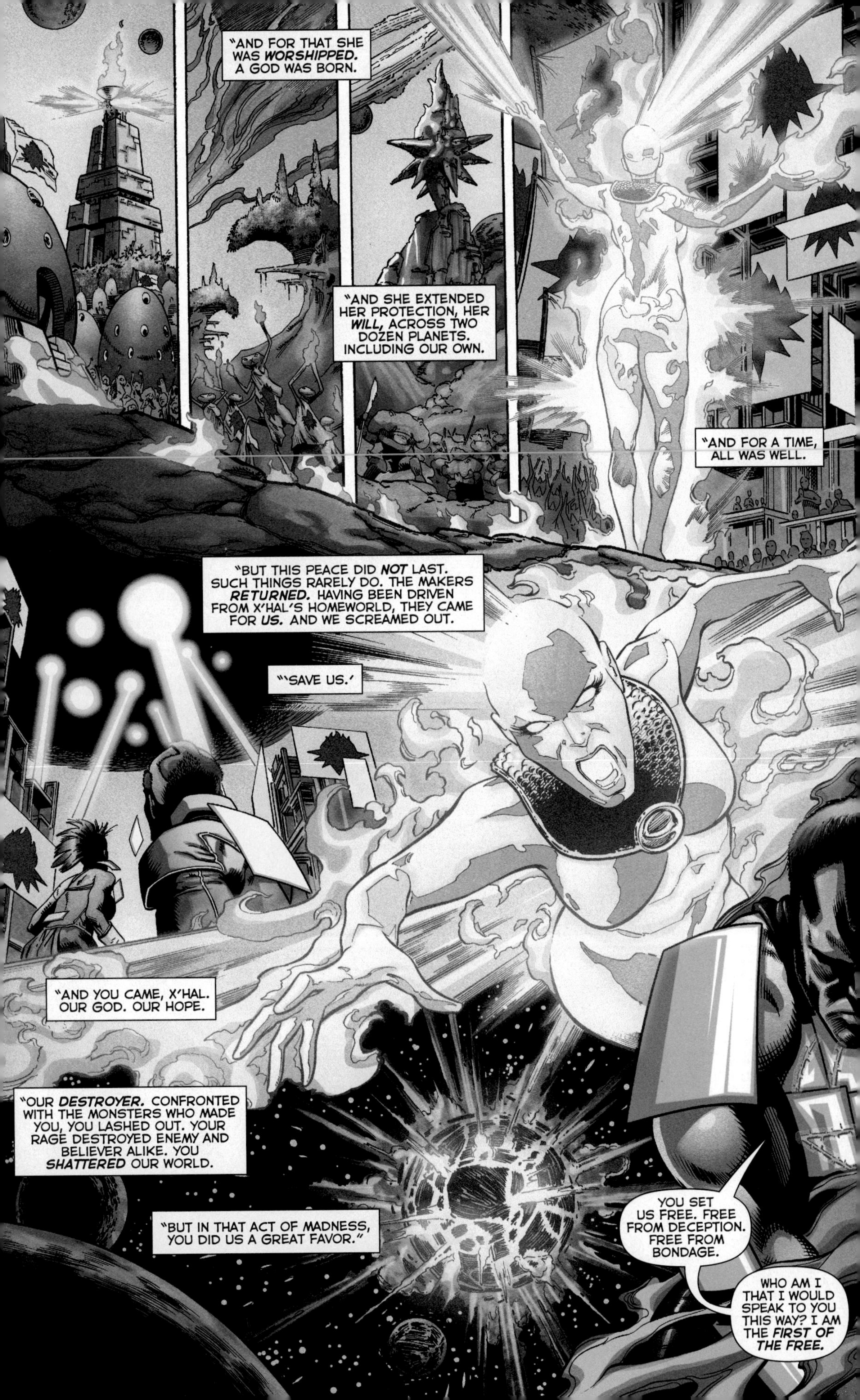
"AND FOR THAT SHE WAS WORSHIPPED. A GOD WAS BORN.
"AND SHE EXTENDED HER PROTECTION, HER WILL, ACROSS TWO DOZEN PLANETS. INCLUDING OUR OWN.
"AND FOR A TIME, ALL WAS WELL.
"BUT THIS PEACE DID NOT LAST. SUCH THINGS RARELY DO. THE MAKERS RETURNED. HAVING BEEN DRIVEN FROM X'HAL'S HOMEWORLD, THEY CAME FOR US. AND WE SCREAMED OUT.
"'SAVE US.'
"AND YOU CAME, X'HAL. OUR GOD. OUR HOPE.
"OUR DESTROYER. CONFRONTED WITH THE MONSTERS WHO MADE YOU, YOU LASHED OUT. YOUR RAGE DESTROYED ENEMY AND BELIEVER ALIKE. YOU SHATTERED OUR WORLD.
"BUT IN THAT ACT OF MADNESS, YOU DID US A GREAT FAVOR."
YOU SET US FREE. FREE FROM DECEPTION. FREE FROM BONDAGE.
WHO AM I THAT I WOULD SPEAK TO YOU THIS WAY? I AM THE FIRST OF THE FREE.

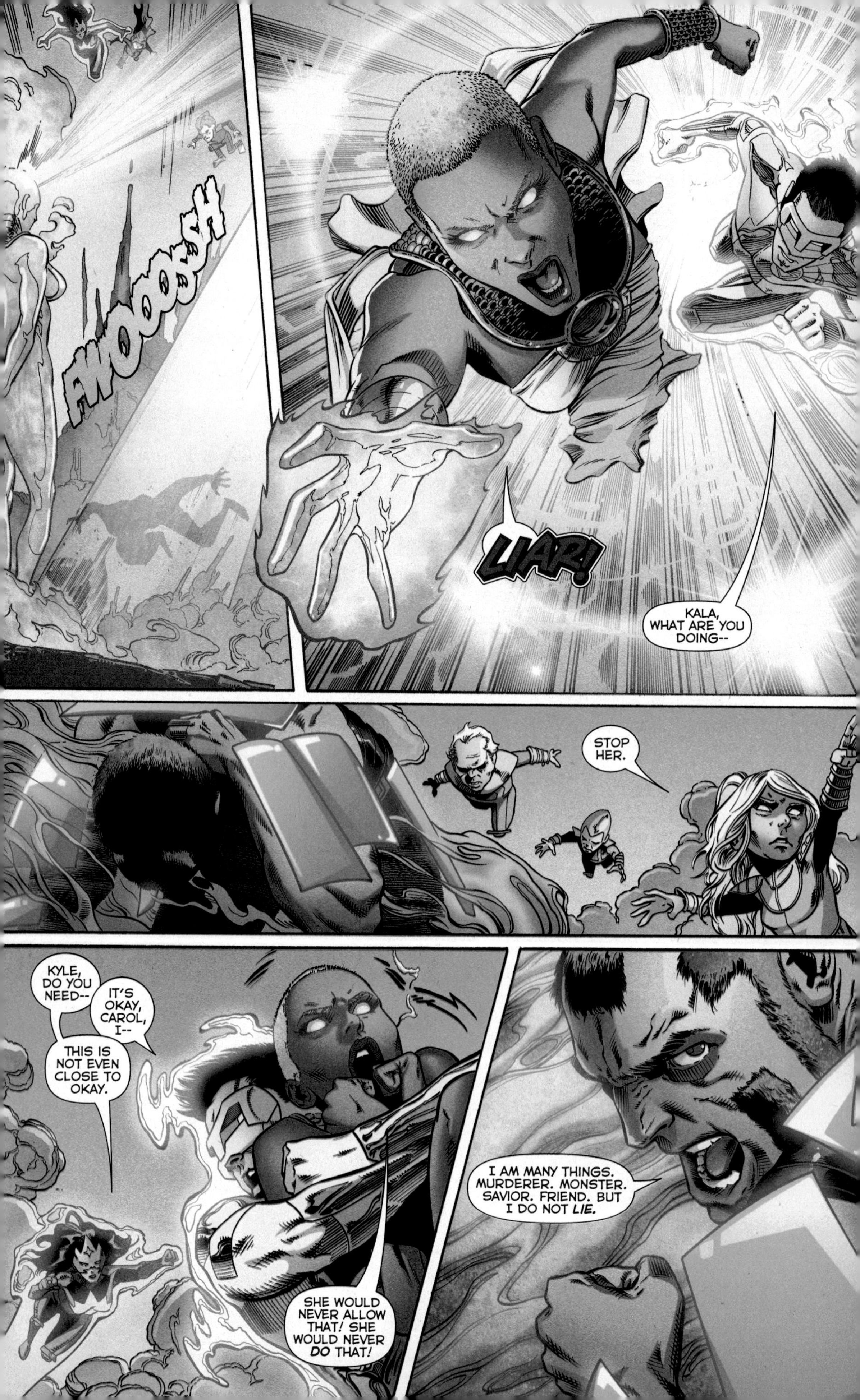
FWOOOSH
LIAR!
KALA, WHAT ARE YOU DOING--
STOP HER.
KYLE, DO YOU NEED--
IT'S OKAY, CAROL, I--
THIS IS NOT EVEN CLOSE TO OKAY.
SHE WOULD NEVER ALLOW THAT! SHE WOULD NEVER DO THAT!
I AM MANY THINGS. MURDERER. MONSTER. SAVIOR. FRIEND. BUT I DO NOT LIE.

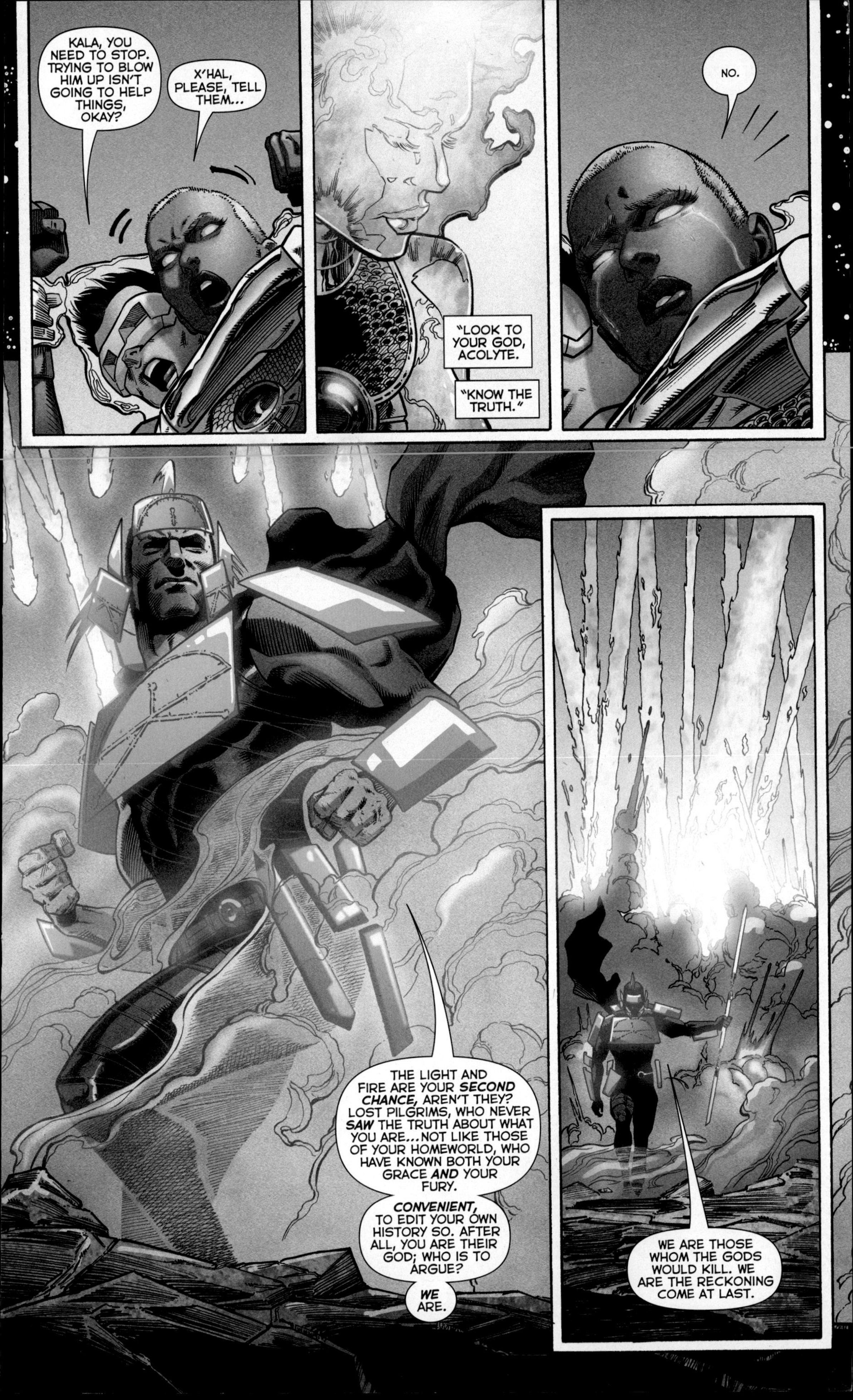
KALA, YOU NEED TO STOP. TRYING TO BLOW HIM UP ISN'T GOING TO HELP THINGS, OKAY?
X'HAL, PLEASE, TELL THEM...
"LOOK TO YOUR GOD, ACOLYTE.
"KNOW THE TRUTH."
NO.
THE LIGHT AND FIRE ARE YOUR SECOND CHANCE, AREN'T THEY? LOST PILGRIMS, WHO NEVER SAW THE TRUTH ABOUT WHAT YOU ARE...NOT LIKE THOSE OF YOUR HOMEWORLD, WHO HAVE KNOWN BOTH YOUR GRACE AND YOUR FURY.
CONVENIENT, TO EDIT YOUR OWN HISTORY SO. AFTER ALL, YOU ARE THEIR GOD; WHO IS TO ARGUE?
WE ARE.
WE ARE THOSE WHOM THE GODS WOULD KILL. WE ARE THE RECKONING COME AT LAST.

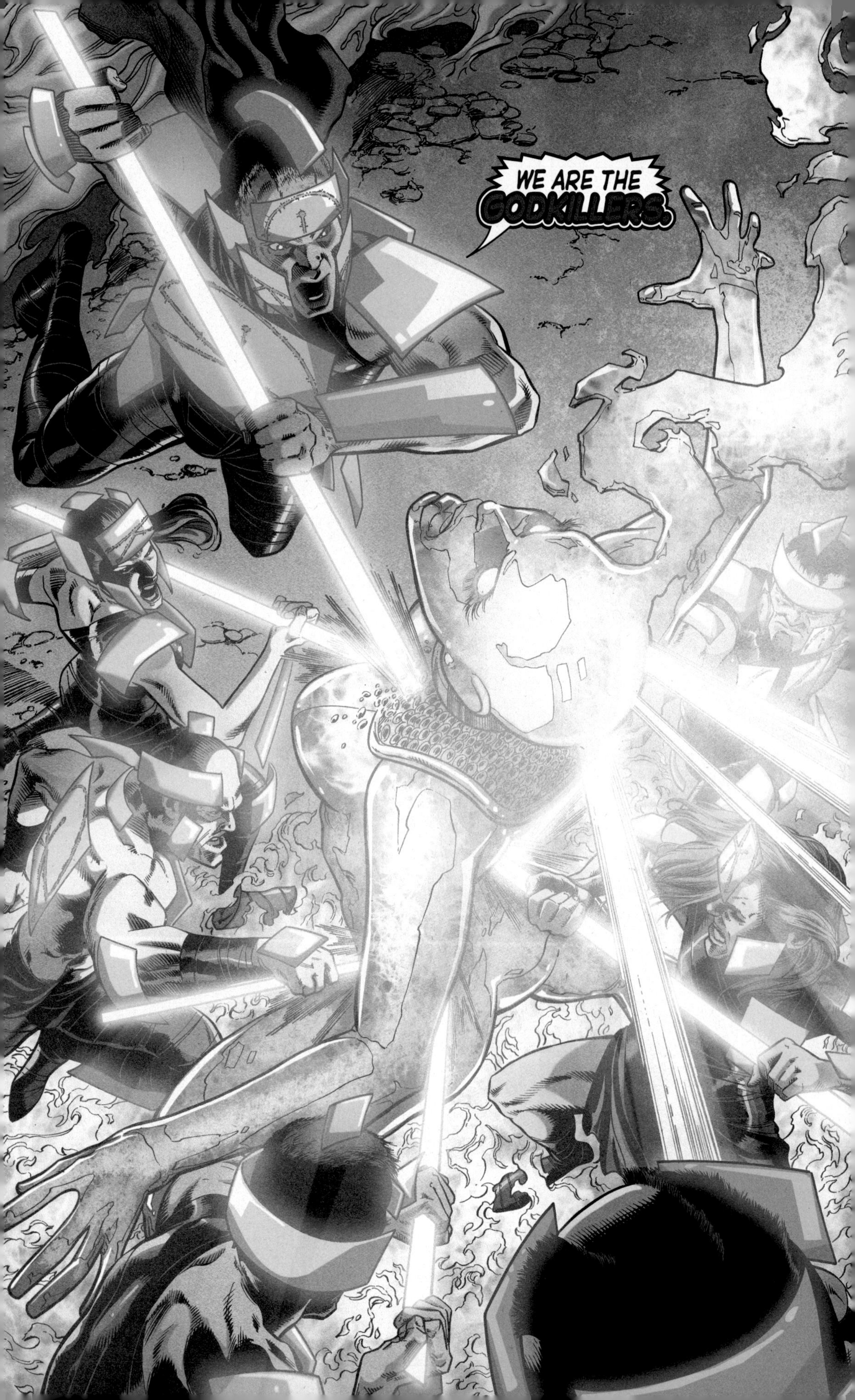
WE ARE THE GODKILLERS.

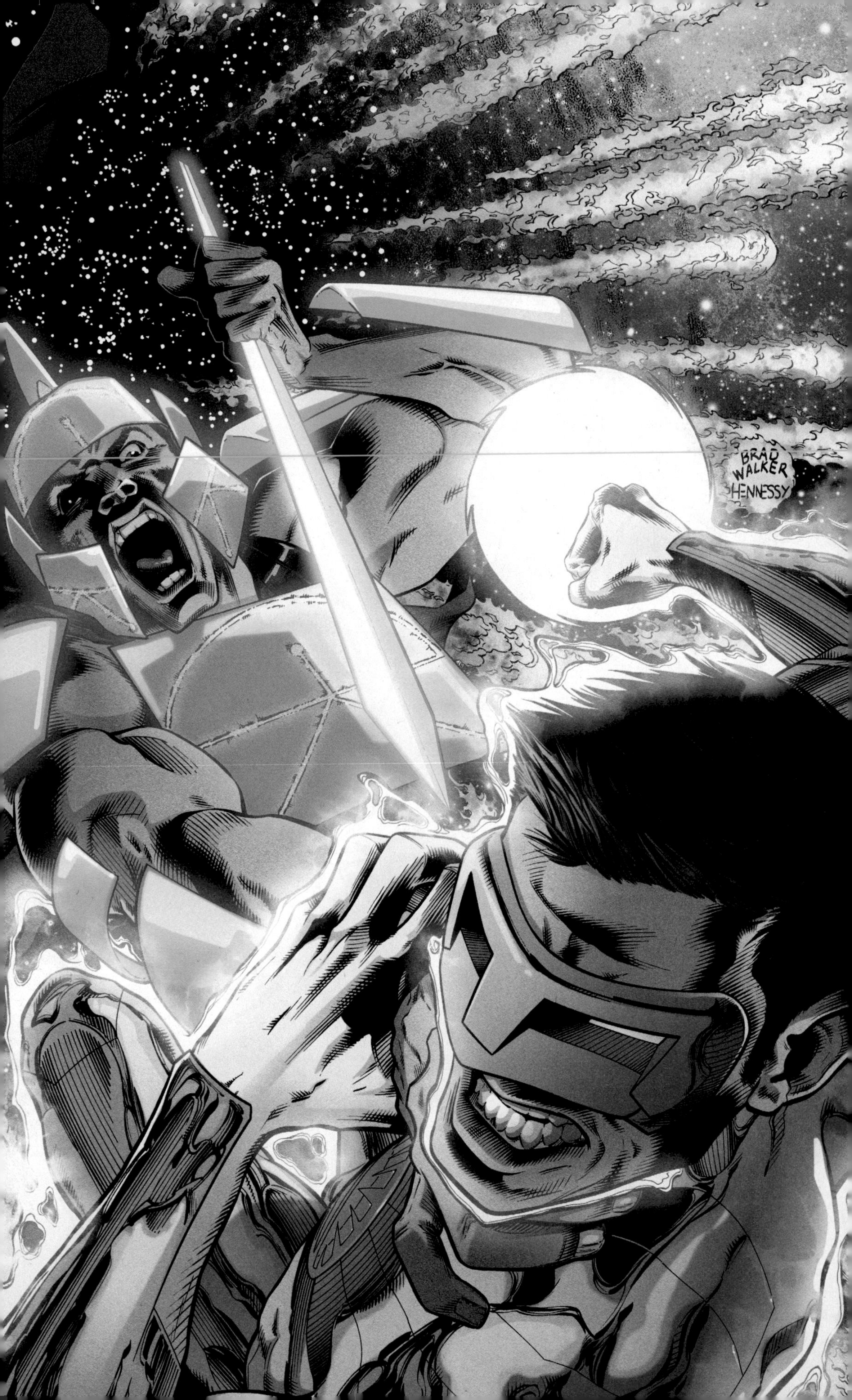
BRAD
WALKER
HENNESSY

HOW THE GODS KILL: THE GODKILLERS PART III

JUSTIN JORDAN writer BRAD WALKER with DIOGENES NEVES (pgs 64-70) pencillers ANDREW HENNESSY with MARC DEERING (pgs 64-70) inkers WIL QUINTANA colorist DAVE SHARPE letterer cover art by BRAD WALKER, ANDREW HENNESSY and WIL QUINTANA

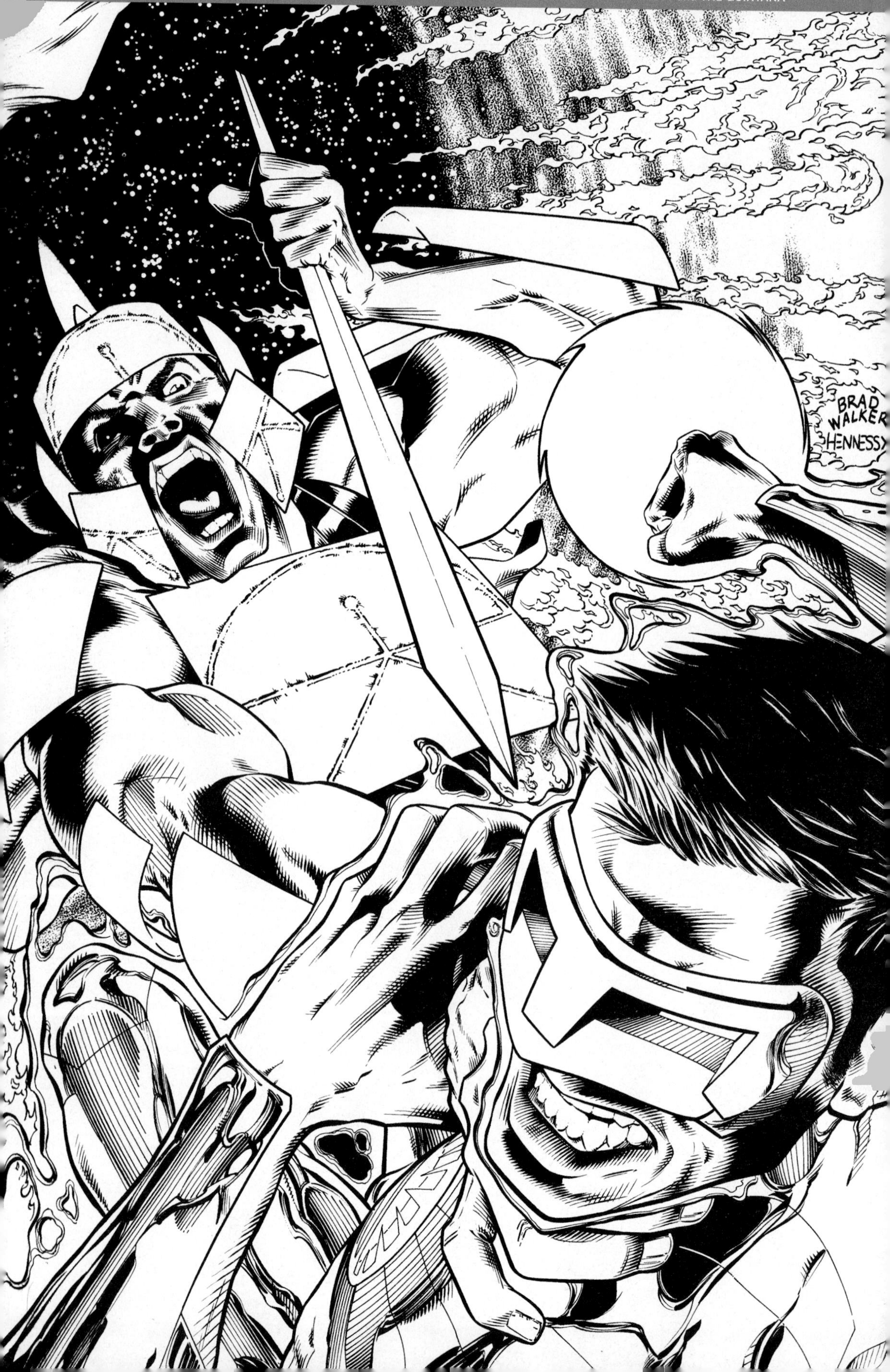
BRAD WALKER
HENNESSY

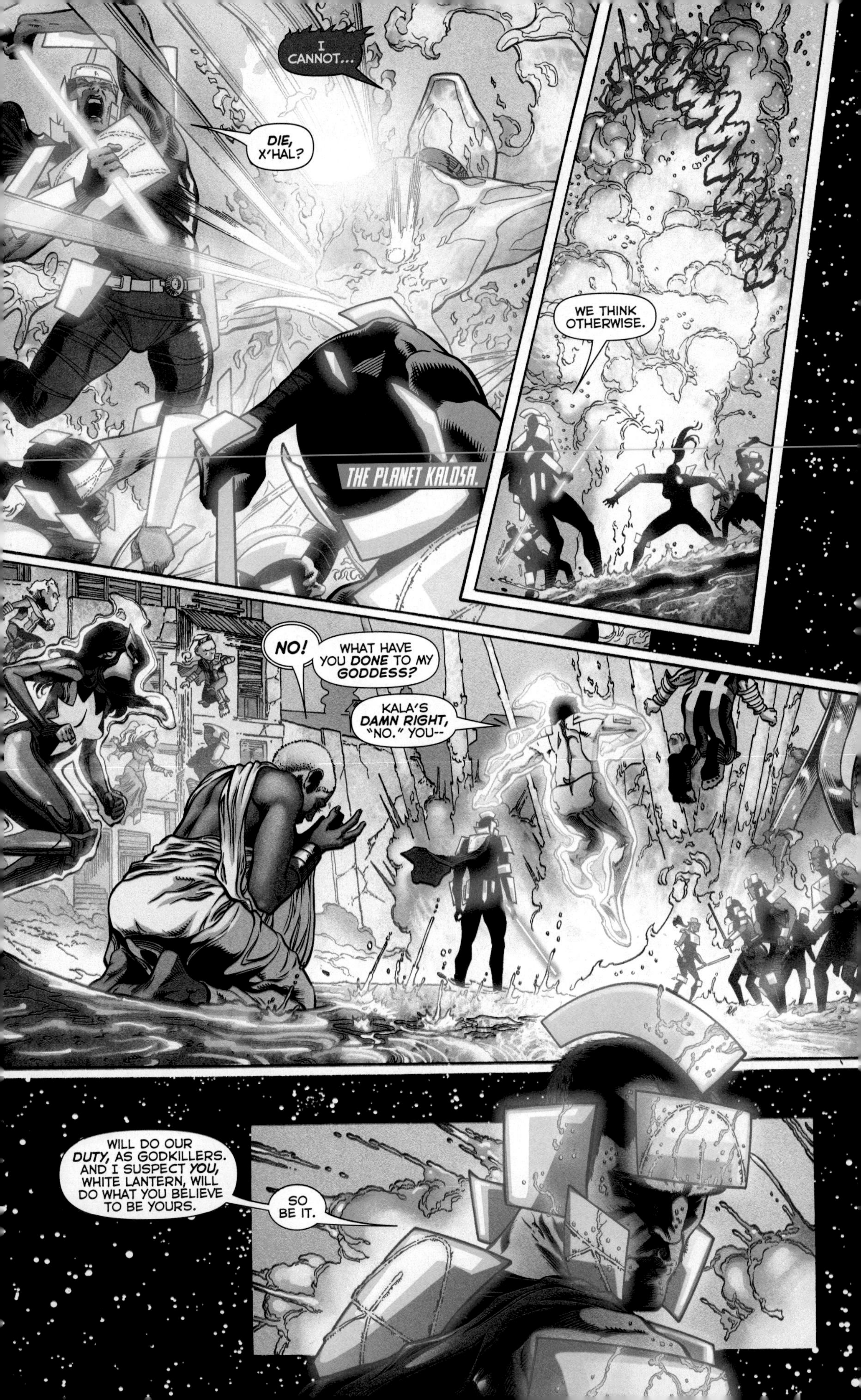
I CANNOT...
DIE, X'HAL?
THE PLANET KALOSA.
WE THINK OTHERWISE.
NO!
WHAT HAVE YOU DONE TO MY GODDESS?
KALA'S DAMN RIGHT, "NO." YOU--
WILL DO OUR DUTY, AS GODKILLERS. AND I SUSPECT YOU, WHITE LANTERN, WILL DO WHAT YOU BELIEVE TO BE YOURS.
SO BE IT.

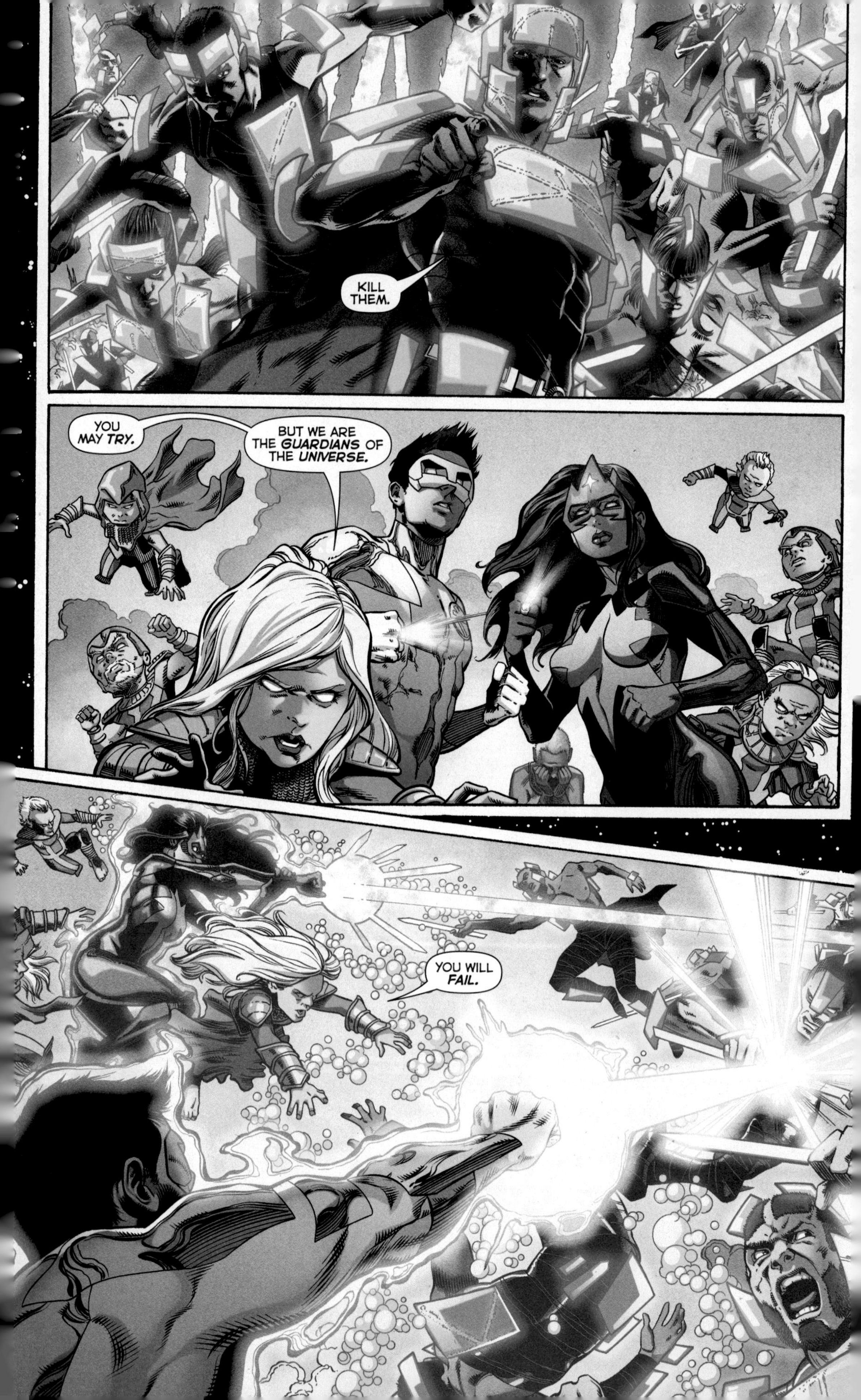
KILL THEM.
YOU MAY TRY.
BUT WE ARE THE GUARDIANS OF THE UNIVERSE.
YOU WILL FAIL.

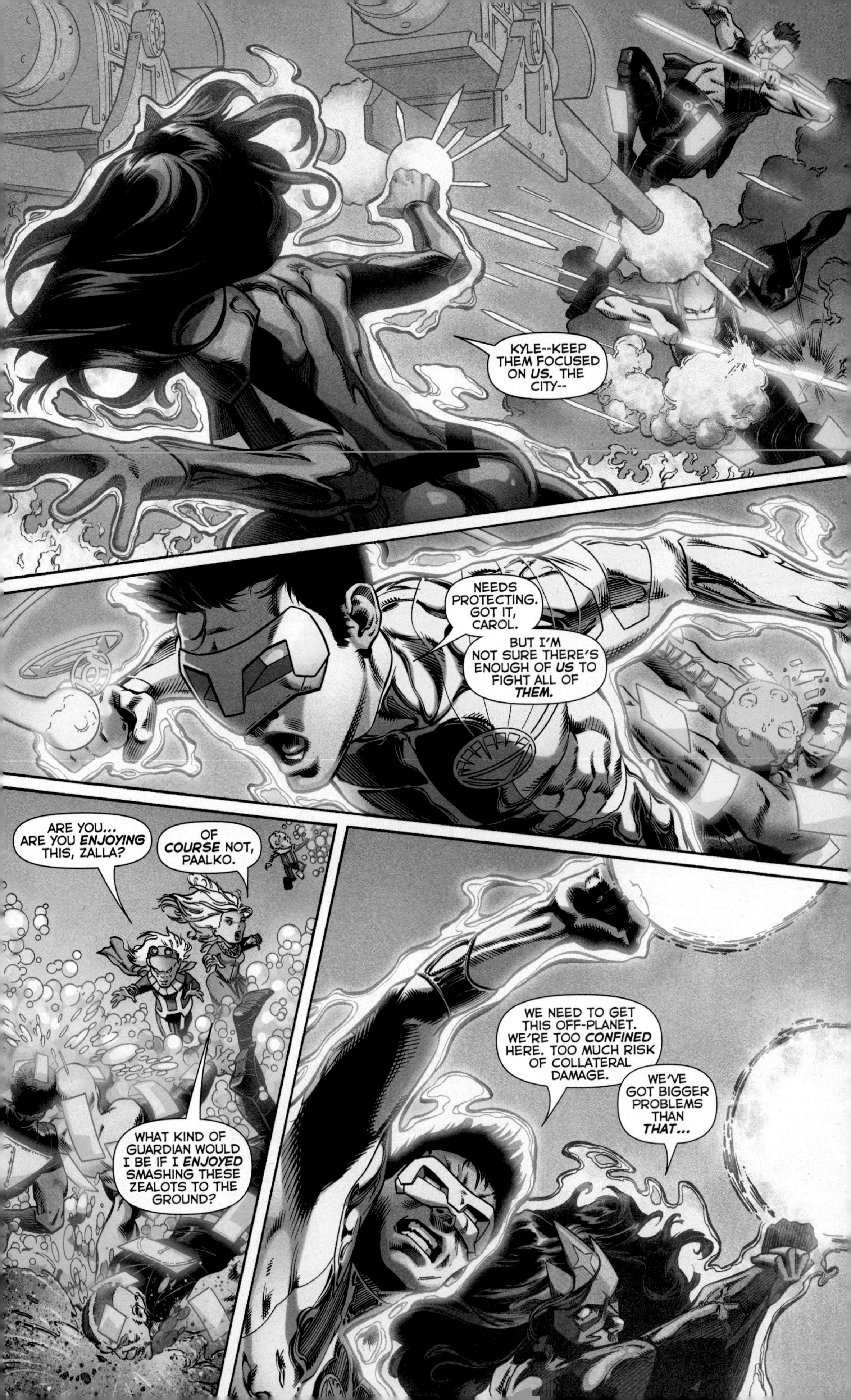
KYLE--KEEP THEM FOCUSED ON US. THE CITY--
NEEDS PROTECTING. GOT IT, CAROL.
BUT I'M NOT SURE THERE'S ENOUGH OF US TO FIGHT ALL OF THEM.
ARE YOU... ARE YOU ENJOYING THIS, ZALLA?
OF COURSE NOT, PAALKO.
WHAT KIND OF GUARDIAN WOULD I BE IF I ENJOYED SMASHING THESE ZEALOTS TO THE GROUND?
WE NEED TO GET THIS OFF-PLANET. WE'RE TOO CONFINED HERE. TOO MUCH RISK OF COLLATERAL DAMAGE.
WE'VE GOT BIGGER PROBLEMS THAN THAT...

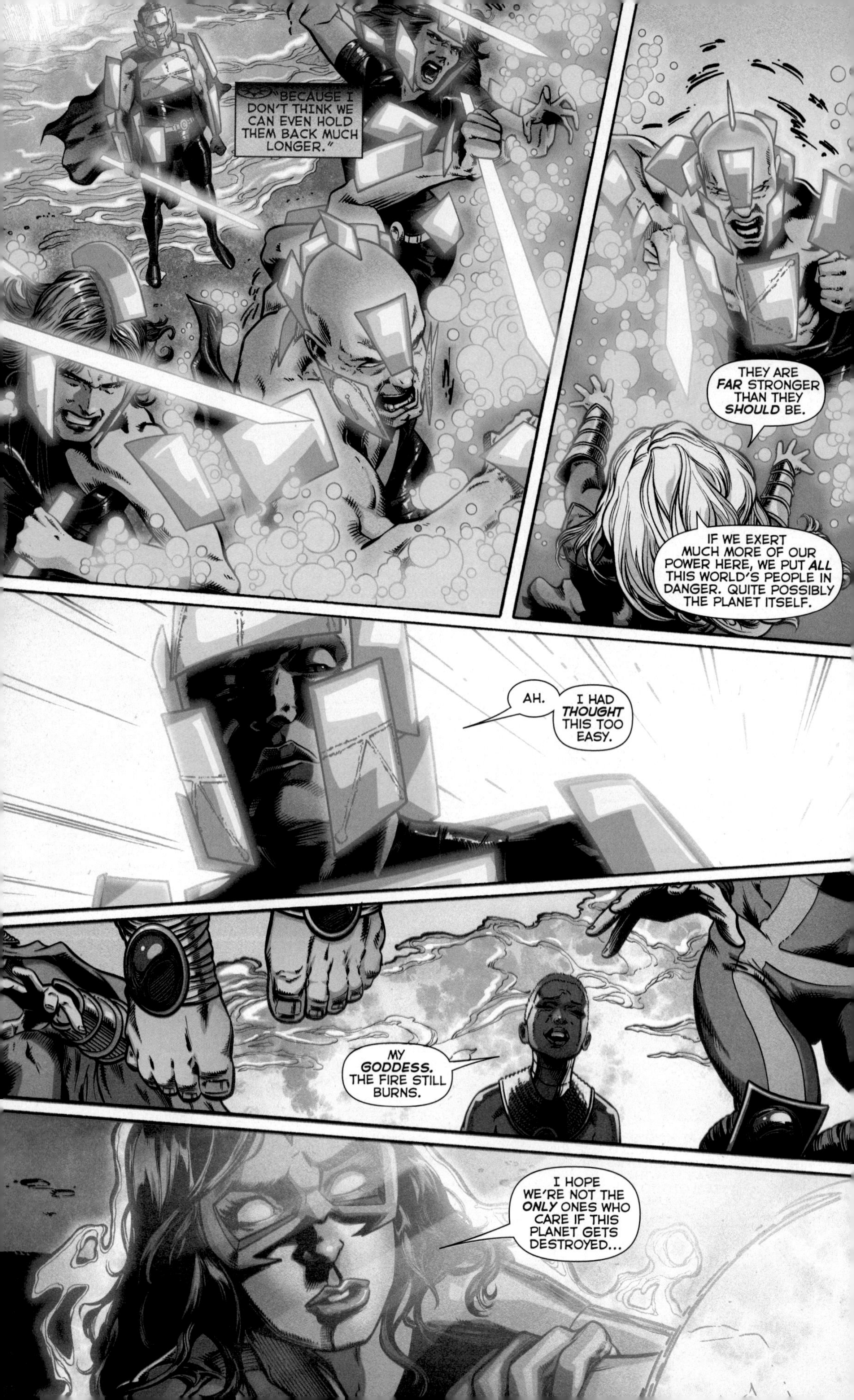
"BECAUSE I DON'T THINK WE CAN EVEN HOLD THEM BACK MUCH LONGER."
THEY ARE FAR STRONGER THAN THEY SHOULD BE.
IF WE EXERT MUCH MORE OF OUR POWER HERE, WE PUT ALL THIS WORLD'S PEOPLE IN DANGER. QUITE POSSIBLY THE PLANET ITSELF.
AH.
I HAD THOUGHT THIS TOO EASY.
MY GODDESS. THE FIRE STILL BURNS.
I HOPE WE'RE NOT THE ONLY ONES WHO CARE IF THIS PLANET GETS DESTROYED...

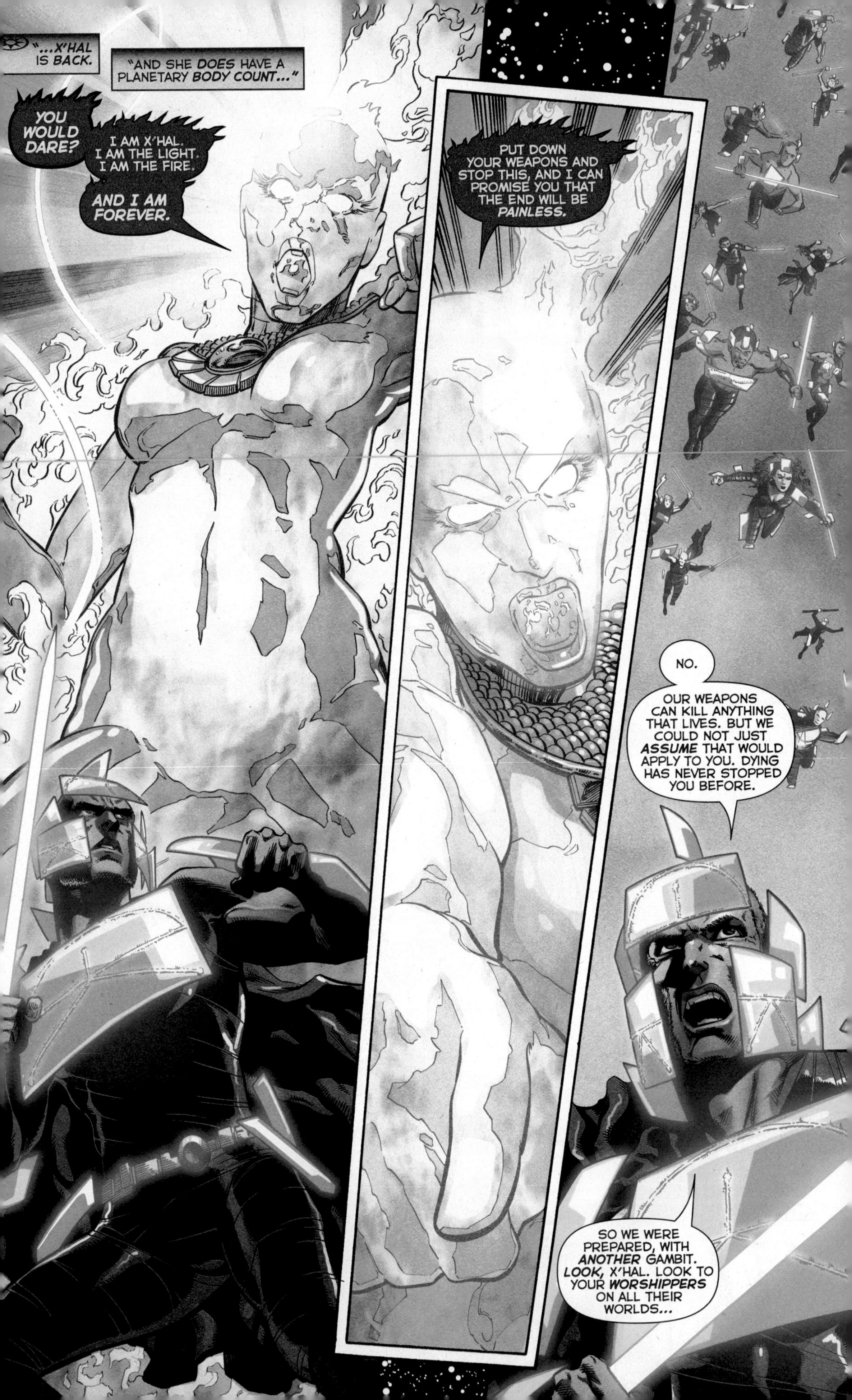
"...X'HAL IS BACK.
"AND SHE DOES HAVE A PLANETARY BODY COUNT..."
YOU WOULD DARE?
I AM X'HAL. I AM THE LIGHT. I AM THE FIRE.
AND I AM FOREVER.
PUT DOWN YOUR WEAPONS AND STOP THIS, AND I CAN PROMISE YOU THAT THE END WILL BE PAINLESS.
NO.
OUR WEAPONS CAN KILL ANYTHING THAT LIVES. BUT WE COULD NOT JUST ASSUME THAT WOULD APPLY TO YOU. DYING HAS NEVER STOPPED YOU BEFORE.
SO WE WERE PREPARED, WITH ANOTHER GAMBIT. LOOK, X'HAL. LOOK TO YOUR WORSHIPPERS ON ALL THEIR WORLDS...

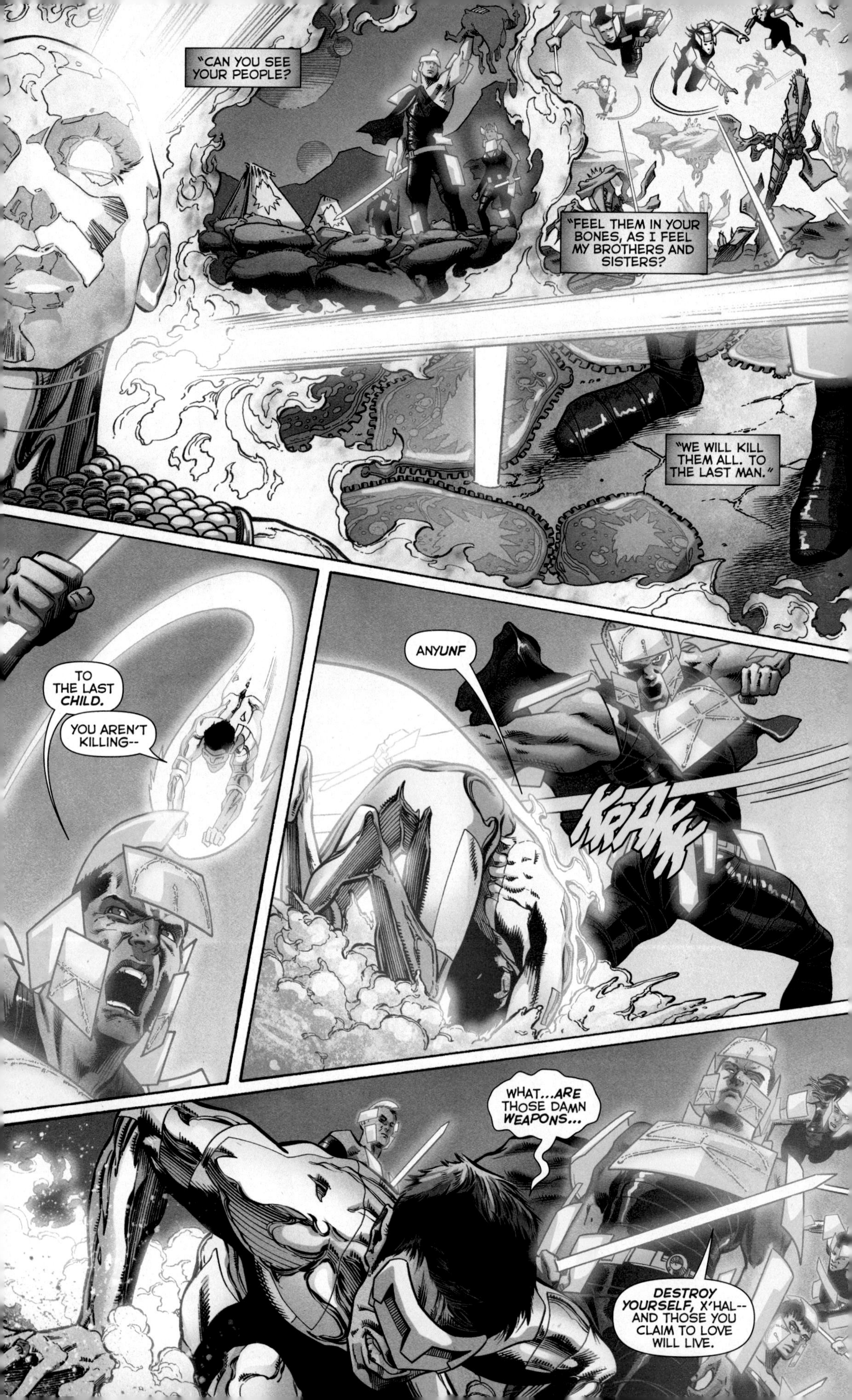
"CAN YOU SEE YOUR PEOPLE?
"FEEL THEM IN YOUR BONES, AS I FEEL MY BROTHERS AND SISTERS?
"WE WILL KILL THEM ALL. TO THE LAST MAN."
TO THE LAST CHILD.
YOU AREN'T KILLING--
ANYUNF
KRAKK
WHAT...ARE THOSE DAMN WEAPONS...
DESTROY YOURSELF, X'HAL-- AND THOSE YOU CLAIM TO LOVE WILL LIVE.

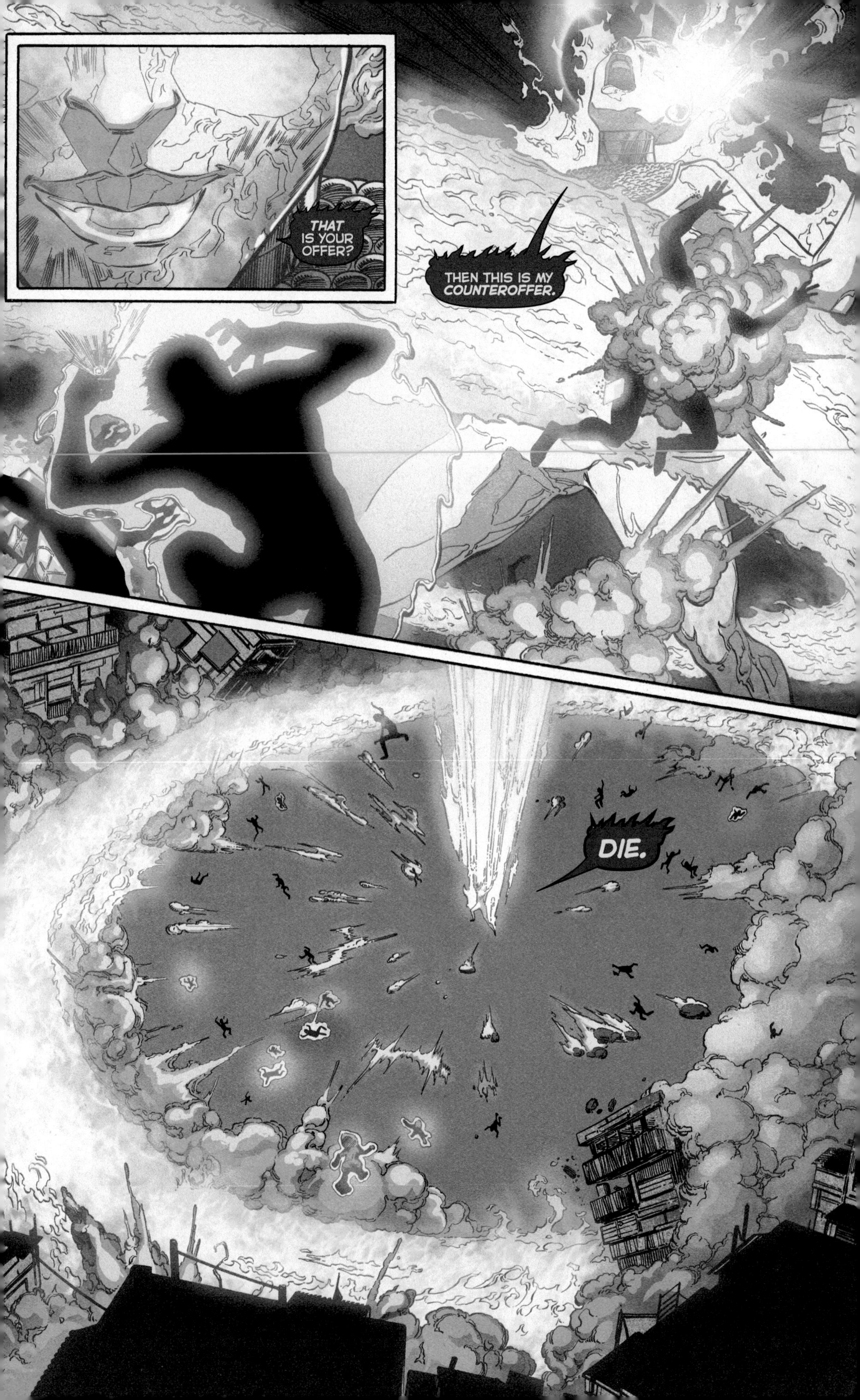
THAT IS YOUR OFFER?
THEN THIS IS MY COUNTEROFFER.
DIE.

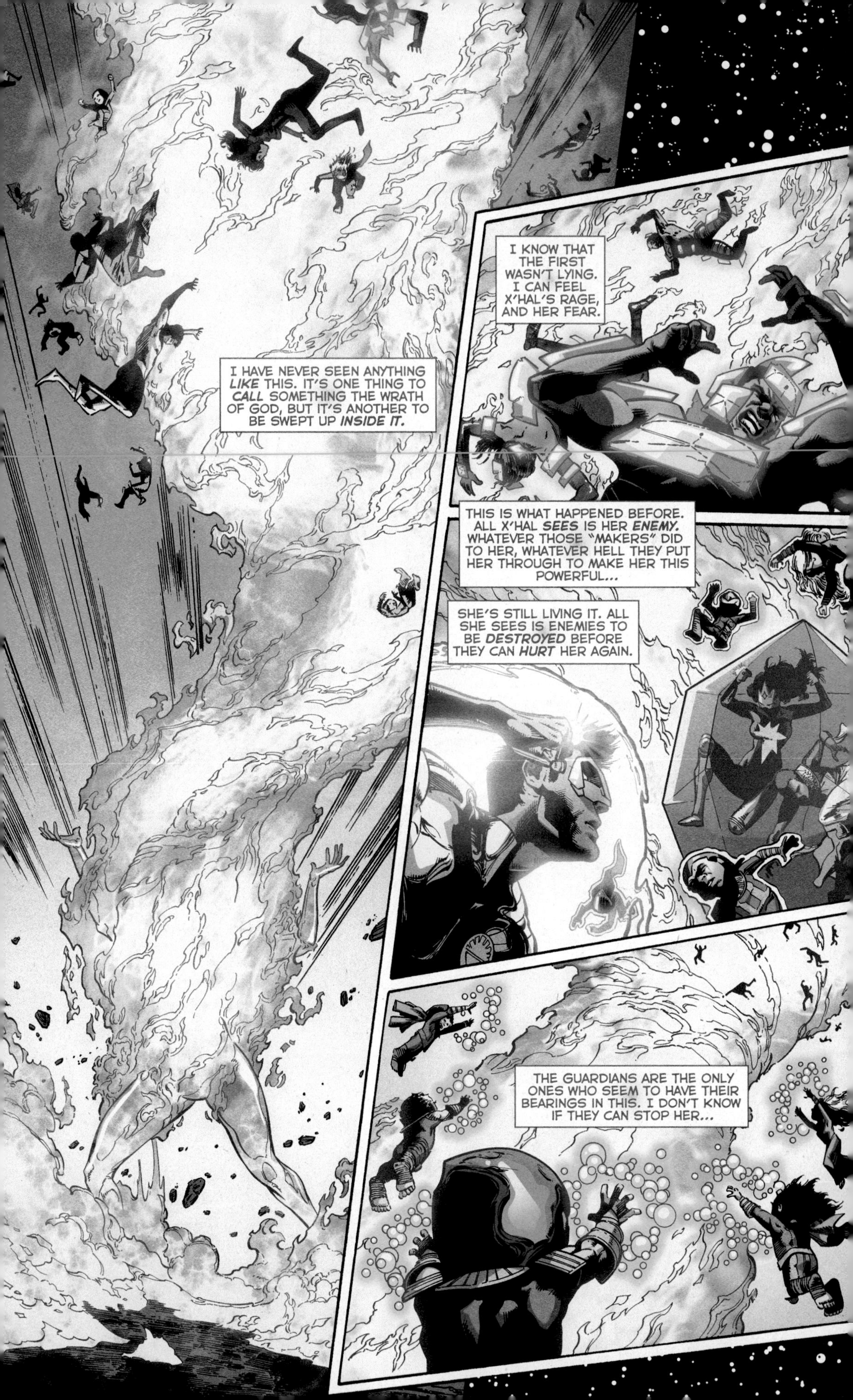
I HAVE NEVER SEEN ANYTHING LIKE THIS. IT'S ONE THING TO CALL SOMETHING THE WRATH OF GOD, BUT IT'S ANOTHER TO BE SWEPT UP INSIDE IT.
I KNOW THAT THE FIRST WASN'T LYING. I CAN FEEL X'HAL'S RAGE, AND HER FEAR.
THIS IS WHAT HAPPENED BEFORE. ALL X'HAL SEES IS HER ENEMY. WHATEVER THOSE "MAKERS" DID TO HER, WHATEVER HELL THEY PUT HER THROUGH TO MAKE HER THIS POWERFUL...
SHE'S STILL LIVING IT. ALL SHE SEES IS ENEMIES TO BE DESTROYED BEFORE THEY CAN HURT HER AGAIN.
THE GUARDIANS ARE THE ONLY ONES WHO SEEM TO HAVE THEIR BEARINGS IN THIS. I DON'T KNOW IF THEY CAN STOP HER...

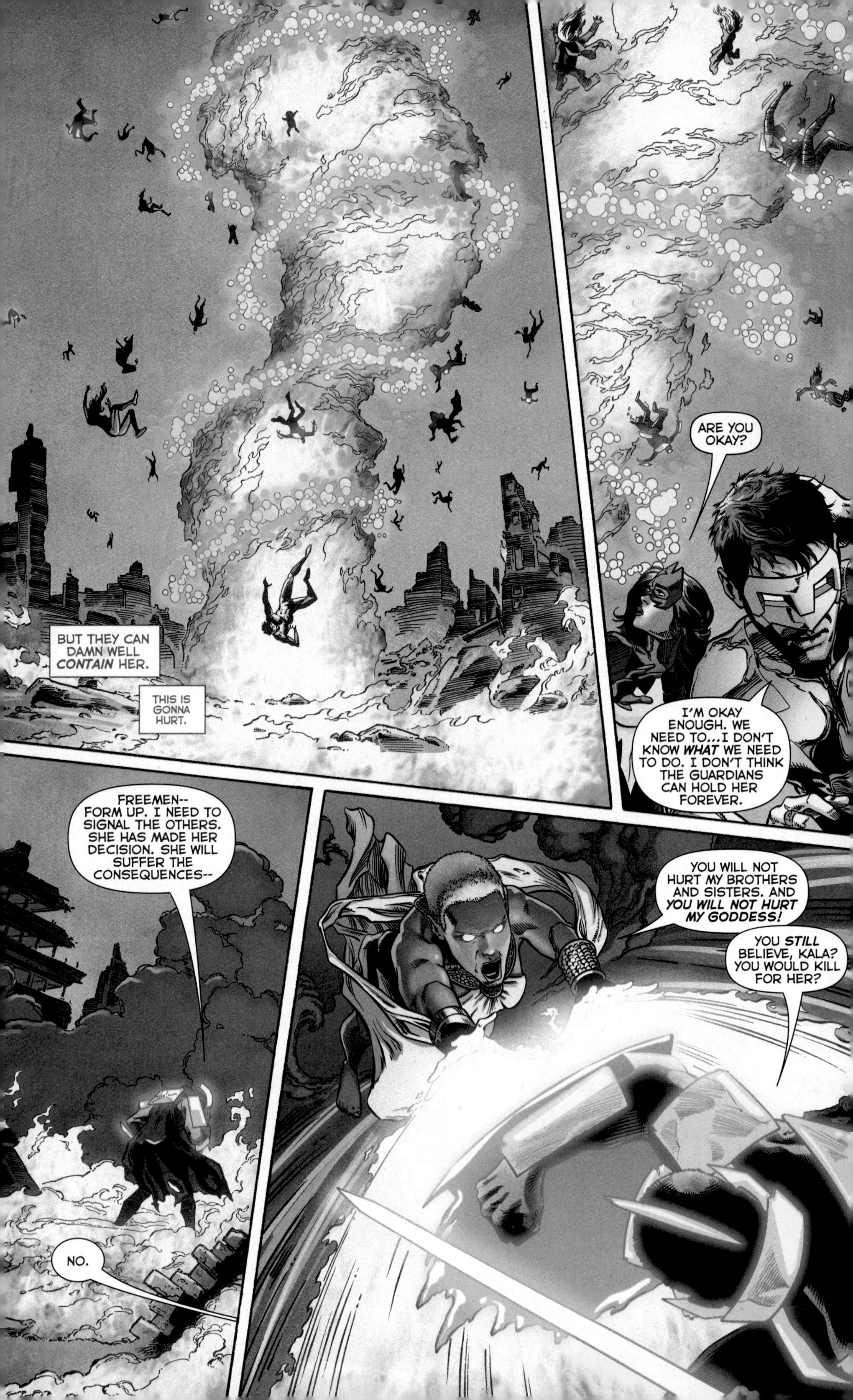
BUT THEY CAN DAMN WELL CONTAIN HER.
THIS IS GONNA HURT.
ARE YOU OKAY?
I'M OKAY ENOUGH. WE NEED TO...I DON'T KNOW WHAT WE NEED TO DO. I DON'T THINK THE GUARDIANS CAN HOLD HER FOREVER.
FREEMEN-- FORM UP. I NEED TO SIGNAL THE OTHERS. SHE HAS MADE HER DECISION. SHE WILL SUFFER THE CONSEQUENCES--
NO.
YOU WILL NOT HURT MY BROTHERS AND SISTERS. AND YOU WILL NOT HURT MY GODDESS!
YOU STILL BELIEVE, KALA? YOU WOULD KILL FOR HER?

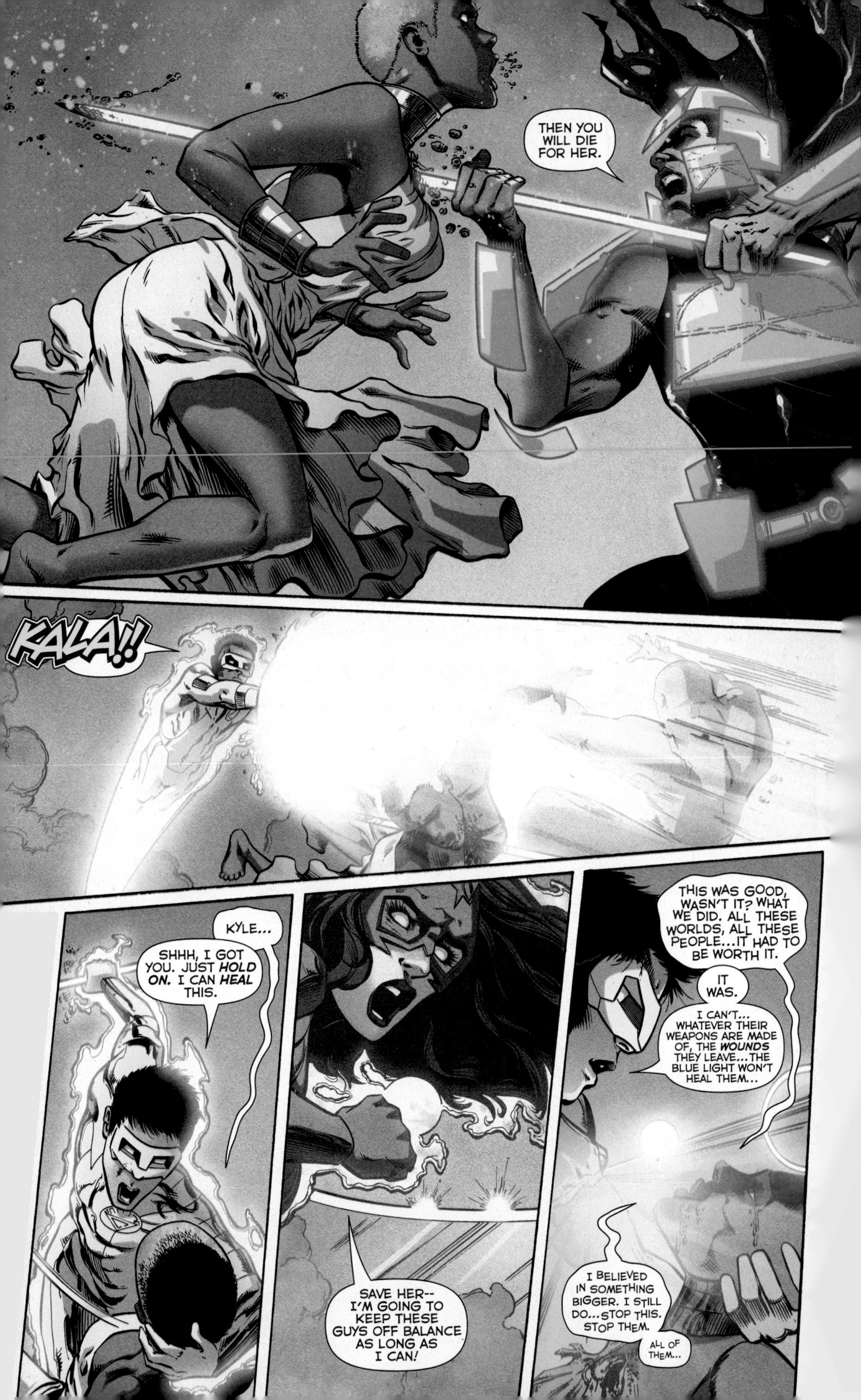
THEN YOU WILL DIE FOR HER.
KALA!!
KYLE...
SHHH, I GOT YOU. JUST HOLD ON. I CAN HEAL THIS.
SAVE HER-- I'M GOING TO KEEP THESE GUYS OFF BALANCE AS LONG AS I CAN!
THIS WAS GOOD, WASN'T IT? WHAT WE DID. ALL THESE WORLDS, ALL THESE PEOPLE...IT HAD TO BE WORTH IT.
IT WAS.
I CAN'T... WHATEVER THEIR WEAPONS ARE MADE OF, THE WOUNDS THEY LEAVE...THE BLUE LIGHT WON'T HEAL THEM...
I BELIEVED IN SOMETHING BIGGER. I STILL DO...STOP THIS. STOP THEM.
ALL OF THEM...

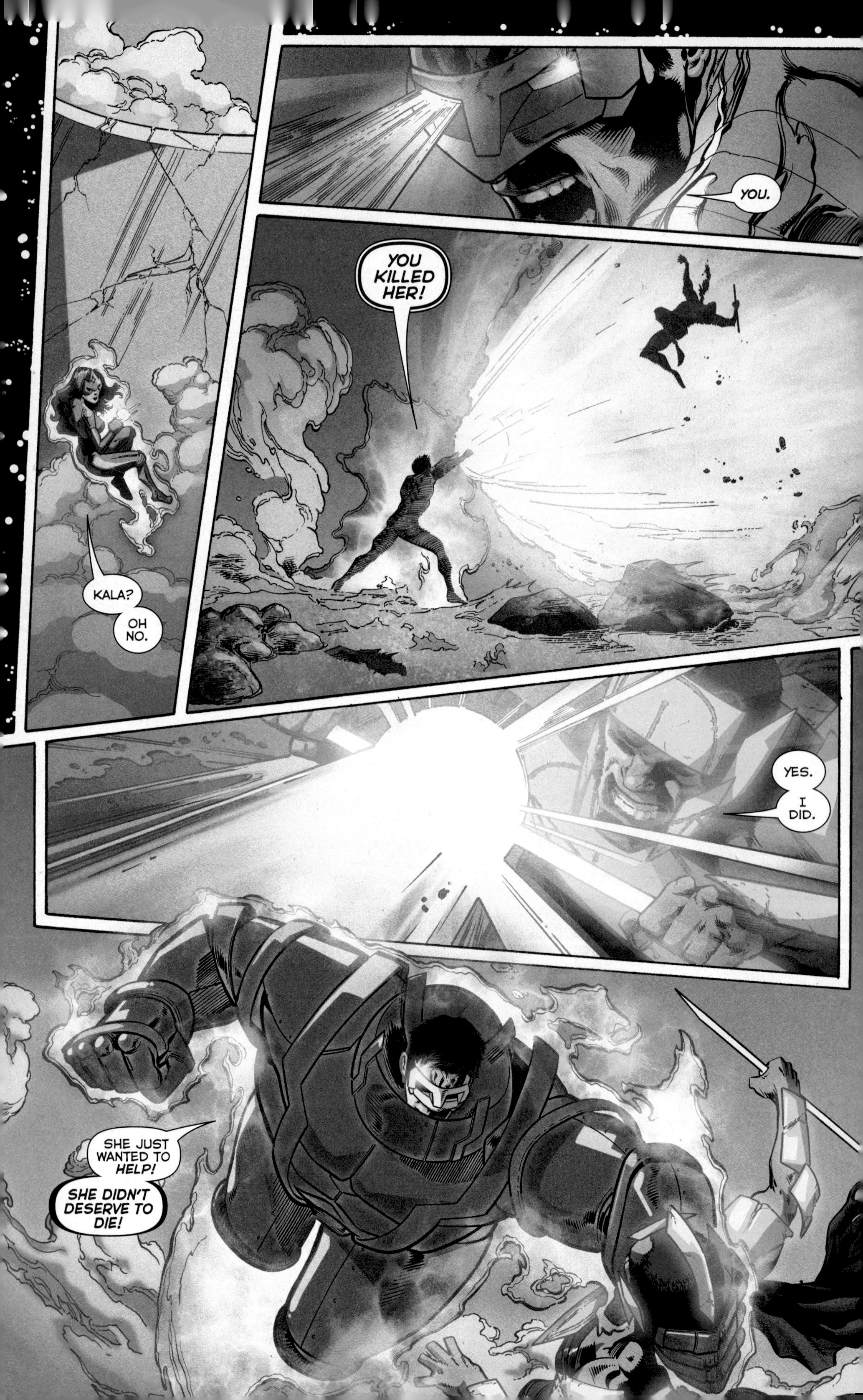
YOU.
YOU KILLED HER!
KALA?
OH NO.
YES.
I DID.
SHE JUST WANTED TO HELP!
SHE DIDN'T DESERVE TO DIE!

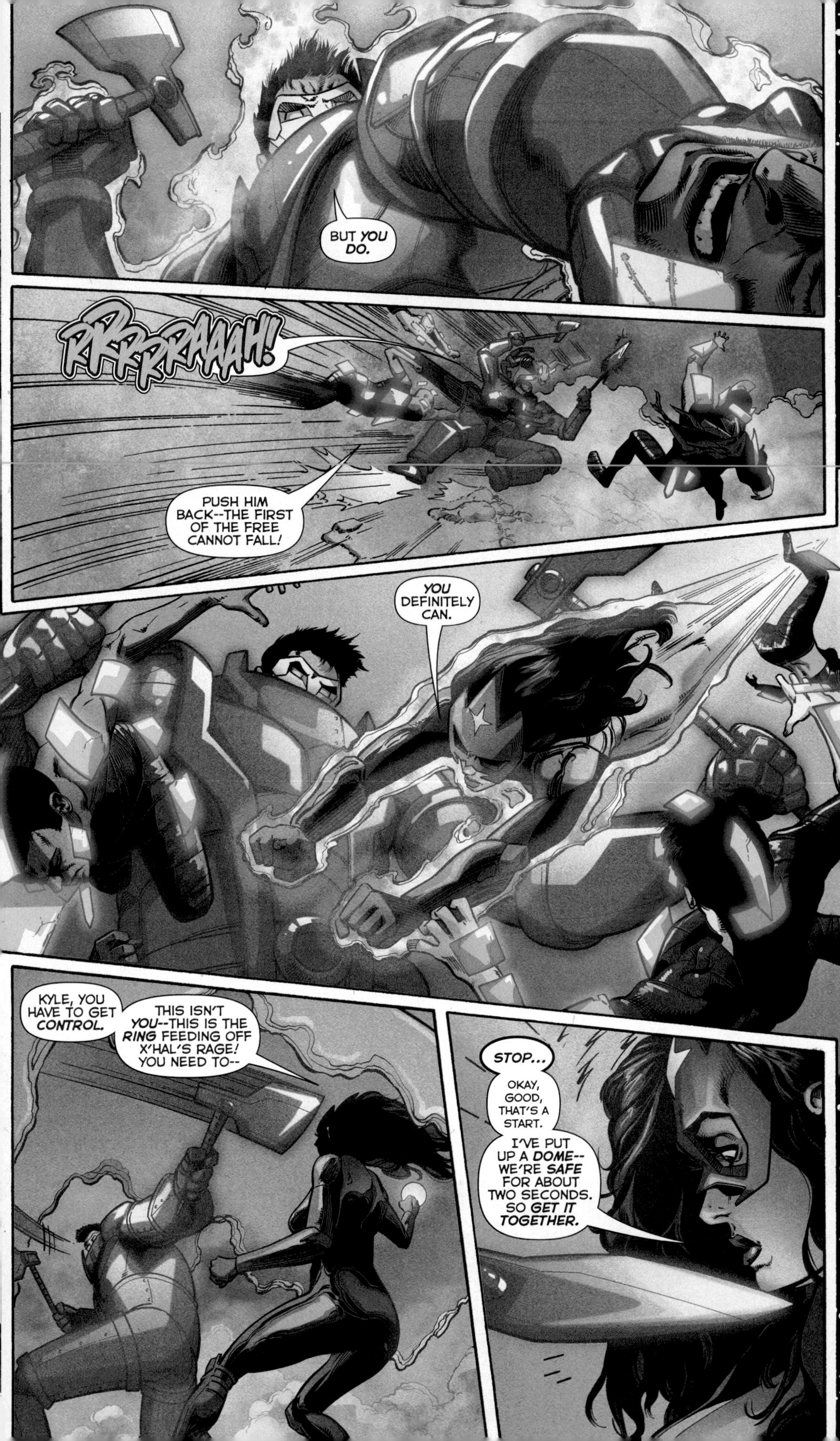
BUT YOU DO.
RRRRRAAAH!
PUSH HIM BACK--THE FIRST OF THE FREE CANNOT FALL!
YOU DEFINITELY CAN.
KYLE, YOU HAVE TO GET CONTROL.
THIS ISN'T YOU--THIS IS THE RING FEEDING OFF X'HAL'S RAGE! YOU NEED TO--
STOP...
OKAY, GOOD, THAT'S A START.
I'VE PUT UP A DOME--WE'RE SAFE FOR ABOUT TWO SECONDS. SO GET IT TOGETHER.

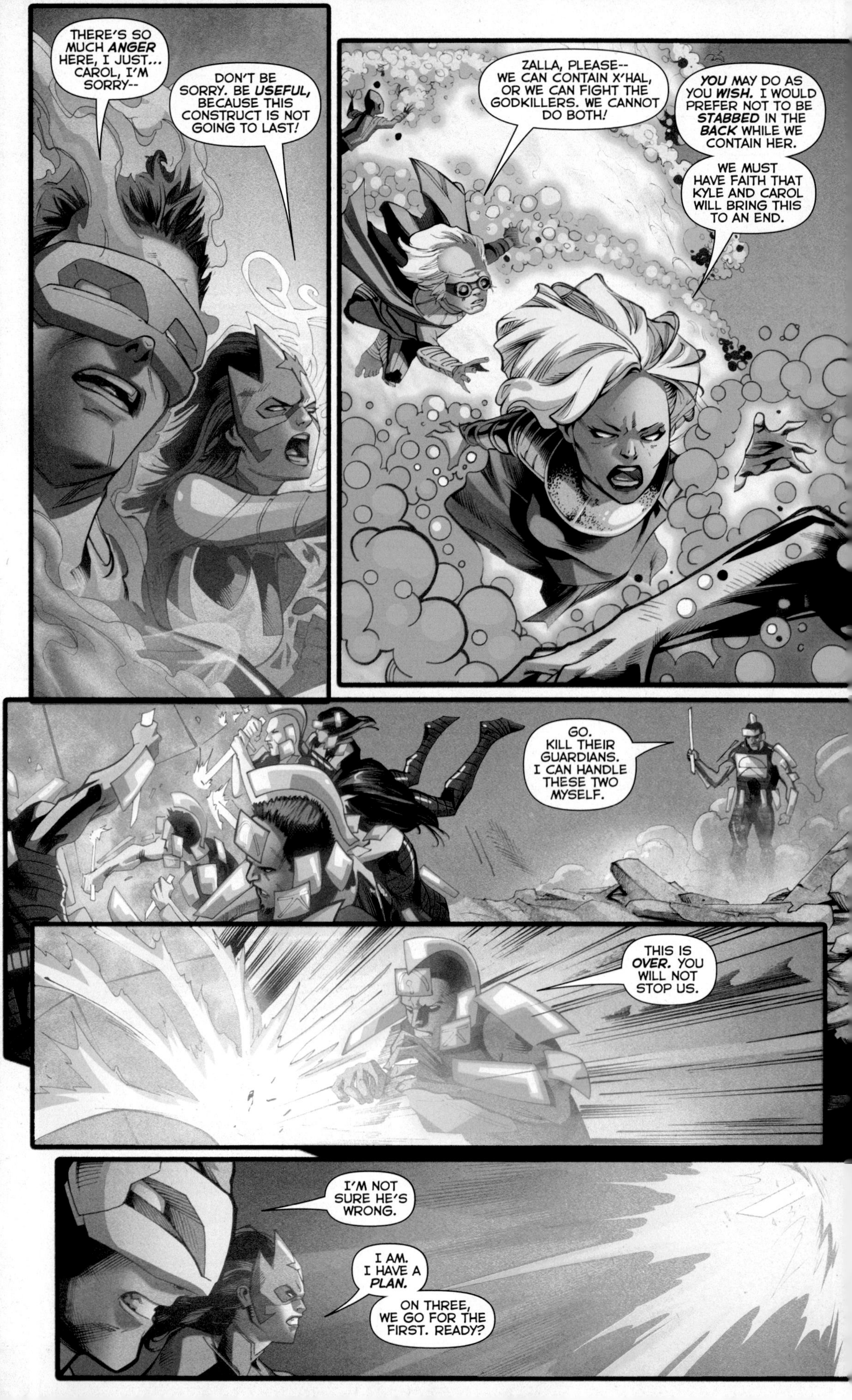
THERE'S SO MUCH ANGER HERE, I JUST... CAROL, I'M SORRY--
DON'T BE SORRY. BE USEFUL, BECAUSE THIS CONSTRUCT IS NOT GOING TO LAST!
ZALLA, PLEASE-- WE CAN CONTAIN X'HAL, OR WE CAN FIGHT THE GODKILLERS. WE CANNOT DO BOTH!
YOU MAY DO AS YOU WISH. I WOULD PREFER NOT TO BE STABBED IN THE BACK WHILE WE CONTAIN HER.
WE MUST HAVE FAITH THAT KYLE AND CAROL WILL BRING THIS TO AN END.
GO. KILL THEIR GUARDIANS. I CAN HANDLE THESE TWO MYSELF.
THIS IS OVER. YOU WILL NOT STOP US.
I'M NOT SURE HE'S WRONG.
I AM. I HAVE A PLAN.
ON THREE, WE GO FOR THE FIRST. READY?

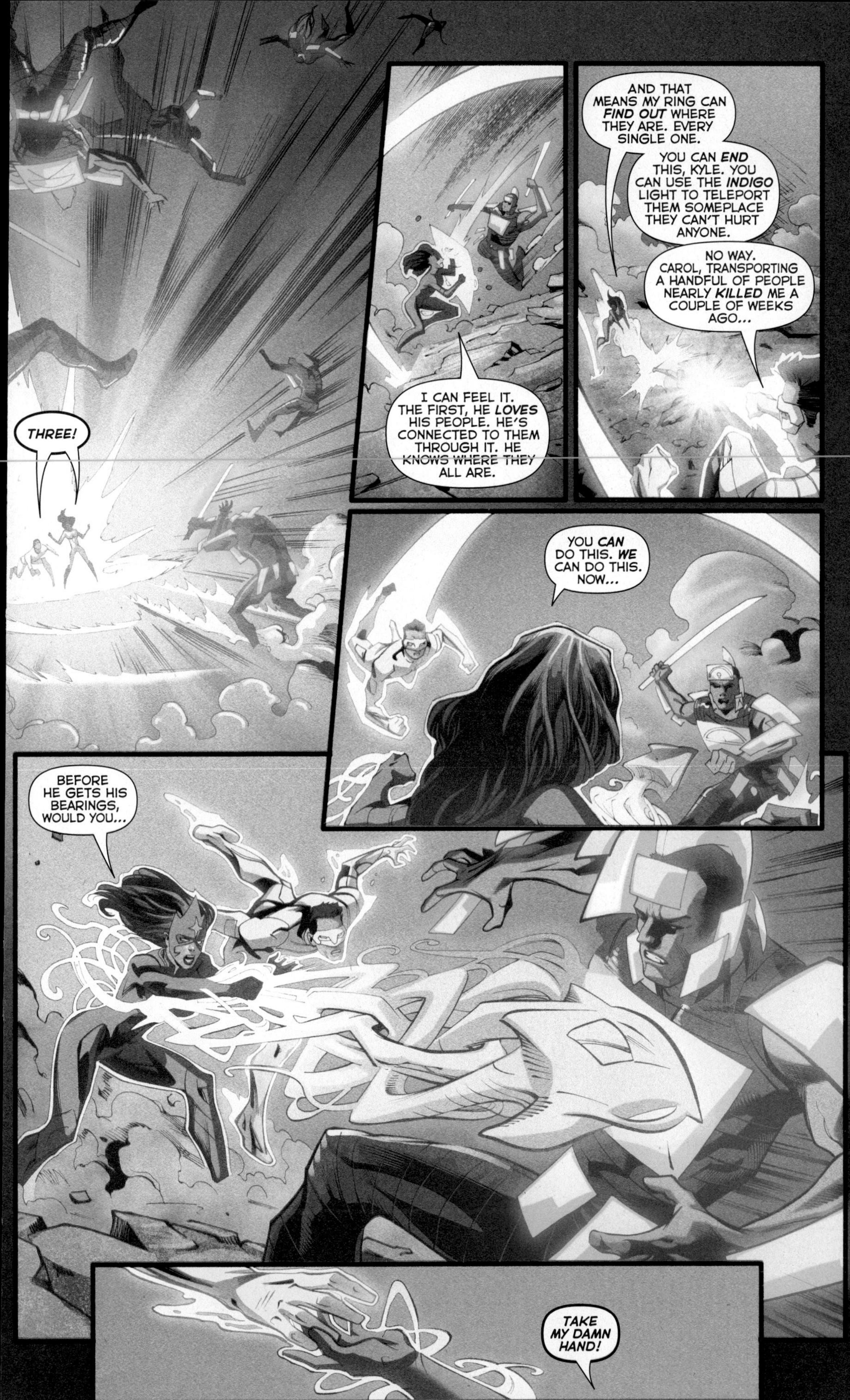
THREE!
I CAN FEEL IT. THE FIRST, HE LOVES HIS PEOPLE. HE'S CONNECTED TO THEM THROUGH IT. HE KNOWS WHERE THEY ALL ARE.
AND THAT MEANS MY RING CAN FIND OUT WHERE THEY ARE. EVERY SINGLE ONE.
YOU CAN END THIS, KYLE. YOU CAN USE THE INDIGO LIGHT TO TELEPORT THEM SOMEPLACE THEY CAN'T HURT ANYONE.
NO WAY. CAROL, TRANSPORTING A HANDFUL OF PEOPLE NEARLY KILLED ME A COUPLE OF WEEKS AGO...
YOU CAN DO THIS. WE CAN DO THIS. NOW...
BEFORE HE GETS HIS BEARINGS, WOULD YOU...
TAKE MY DAMN HAND!

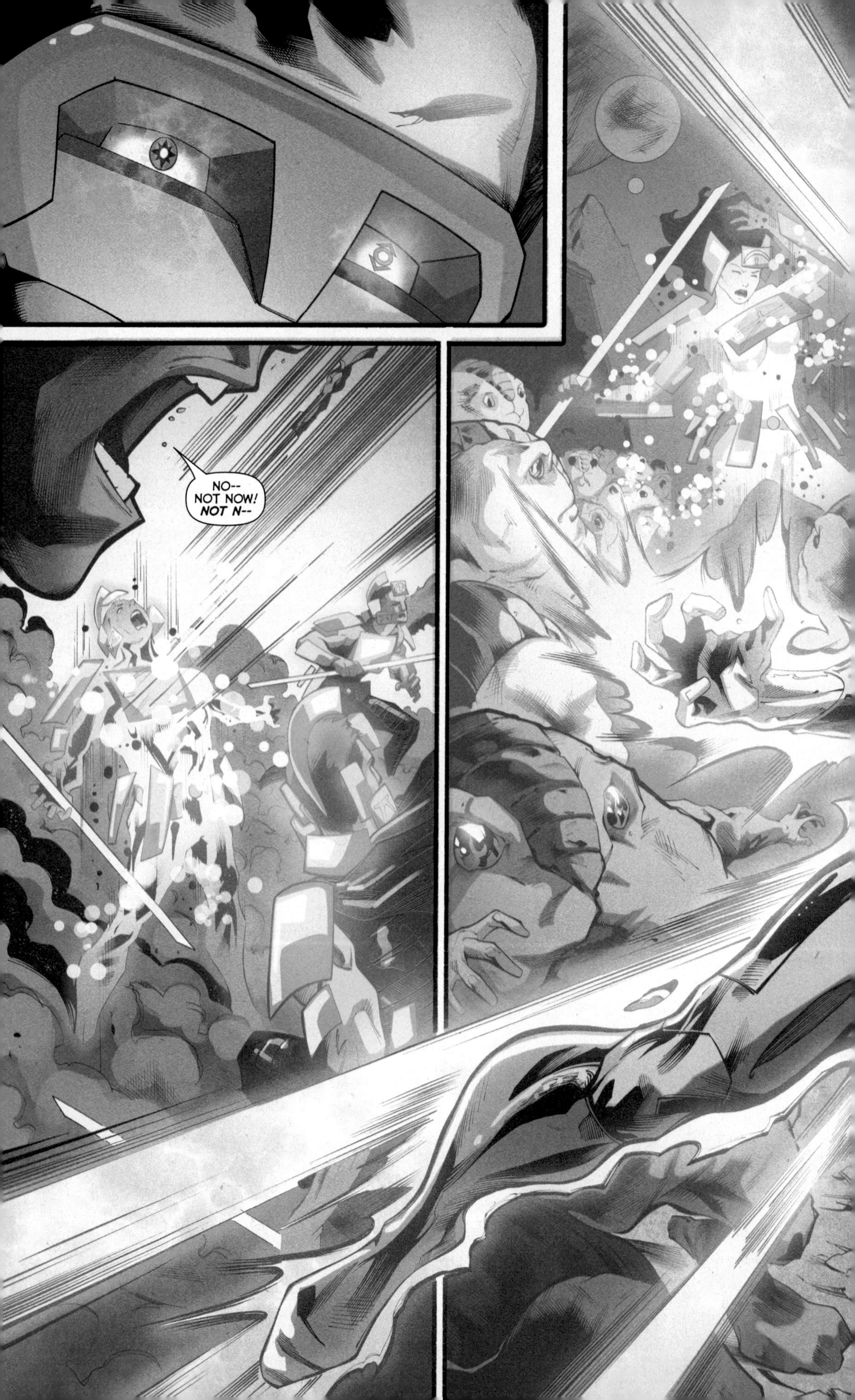
NO--
NOT NOW!
NOT N--

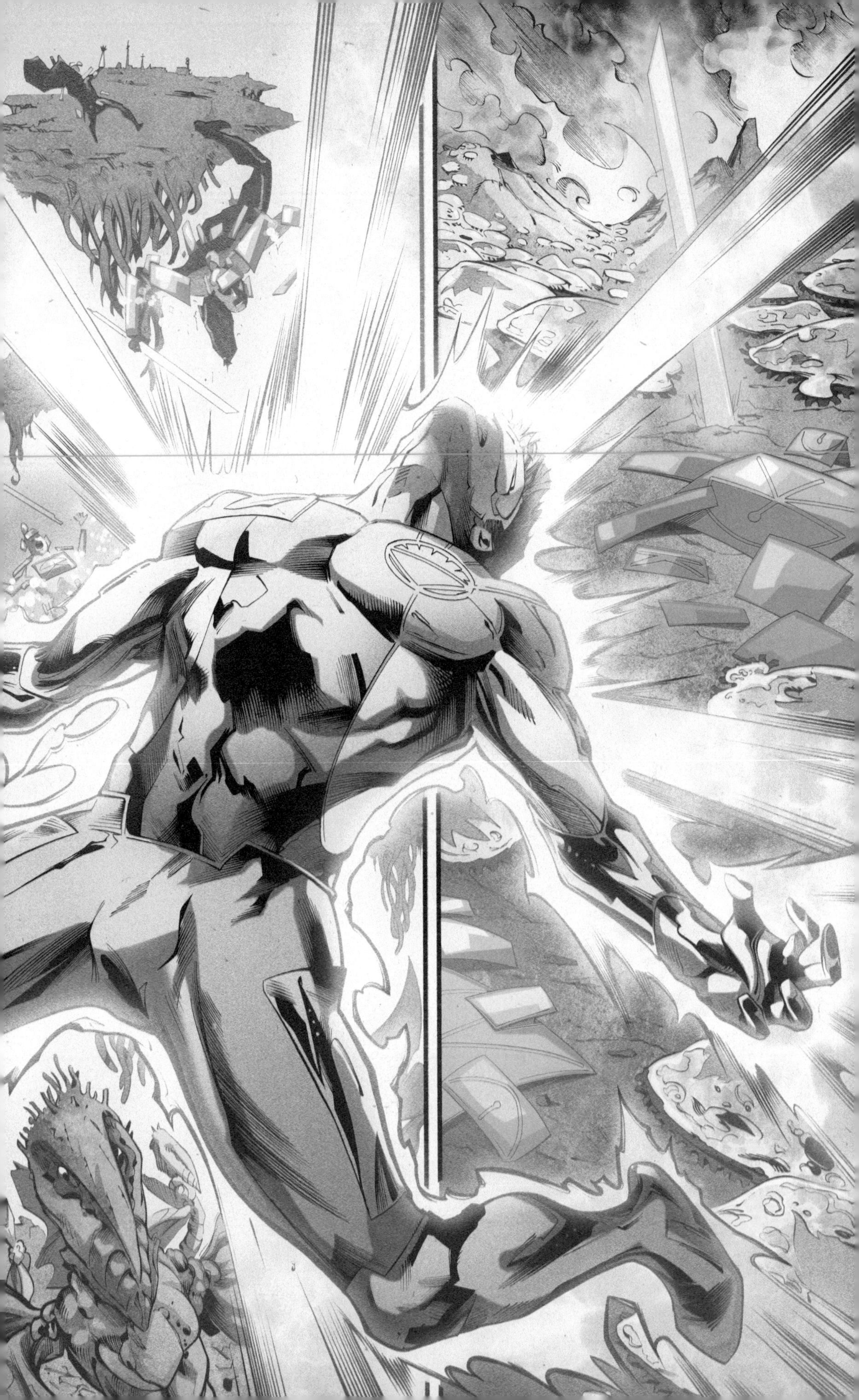

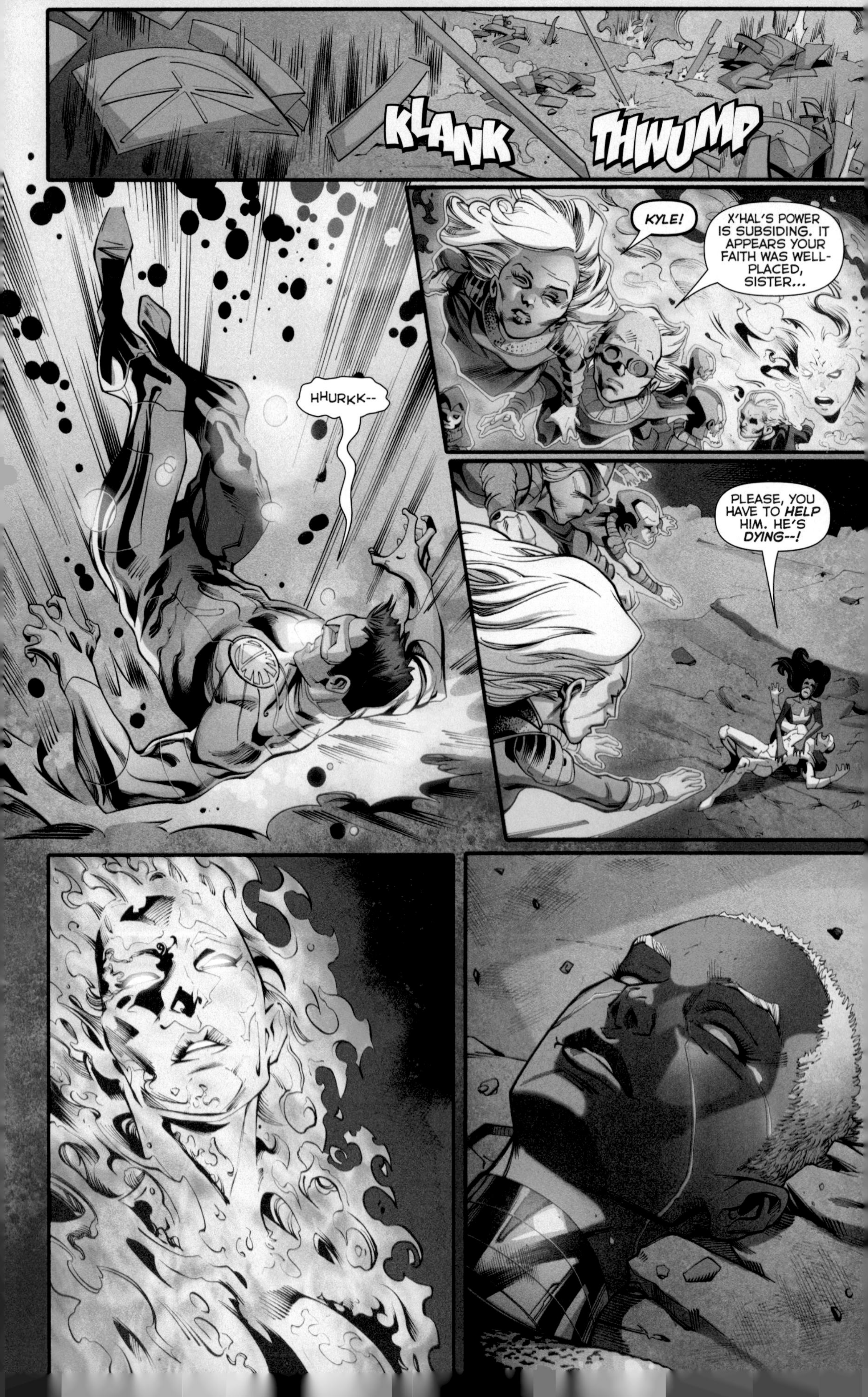
KLANK
THWUMP
HHURKK--
KYLE!
X'HAL'S POWER IS SUBSIDING. IT APPEARS YOUR FAITH WAS WELL-PLACED, SISTER...
PLEASE, YOU HAVE TO HELP HIM. HE'S DYING--!

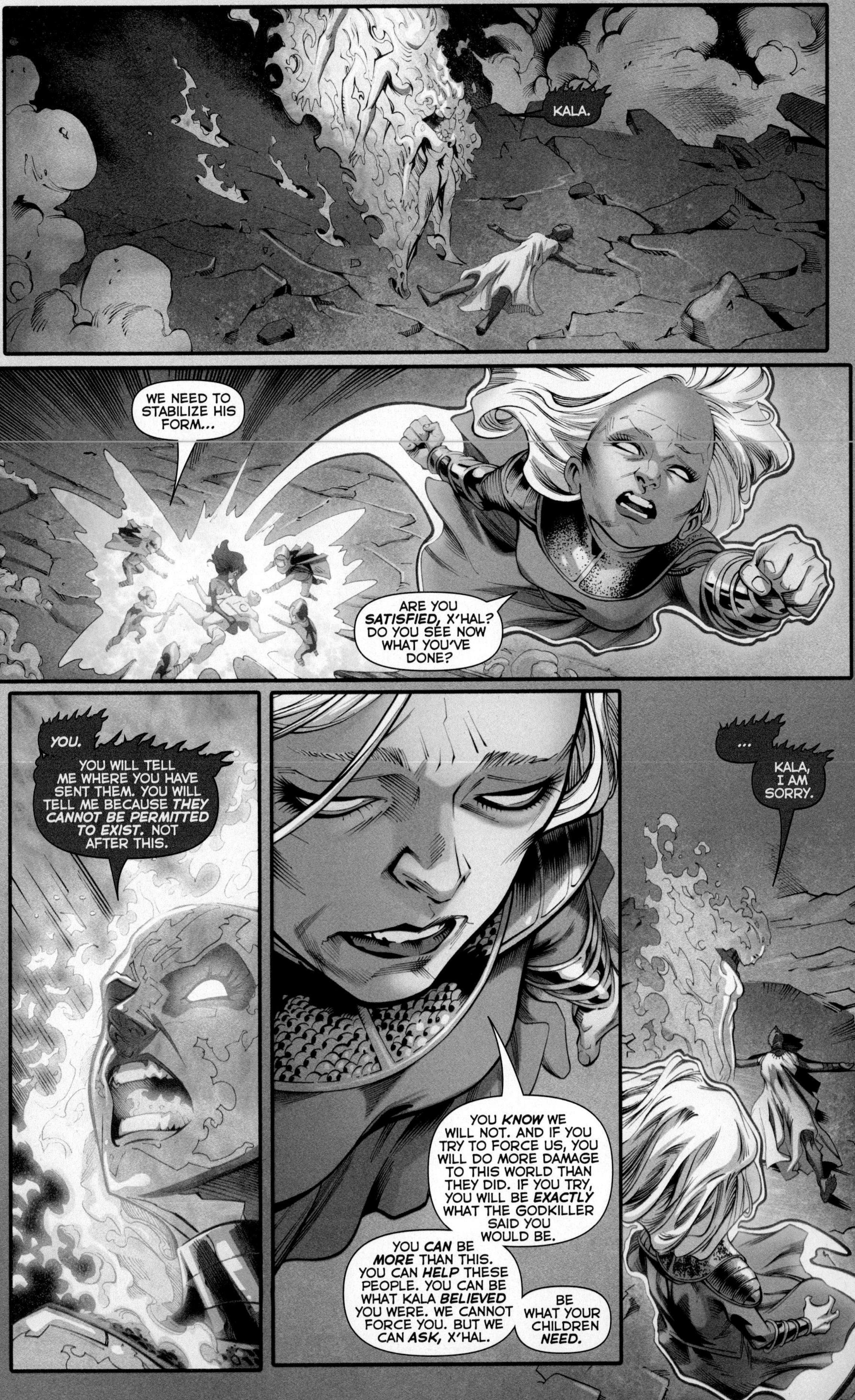
KALA.
WE NEED TO STABILIZE HIS FORM...
ARE YOU SATISFIED, X'HAL? DO YOU SEE NOW WHAT YOU'VE DONE?
YOU.
YOU WILL TELL ME WHERE YOU HAVE SENT THEM. YOU WILL TELL ME BECAUSE THEY CANNOT BE PERMITTED TO EXIST. NOT AFTER THIS.
YOU KNOW WE WILL NOT. AND IF YOU TRY TO FORCE US, YOU WILL DO MORE DAMAGE TO THIS WORLD THAN THEY DID. IF YOU TRY, YOU WILL BE EXACTLY WHAT THE GODKILLER SAID YOU WOULD BE.
YOU CAN BE MORE THAN THIS. YOU CAN HELP THESE PEOPLE. YOU CAN BE WHAT KALA BELIEVED YOU WERE. WE CANNOT FORCE YOU. BUT WE CAN ASK, X'HAL.
BE WHAT YOUR CHILDREN NEED.
...
KALA, I AM SORRY.

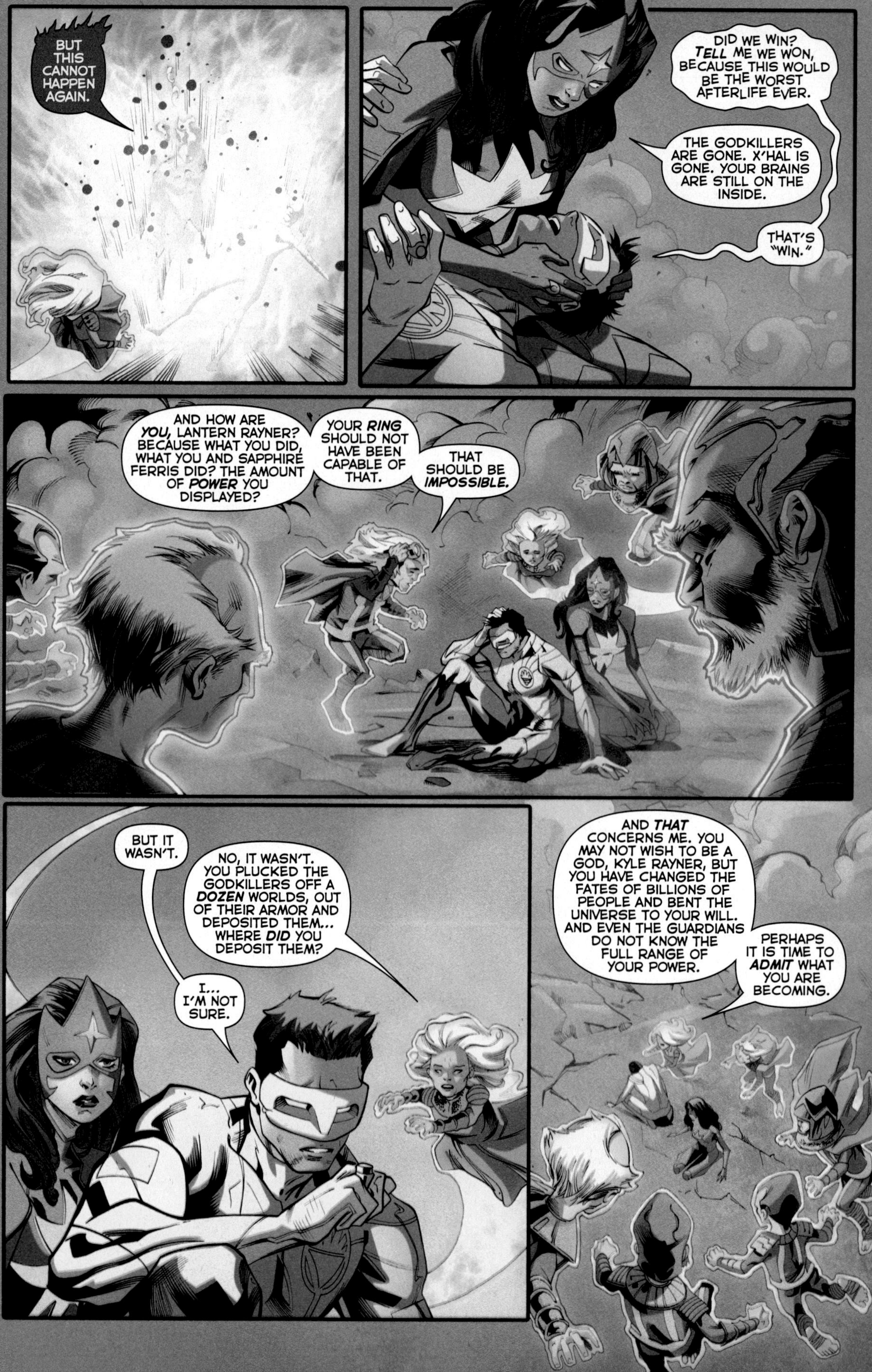
BUT THIS CANNOT HAPPEN AGAIN.
DID WE WIN? TELL ME WE WON, BECAUSE THIS WOULD BE THE WORST AFTERLIFE EVER.
THE GODKILLERS ARE GONE. X'HAL IS GONE. YOUR BRAINS ARE STILL ON THE INSIDE.
THAT'S "WIN."
AND HOW ARE YOU, LANTERN RAYNER? BECAUSE WHAT YOU DID, WHAT YOU AND SAPPHIRE FERRIS DID? THE AMOUNT OF POWER YOU DISPLAYED?
YOUR RING SHOULD NOT HAVE BEEN CAPABLE OF THAT.
THAT SHOULD BE IMPOSSIBLE.
BUT IT WASN'T.
NO, IT WASN'T. YOU PLUCKED THE GODKILLERS OFF A DOZEN WORLDS, OUT OF THEIR ARMOR AND DEPOSITED THEM... WHERE DID YOU DEPOSIT THEM?
I... I'M NOT SURE.
AND THAT CONCERNS ME. YOU MAY NOT WISH TO BE A GOD, KYLE RAYNER, BUT YOU HAVE CHANGED THE FATES OF BILLIONS OF PEOPLE AND BENT THE UNIVERSE TO YOUR WILL. AND EVEN THE GUARDIANS DO NOT KNOW THE FULL RANGE OF YOUR POWER.
PERHAPS IT IS TIME TO ADMIT WHAT YOU ARE BECOMING.

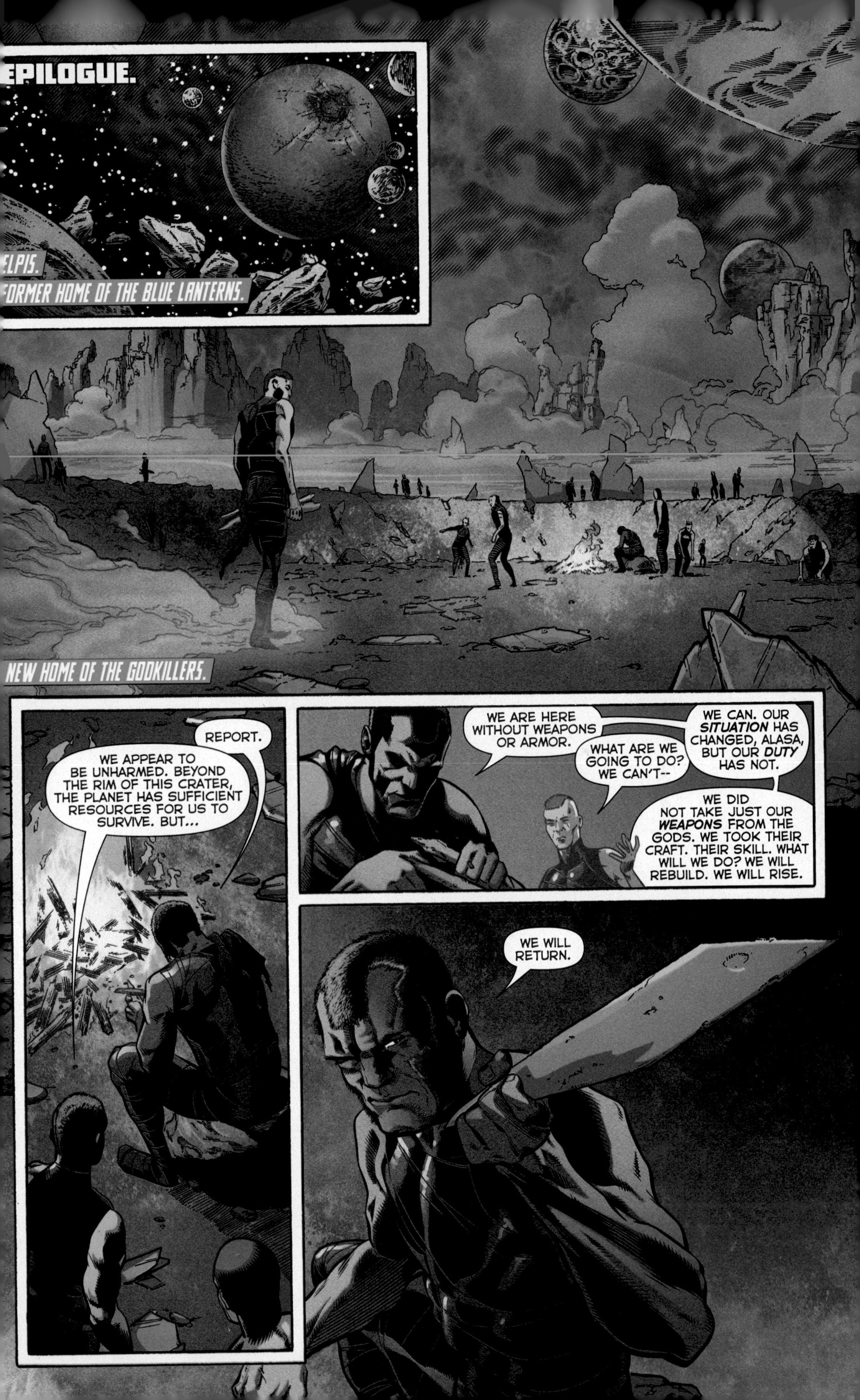
EPILOGUE.
ELPIS.
FORMER HOME OF THE BLUE LANTERNS.
NEW HOME OF THE GODKILLERS.
REPORT.
WE APPEAR TO BE UNHARMED. BEYOND THE RIM OF THIS CRATER, THE PLANET HAS SUFFICIENT RESOURCES FOR US TO SURVIVE. BUT...
WE ARE HERE WITHOUT WEAPONS OR ARMOR.
WHAT ARE WE GOING TO DO? WE CAN'T--
WE CAN. OUR SITUATION HAS CHANGED, ALASA, BUT OUR DUTY HAS NOT.
WE DID NOT TAKE JUST OUR WEAPONS FROM THE GODS. WE TOOK THEIR CRAFT. THEIR SKILL. WHAT WILL WE DO? WE WILL REBUILD. WE WILL RISE.
WE WILL RETURN.

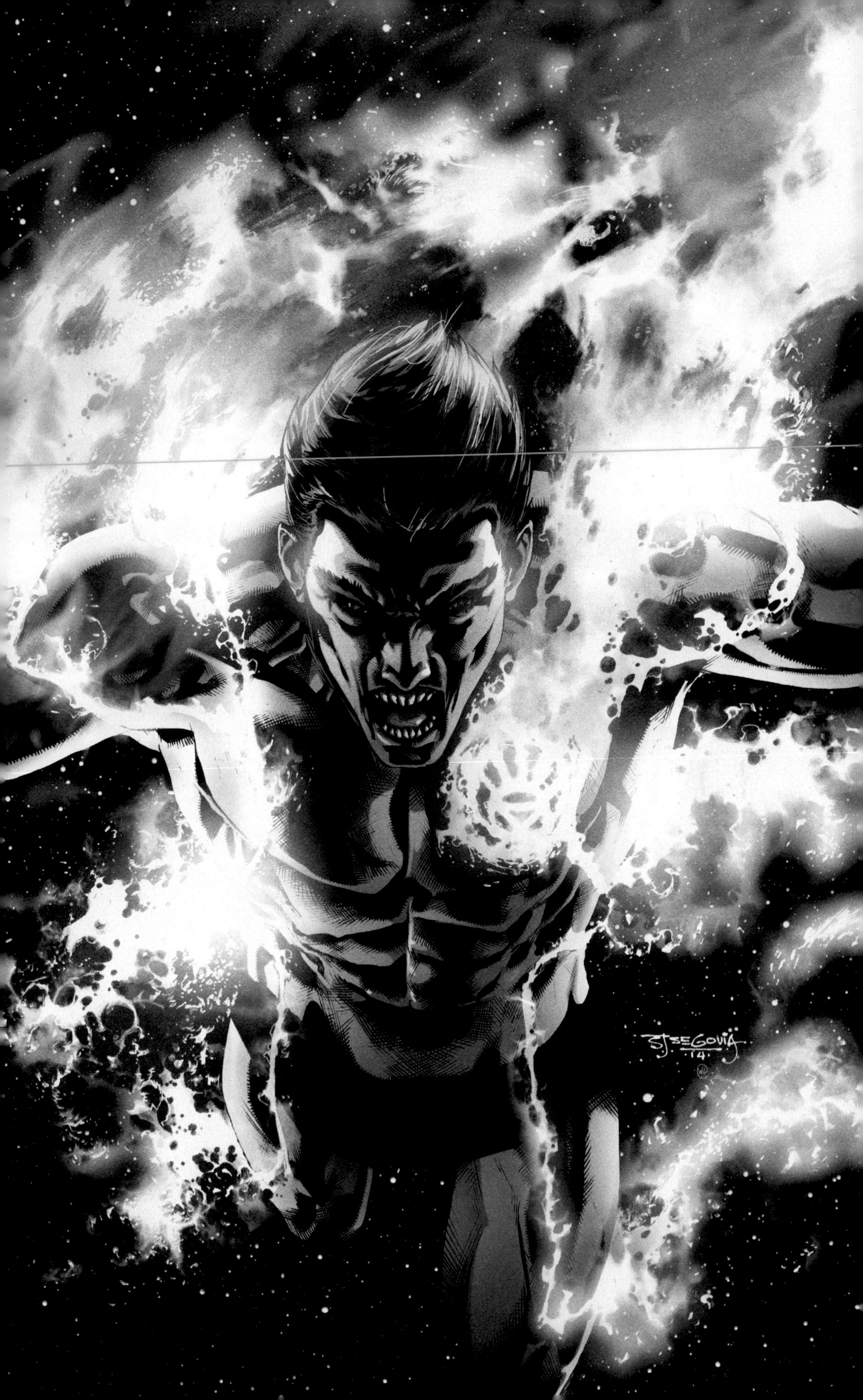

LIFE/NOT-LIFE

JUSTIN JORDAN writer **STEPHEN SEGOVIA, EDGAR SALAZAR** (pgs 104-110) and **JED DOUGHERTY** (pgs 111-112) pencillers
STEPHEN SEGOVIA, JASON PAZ (pgs 90-103), **JASON GORDER** (pgs 104-110) **and JED DOUGHERTY** (pgs 111-112) inkers
ANDREW DALHOUSE and **HI-FI** (pgs 96-112) colorists **DAVE SHARPE** letterer cover art by **STEPHEN SEGOVIA** and **WIL QUINTANA**

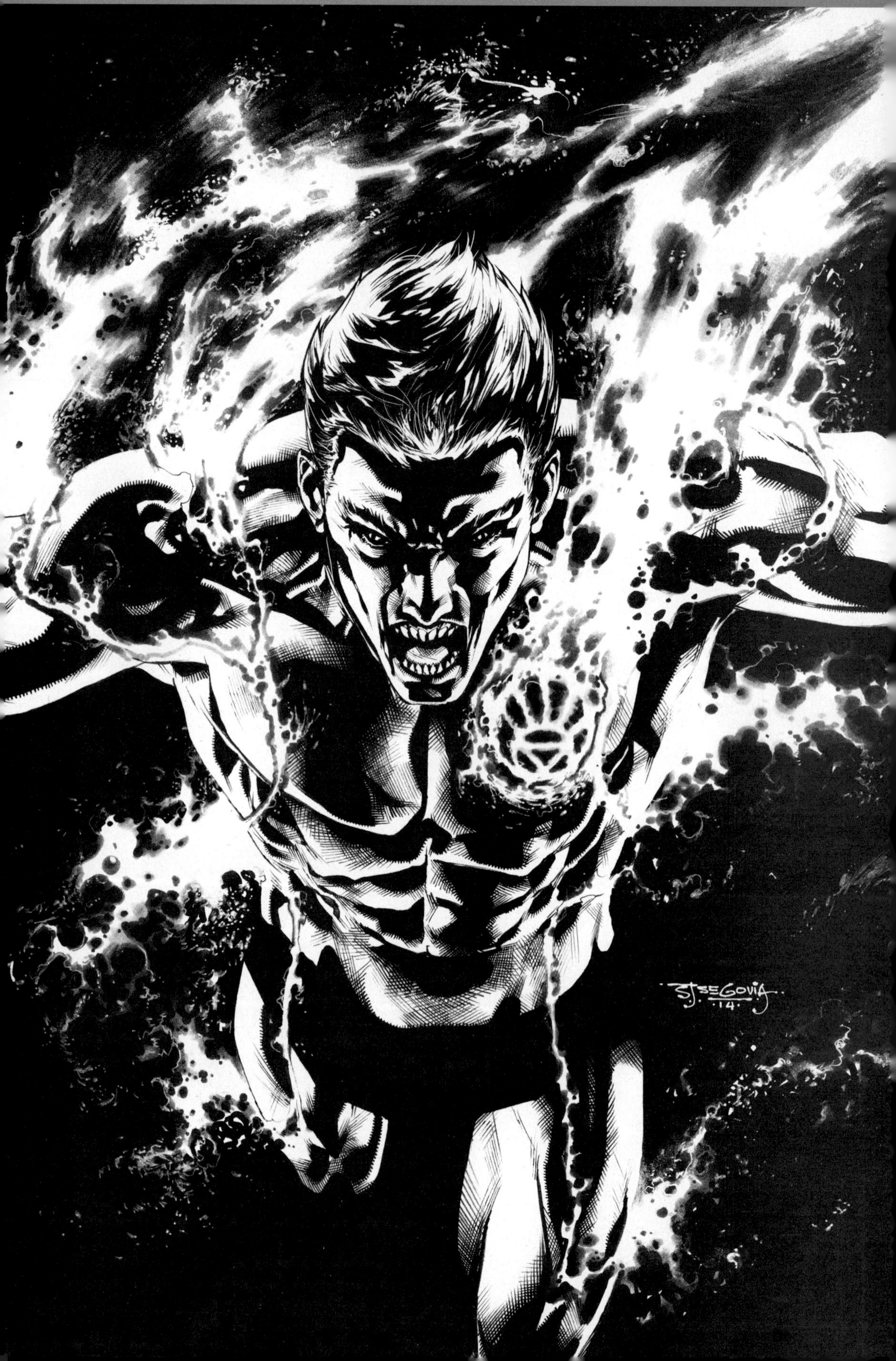
SJ SEGOVIA '14

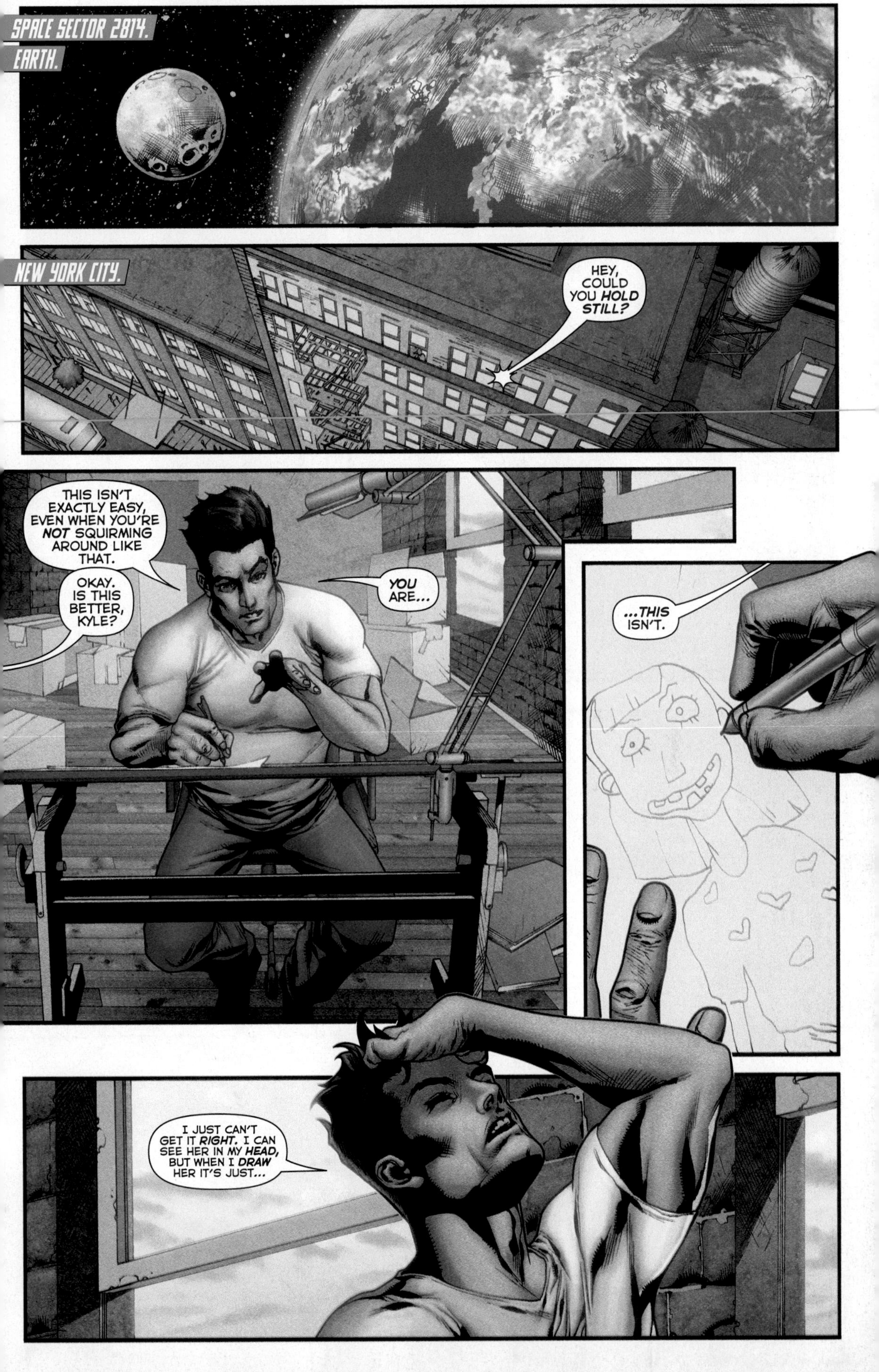
SPACE SECTOR 2814.
EARTH.
NEW YORK CITY.
HEY, COULD YOU HOLD STILL?
THIS ISN'T EXACTLY EASY, EVEN WHEN YOU'RE NOT SQUIRMING AROUND LIKE THAT.
OKAY. IS THIS BETTER, KYLE?
YOU ARE...
...THIS ISN'T.
I JUST CAN'T GET IT RIGHT. I CAN SEE HER IN MY HEAD, BUT WHEN I DRAW HER IT'S JUST...

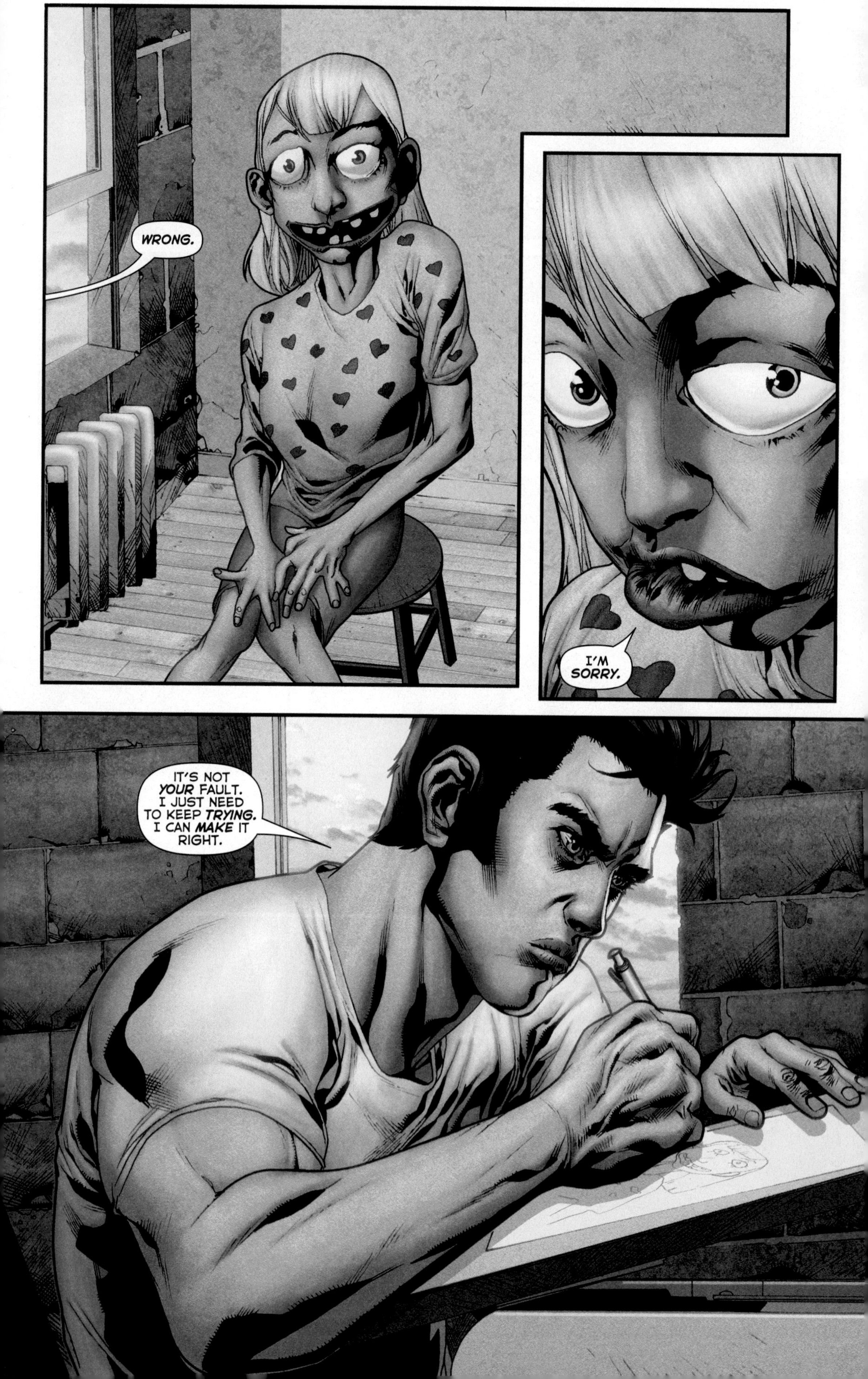
WRONG.
I'M SORRY.
IT'S NOT *YOUR* FAULT. I JUST NEED TO KEEP *TRYING*. I CAN *MAKE* IT RIGHT.

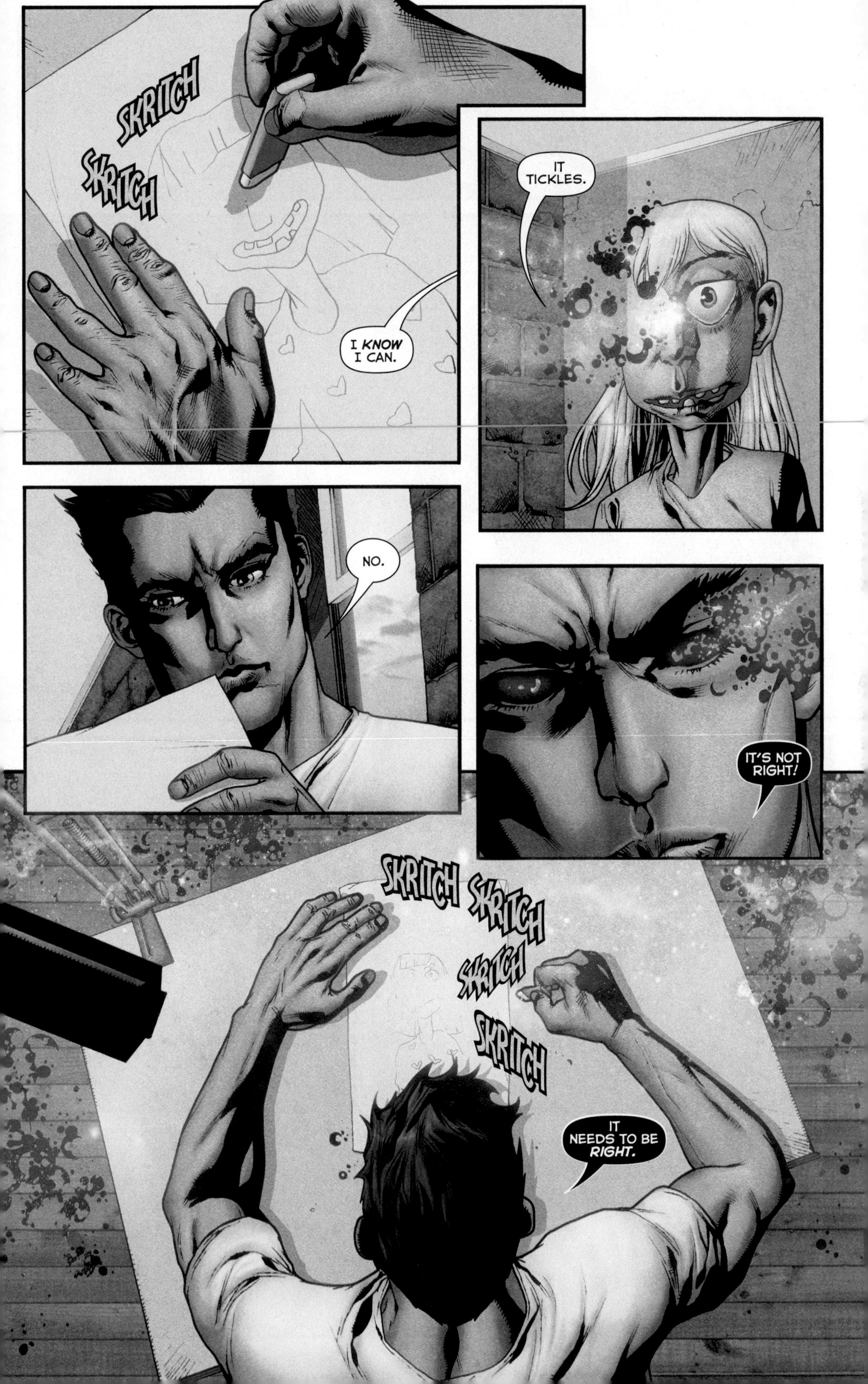
SKRITCH
SKRITCH
I KNOW I CAN.
IT TICKLES.
NO.
IT'S NOT RIGHT!
SKRITCH SKRITCH
SKRITCH
SKRITCH
IT NEEDS TO BE RIGHT.

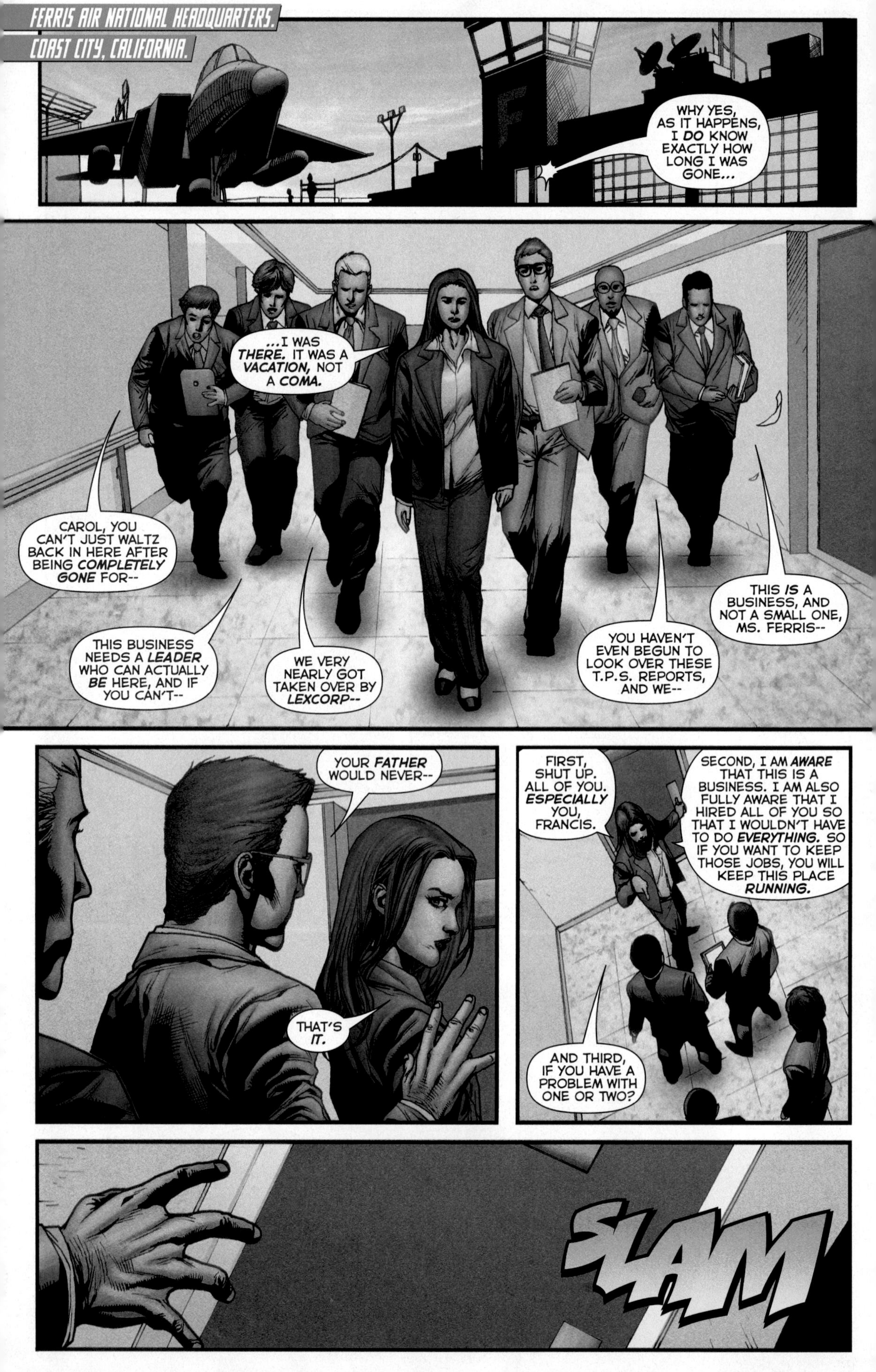
FERRIS AIR NATIONAL HEADQUARTERS.
COAST CITY, CALIFORNIA.
WHY YES, AS IT HAPPENS, I DO KNOW EXACTLY HOW LONG I WAS GONE...
CAROL, YOU CAN'T JUST WALTZ BACK IN HERE AFTER BEING COMPLETELY GONE FOR--
...I WAS THERE. IT WAS A VACATION, NOT A COMA.
THIS BUSINESS NEEDS A LEADER WHO CAN ACTUALLY BE HERE, AND IF YOU CAN'T--
WE VERY NEARLY GOT TAKEN OVER BY LEXCORP--
YOU HAVEN'T EVEN BEGUN TO LOOK OVER THESE T.P.S. REPORTS, AND WE--
THIS IS A BUSINESS, AND NOT A SMALL ONE, MS. FERRIS--
YOUR FATHER WOULD NEVER--
THAT'S IT.
FIRST, SHUT UP. ALL OF YOU. ESPECIALLY YOU, FRANCIS.
SECOND, I AM AWARE THAT THIS IS A BUSINESS. I AM ALSO FULLY AWARE THAT I HIRED ALL OF YOU SO THAT I WOULDN'T HAVE TO DO EVERYTHING. SO IF YOU WANT TO KEEP THOSE JOBS, YOU WILL KEEP THIS PLACE RUNNING.
AND THIRD, IF YOU HAVE A PROBLEM WITH ONE OR TWO?
SLAM

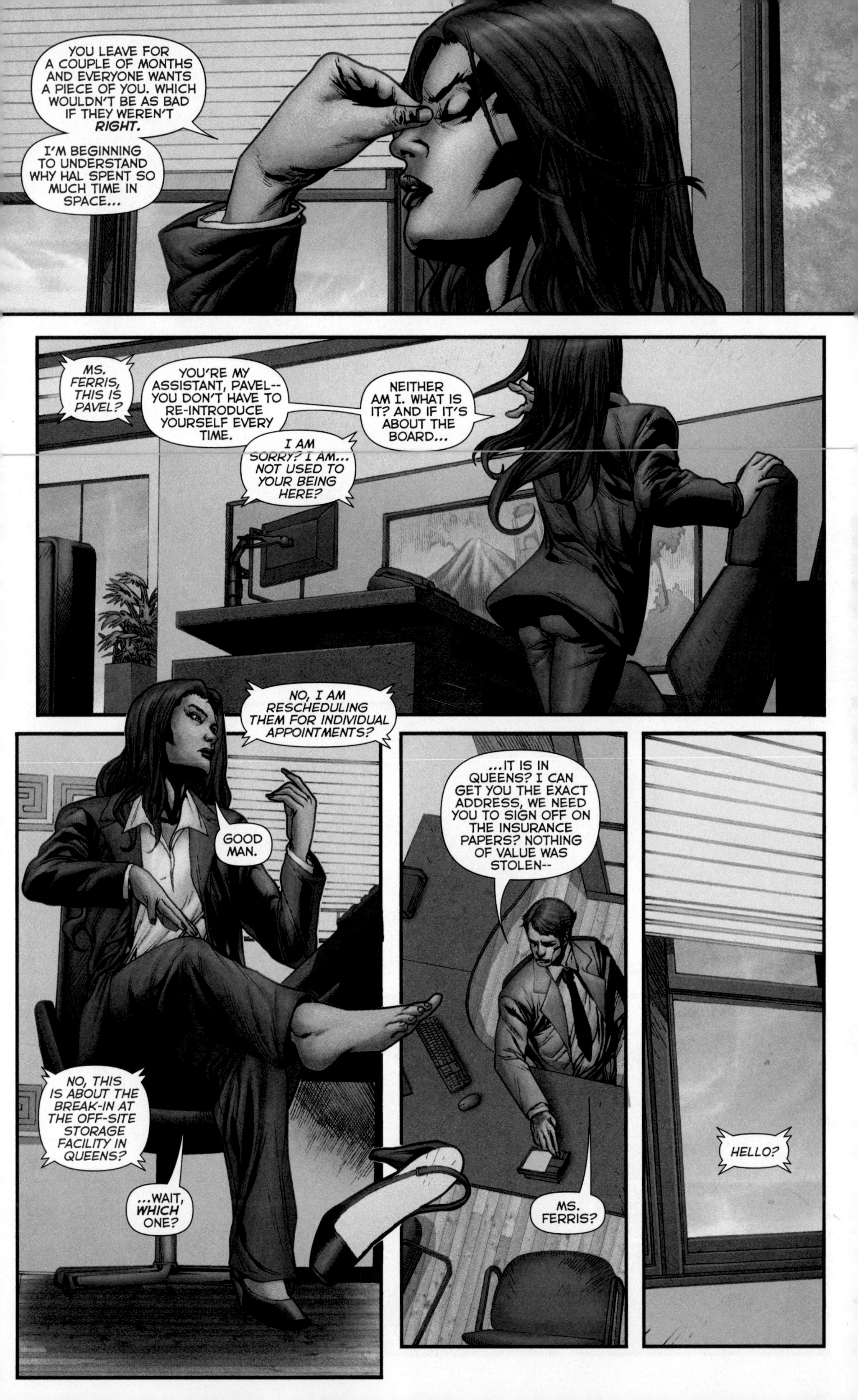
YOU LEAVE FOR A COUPLE OF MONTHS AND EVERYONE WANTS A PIECE OF YOU. WHICH WOULDN'T BE AS BAD IF THEY WEREN'T ***RIGHT.***
I'M BEGINNING TO UNDERSTAND WHY HAL SPENT SO MUCH TIME IN SPACE...
MS. FERRIS, THIS IS PAVEL?
YOU'RE MY ASSISTANT, PAVEL-- YOU DON'T HAVE TO RE-INTRODUCE YOURSELF EVERY TIME.
I AM SORRY? I AM... NOT USED TO YOUR BEING HERE?
NEITHER AM I. WHAT IS IT? AND IF IT'S ABOUT THE BOARD...
NO, I AM RESCHEDULING THEM FOR INDIVIDUAL APPOINTMENTS?
GOOD MAN.
NO, THIS IS ABOUT THE BREAK-IN AT THE OFF-SITE STORAGE FACILITY IN QUEENS?
...WAIT, ***WHICH*** ONE?
...IT IS IN QUEENS? I CAN GET YOU THE EXACT ADDRESS, WE NEED YOU TO SIGN OFF ON THE INSURANCE PAPERS? NOTHING OF VALUE WAS STOLEN--
MS. FERRIS?
HELLO?

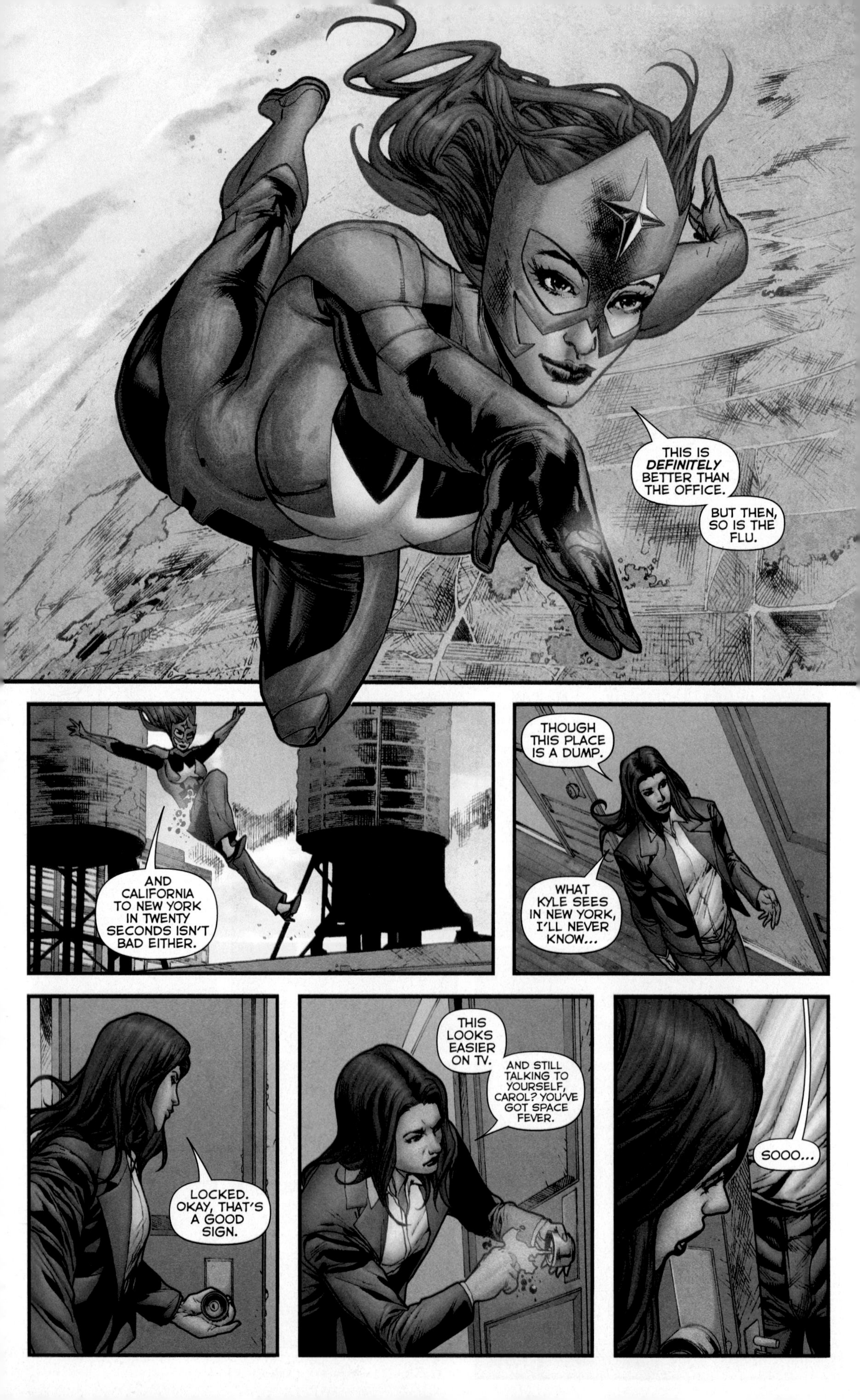
THIS IS *DEFINITELY* BETTER THAN THE OFFICE.
BUT THEN, SO IS THE FLU.
AND CALIFORNIA TO NEW YORK IN TWENTY SECONDS ISN'T BAD EITHER.
THOUGH THIS PLACE IS A DUMP.
WHAT KYLE SEES IN NEW YORK, I'LL NEVER KNOW...
LOCKED. OKAY, THAT'S A GOOD SIGN.
THIS LOOKS EASIER ON TV.
AND STILL TALKING TO YOURSELF, CAROL? YOU'VE GOT SPACE FEVER.
SOOO...

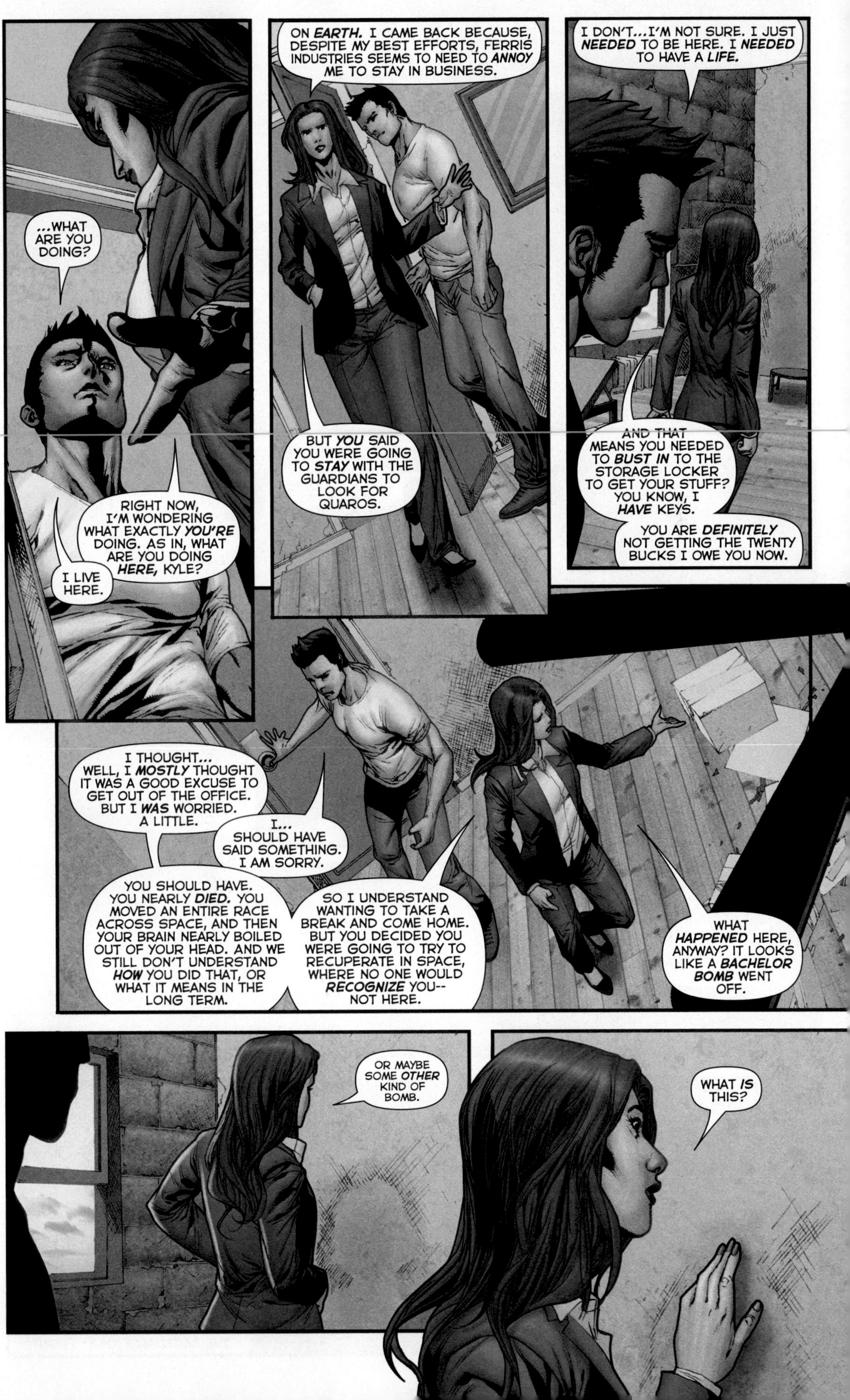
...WHAT ARE YOU DOING?
RIGHT NOW, I'M WONDERING WHAT EXACTLY YOU'RE DOING. AS IN, WHAT ARE YOU DOING HERE, KYLE?
I LIVE HERE.
ON EARTH. I CAME BACK BECAUSE, DESPITE MY BEST EFFORTS, FERRIS INDUSTRIES SEEMS TO NEED TO ANNOY ME TO STAY IN BUSINESS.
BUT YOU SAID YOU WERE GOING TO STAY WITH THE GUARDIANS TO LOOK FOR QUAROS.
I DON'T...I'M NOT SURE. I JUST NEEDED TO BE HERE. I NEEDED TO HAVE A LIFE.
AND THAT MEANS YOU NEEDED TO BUST IN TO THE STORAGE LOCKER TO GET YOUR STUFF? YOU KNOW, I HAVE KEYS.
YOU ARE DEFINITELY NOT GETTING THE TWENTY BUCKS I OWE YOU NOW.
I THOUGHT... WELL, I MOSTLY THOUGHT IT WAS A GOOD EXCUSE TO GET OUT OF THE OFFICE. BUT I WAS WORRIED. A LITTLE.
I... SHOULD HAVE SAID SOMETHING. I AM SORRY.
YOU SHOULD HAVE. YOU NEARLY DIED. YOU MOVED AN ENTIRE RACE ACROSS SPACE, AND THEN YOUR BRAIN NEARLY BOILED OUT OF YOUR HEAD. AND WE STILL DON'T UNDERSTAND HOW YOU DID THAT, OR WHAT IT MEANS IN THE LONG TERM.
SO I UNDERSTAND WANTING TO TAKE A BREAK AND COME HOME. BUT YOU DECIDED YOU WERE GOING TO TRY TO RECUPERATE IN SPACE, WHERE NO ONE WOULD RECOGNIZE YOU-- NOT HERE.
WHAT HAPPENED HERE, ANYWAY? IT LOOKS LIKE A BACHELOR BOMB WENT OFF.
OR MAYBE SOME OTHER KIND OF BOMB.
WHAT IS THIS?

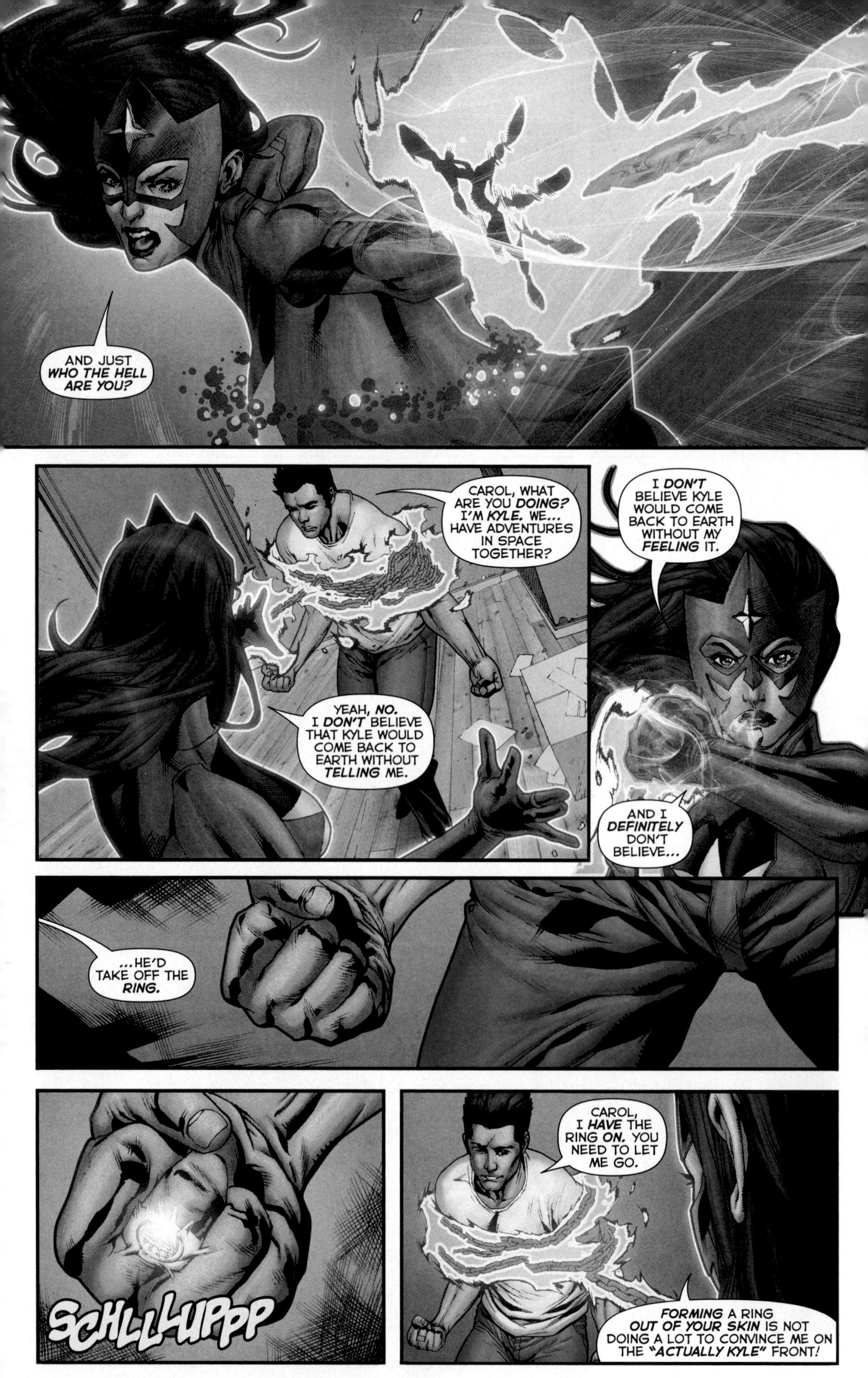

AND JUST WHO THE HELL ARE YOU?
CAROL, WHAT ARE YOU DOING? I'M KYLE. WE... HAVE ADVENTURES IN SPACE TOGETHER?
YEAH, NO. I DON'T BELIEVE THAT KYLE WOULD COME BACK TO EARTH WITHOUT TELLING ME.
I DON'T BELIEVE KYLE WOULD COME BACK TO EARTH WITHOUT MY FEELING IT.
AND I DEFINITELY DON'T BELIEVE...
...HE'D TAKE OFF THE RING.
SCHLLLUPPP
CAROL, I HAVE THE RING ON. YOU NEED TO LET ME GO.
FORMING A RING OUT OF YOUR SKIN IS NOT DOING A LOT TO CONVINCE ME ON THE "ACTUALLY KYLE" FRONT!

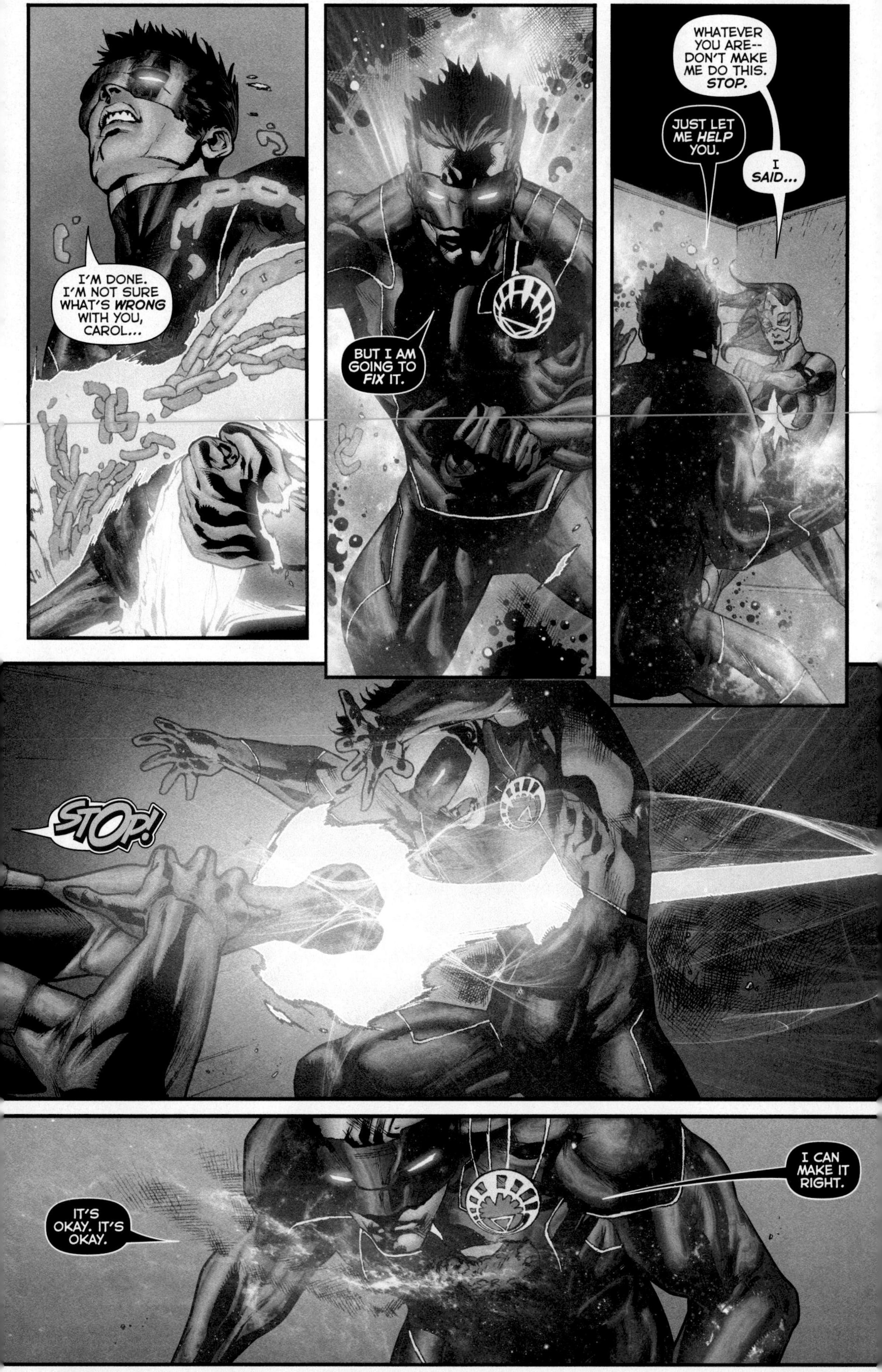
I'M DONE. I'M NOT SURE WHAT'S WRONG WITH YOU, CAROL...
BUT I AM GOING TO FIX IT.
WHATEVER YOU ARE-- DON'T MAKE ME DO THIS. STOP.
JUST LET ME HELP YOU.
I SAID...
STOP!
I CAN MAKE IT RIGHT.
IT'S OKAY. IT'S OKAY.

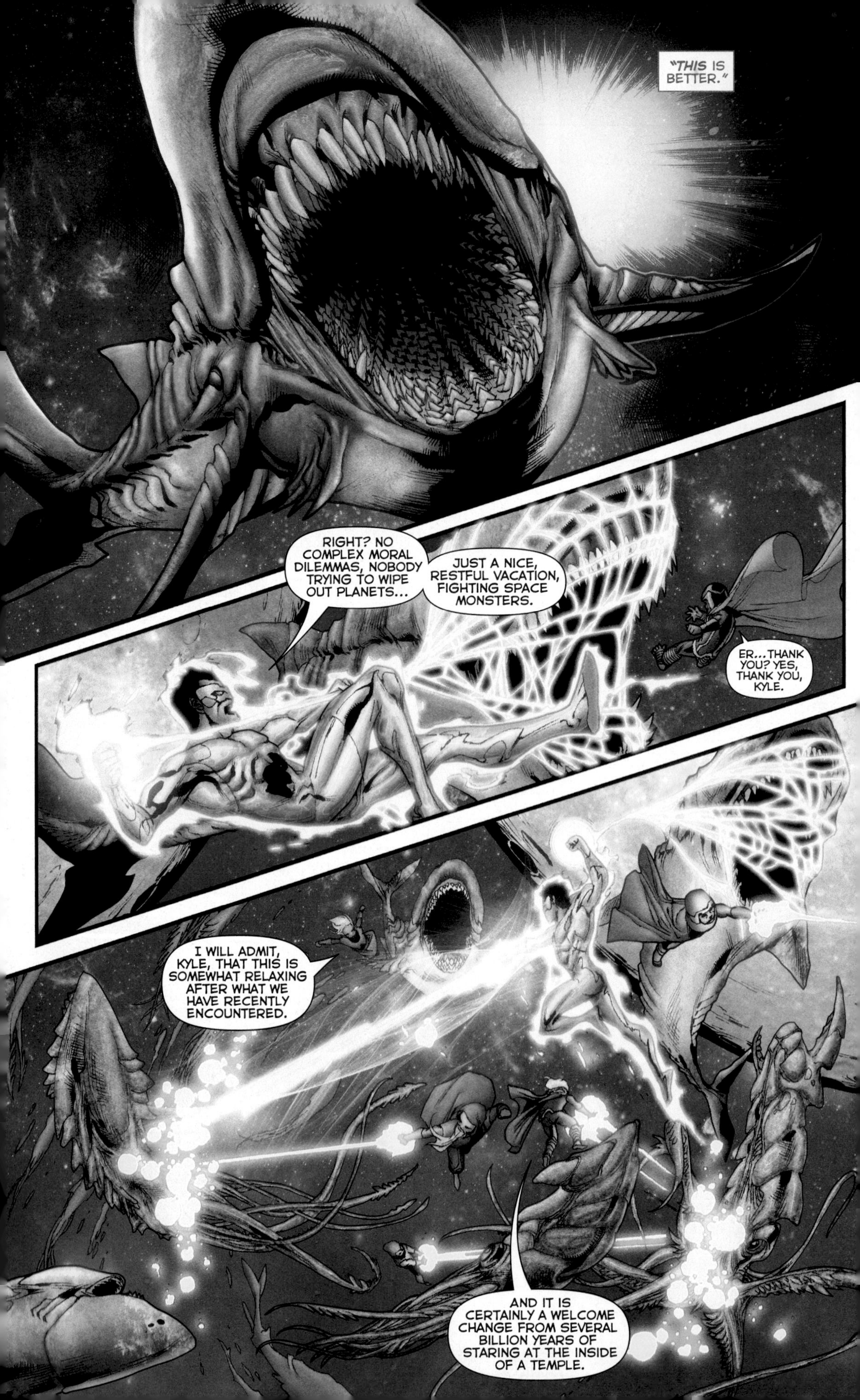
"THIS IS BETTER."
RIGHT? NO COMPLEX MORAL DILEMMAS, NOBODY TRYING TO WIPE OUT PLANETS...
JUST A NICE, RESTFUL VACATION, FIGHTING SPACE MONSTERS.
ER...THANK YOU? YES, THANK YOU, KYLE.
I WILL ADMIT, KYLE, THAT THIS IS SOMEWHAT RELAXING AFTER WHAT WE HAVE RECENTLY ENCOUNTERED.
AND IT IS CERTAINLY A WELCOME CHANGE FROM SEVERAL BILLION YEARS OF STARING AT THE INSIDE OF A TEMPLE.

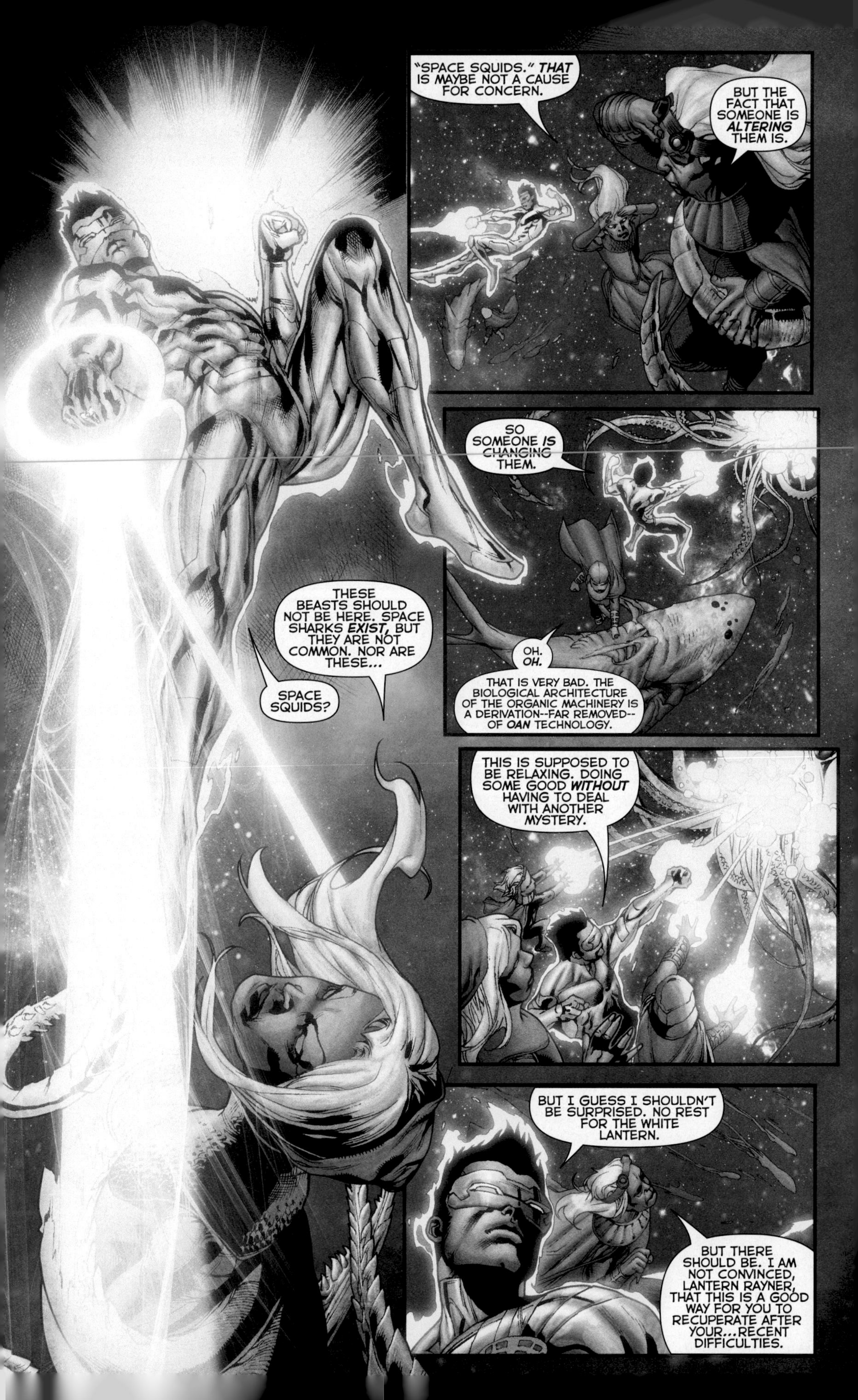

"SPACE SQUIDS." THAT IS MAYBE NOT A CAUSE FOR CONCERN.
BUT THE FACT THAT SOMEONE IS ALTERING THEM IS.
THESE BEASTS SHOULD NOT BE HERE. SPACE SHARKS EXIST, BUT THEY ARE NOT COMMON. NOR ARE THESE...
SPACE SQUIDS?
SO SOMEONE IS CHANGING THEM.
OH. OH.
THAT IS VERY BAD. THE BIOLOGICAL ARCHITECTURE OF THE ORGANIC MACHINERY IS A DERIVATION--FAR REMOVED--OF OAN TECHNOLOGY.
THIS IS SUPPOSED TO BE RELAXING. DOING SOME GOOD WITHOUT HAVING TO DEAL WITH ANOTHER MYSTERY.
BUT I GUESS I SHOULDN'T BE SURPRISED. NO REST FOR THE WHITE LANTERN.
BUT THERE SHOULD BE. I AM NOT CONVINCED, LANTERN RAYNER, THAT THIS IS A GOOD WAY FOR YOU TO RECUPERATE AFTER YOUR...RECENT DIFFICULTIES.

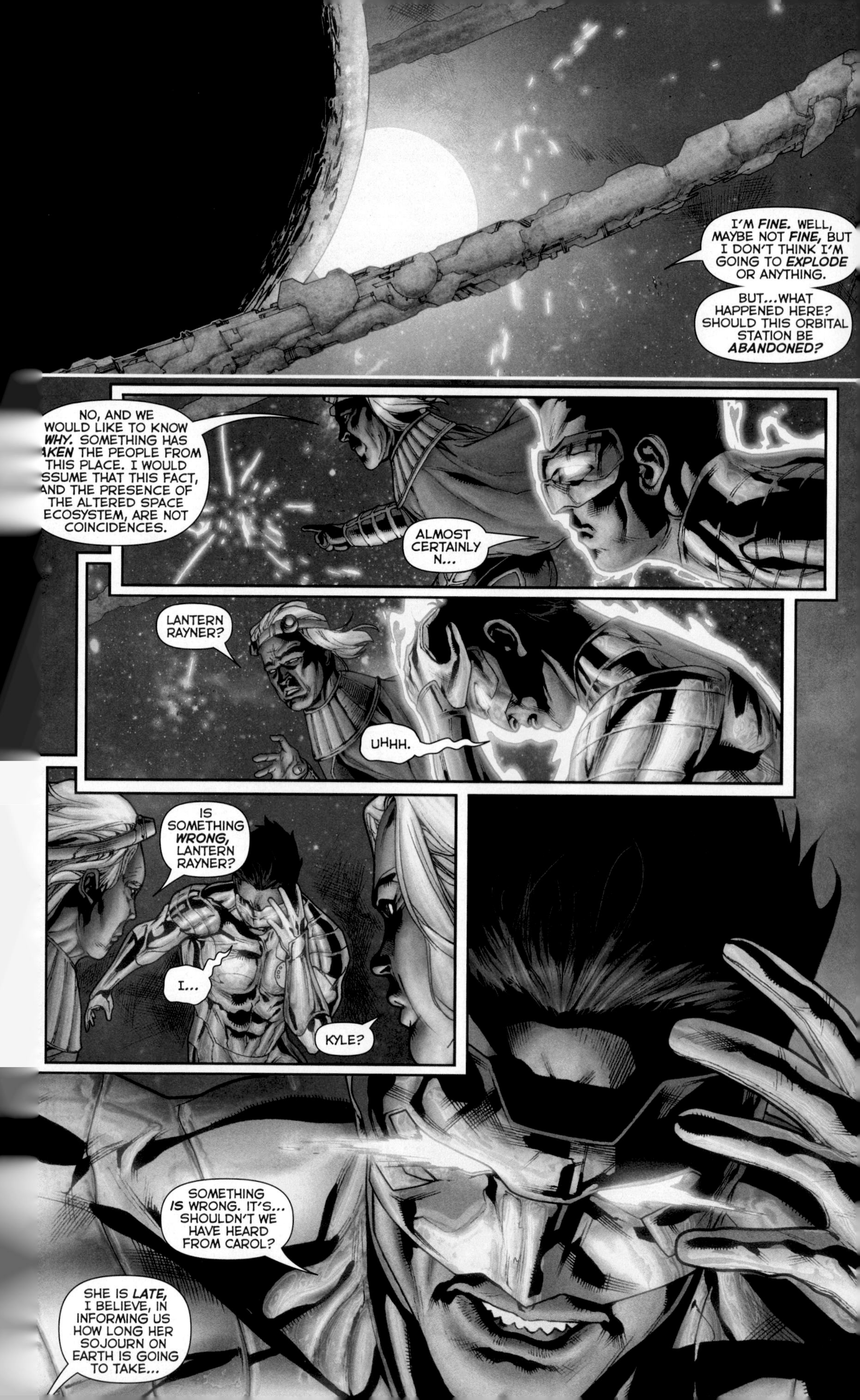
I'M FINE. WELL, MAYBE NOT FINE, BUT I DON'T THINK I'M GOING TO EXPLODE OR ANYTHING.
BUT...WHAT HAPPENED HERE? SHOULD THIS ORBITAL STATION BE ABANDONED?
NO, AND WE WOULD LIKE TO KNOW WHY. SOMETHING HAS AKEN THE PEOPLE FROM THIS PLACE. I WOULD SSUME THAT THIS FACT, AND THE PRESENCE OF THE ALTERED SPACE ECOSYSTEM, ARE NOT COINCIDENCES.
ALMOST CERTAINLY N...
LANTERN RAYNER?
UHHH.
IS SOMETHING WRONG, LANTERN RAYNER?
I...
KYLE?
SOMETHING IS WRONG. IT'S... SHOULDN'T WE HAVE HEARD FROM CAROL?
SHE IS LATE, I BELIEVE, IN INFORMING US HOW LONG HER SOJOURN ON EARTH IS GOING TO TAKE...

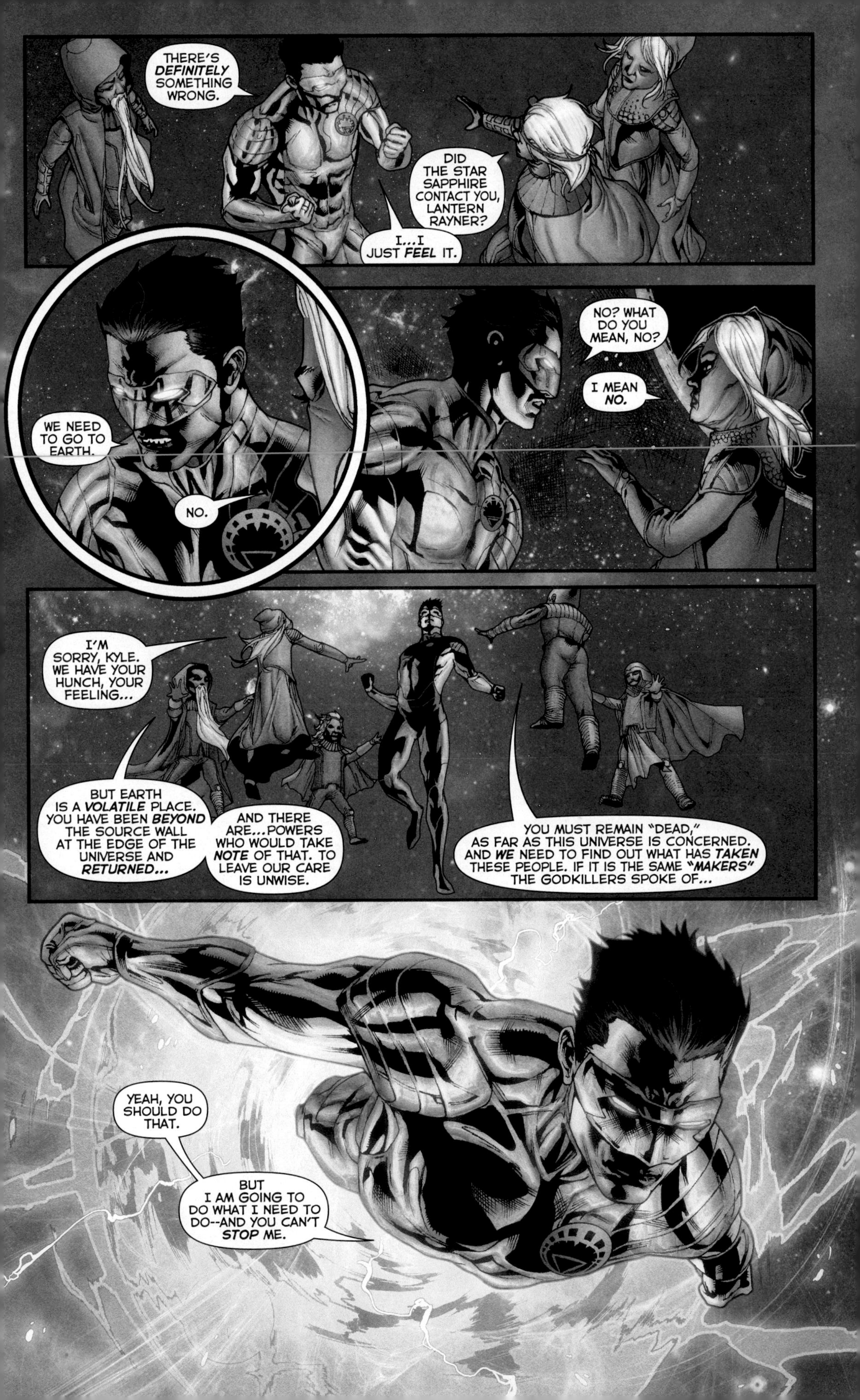
THERE'S DEFINITELY SOMETHING WRONG.
DID THE STAR SAPPHIRE CONTACT YOU, LANTERN RAYNER?
I...I JUST FEEL IT.
WE NEED TO GO TO EARTH.
NO.
NO? WHAT DO YOU MEAN, NO?
I MEAN NO.
I'M SORRY, KYLE. WE HAVE YOUR HUNCH, YOUR FEELING...
BUT EARTH IS A VOLATILE PLACE. YOU HAVE BEEN BEYOND THE SOURCE WALL AT THE EDGE OF THE UNIVERSE AND RETURNED...
AND THERE ARE...POWERS WHO WOULD TAKE NOTE OF THAT. TO LEAVE OUR CARE IS UNWISE.
YOU MUST REMAIN "DEAD," AS FAR AS THIS UNIVERSE IS CONCERNED. AND WE NEED TO FIND OUT WHAT HAS TAKEN THESE PEOPLE. IF IT IS THE SAME "MAKERS" THE GODKILLERS SPOKE OF...
YEAH, YOU SHOULD DO THAT.
BUT I AM GOING TO DO WHAT I NEED TO DO--AND YOU CAN'T STOP ME.

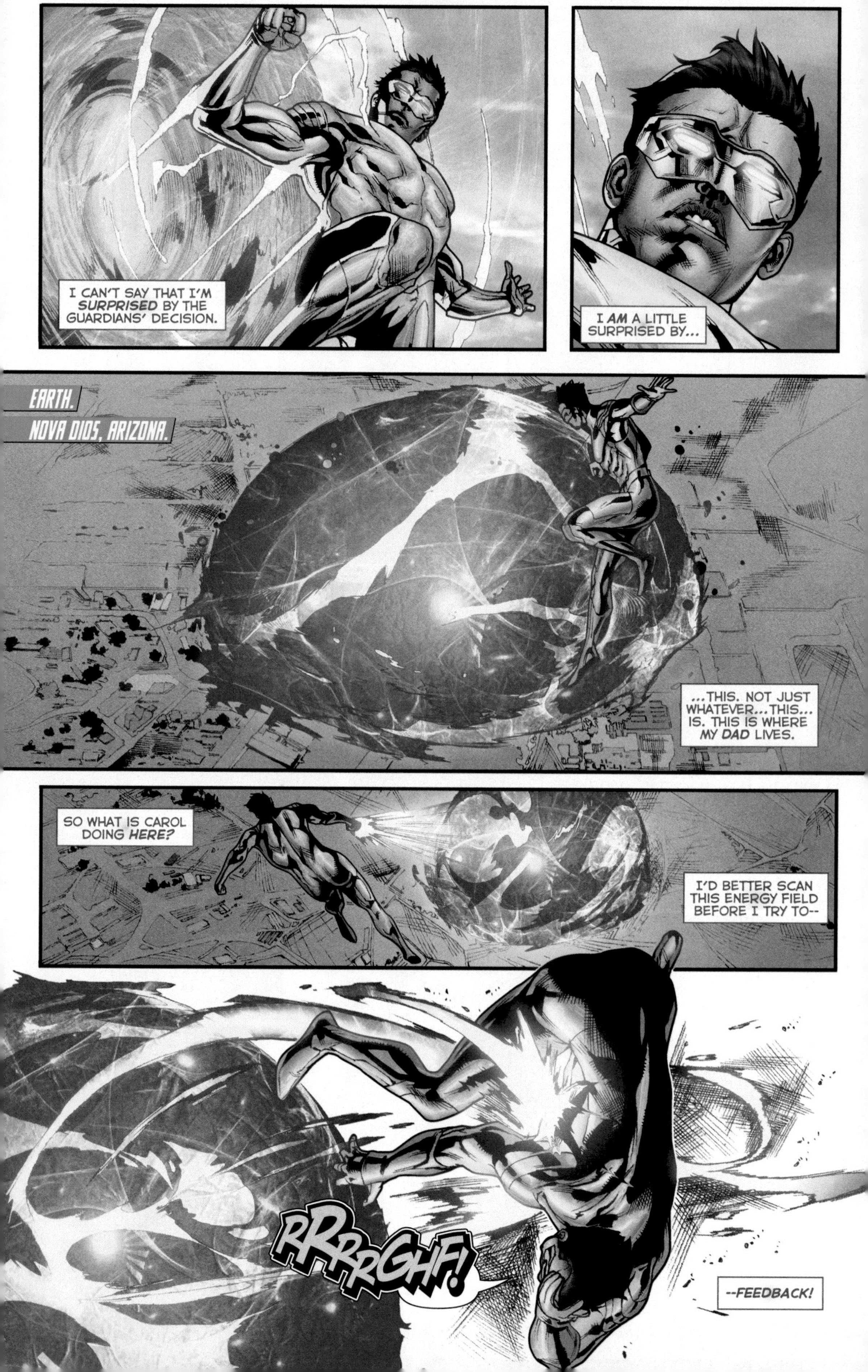

I CAN'T SAY THAT I'M *SURPRISED* BY THE GUARDIANS' DECISION.
I *AM* A LITTLE SURPRISED BY...
EARTH.
NOVA DIOS, ARIZONA.
...THIS. NOT JUST WHATEVER...THIS... IS. THIS IS WHERE MY *DAD* LIVES.
SO WHAT IS CAROL DOING *HERE?*
I'D BETTER SCAN THIS ENERGY FIELD BEFORE I TRY TO--
RRRRRGHF!
--FEEDBACK!

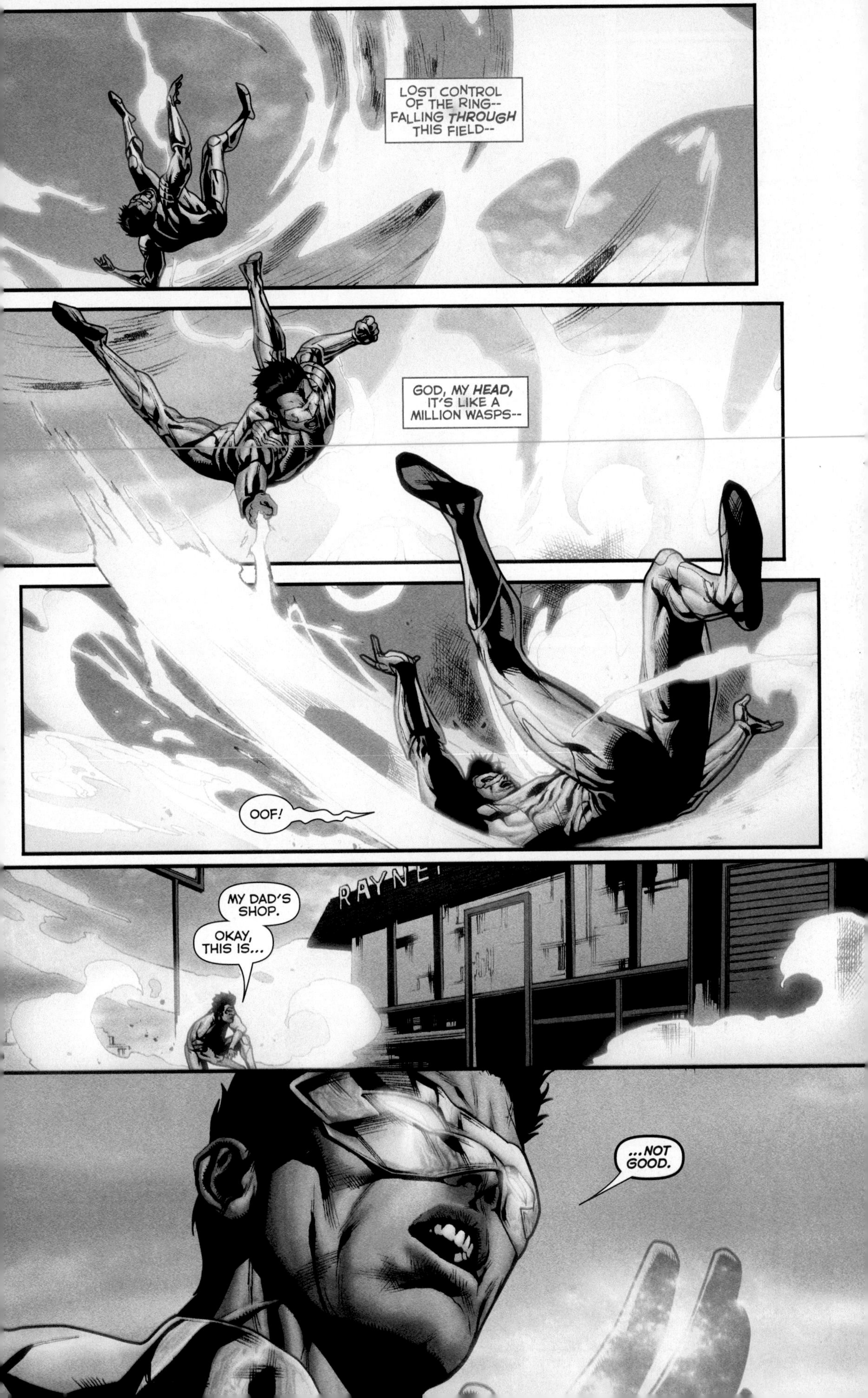
LOST CONTROL OF THE RING-- FALLING THROUGH THIS FIELD--
GOD, MY HEAD, IT'S LIKE A MILLION WASPS--
OOF!
RAYNE
MY DAD'S SHOP.
OKAY, THIS IS...
...NOT GOOD.

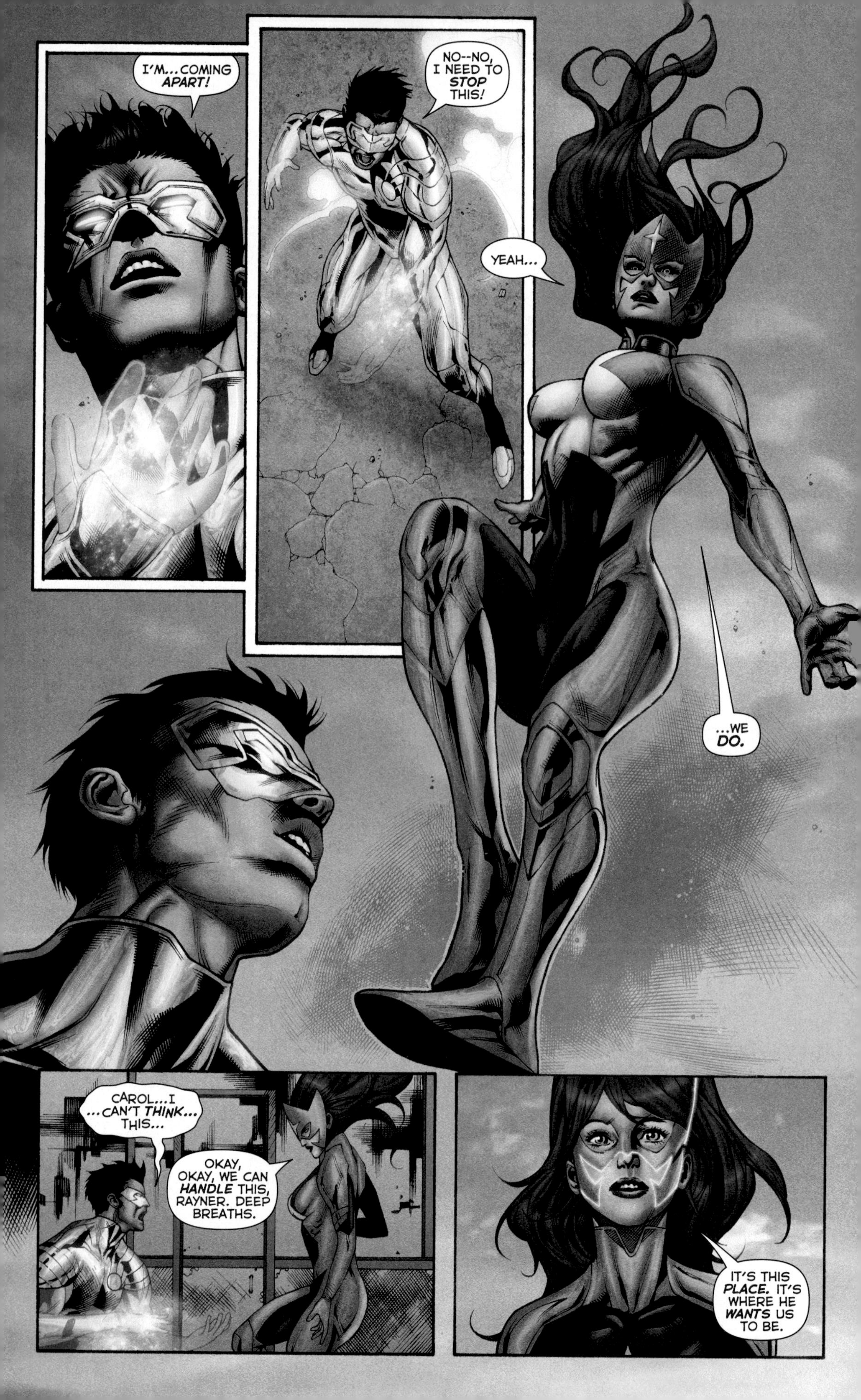
I'M...COMING APART!
NO--NO, I NEED TO STOP THIS!
YEAH...
...WE DO.
CAROL...I ...CAN'T THINK... THIS...
OKAY, OKAY, WE CAN HANDLE THIS, RAYNER. DEEP BREATHS.
IT'S THIS PLACE. IT'S WHERE HE WANTS US TO BE.

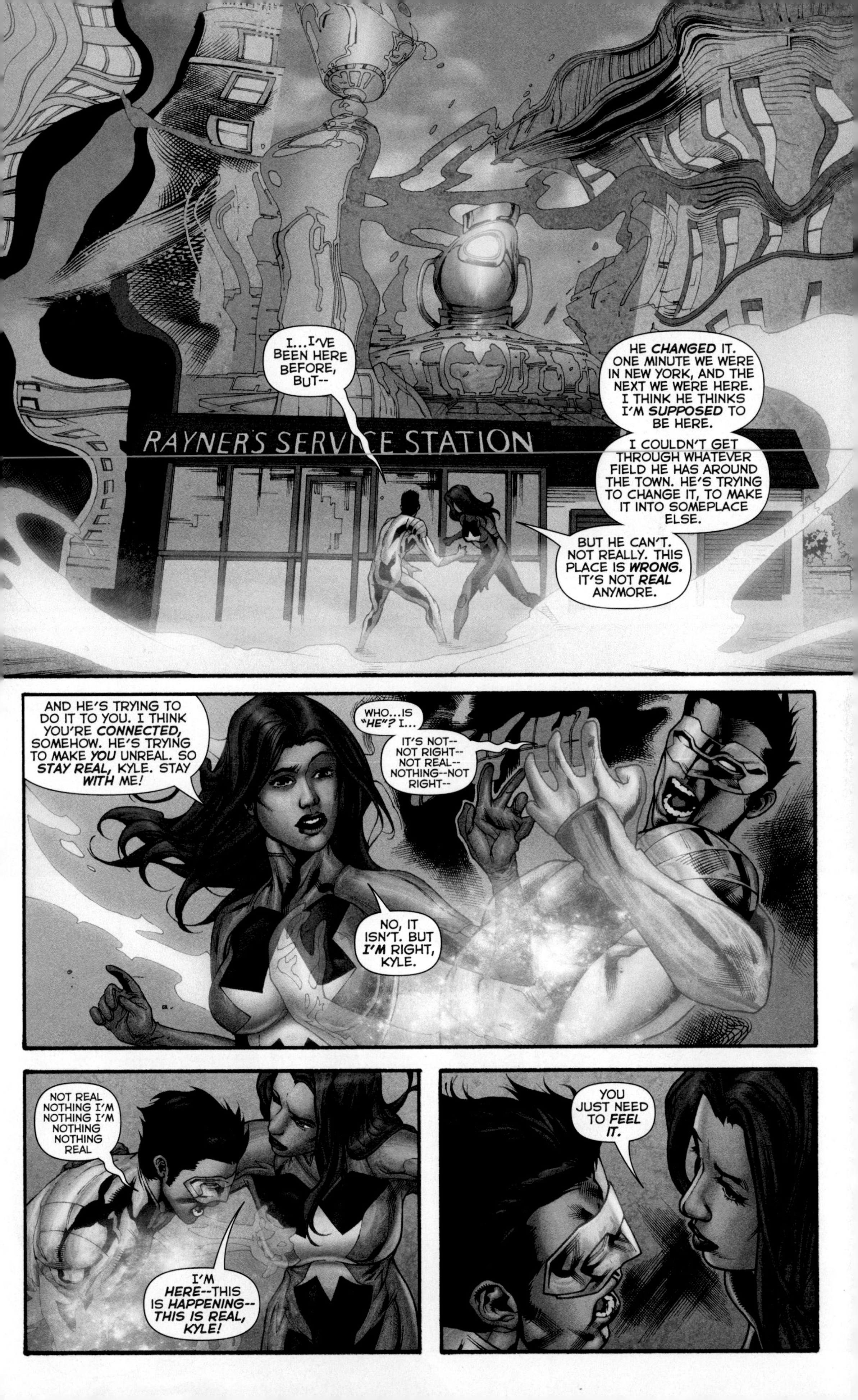
RAYNER'S SERVICE STATION
I...I'VE BEEN HERE BEFORE, BUT--
HE CHANGED IT. ONE MINUTE WE WERE IN NEW YORK, AND THE NEXT WE WERE HERE. I THINK HE THINKS I'M SUPPOSED TO BE HERE.
I COULDN'T GET THROUGH WHATEVER FIELD HE HAS AROUND THE TOWN. HE'S TRYING TO CHANGE IT, TO MAKE IT INTO SOMEPLACE ELSE.
BUT HE CAN'T. NOT REALLY. THIS PLACE IS WRONG. IT'S NOT REAL ANYMORE.
AND HE'S TRYING TO DO IT TO YOU. I THINK YOU'RE CONNECTED, SOMEHOW. HE'S TRYING TO MAKE YOU UNREAL. SO STAY REAL, KYLE. STAY WITH ME!
WHO...IS "HE"? I...
IT'S NOT-- NOT RIGHT-- NOT REAL-- NOTHING--NOT RIGHT--
NO, IT ISN'T. BUT I'M RIGHT, KYLE.
NOT REAL NOTHING I'M NOTHING I'M NOTHING NOTHING REAL
I'M HERE--THIS IS HAPPENING-- THIS IS REAL, KYLE!
YOU JUST NEED TO FEEL IT.

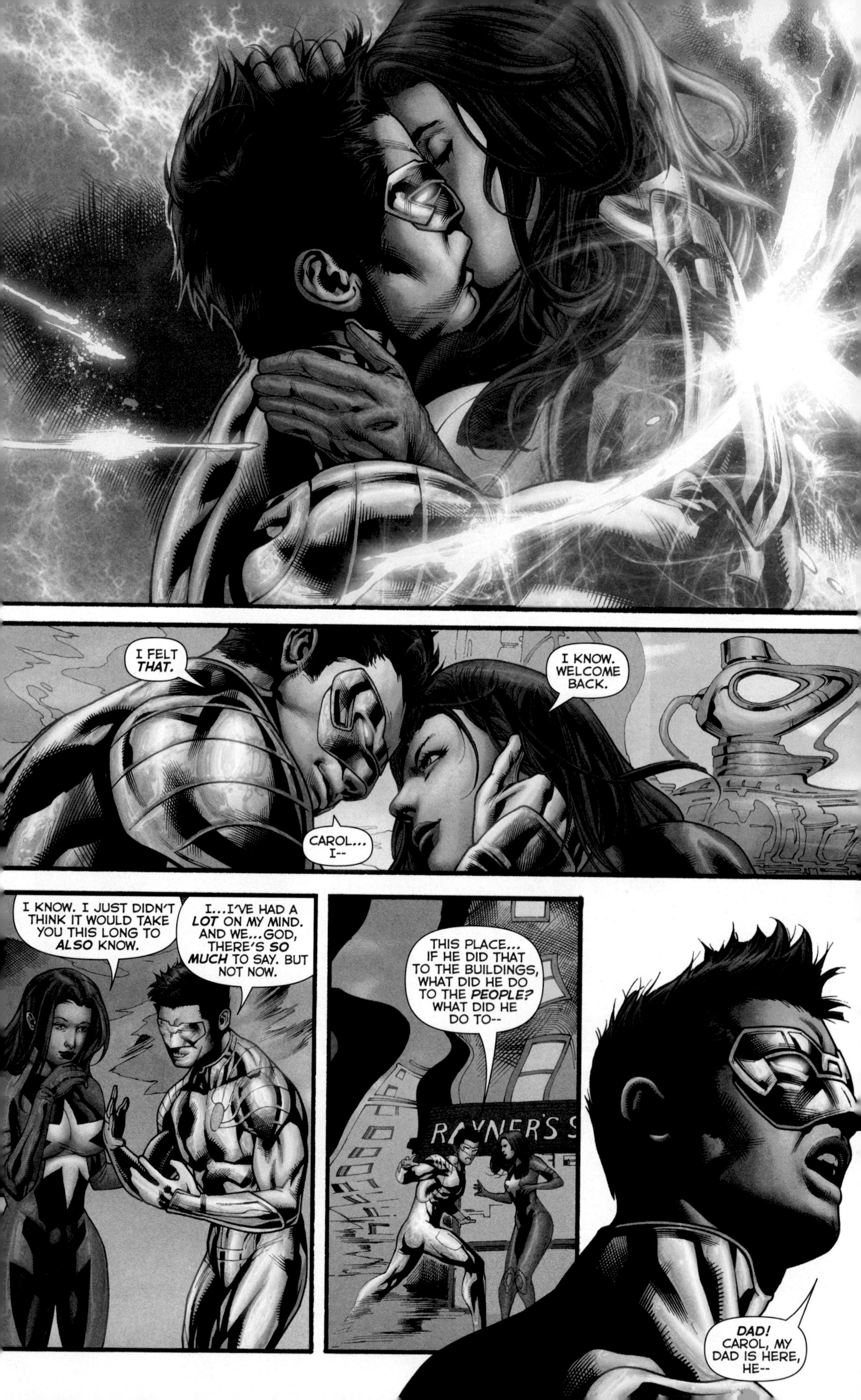
I FELT THAT.
I KNOW. WELCOME BACK.
CAROL... I--
I KNOW. I JUST DIDN'T THINK IT WOULD TAKE YOU THIS LONG TO ALSO KNOW.
I...I'VE HAD A LOT ON MY MIND. AND WE...GOD, THERE'S SO MUCH TO SAY. BUT NOT NOW.
THIS PLACE... IF HE DID THAT TO THE BUILDINGS, WHAT DID HE DO TO THE PEOPLE? WHAT DID HE DO TO--
RAYNER'S S
DAD! CAROL, MY DAD IS HERE, HE--

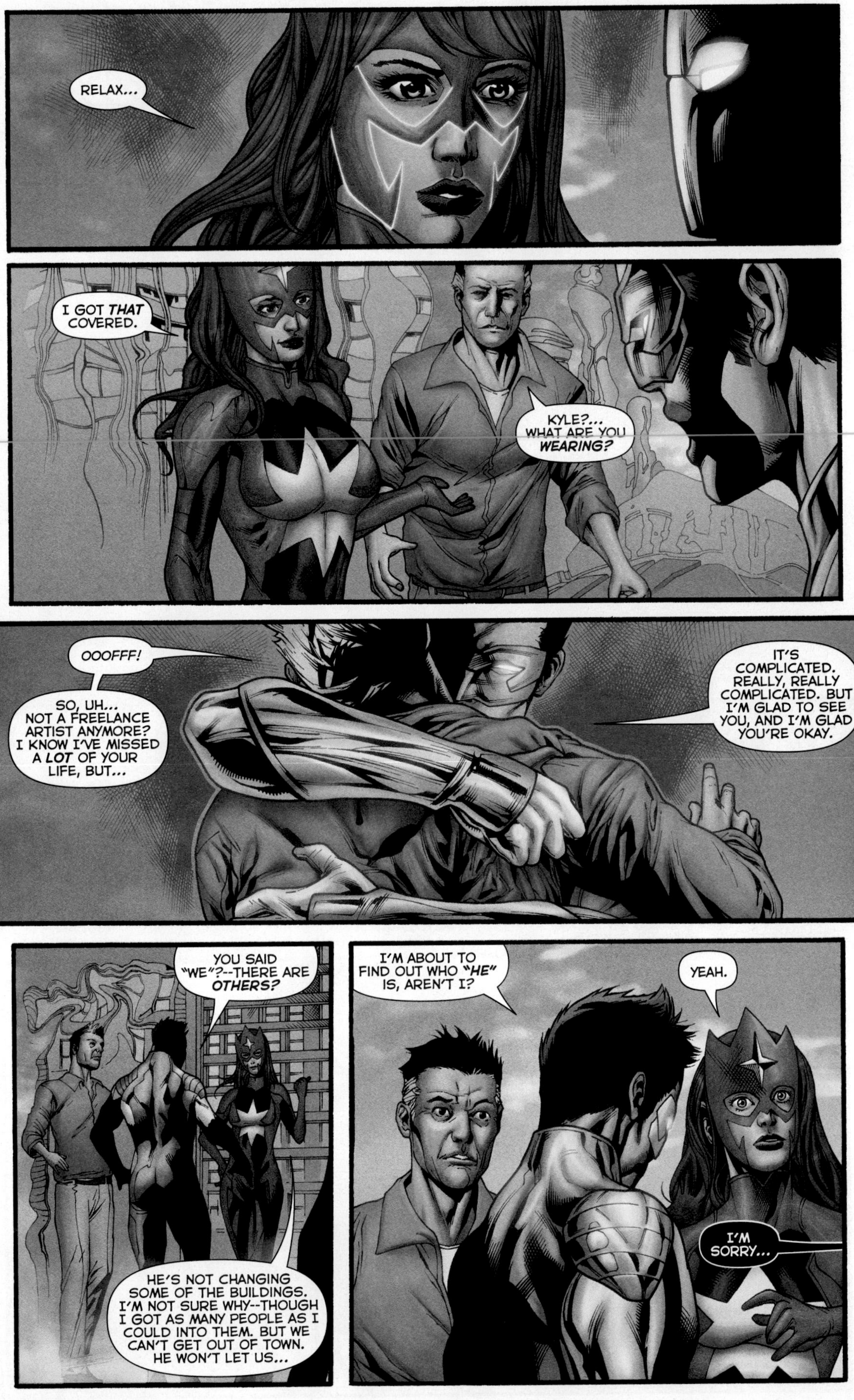
RELAX...
I GOT *THAT* COVERED.
KYLE?... WHAT ARE YOU *WEARING?*
OOOFFF!
SO, UH... NOT A FREELANCE ARTIST ANYMORE? I KNOW I'VE MISSED A *LOT* OF YOUR LIFE, BUT...
IT'S COMPLICATED. REALLY, REALLY COMPLICATED. BUT I'M GLAD TO SEE YOU, AND I'M GLAD YOU'RE OKAY.
YOU SAID "WE"?--THERE ARE *OTHERS?*
HE'S NOT CHANGING SOME OF THE BUILDINGS. I'M NOT SURE WHY--THOUGH I GOT AS MANY PEOPLE AS I COULD INTO THEM. BUT WE CAN'T GET OUT OF TOWN. HE WON'T LET US...
I'M ABOUT TO FIND OUT WHO *"HE"* IS, AREN'T I?
YEAH.
I'M SORRY...

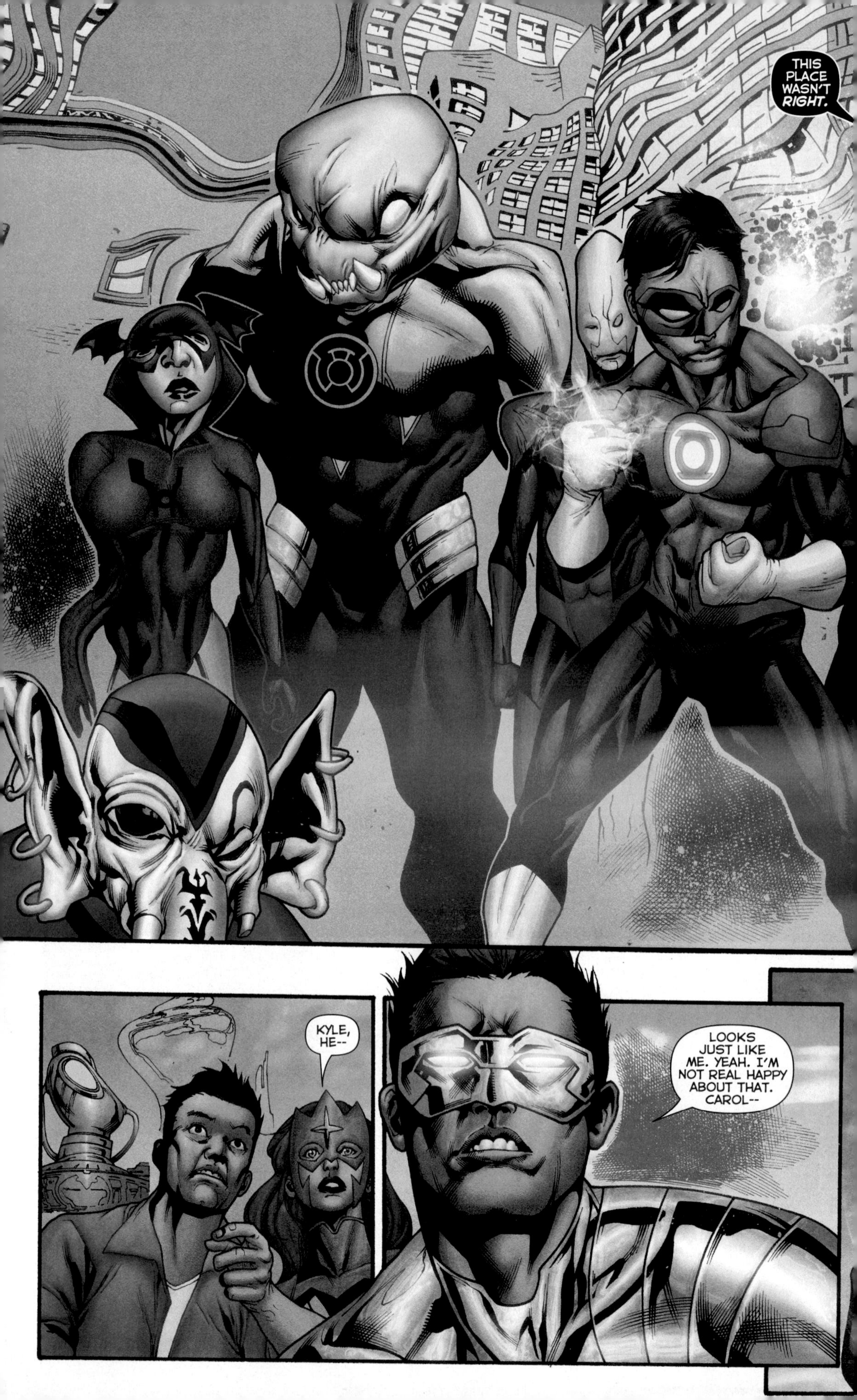
THIS PLACE WASN'T *RIGHT.*
KYLE, HE--
LOOKS JUST LIKE ME. YEAH. I'M NOT REAL HAPPY ABOUT THAT. CAROL--

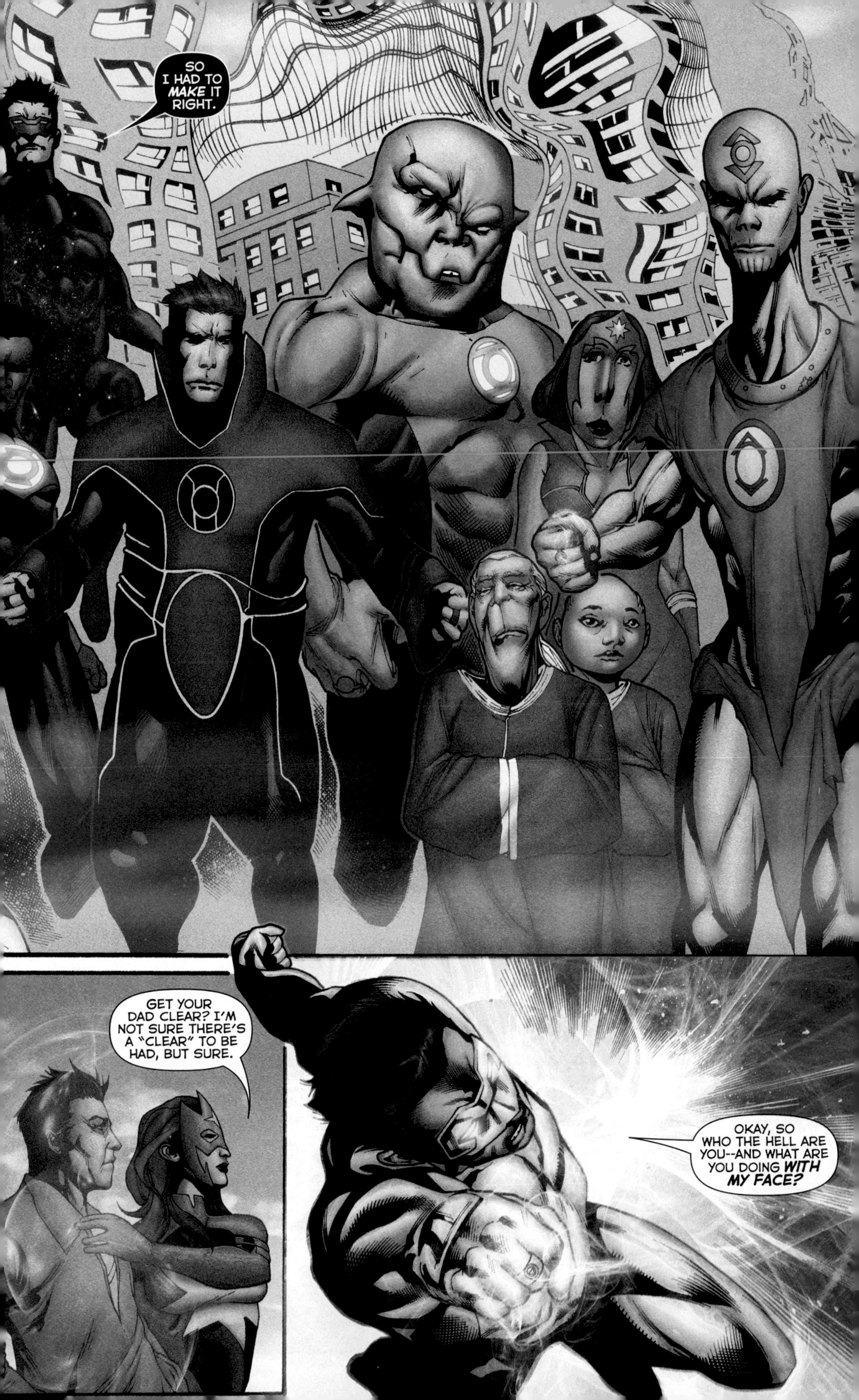
SO I HAD TO MAKE IT RIGHT.
GET YOUR DAD CLEAR? I'M NOT SURE THERE'S A "CLEAR" TO BE HAD, BUT SURE.
OKAY, SO WHO THE HELL ARE YOU--AND WHAT ARE YOU DOING WITH MY FACE?

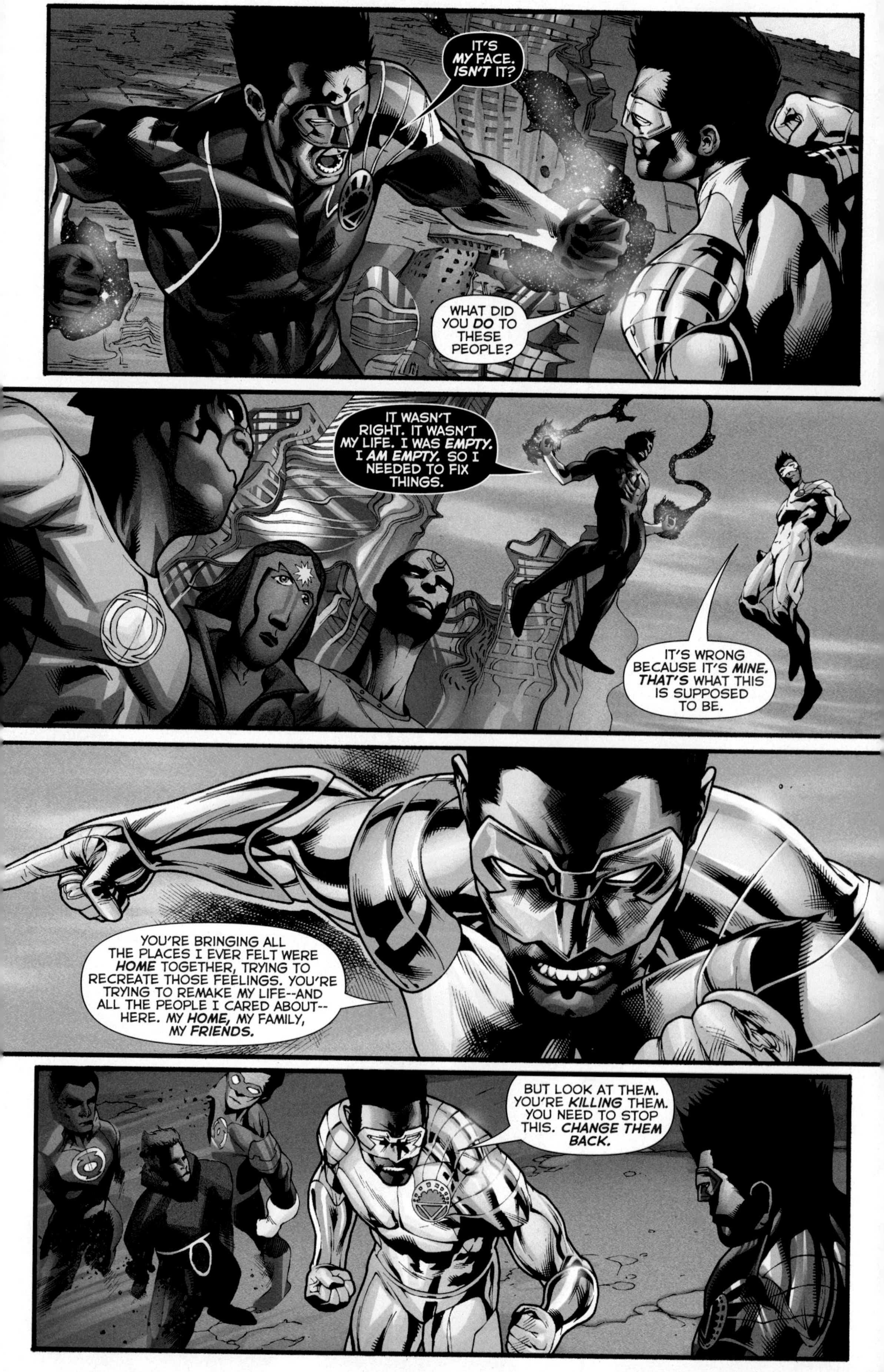
IT'S *MY* FACE. *ISN'T* IT?
WHAT DID YOU *DO* TO THESE PEOPLE?
IT WASN'T RIGHT. IT WASN'T MY LIFE. I WAS *EMPTY.* I *AM EMPTY.* SO I NEEDED TO FIX THINGS.
IT'S WRONG BECAUSE IT'S *MINE. THAT'S* WHAT THIS IS SUPPOSED TO BE.
YOU'RE BRINGING ALL THE PLACES I EVER FELT WERE *HOME* TOGETHER, TRYING TO RECREATE THOSE FEELINGS. YOU'RE TRYING TO REMAKE MY LIFE--AND ALL THE PEOPLE I CARED ABOUT--HERE. MY *HOME,* MY FAMILY, MY *FRIENDS.*
BUT LOOK AT THEM. YOU'RE *KILLING* THEM. YOU NEED TO STOP THIS. *CHANGE THEM BACK.*

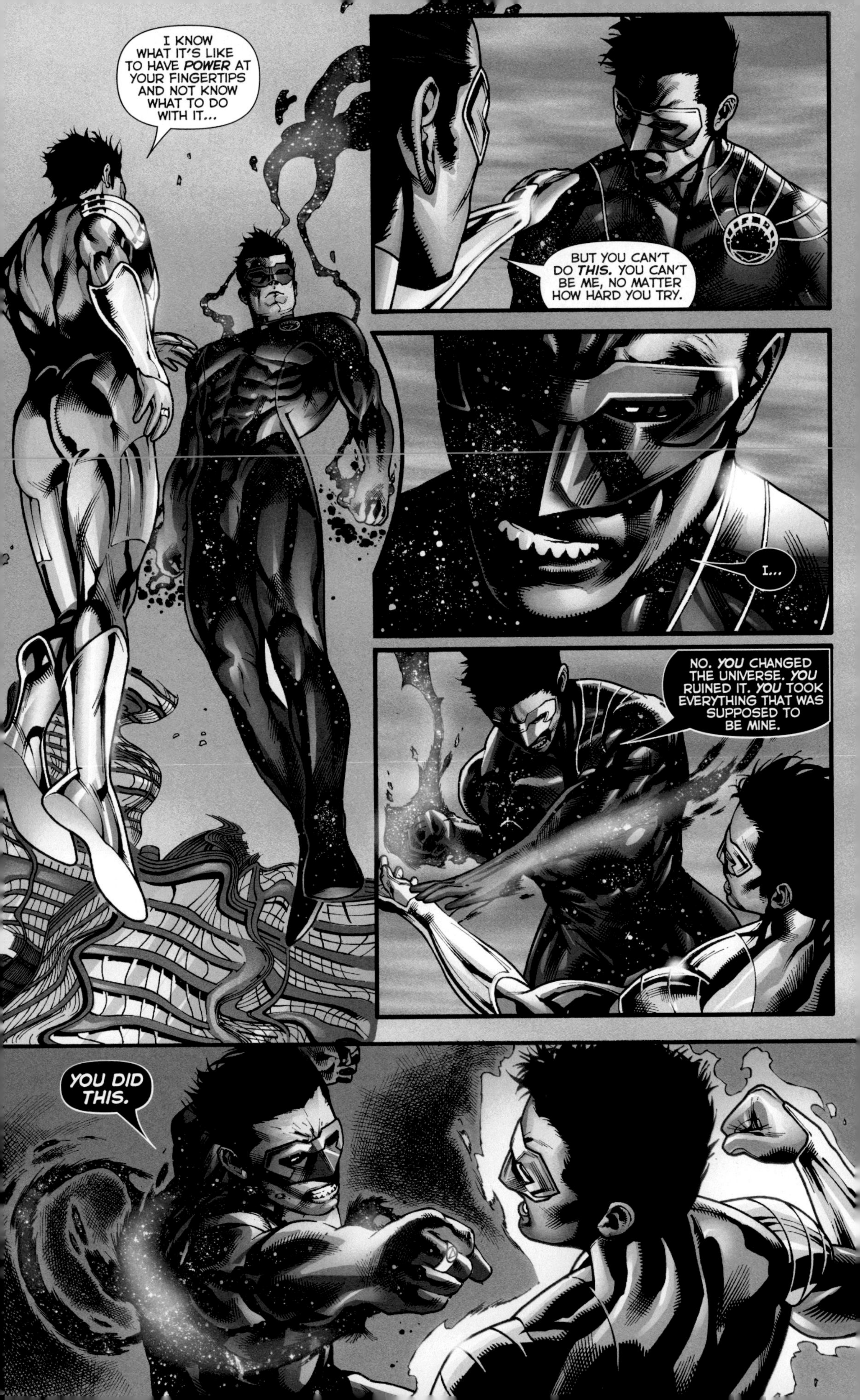
I KNOW WHAT IT'S LIKE TO HAVE *POWER* AT YOUR FINGERTIPS AND NOT KNOW WHAT TO DO WITH IT...
BUT YOU CAN'T DO *THIS.* YOU CAN'T BE ME, NO MATTER HOW HARD YOU TRY.
I...
NO. *YOU* CHANGED THE UNIVERSE. *YOU* RUINED IT. *YOU* TOOK EVERYTHING THAT WAS SUPPOSED TO BE MINE.
YOU DID THIS.

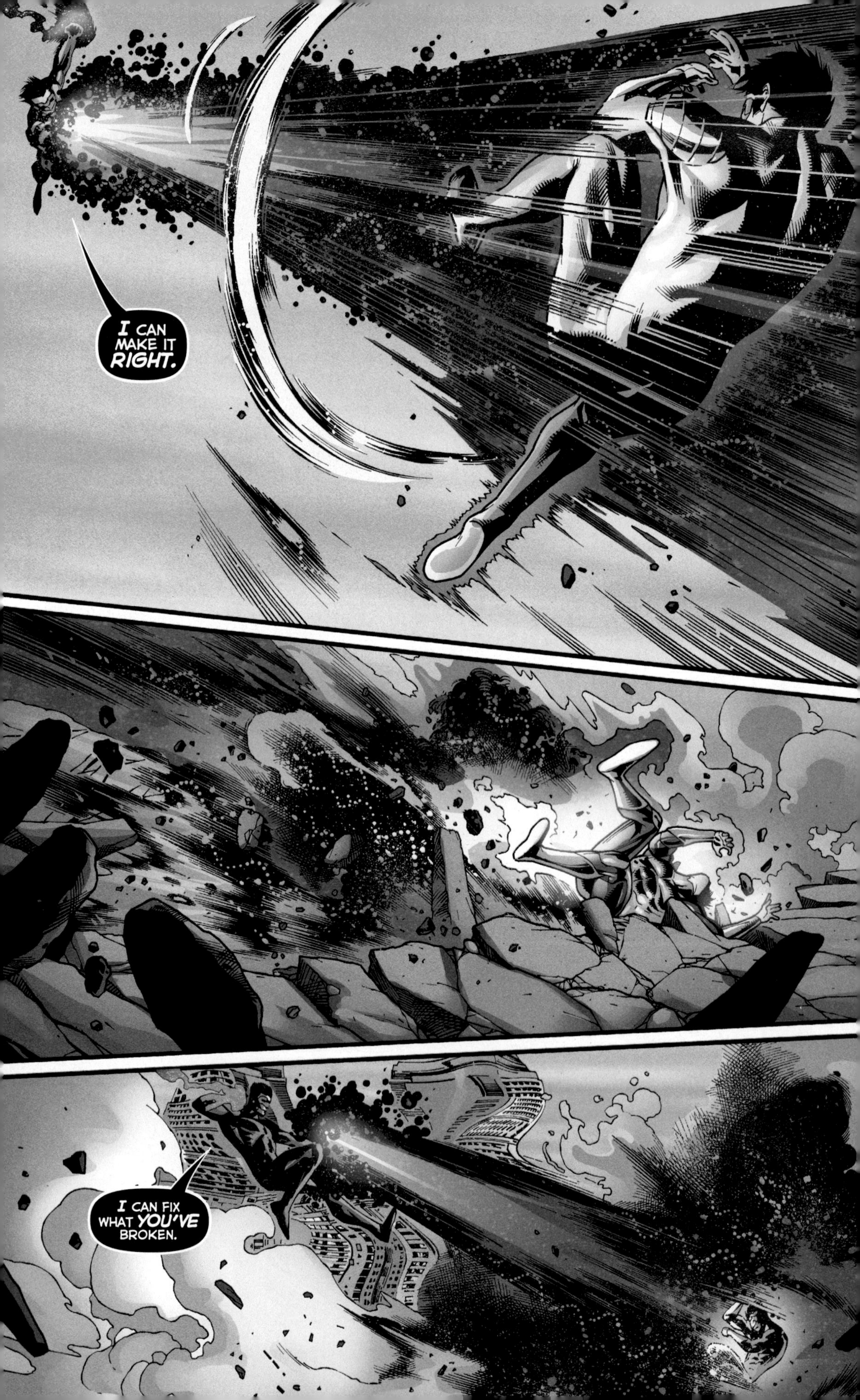
I CAN MAKE IT RIGHT.
I CAN FIX WHAT YOU'VE BROKEN.

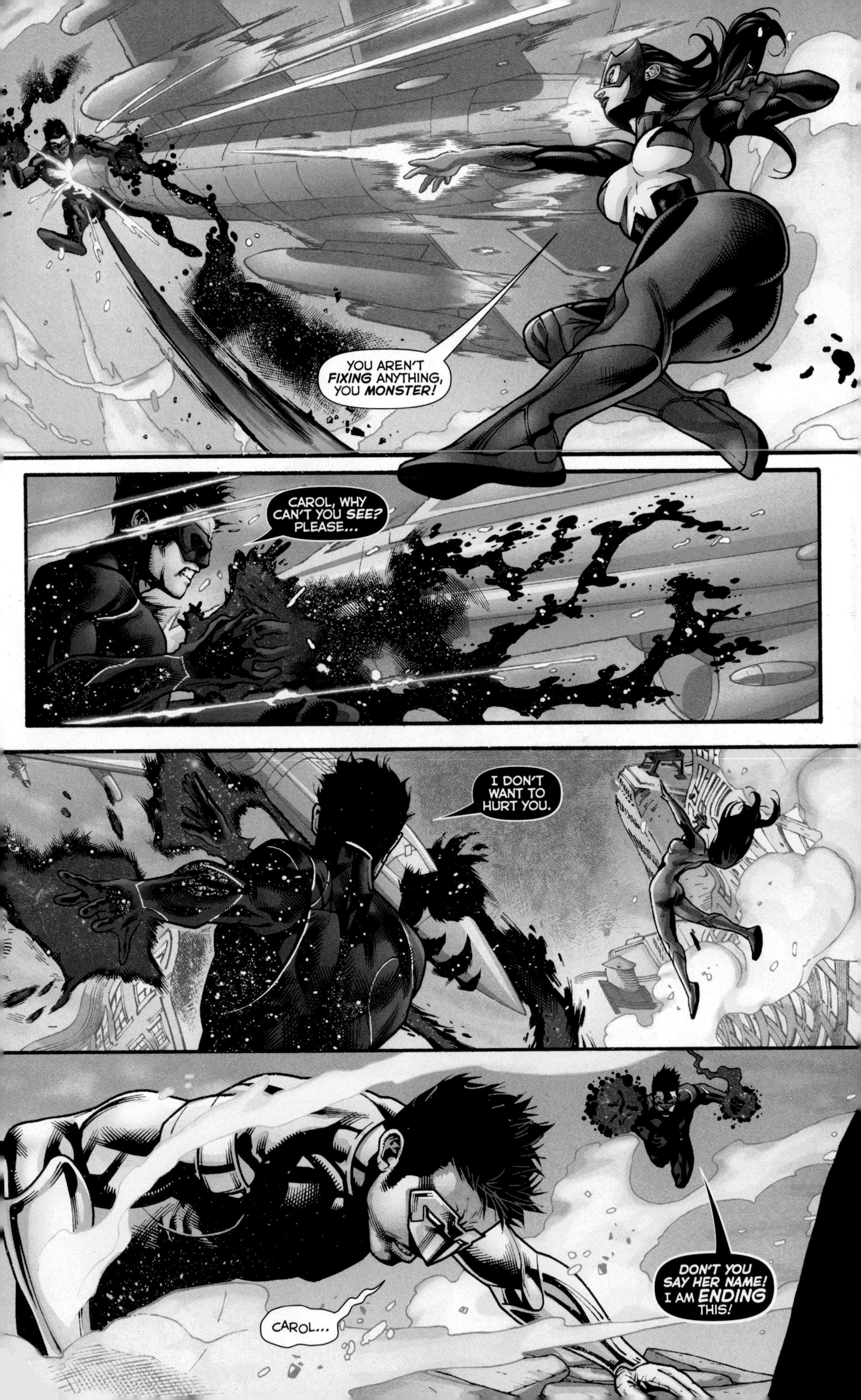
YOU AREN'T FIXING ANYTHING, YOU MONSTER!
CAROL, WHY CAN'T YOU SEE? PLEASE...
I DON'T WANT TO HURT YOU.
CAROL...
DON'T YOU SAY HER NAME! I AM ENDING THIS!

STOP! THIS IS MADNESS.

DAD, *PLEASE*, I...I HAVE TO *END* THIS.

I HAVE TO GET MY *LIFE* BACK.

WHY CAN'T YOU *SEE* THAT? DON'T YOU *LOVE ME*?

IF YOU REALLY BELIEVE YOU'RE MY *SON*...THEN PLEASE, JUST LOOK, OKAY? LOOK WHAT YOU'RE DOING.

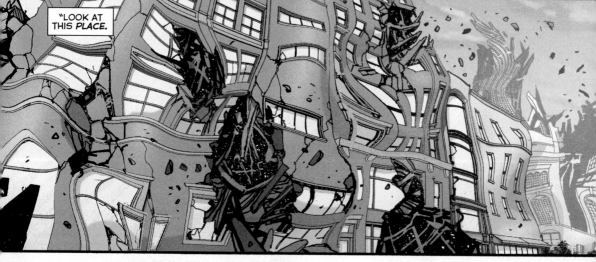

"LOOK AT THIS *PLACE.*"

"LOOK AT THESE *PEOPLE.*"

"IF THERE'S *ONE THING* I KNOW ABOUT KYLE, IT'S THAT HE *CARES.* DEEPLY. ABOUT *EVERYONE* IN HIS LIFE. HE WOULDN'T HURT THEM. NOT LIKE THIS."

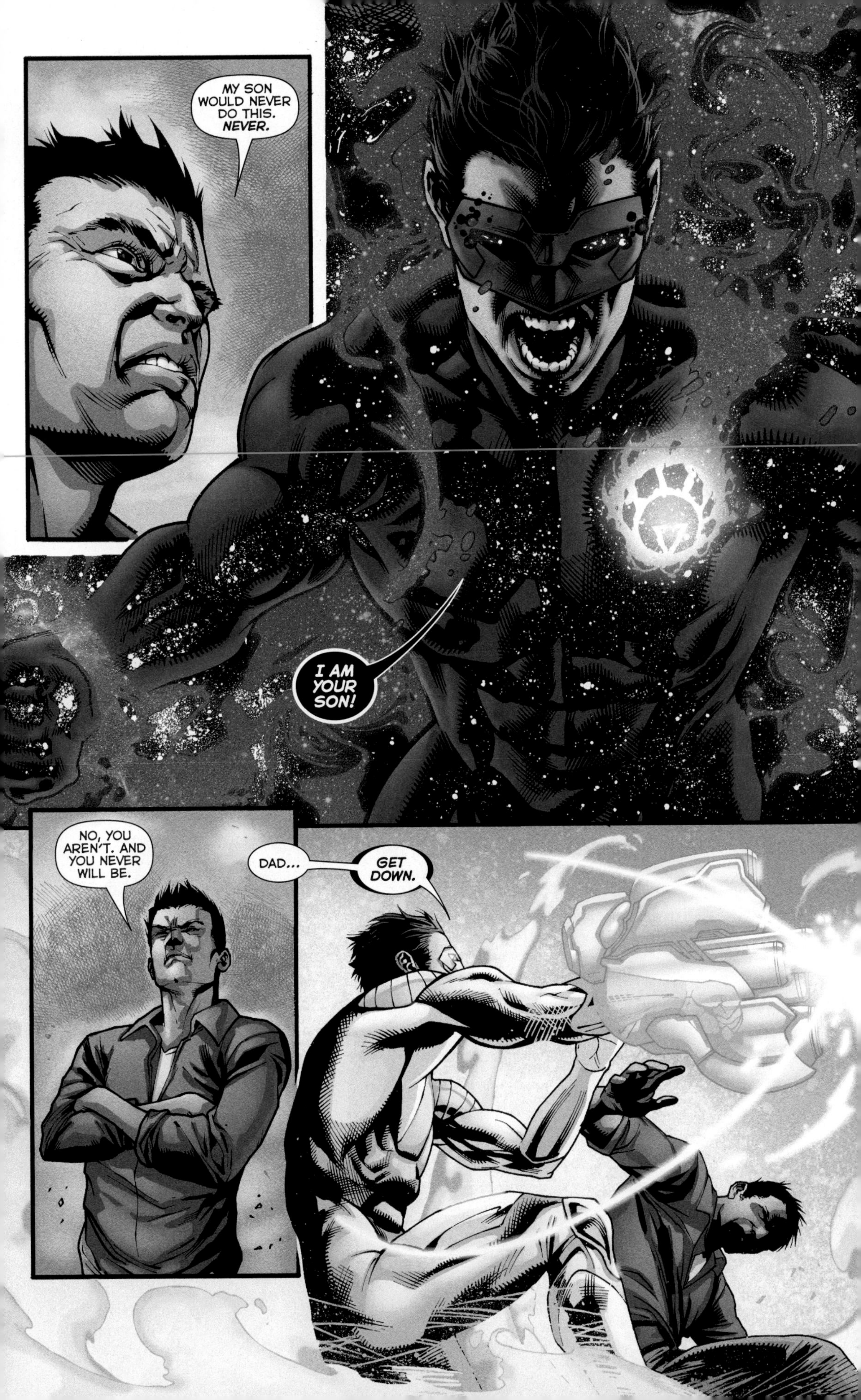
MY SON WOULD NEVER DO THIS. NEVER.
I AM YOUR SON!
NO, YOU AREN'T. AND YOU NEVER WILL BE.
DAD...
GET DOWN.

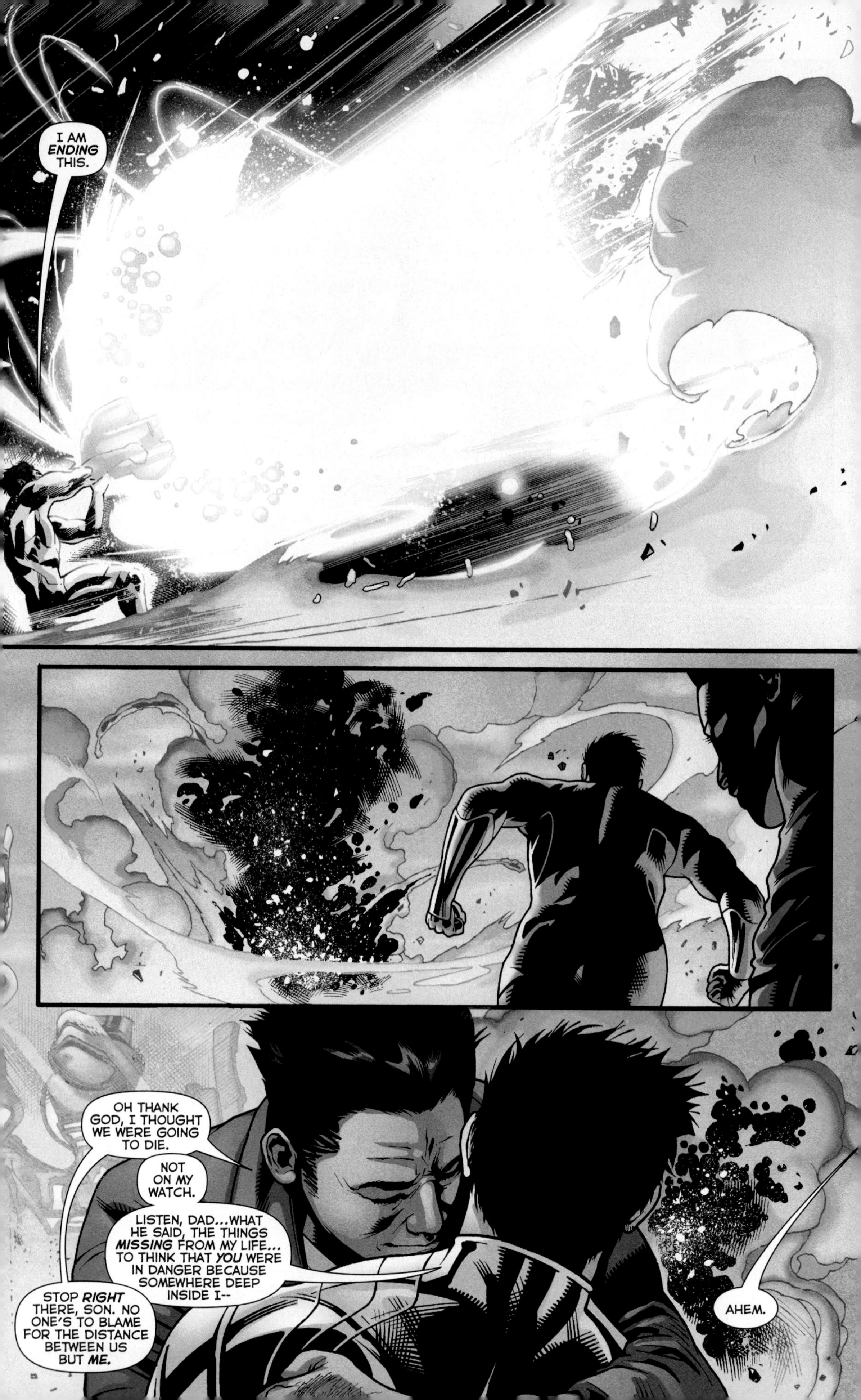
I AM ENDING THIS.
OH THANK GOD, I THOUGHT WE WERE GOING TO DIE.
NOT ON MY WATCH.
LISTEN, DAD...WHAT HE SAID, THE THINGS MISSING FROM MY LIFE... TO THINK THAT YOU WERE IN DANGER BECAUSE SOMEWHERE DEEP INSIDE I--
STOP RIGHT THERE, SON. NO ONE'S TO BLAME FOR THE DISTANCE BETWEEN US BUT ME.
AHEM.

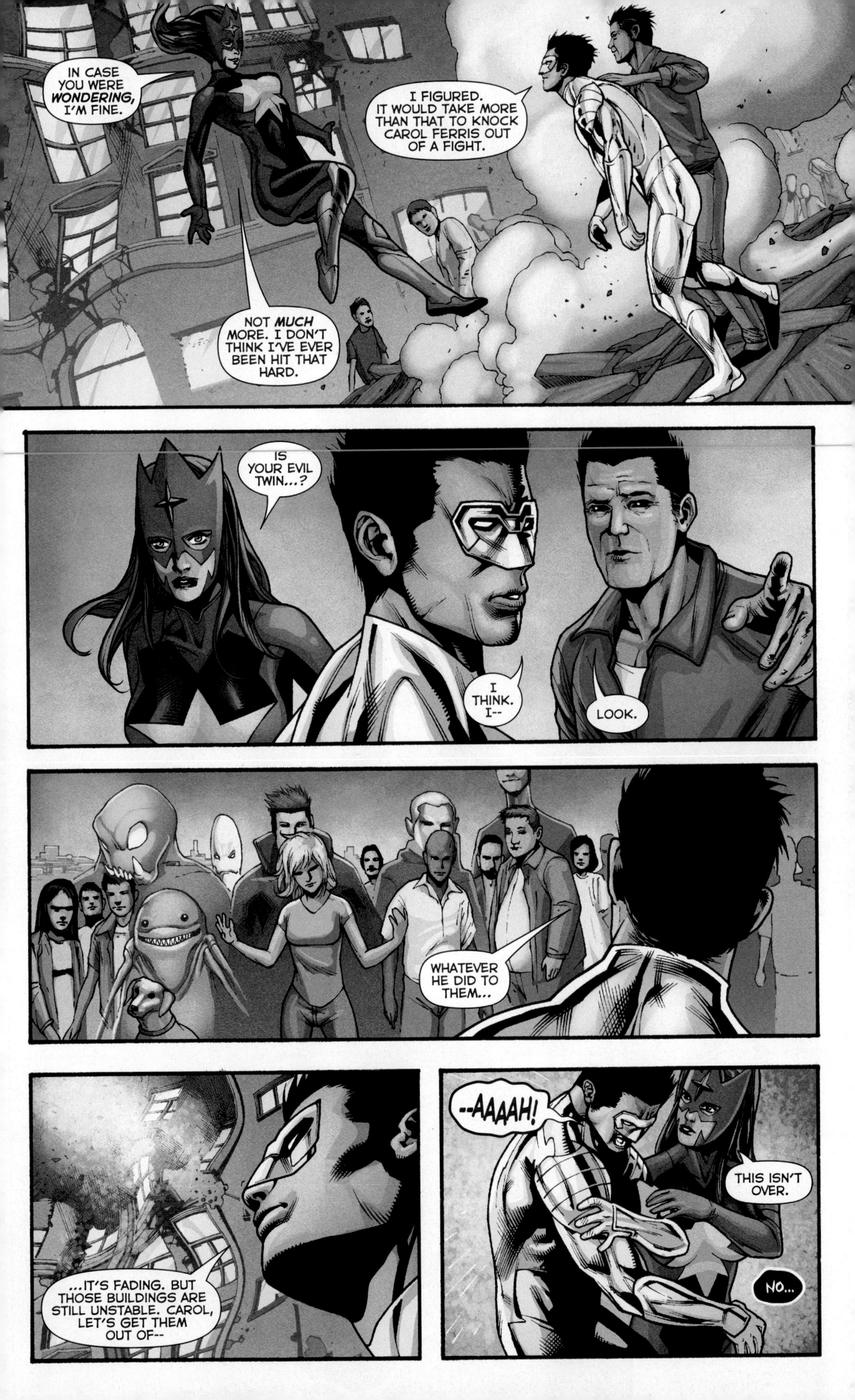
IN CASE YOU WERE WONDERING, I'M FINE.
I FIGURED. IT WOULD TAKE MORE THAN THAT TO KNOCK CAROL FERRIS OUT OF A FIGHT.
NOT MUCH MORE. I DON'T THINK I'VE EVER BEEN HIT THAT HARD.
IS YOUR EVIL TWIN...?
I THINK. I--
LOOK.
WHATEVER HE DID TO THEM...
...IT'S FADING. BUT THOSE BUILDINGS ARE STILL UNSTABLE. CAROL, LET'S GET THEM OUT OF--
--AAAAH!
THIS ISN'T OVER.
NO...

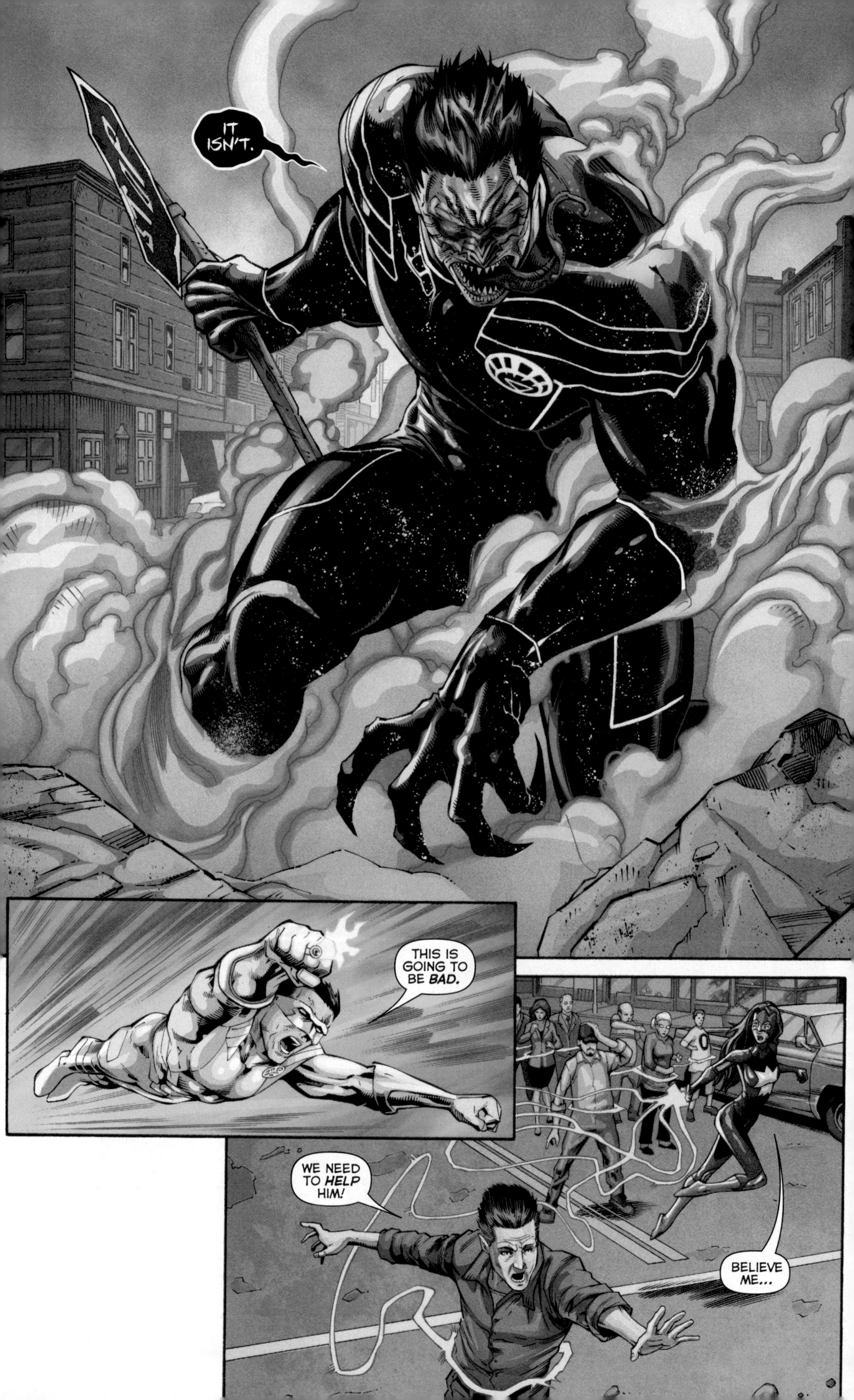
IT ISN'T.
THIS IS GOING TO BE *BAD.*
WE NEED TO *HELP* HIM!
BELIEVE ME...

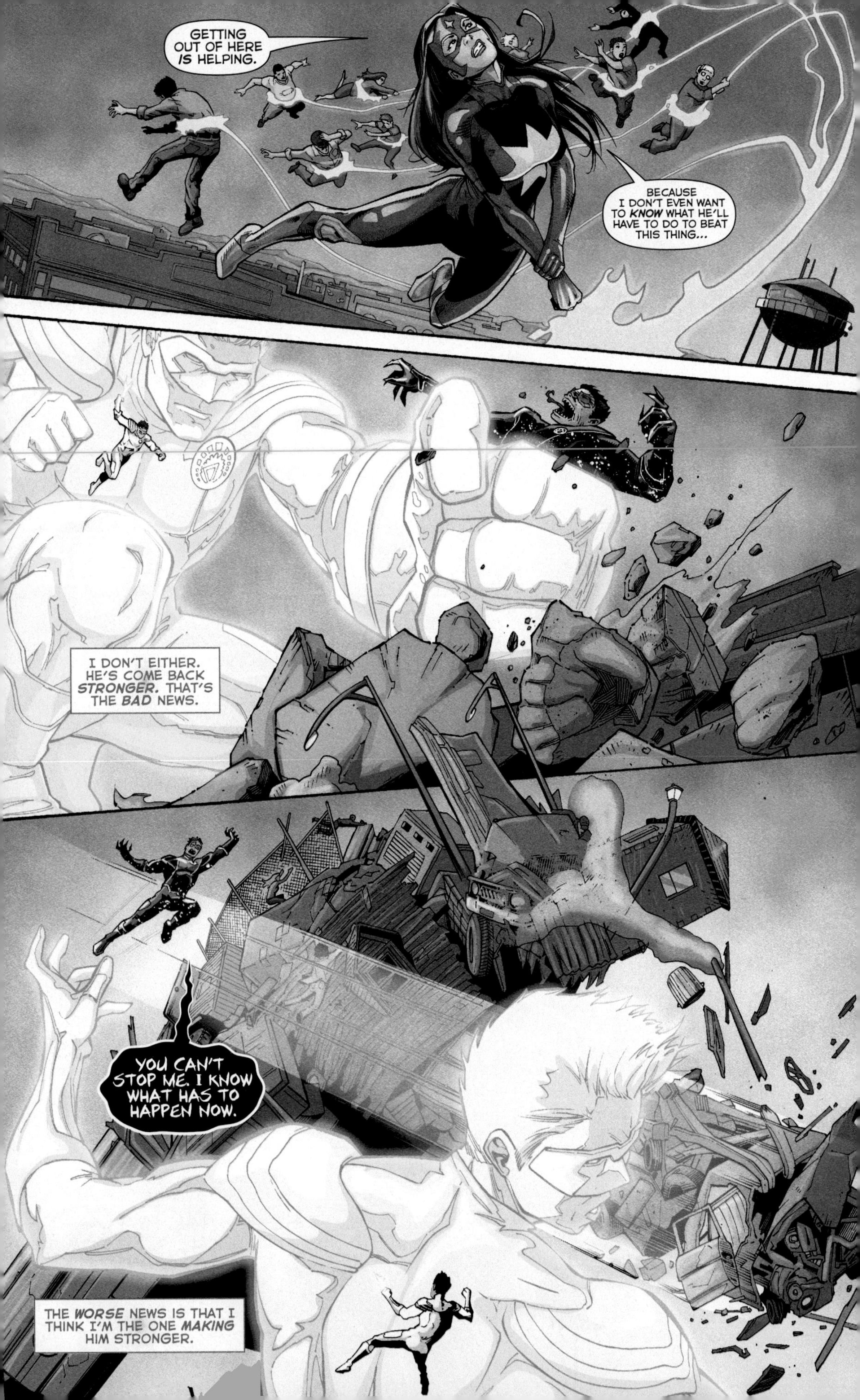
GETTING OUT OF HERE IS HELPING.
BECAUSE I DON'T EVEN WANT TO KNOW WHAT HE'LL HAVE TO DO TO BEAT THIS THING...
I DON'T EITHER. HE'S COME BACK STRONGER. THAT'S THE BAD NEWS.
YOU CAN'T STOP ME. I KNOW WHAT HAS TO HAPPEN NOW.
THE WORSE NEWS IS THAT I THINK I'M THE ONE MAKING HIM STRONGER.

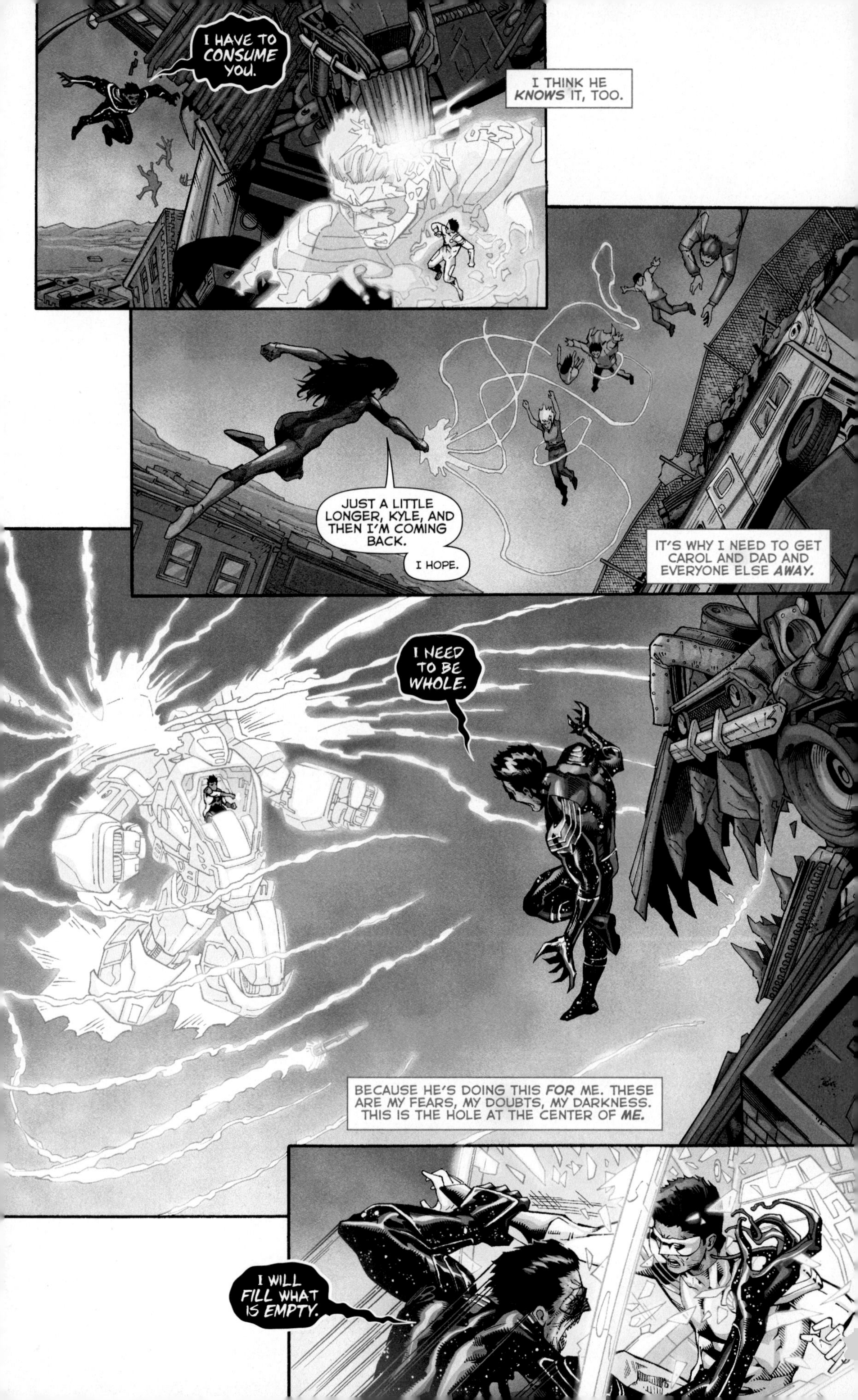
I HAVE TO CONSUME YOU.
I THINK HE KNOWS IT, TOO.
JUST A LITTLE LONGER, KYLE, AND THEN I'M COMING BACK.
I HOPE.
IT'S WHY I NEED TO GET CAROL AND DAD AND EVERYONE ELSE AWAY.
I NEED TO BE WHOLE.
BECAUSE HE'S DOING THIS FOR ME. THESE ARE MY FEARS, MY DOUBTS, MY DARKNESS. THIS IS THE HOLE AT THE CENTER OF ME.
I WILL FILL WHAT IS EMPTY.

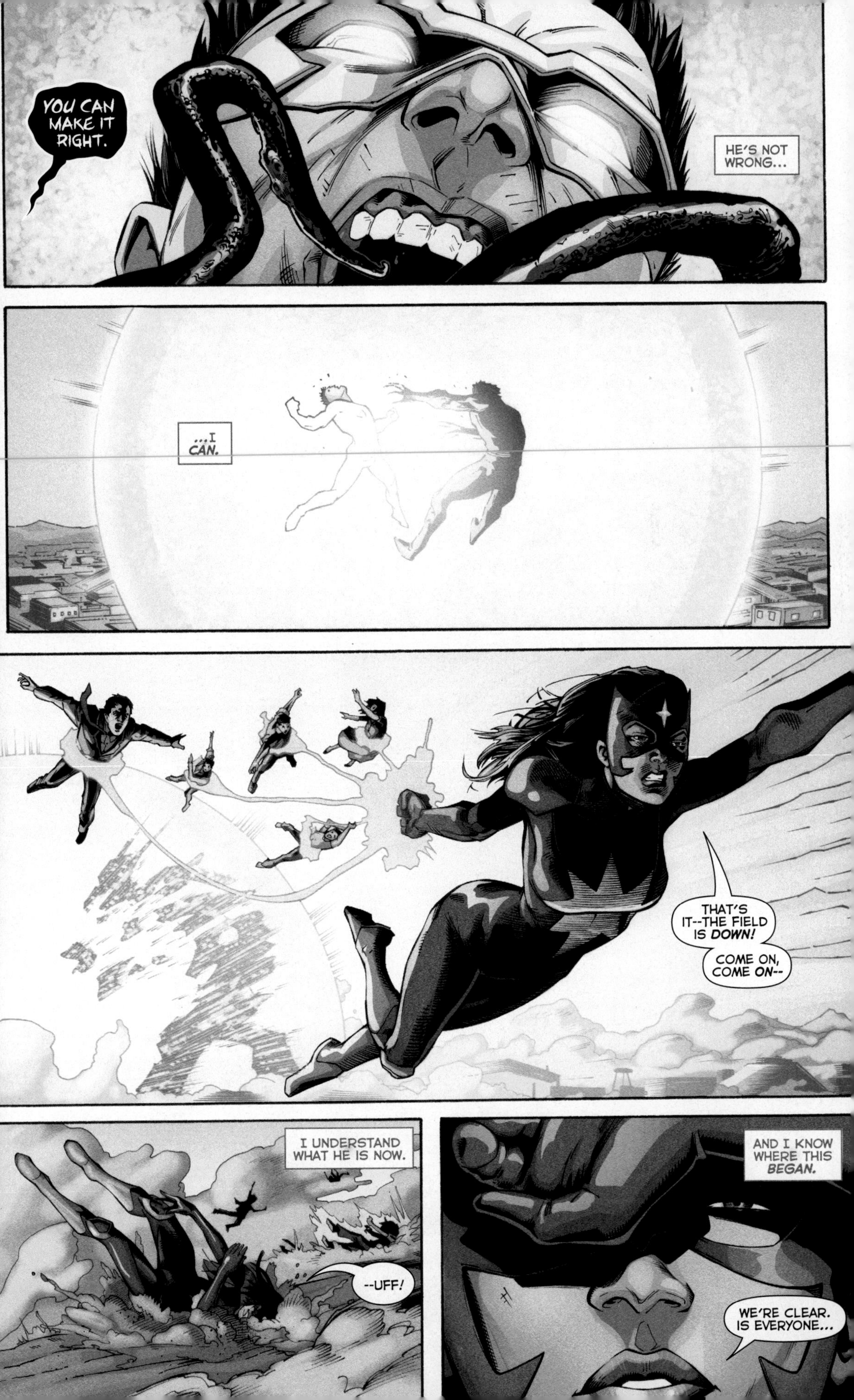
YOU CAN MAKE IT RIGHT.
HE'S NOT WRONG...
...I CAN.
THAT'S IT--THE FIELD IS DOWN!
COME ON, COME ON--
I UNDERSTAND WHAT HE IS NOW.
--UFF!
AND I KNOW WHERE THIS BEGAN.
WE'RE CLEAR. IS EVERYONE...

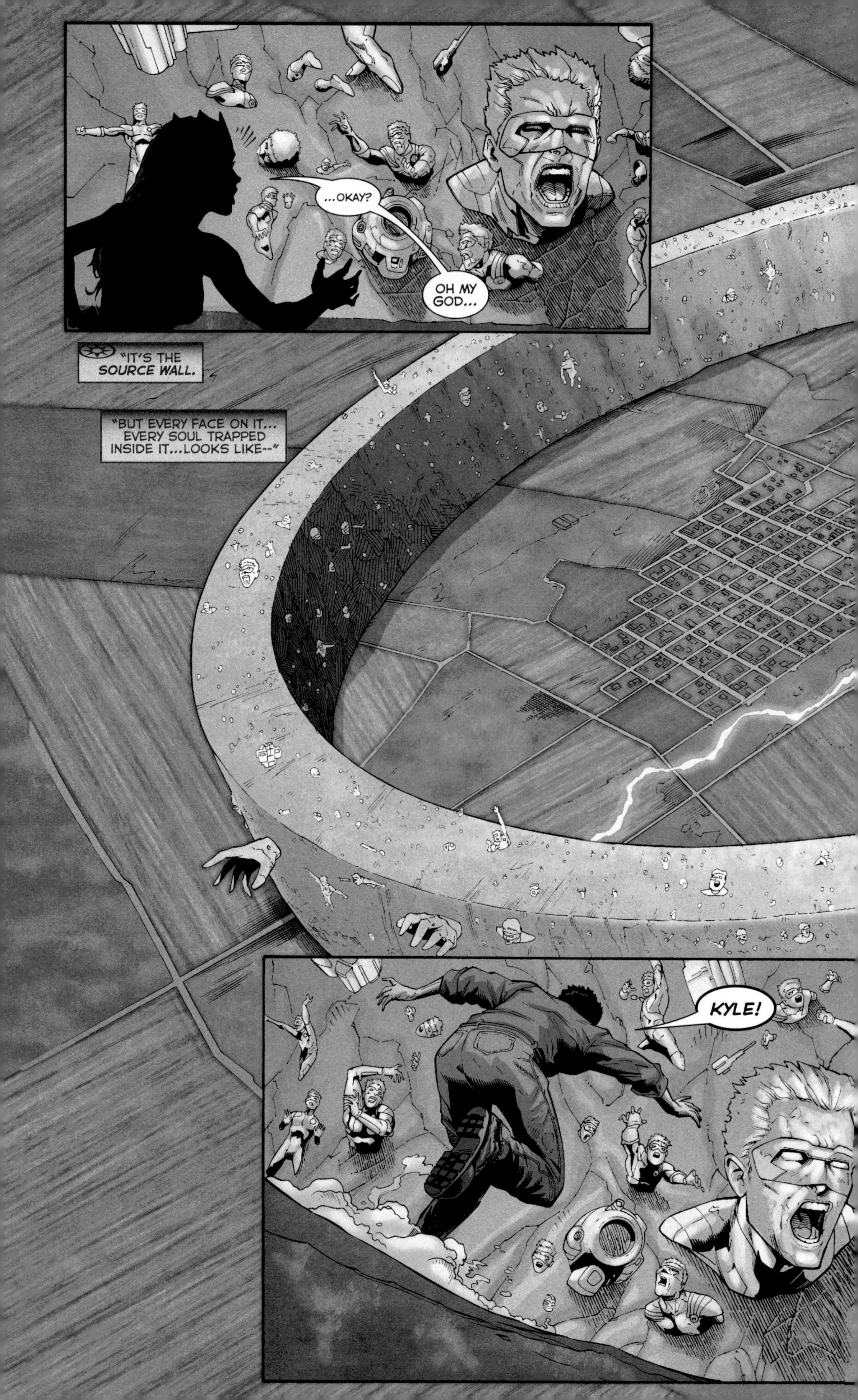
...OKAY?
OH MY GOD...
"IT'S THE SOURCE WALL.
"BUT EVERY FACE ON IT... EVERY SOUL TRAPPED INSIDE IT...LOOKS LIKE--"
KYLE!

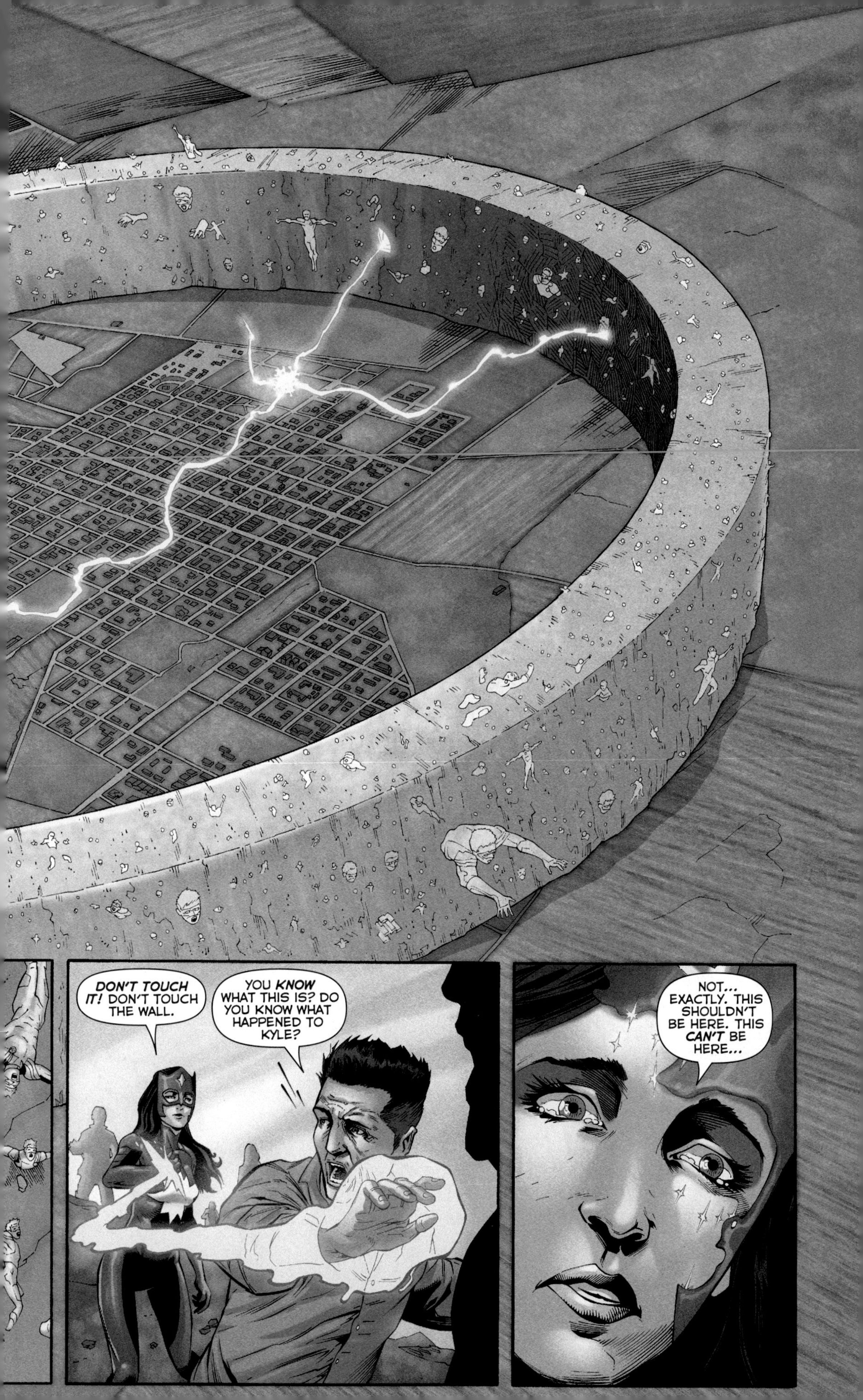
DON'T TOUCH IT! DON'T TOUCH THE WALL.
YOU KNOW WHAT THIS IS? DO YOU KNOW WHAT HAPPENED TO KYLE?
NOT... EXACTLY. THIS SHOULDN'T BE HERE. THIS CAN'T BE HERE...

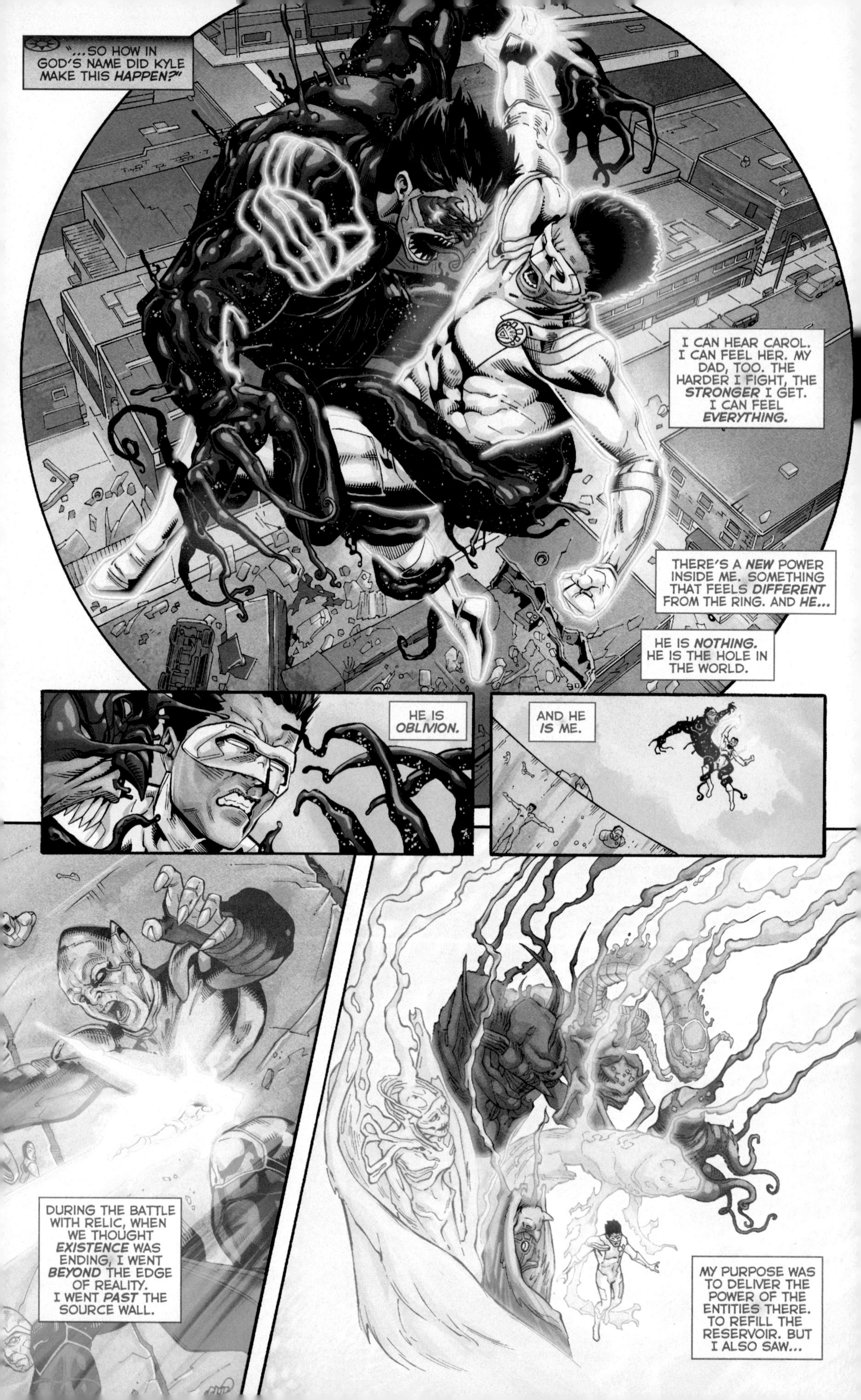
"...SO HOW IN GOD'S NAME DID KYLE MAKE THIS *HAPPEN?*"
I CAN HEAR CAROL. I CAN FEEL HER. MY DAD, TOO. THE HARDER I FIGHT, THE *STRONGER* I GET. I CAN FEEL *EVERYTHING.*
THERE'S A *NEW* POWER INSIDE ME. SOMETHING THAT FEELS *DIFFERENT* FROM THE RING. AND *HE...*
HE IS *NOTHING.* HE IS THE HOLE IN THE WORLD.
HE IS *OBLIVION.*
AND HE *IS* ME.
DURING THE BATTLE WITH RELIC, WHEN WE THOUGHT *EXISTENCE* WAS ENDING, I WENT *BEYOND* THE EDGE OF REALITY. I WENT *PAST* THE SOURCE WALL.
MY PURPOSE WAS TO DELIVER THE POWER OF THE ENTITIES THERE. TO REFILL THE RESERVOIR. BUT I ALSO SAW...

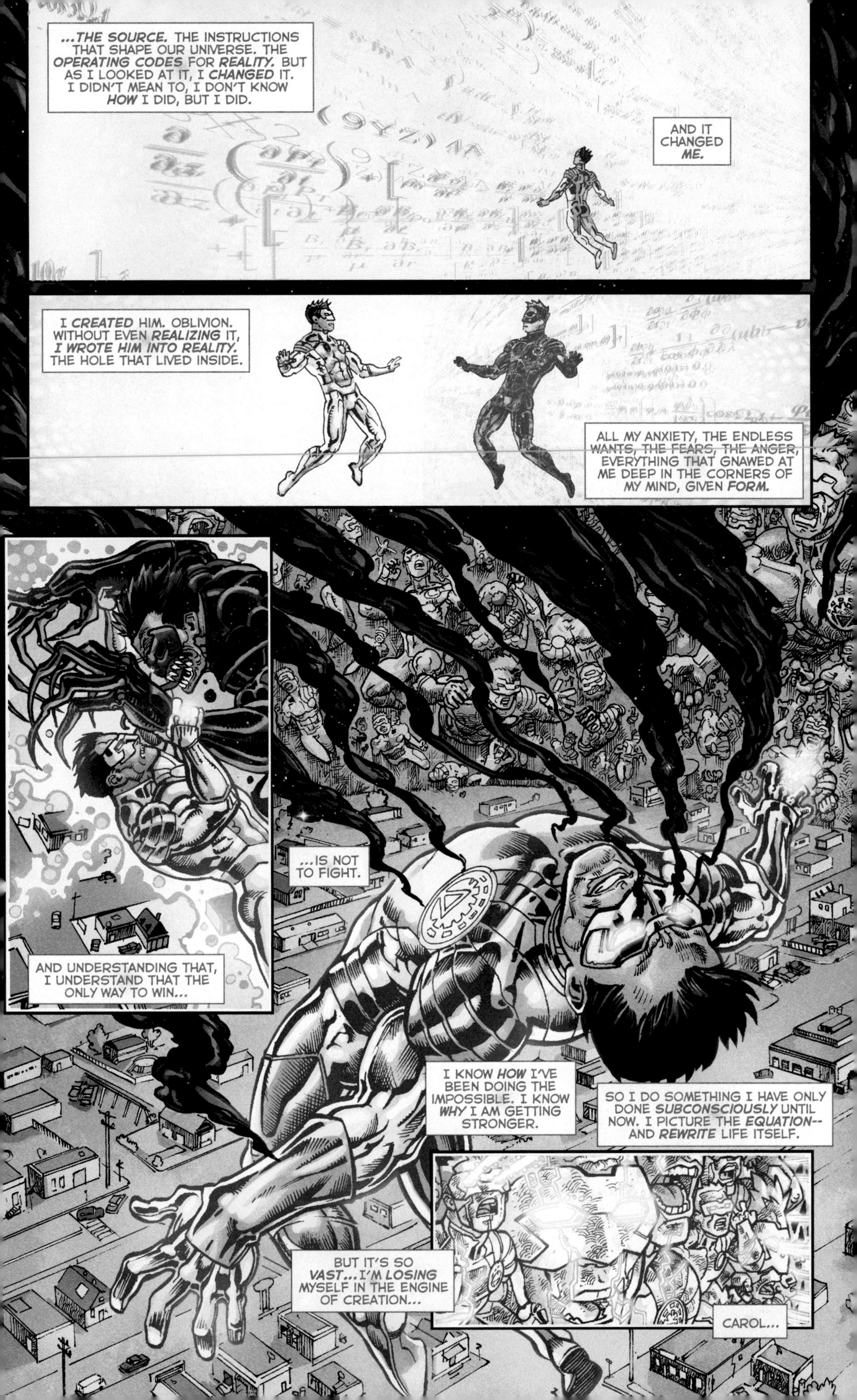
...THE SOURCE. THE INSTRUCTIONS THAT SHAPE OUR UNIVERSE. THE OPERATING CODES FOR REALITY. BUT AS I LOOKED AT IT, I CHANGED IT. I DIDN'T MEAN TO, I DON'T KNOW HOW I DID, BUT I DID.
AND IT CHANGED ME.
I CREATED HIM. OBLIVION. WITHOUT EVEN REALIZING IT, I WROTE HIM INTO REALITY. THE HOLE THAT LIVED INSIDE.
ALL MY ANXIETY, THE ENDLESS WANTS, THE FEARS, THE ANGER, EVERYTHING THAT GNAWED AT ME DEEP IN THE CORNERS OF MY MIND, GIVEN FORM.
AND UNDERSTANDING THAT, I UNDERSTAND THAT THE ONLY WAY TO WIN...
...IS NOT TO FIGHT.
I KNOW HOW I'VE BEEN DOING THE IMPOSSIBLE. I KNOW WHY I AM GETTING STRONGER.
SO I DO SOMETHING I HAVE ONLY DONE SUBCONSCIOUSLY UNTIL NOW. I PICTURE THE EQUATION-- AND REWRITE LIFE ITSELF.
BUT IT'S SO VAST...I'M LOSING MYSELF IN THE ENGINE OF CREATION...
CAROL...

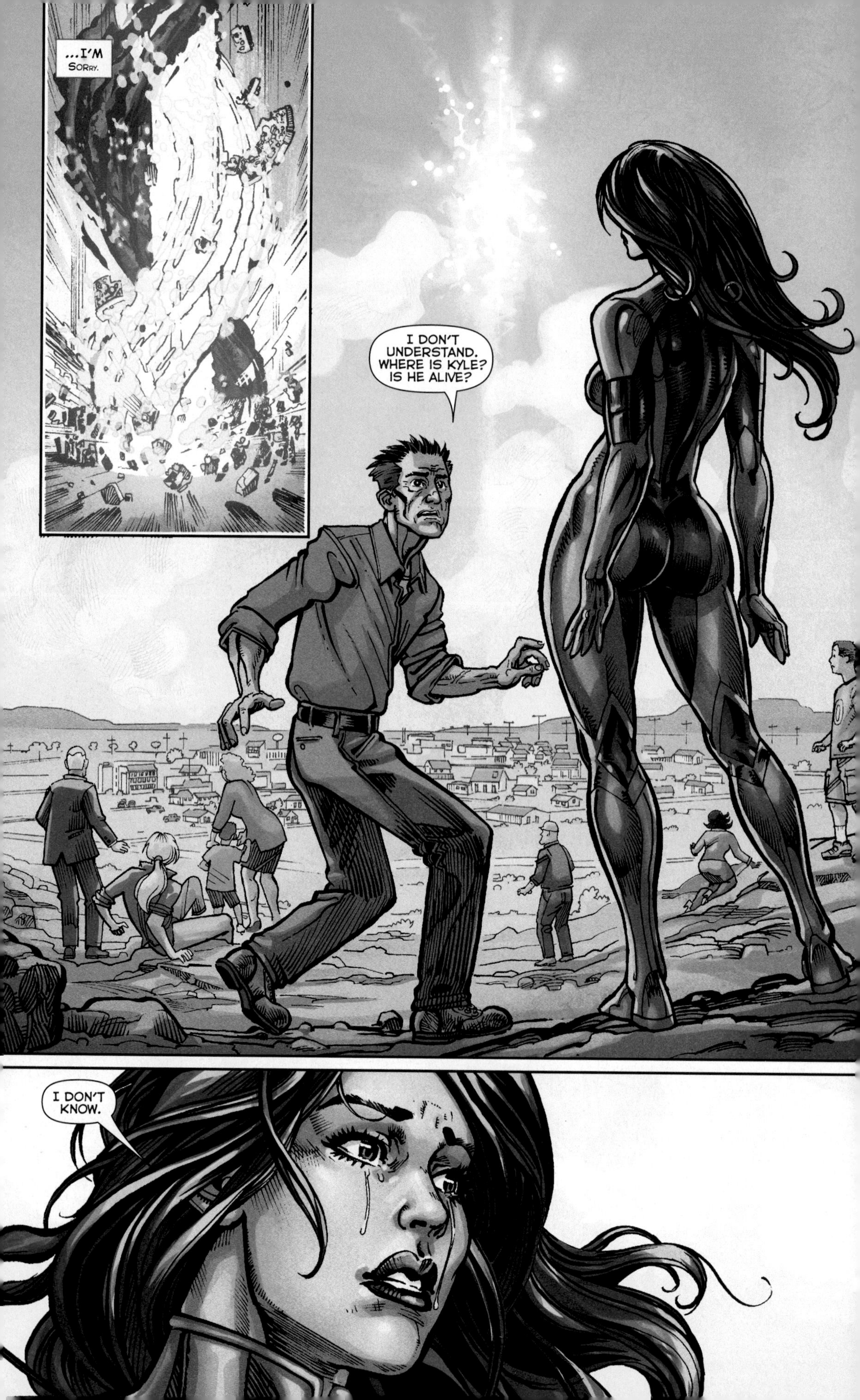
...I'M SORRY.
I DON'T UNDERSTAND. WHERE IS KYLE? IS HE ALIVE?
I DON'T KNOW.

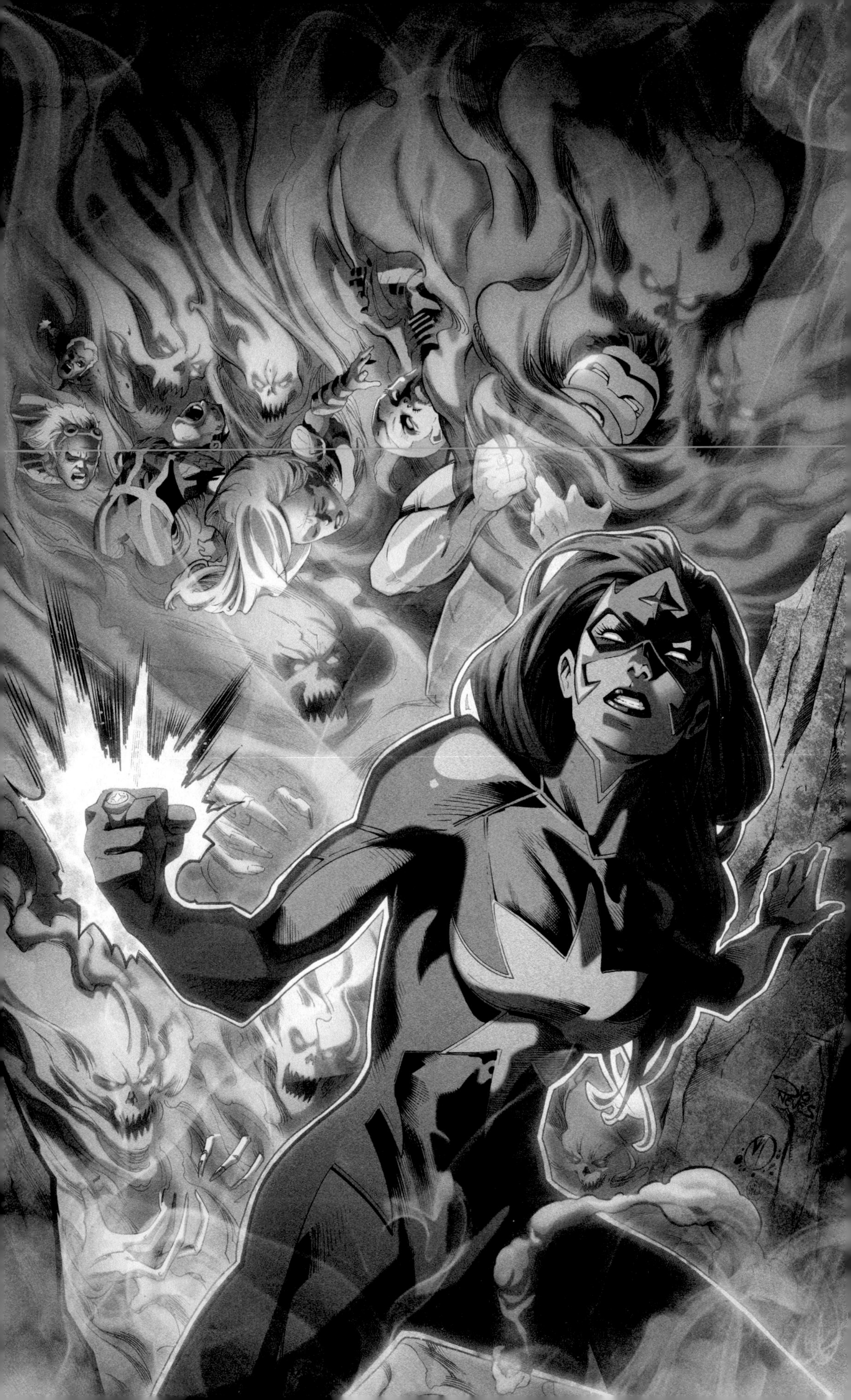

DEADWORLD

JUSTIN JORDAN writer **DIOGENES NEVES** penciller **MARC DEERING** inker **WIL QUINTANA** colorist **DAVE SHARPE** letterer
cover art by **DIOGENES NEVES, MARC DEERING** and **WIL QUINTANA**

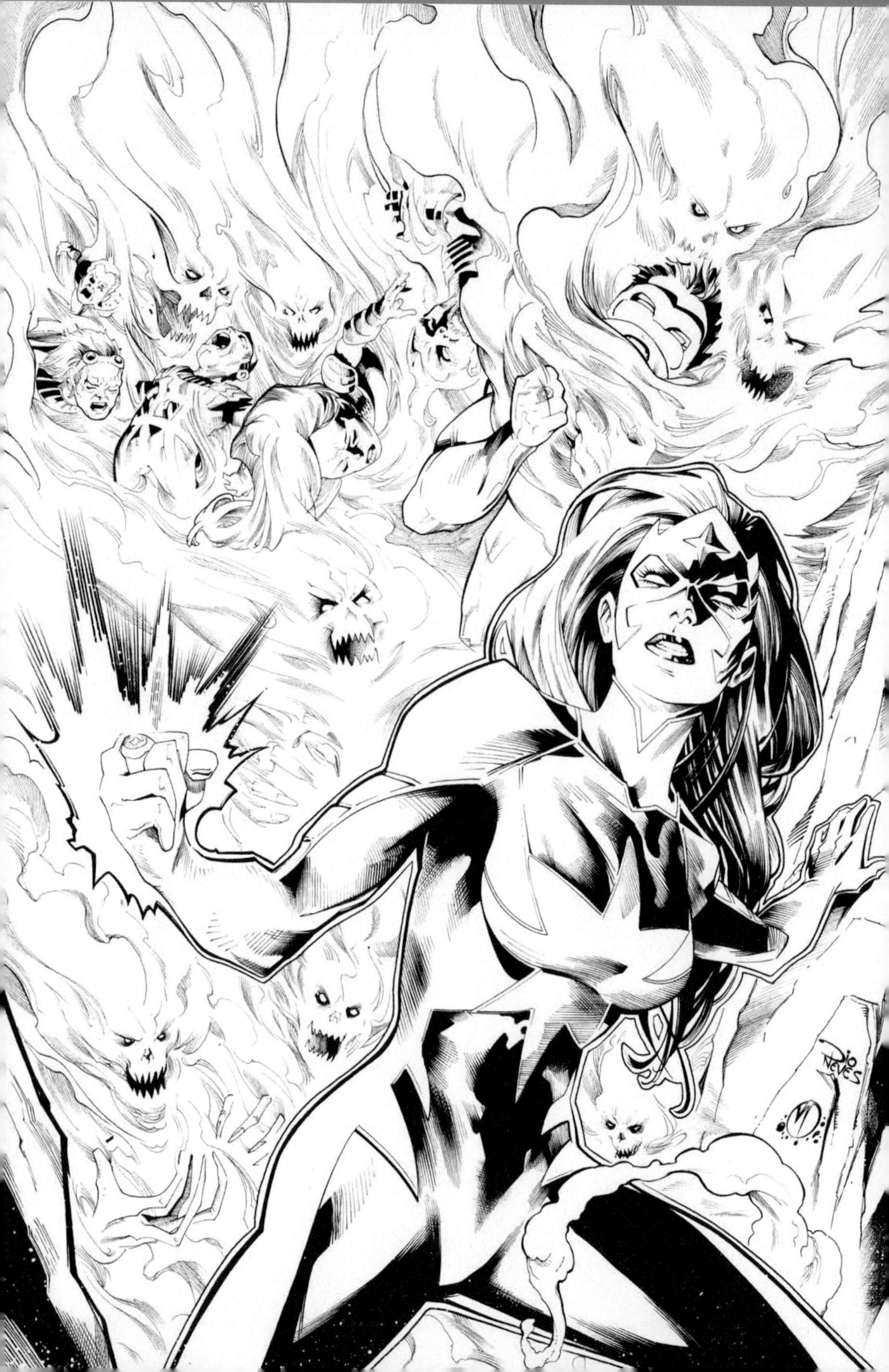
DIO NEVES

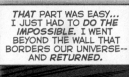

I KNOW HOW I GOT HERE.

THAT PART WAS EASY... I JUST HAD TO *DO THE IMPOSSIBLE.* I WENT BEYOND THE WALL THAT BORDERS OUR UNIVERSE-- AND *RETURNED.*

IMPOSSIBLE, RIGHT? BUT I CAME BACK, ALIVE AND WELL...

...BUT NOT THE SAME. WHAT I *SAW* ON THE OTHER SIDE OF THE SOURCE WALL...IT CHANGED ME.

OR MAYBE IT DIDN'T. MAYBE I *WAS* THIS, ALL ALONG.

WHAT IT DID FOR SURE WAS *CREATE OBLIVION,* A MONSTER FROM MY ID THAT WAS DETERMINED TO "FIX" REALITY. *I* CREATED HIM.

SO I HAD TO *UN-CREATE* HIM. I UNMADE US BOTH. IN THAT MOMENT, I EXPECTED TO DIE.

BUT IT DIDN'T *TAKE.* I'M NOT GOOD AT DYING. OR AT LEAST, I'M NOT GOOD AT *STAYING* DEAD.

SO WHEN I SAY I KNOW HOW I GOT HERE, I MEAN IT IN THE METAPHORICAL SENSE, BECAUSE...

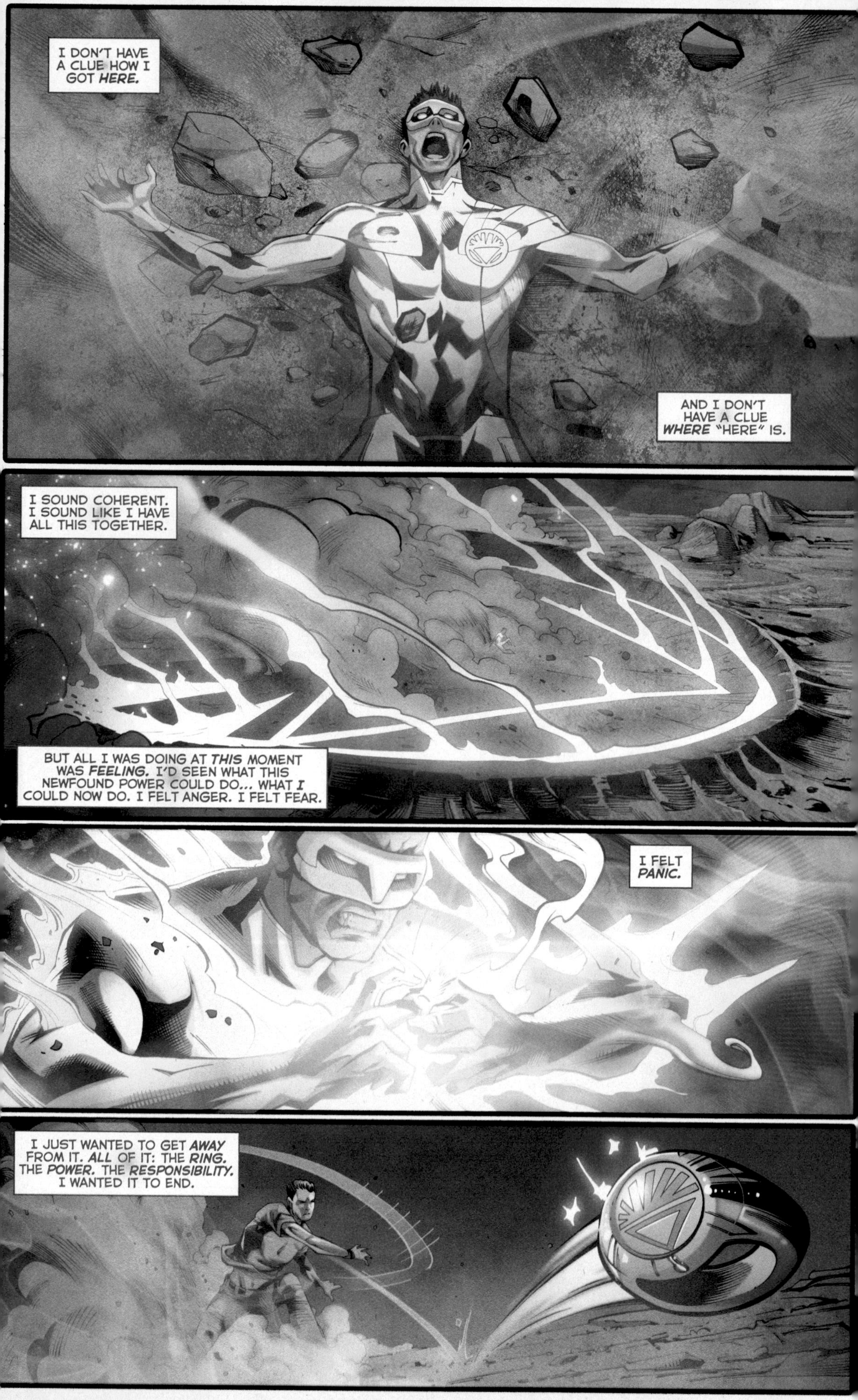
I DON'T HAVE A CLUE HOW I GOT HERE.
AND I DON'T HAVE A CLUE WHERE "HERE" IS.
I SOUND COHERENT. I SOUND LIKE I HAVE ALL THIS TOGETHER.
BUT ALL I WAS DOING AT THIS MOMENT WAS FEELING. I'D SEEN WHAT THIS NEWFOUND POWER COULD DO... WHAT I COULD NOW DO. I FELT ANGER. I FELT FEAR.
I FELT PANIC.
I JUST WANTED TO GET AWAY FROM IT. ALL OF IT: THE RING. THE POWER. THE RESPONSIBILITY. I WANTED IT TO END.

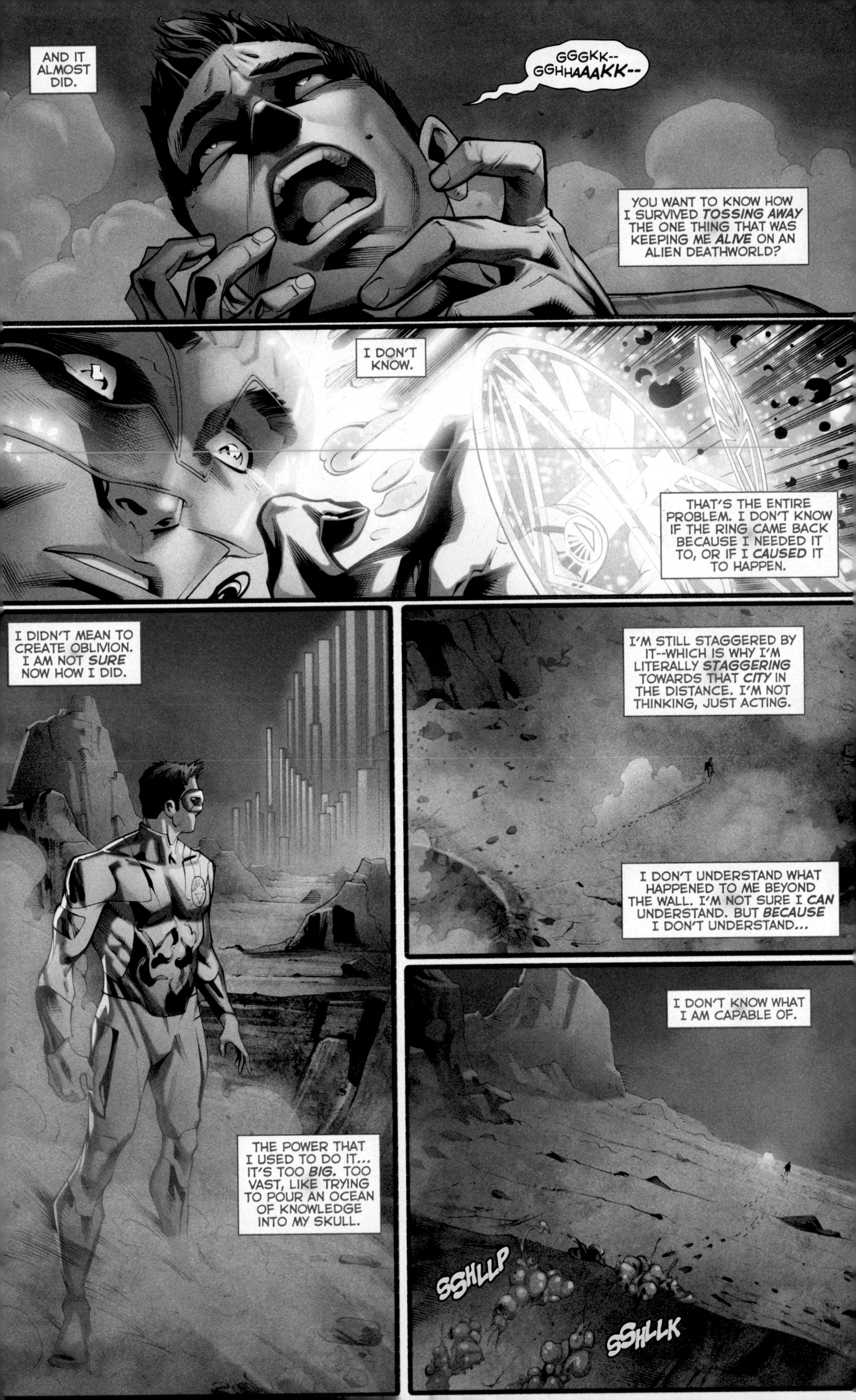
AND IT ALMOST DID.
GGGKK-- GGHHAAAKK--
YOU WANT TO KNOW HOW I SURVIVED TOSSING AWAY THE ONE THING THAT WAS KEEPING ME ALIVE ON AN ALIEN DEATHWORLD?
I DON'T KNOW.
THAT'S THE ENTIRE PROBLEM. I DON'T KNOW IF THE RING CAME BACK BECAUSE I NEEDED IT TO, OR IF I CAUSED IT TO HAPPEN.
I DIDN'T MEAN TO CREATE OBLIVION. I AM NOT SURE NOW HOW I DID.
THE POWER THAT I USED TO DO IT... IT'S TOO BIG. TOO VAST, LIKE TRYING TO POUR AN OCEAN OF KNOWLEDGE INTO MY SKULL.
I'M STILL STAGGERED BY IT--WHICH IS WHY I'M LITERALLY STAGGERING TOWARDS THAT CITY IN THE DISTANCE. I'M NOT THINKING, JUST ACTING.
I DON'T UNDERSTAND WHAT HAPPENED TO ME BEYOND THE WALL. I'M NOT SURE I CAN UNDERSTAND. BUT BECAUSE I DON'T UNDERSTAND...
I DON'T KNOW WHAT I AM CAPABLE OF.
SSHLLP
SSHLLK

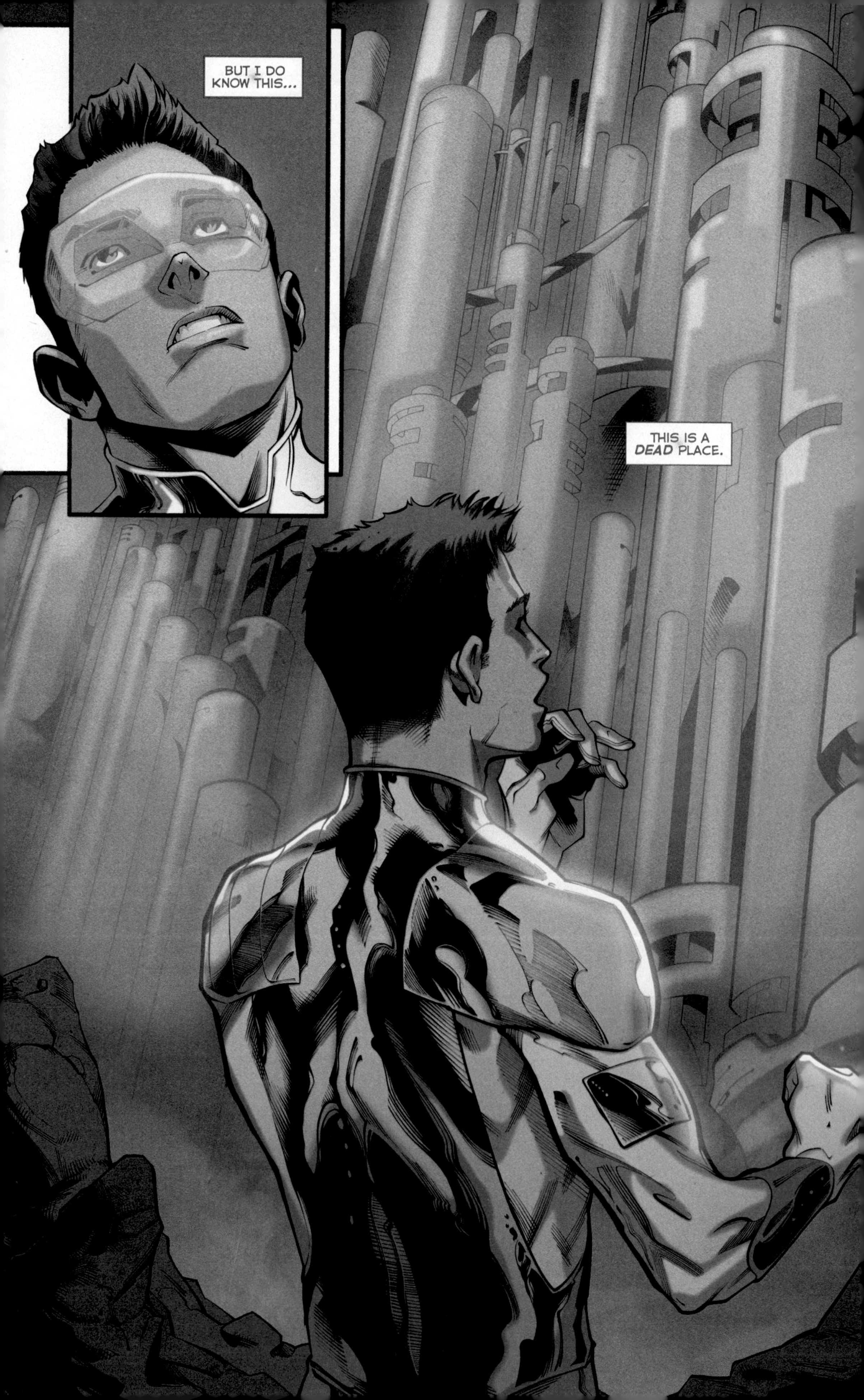
BUT I DO KNOW THIS...
THIS IS A *DEAD* PLACE.

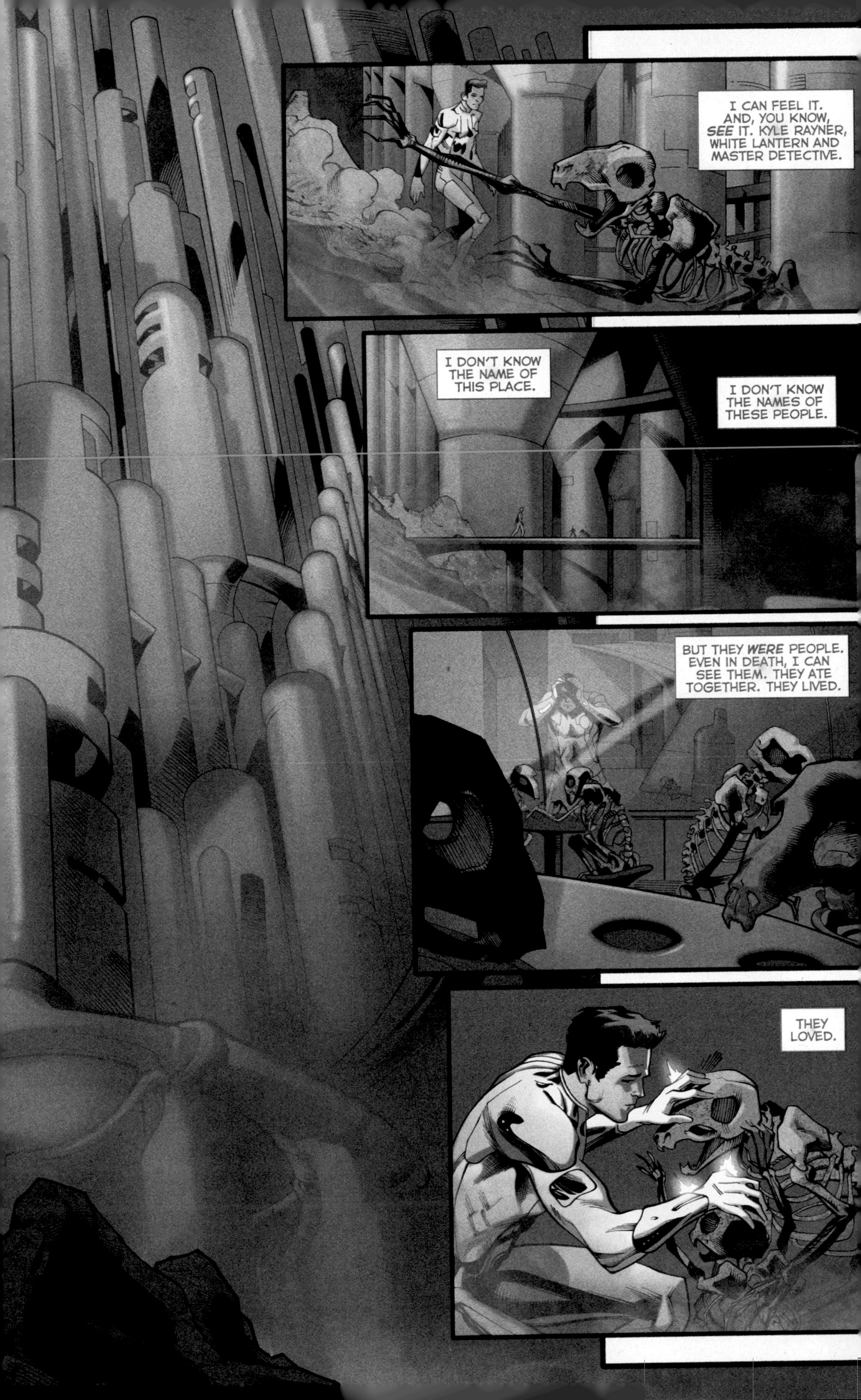
I CAN FEEL IT. AND, YOU KNOW, SEE IT. KYLE RAYNER, WHITE LANTERN AND MASTER DETECTIVE.
I DON'T KNOW THE NAME OF THIS PLACE.
I DON'T KNOW THE NAMES OF THESE PEOPLE.
BUT THEY WERE PEOPLE. EVEN IN DEATH, I CAN SEE THEM. THEY ATE TOGETHER. THEY LIVED.
THEY LOVED.

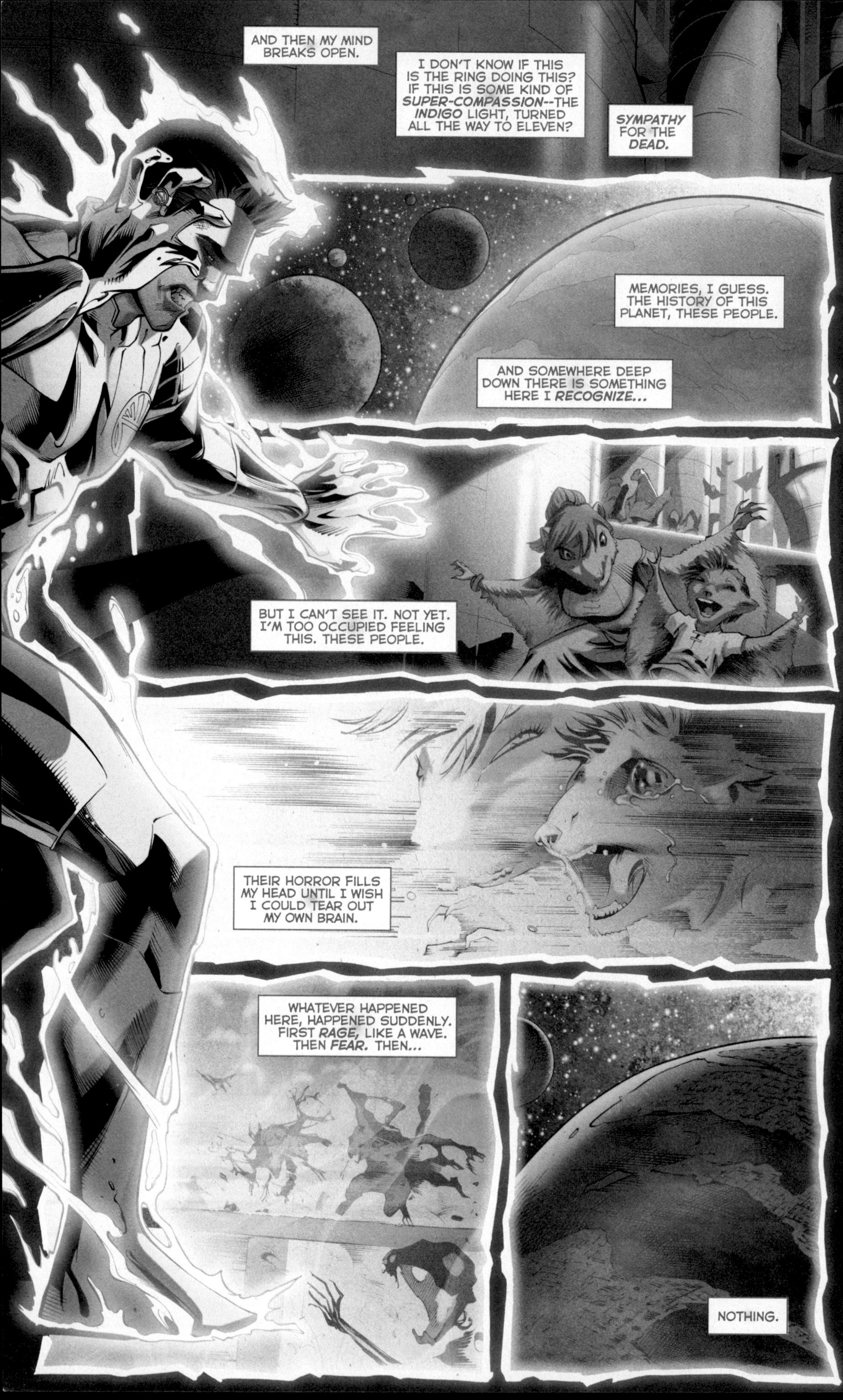
AND THEN MY MIND BREAKS OPEN.
I DON'T KNOW IF THIS IS THE RING DOING THIS? IF THIS IS SOME KIND OF *SUPER-COMPASSION*--THE *INDIGO* LIGHT, TURNED ALL THE WAY TO ELEVEN?
SYMPATHY FOR THE *DEAD.*
MEMORIES, I GUESS. THE HISTORY OF THIS PLANET, THESE PEOPLE.
AND SOMEWHERE DEEP DOWN THERE IS SOMETHING HERE I *RECOGNIZE...*
BUT I CAN'T SEE IT. NOT YET. I'M TOO OCCUPIED FEELING THIS. THESE PEOPLE.
THEIR HORROR FILLS MY HEAD UNTIL I WISH I COULD TEAR OUT MY OWN BRAIN.
WHATEVER HAPPENED HERE, HAPPENED SUDDENLY. FIRST *RAGE,* LIKE A WAVE. THEN *FEAR.* THEN...
NOTHING.

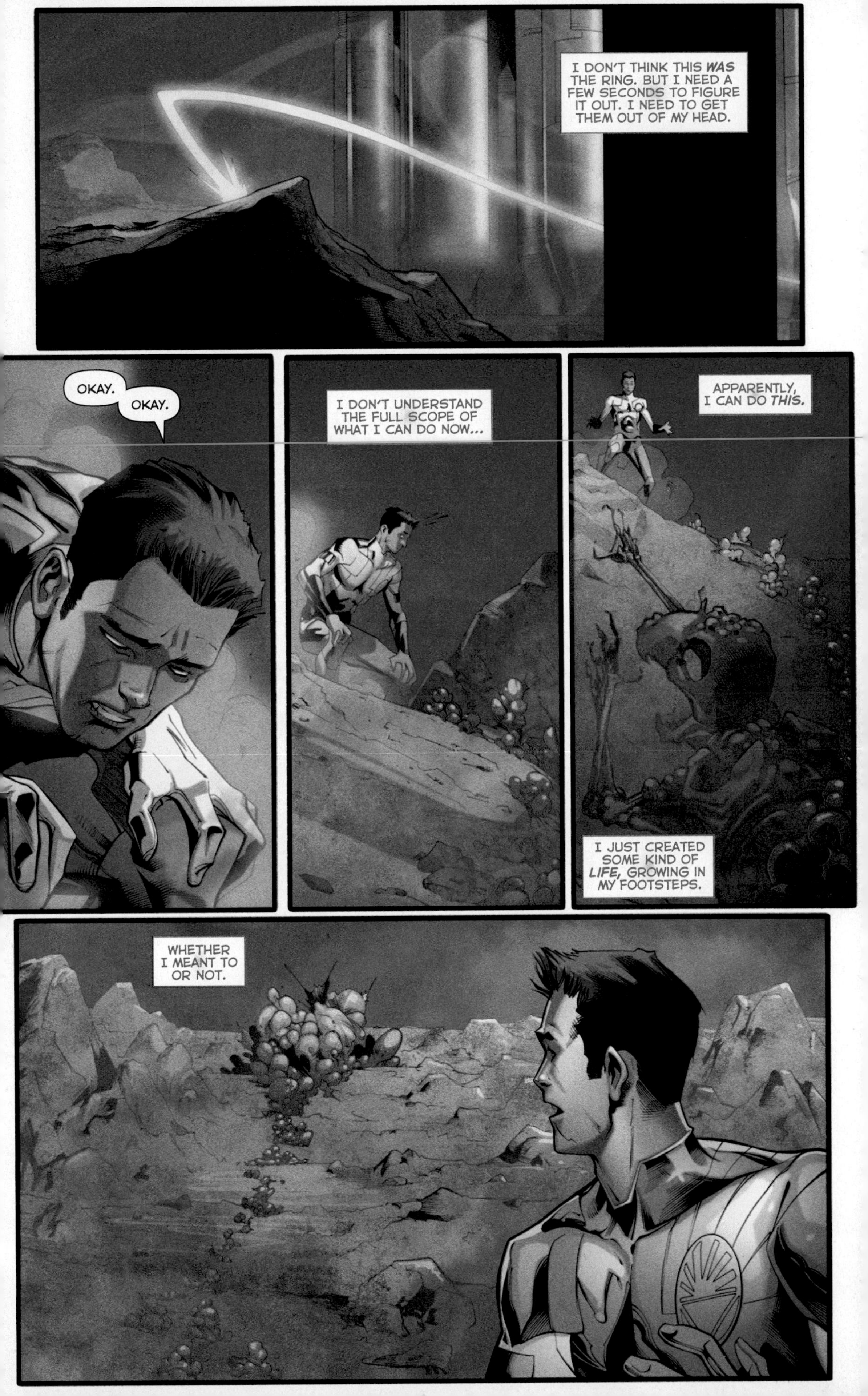
I DON'T THINK THIS WAS THE RING. BUT I NEED A FEW SECONDS TO FIGURE IT OUT. I NEED TO GET THEM OUT OF MY HEAD.
OKAY.
OKAY.
I DON'T UNDERSTAND THE FULL SCOPE OF WHAT I CAN DO NOW...
APPARENTLY, I CAN DO THIS.
I JUST CREATED SOME KIND OF LIFE, GROWING IN MY FOOTSTEPS.
WHETHER I MEANT TO OR NOT.

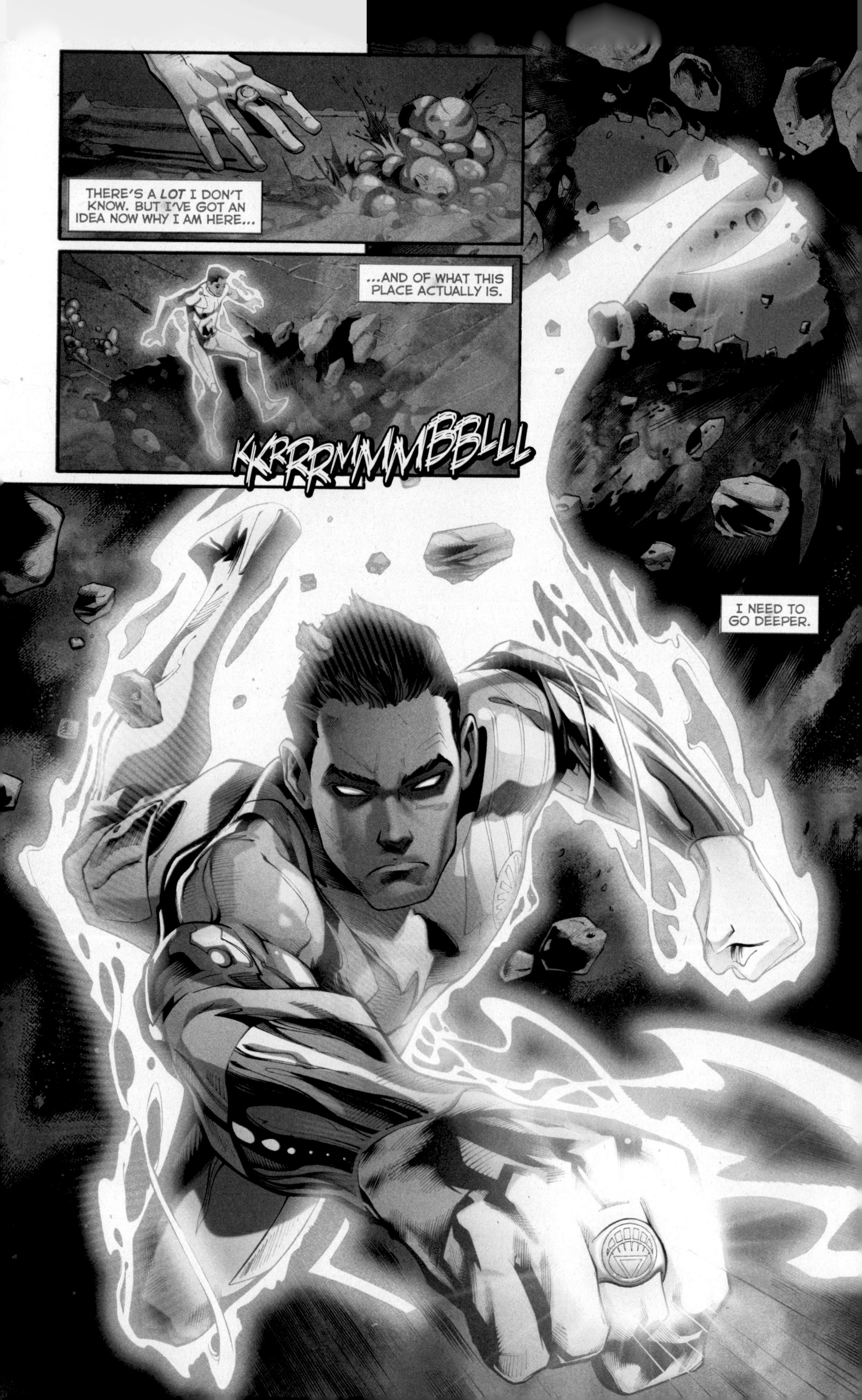
THERE'S A *LOT* I DON'T KNOW. BUT I'VE GOT AN IDEA NOW WHY I AM HERE...
...AND OF WHAT THIS PLACE ACTUALLY IS.
KKRRRMMMBBLLL
I NEED TO GO DEEPER.

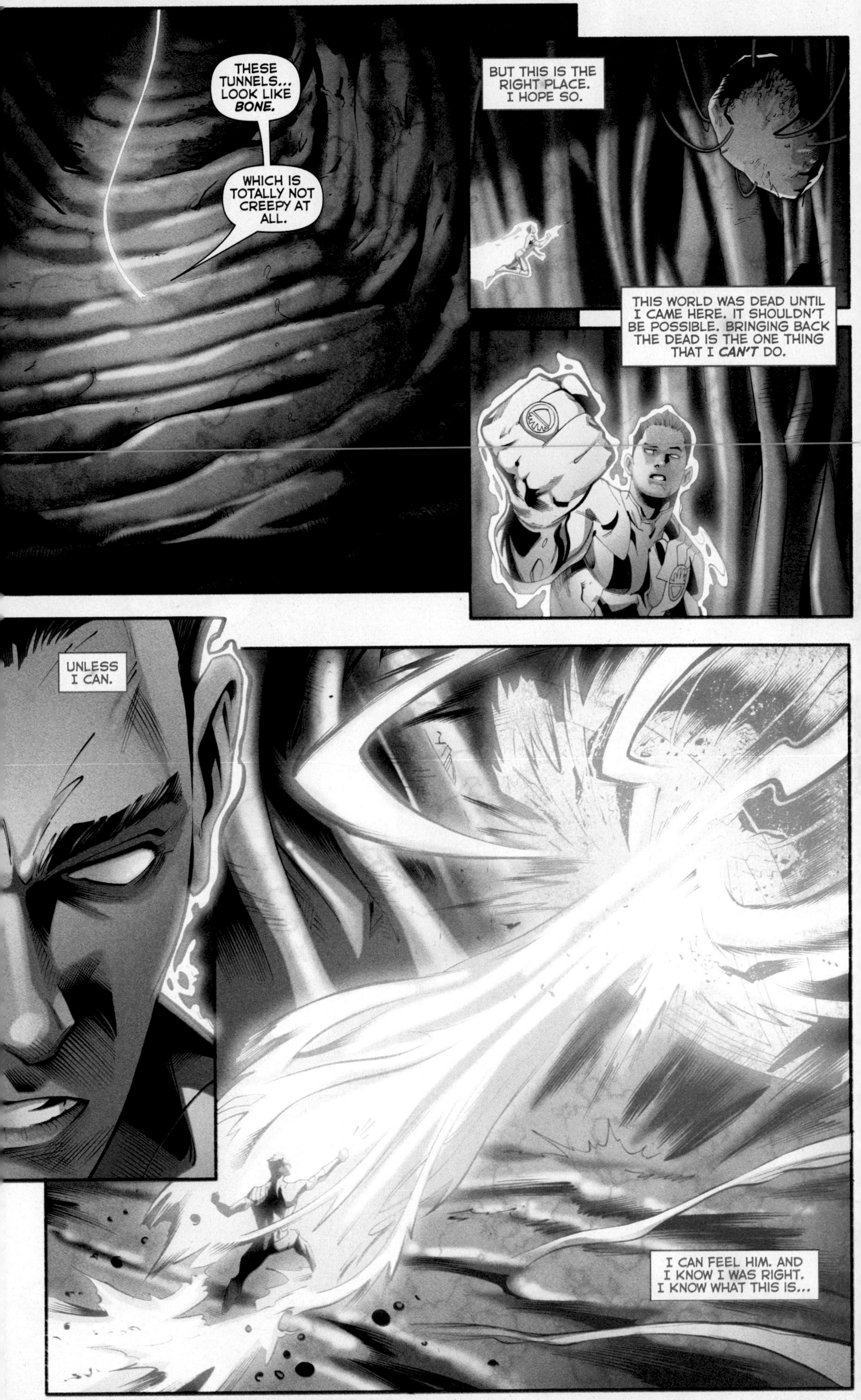

THESE TUNNELS... LOOK LIKE BONE.
WHICH IS TOTALLY NOT CREEPY AT ALL.
BUT THIS IS THE RIGHT PLACE. I HOPE SO.
THIS WORLD WAS DEAD UNTIL I CAME HERE. IT SHOULDN'T BE POSSIBLE. BRINGING BACK THE DEAD IS THE ONE THING THAT I CAN'T DO.
UNLESS I CAN.
I CAN FEEL HIM. AND I KNOW I WAS RIGHT. I KNOW WHAT THIS IS...

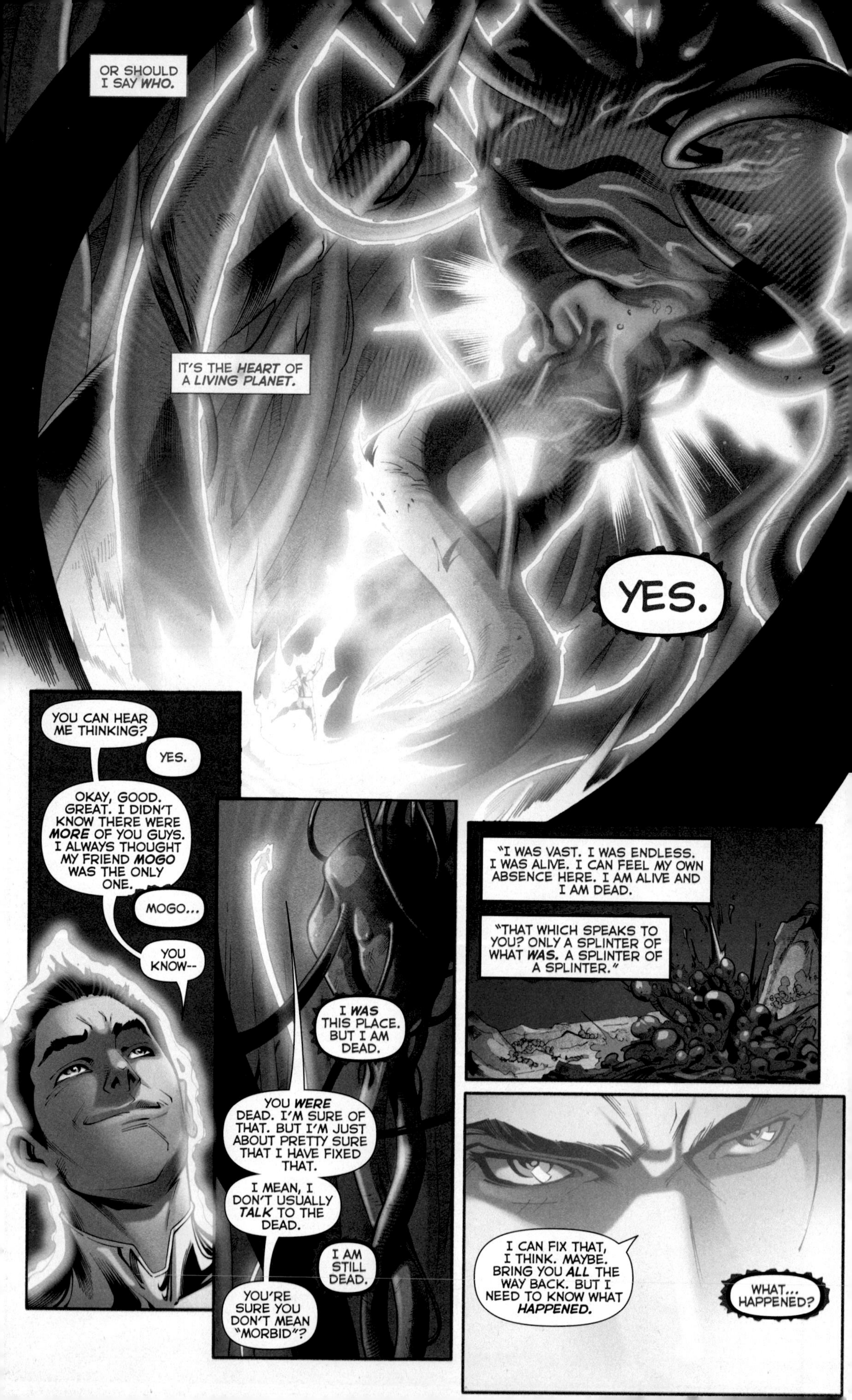

OR SHOULD I SAY WHO.
IT'S THE HEART OF A LIVING PLANET.
YES.
YOU CAN HEAR ME THINKING?
YES.
OKAY, GOOD. GREAT. I DIDN'T KNOW THERE WERE MORE OF YOU GUYS. I ALWAYS THOUGHT MY FRIEND MOGO WAS THE ONLY ONE.
MOGO...
YOU KNOW--
I WAS THIS PLACE. BUT I AM DEAD.
YOU WERE DEAD. I'M SURE OF THAT. BUT I'M JUST ABOUT PRETTY SURE THAT I HAVE FIXED THAT.
I MEAN, I DON'T USUALLY TALK TO THE DEAD.
I AM STILL DEAD.
YOU'RE SURE YOU DON'T MEAN "MORBID"?
"I WAS VAST. I WAS ENDLESS. I WAS ALIVE. I CAN FEEL MY OWN ABSENCE HERE. I AM ALIVE AND I AM DEAD.
"THAT WHICH SPEAKS TO YOU? ONLY A SPLINTER OF WHAT WAS. A SPLINTER OF A SPLINTER."
I CAN FIX THAT, I THINK. MAYBE. BRING YOU ALL THE WAY BACK. BUT I NEED TO KNOW WHAT HAPPENED.
WHAT... HAPPENED?

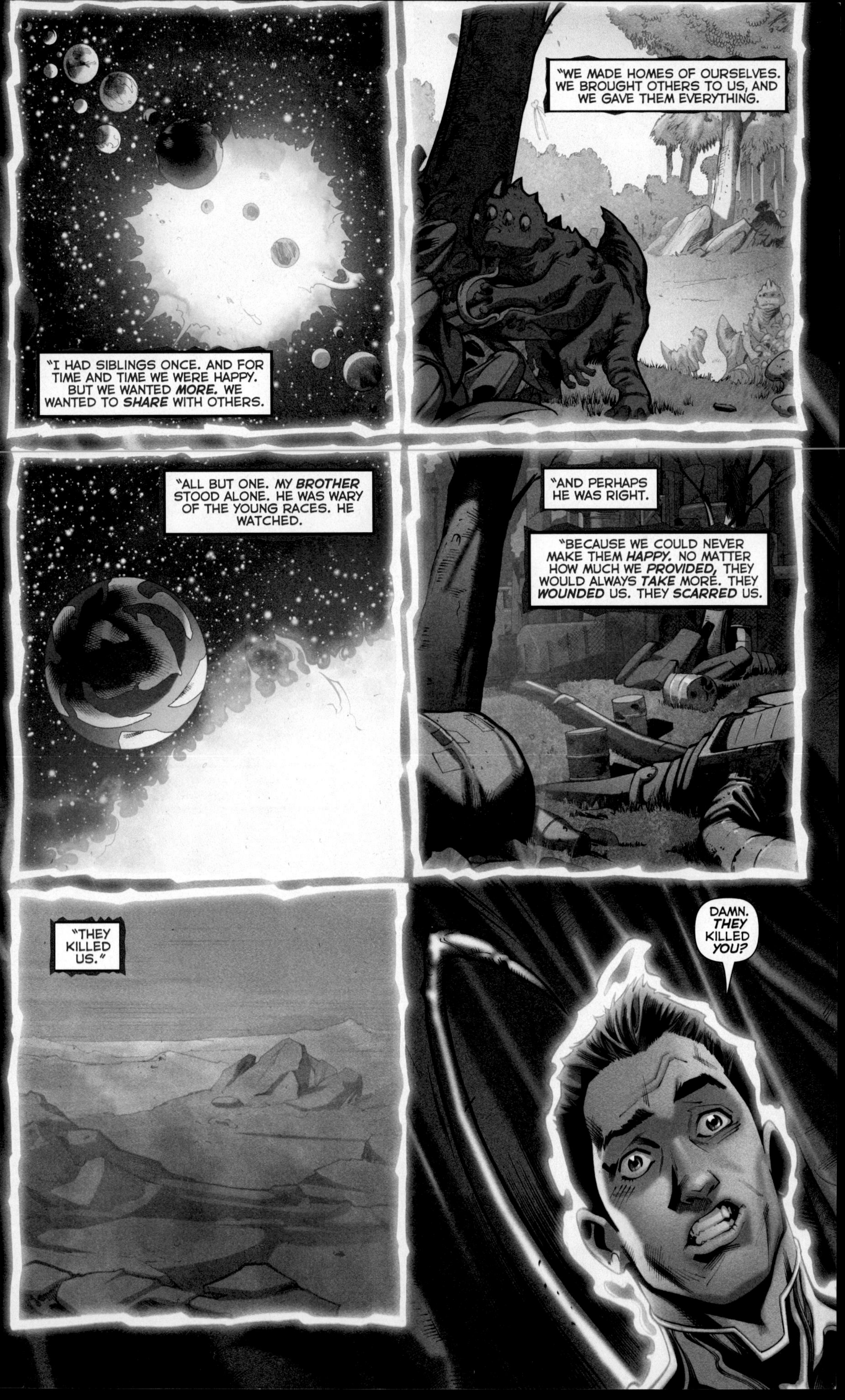
"I HAD SIBLINGS ONCE. AND FOR TIME AND TIME WE WERE HAPPY. BUT WE WANTED *MORE.* WE WANTED TO *SHARE* WITH OTHERS.
"WE MADE HOMES OF OURSELVES. WE BROUGHT OTHERS TO US, AND WE GAVE THEM EVERYTHING.
"ALL BUT ONE. *MY BROTHER* STOOD ALONE. HE WAS WARY OF THE YOUNG RACES. HE WATCHED.
"AND PERHAPS HE WAS RIGHT.
"BECAUSE WE COULD NEVER MAKE THEM *HAPPY.* NO MATTER HOW MUCH WE *PROVIDED,* THEY WOULD ALWAYS *TAKE* MORE. THEY *WOUNDED* US. THEY *SCARRED* US.
"THEY KILLED US."
DAMN. *THEY* KILLED *YOU?*

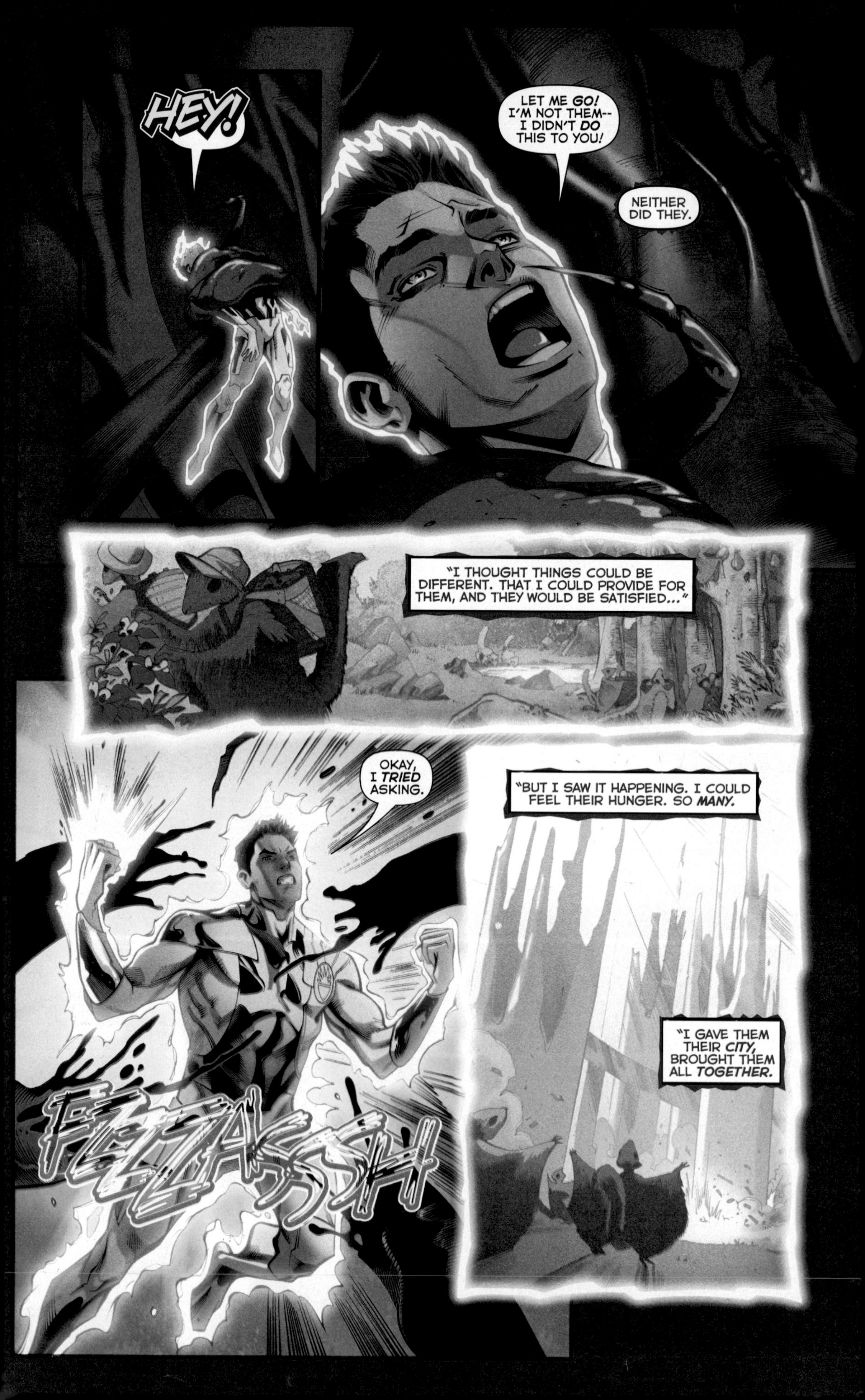
HEY!
LET ME GO! I'M NOT THEM-- I DIDN'T DO THIS TO YOU!
NEITHER DID THEY.
"I THOUGHT THINGS COULD BE DIFFERENT. THAT I COULD PROVIDE FOR THEM, AND THEY WOULD BE SATISFIED..."
OKAY, I TRIED ASKING.
FFZZASSSH
"BUT I SAW IT HAPPENING. I COULD FEEL THEIR HUNGER. SO MANY.
"I GAVE THEM THEIR CITY, BROUGHT THEM ALL TOGETHER.

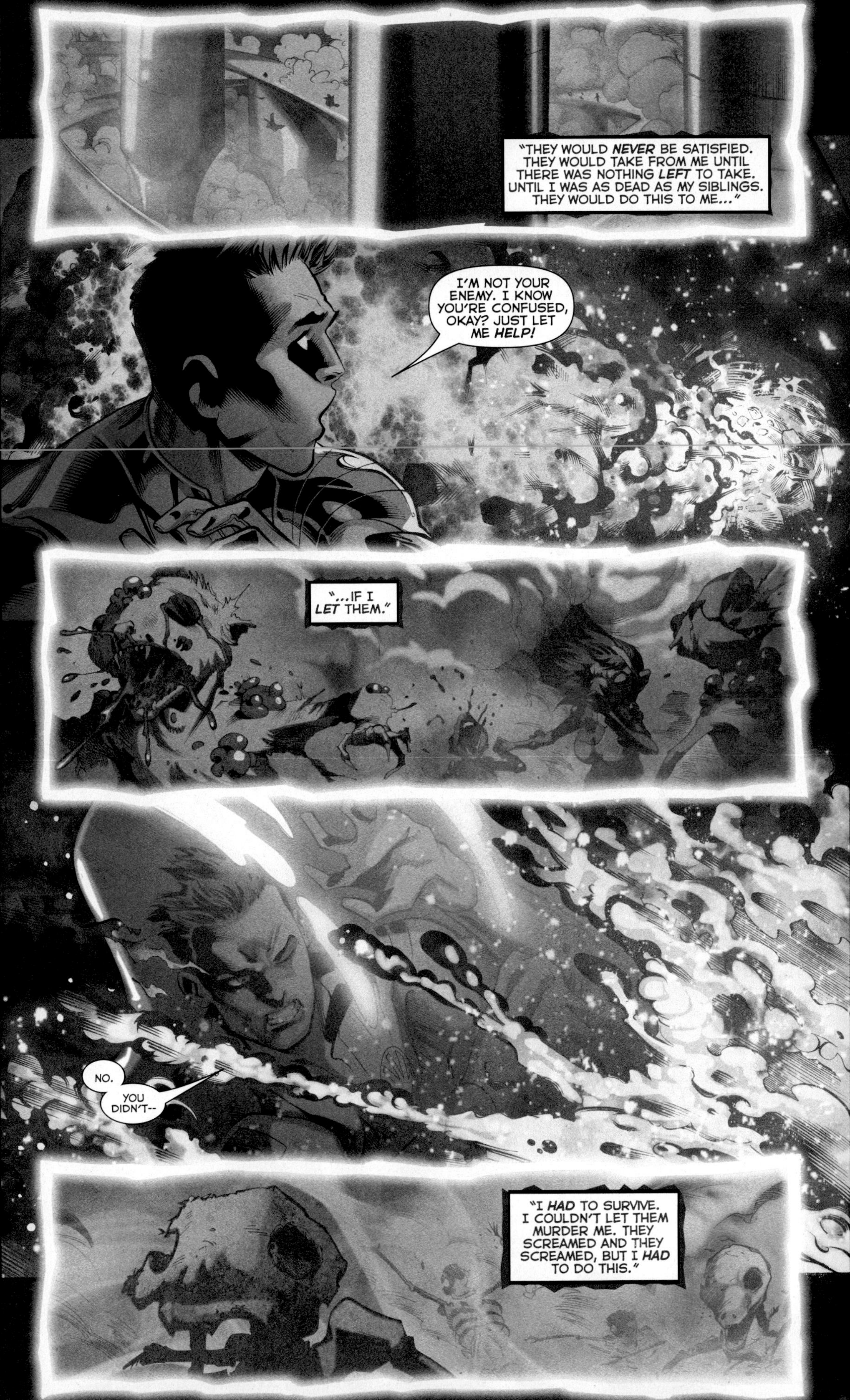
"THEY WOULD NEVER BE SATISFIED. THEY WOULD TAKE FROM ME UNTIL THERE WAS NOTHING LEFT TO TAKE. UNTIL I WAS AS DEAD AS MY SIBLINGS. THEY WOULD DO THIS TO ME..."
I'M NOT YOUR ENEMY. I KNOW YOU'RE CONFUSED, OKAY? JUST LET ME HELP!
"...IF I LET THEM."
NO.
YOU DIDN'T--
"I HAD TO SURVIVE. I COULDN'T LET THEM MURDER ME. THEY SCREAMED AND THEY SCREAMED, BUT I HAD TO DO THIS."

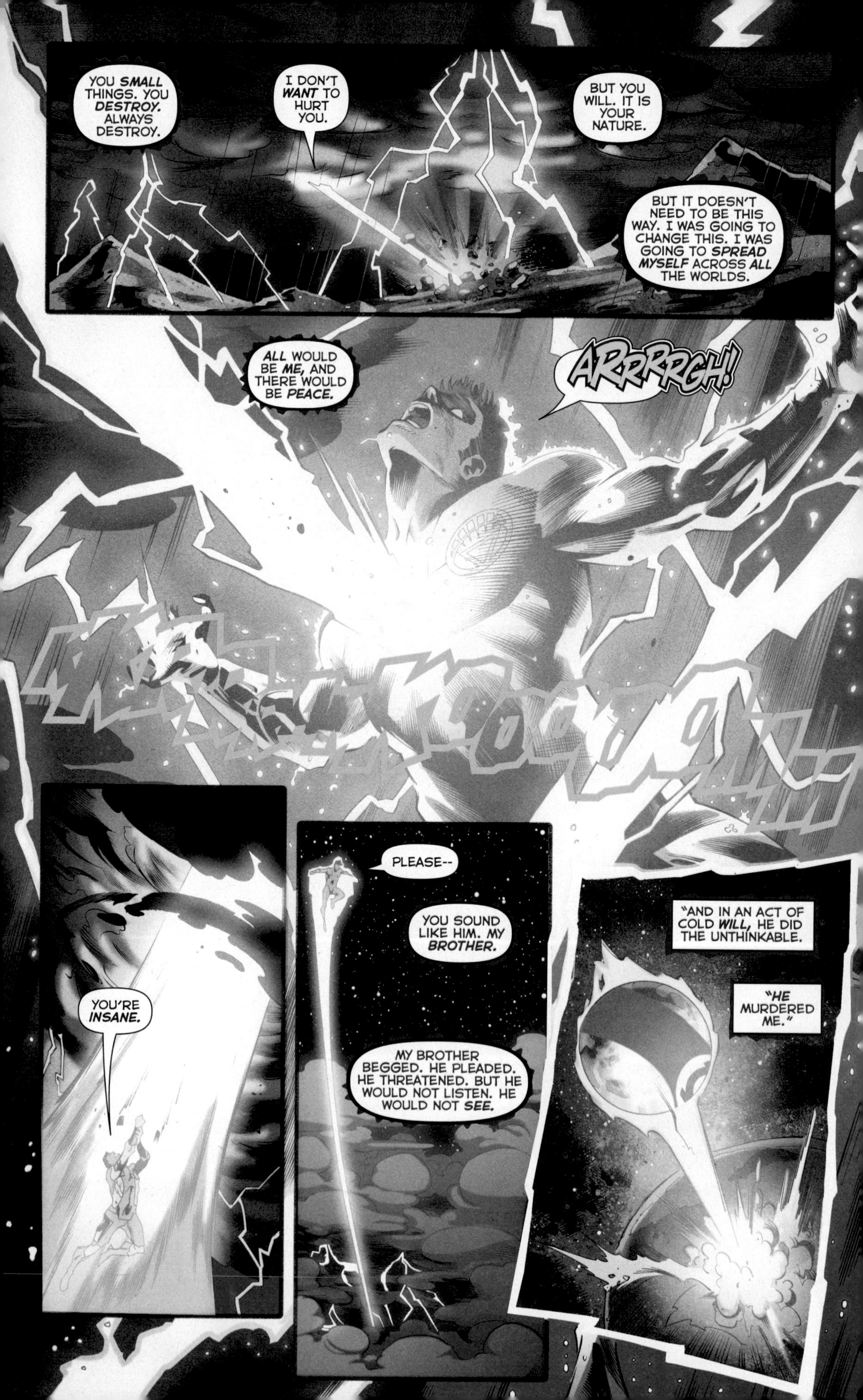
YOU SMALL THINGS. YOU DESTROY. ALWAYS DESTROY.
I DON'T WANT TO HURT YOU.
BUT YOU WILL. IT IS YOUR NATURE.
BUT IT DOESN'T NEED TO BE THIS WAY. I WAS GOING TO CHANGE THIS. I WAS GOING TO SPREAD MYSELF ACROSS ALL THE WORLDS.
ALL WOULD BE ME, AND THERE WOULD BE PEACE.
ARRRRGH!
YOU'RE INSANE.
PLEASE--
YOU SOUND LIKE HIM. MY BROTHER.
MY BROTHER BEGGED. HE PLEADED. HE THREATENED. BUT HE WOULD NOT LISTEN. HE WOULD NOT SEE.
"AND IN AN ACT OF COLD WILL, HE DID THE UNTHINKABLE.
"HE MURDERED ME."

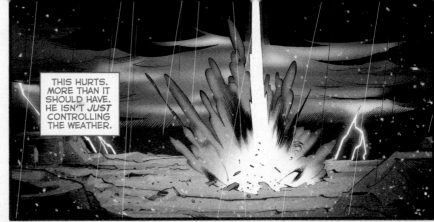

THIS HURTS. MORE THAN IT SHOULD HAVE. HE ISN'T *JUST* CONTROLLING THE WEATHER.

YOU WILL NOT LEAVE ME.

IT'S EVERYTHING. WEATHER. LIFE. *GRAVITY...*

AND LIKE HE SAID, HE'S NOT EVEN ALIVE YET. NOT REALLY. THIS IS WHAT JUST A FRACTION OF HIM CAN DO.

EVERYTHING FEELS WRONG. HE'S-- *CRUSHING ME*--

AND I'M NOT SURE I CAN STOP HIM.

THERE CAN BE ONLY ONE LIFE.

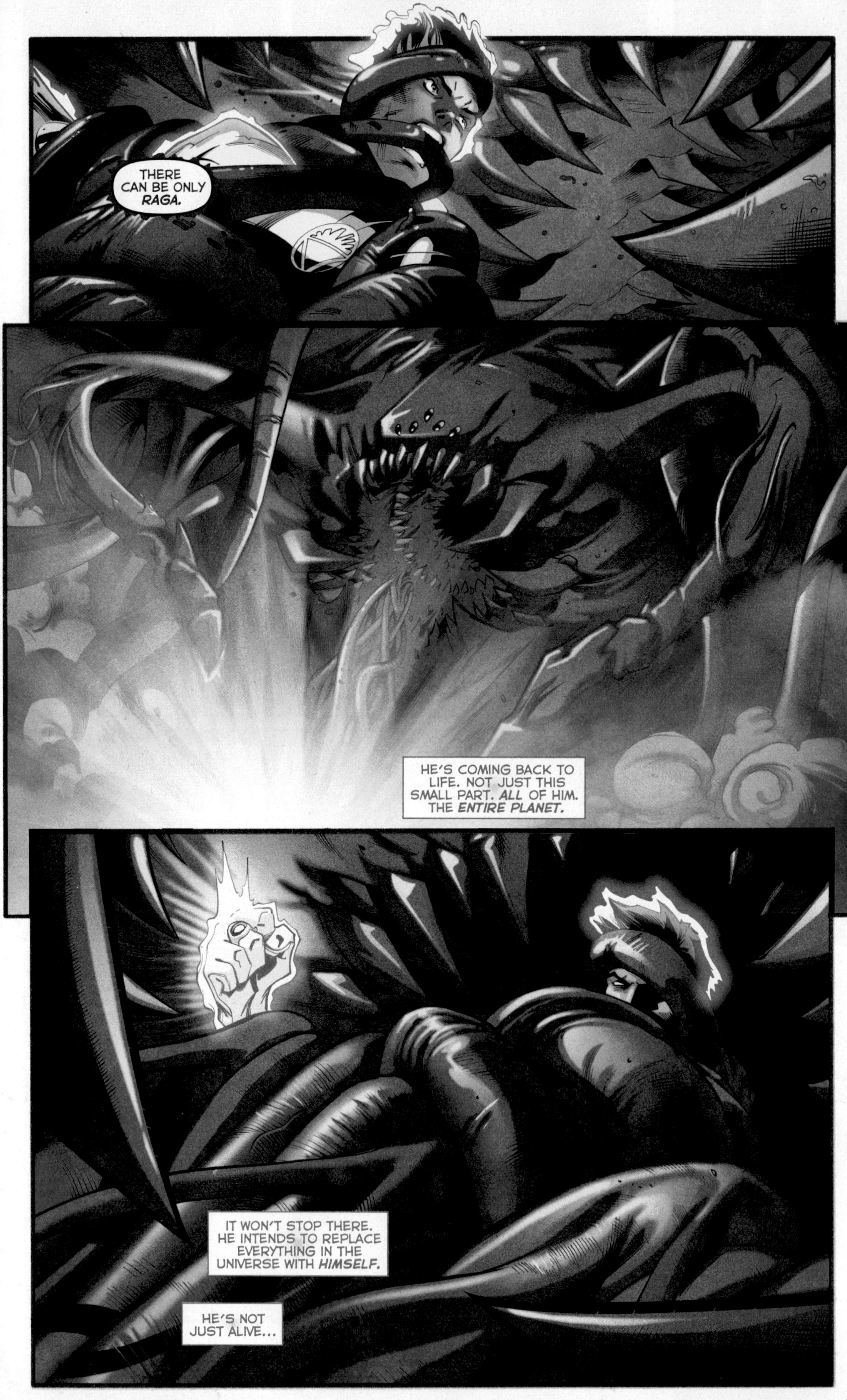
THERE CAN BE ONLY RAGA.
HE'S COMING BACK TO LIFE. NOT JUST THIS SMALL PART. ALL OF HIM. THE ENTIRE PLANET.
IT WON'T STOP THERE. HE INTENDS TO REPLACE EVERYTHING IN THE UNIVERSE WITH HIMSELF.
HE'S NOT JUST ALIVE...

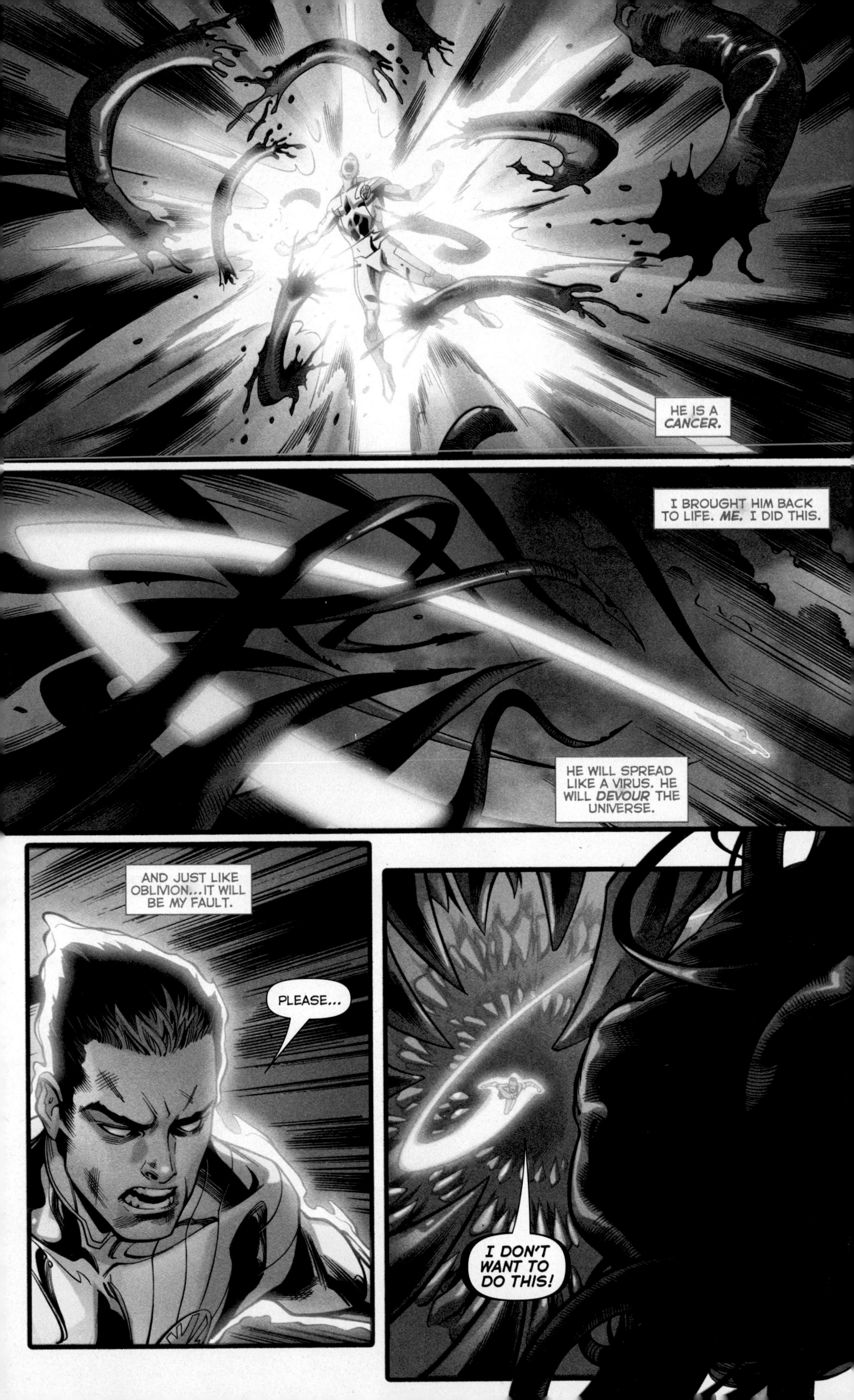
HE IS A CANCER.
I BROUGHT HIM BACK TO LIFE. ME. I DID THIS.
HE WILL SPREAD LIKE A VIRUS. HE WILL DEVOUR THE UNIVERSE.
AND JUST LIKE OBLIVION...IT WILL BE MY FAULT.
PLEASE...
I DON'T WANT TO DO THIS!

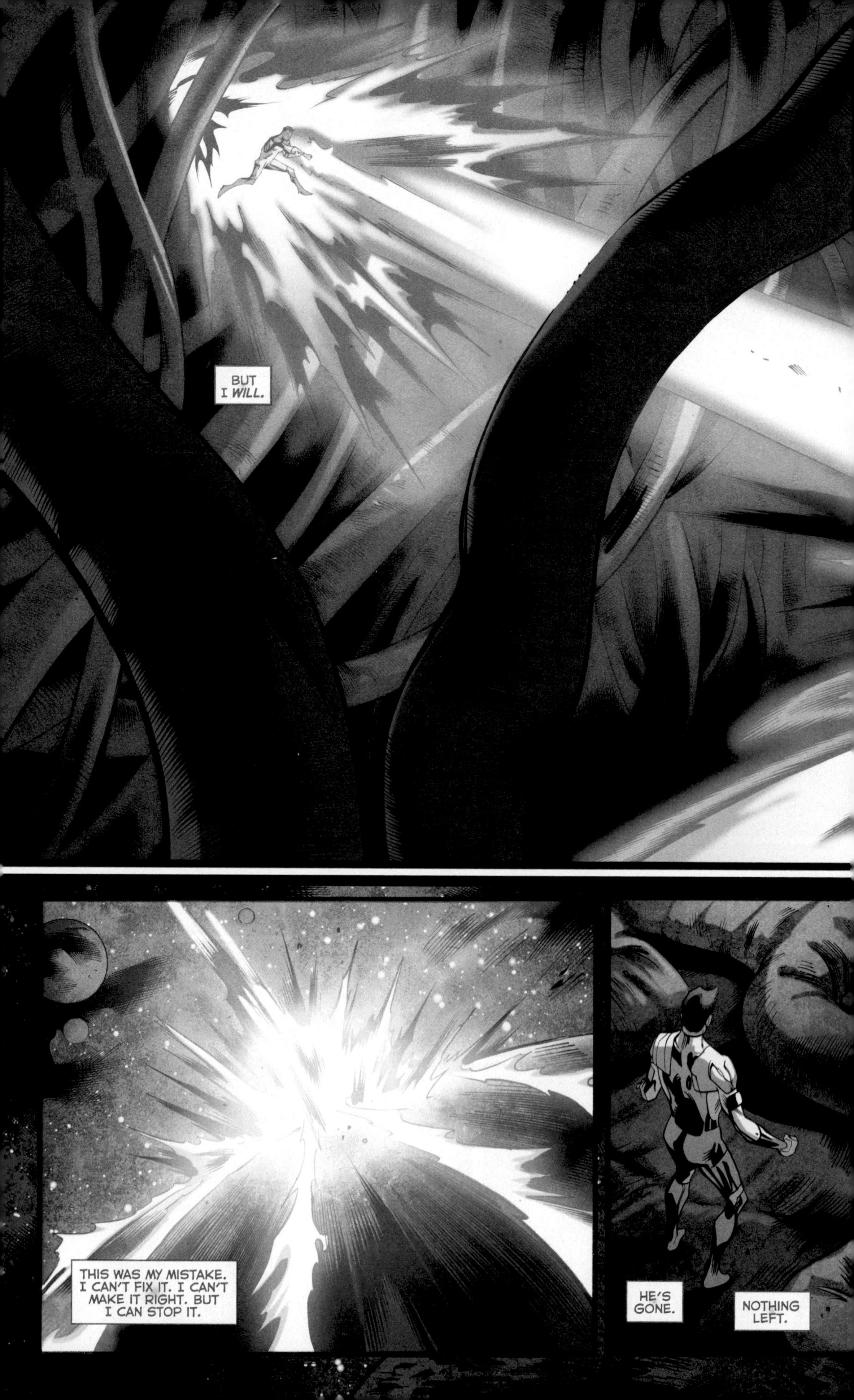
BUT I *WILL.*
THIS WAS MY MISTAKE. I CAN'T FIX IT. I CAN'T MAKE IT RIGHT. BUT I CAN STOP IT.
HE'S GONE.
NOTHING LEFT.

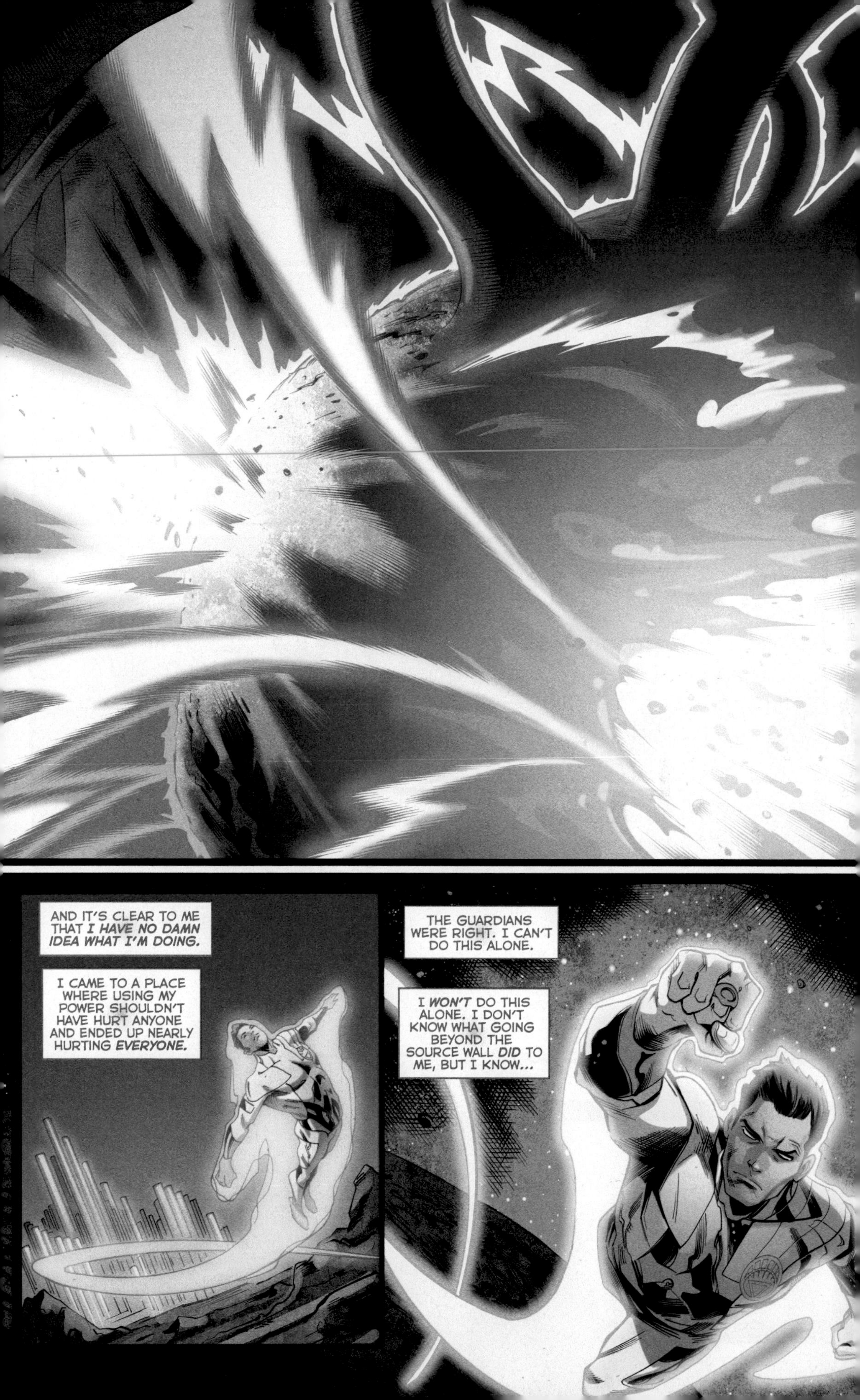
AND IT'S CLEAR TO ME THAT *I HAVE NO DAMN IDEA WHAT I'M DOING.*
I CAME TO A PLACE WHERE USING MY POWER SHOULDN'T HAVE HURT ANYONE AND ENDED UP NEARLY HURTING *EVERYONE.*
THE GUARDIANS WERE RIGHT. I CAN'T DO THIS ALONE.
I *WON'T* DO THIS ALONE. I DON'T KNOW WHAT GOING BEYOND THE SOURCE WALL *DID* TO ME, BUT I KNOW...

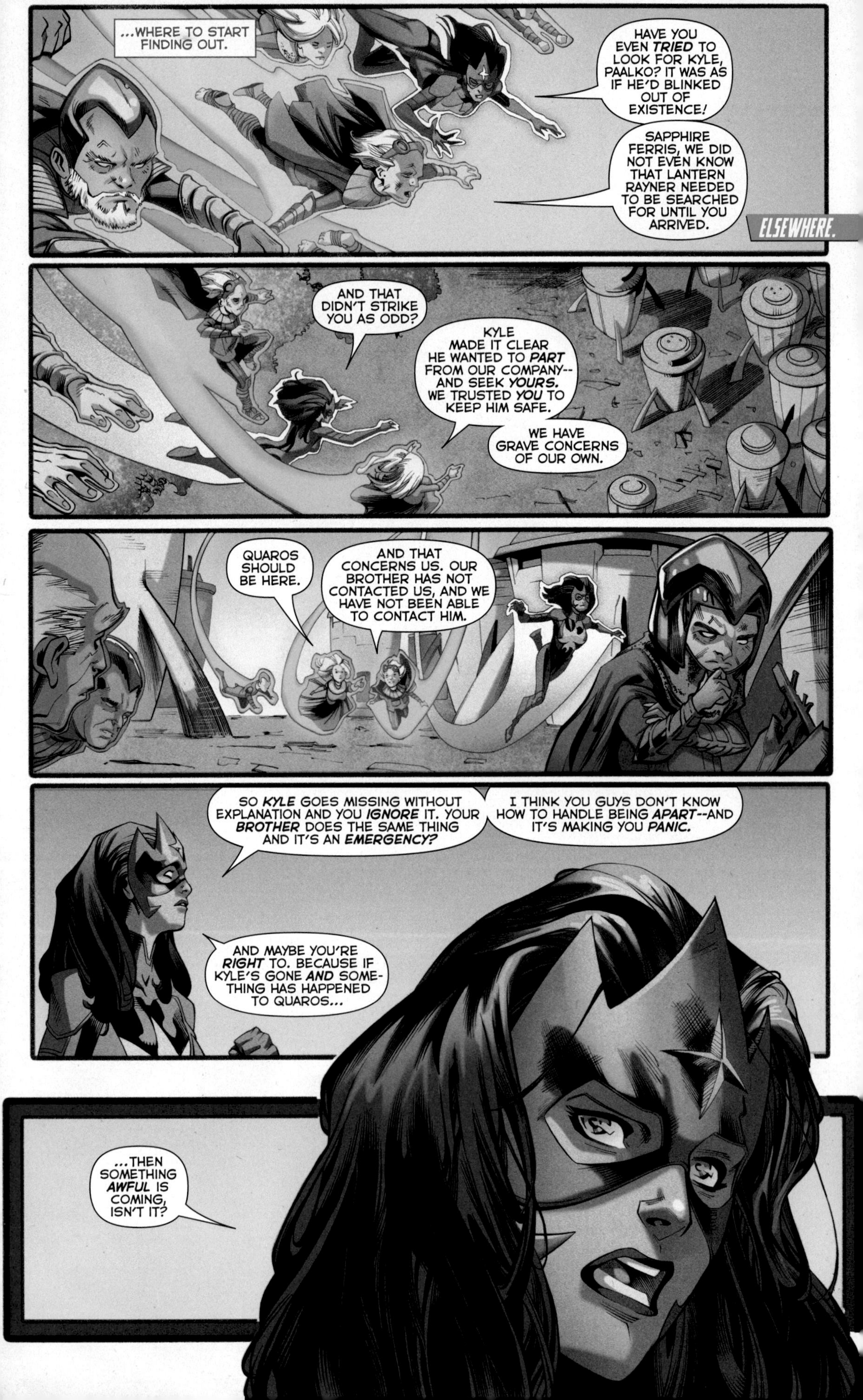
...WHERE TO START FINDING OUT.
HAVE YOU EVEN TRIED TO LOOK FOR KYLE, PAALKO? IT WAS AS IF HE'D BLINKED OUT OF EXISTENCE!
SAPPHIRE FERRIS, WE DID NOT EVEN KNOW THAT LANTERN RAYNER NEEDED TO BE SEARCHED FOR UNTIL YOU ARRIVED.
ELSEWHERE.
AND THAT DIDN'T STRIKE YOU AS ODD?
KYLE MADE IT CLEAR HE WANTED TO PART FROM OUR COMPANY-- AND SEEK YOURS. WE TRUSTED YOU TO KEEP HIM SAFE.
WE HAVE GRAVE CONCERNS OF OUR OWN.
QUAROS SHOULD BE HERE.
AND THAT CONCERNS US. OUR BROTHER HAS NOT CONTACTED US, AND WE HAVE NOT BEEN ABLE TO CONTACT HIM.
SO KYLE GOES MISSING WITHOUT EXPLANATION AND YOU IGNORE IT. YOUR BROTHER DOES THE SAME THING AND IT'S AN EMERGENCY?
I THINK YOU GUYS DON'T KNOW HOW TO HANDLE BEING APART--AND IT'S MAKING YOU PANIC.
AND MAYBE YOU'RE RIGHT TO. BECAUSE IF KYLE'S GONE AND SOMETHING HAS HAPPENED TO QUAROS...
...THEN SOMETHING AWFUL IS COMING, ISN'T IT?

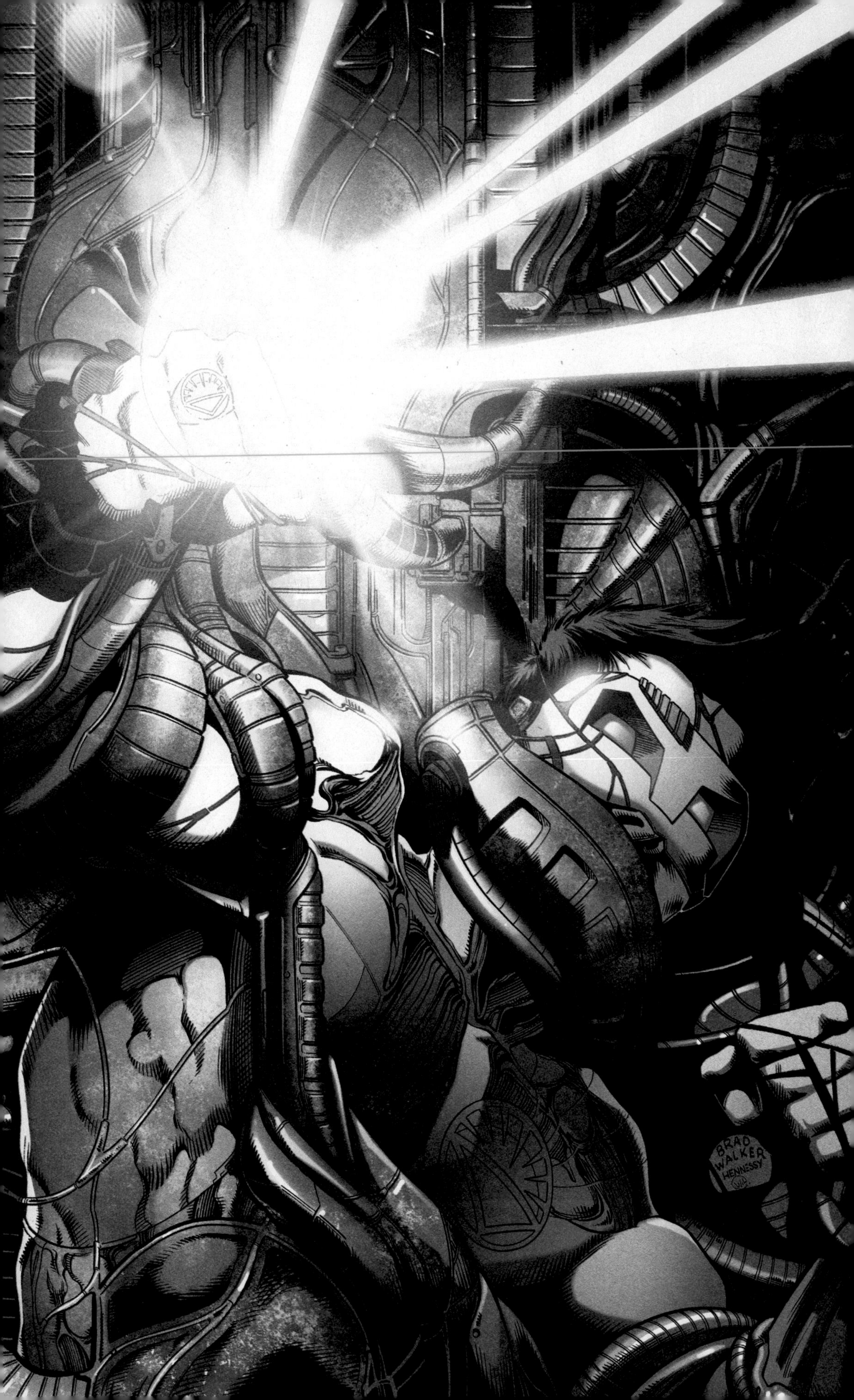
BRAD
WALKER
HENNESSY

BODY SNATCHERS

JUSTIN JORDAN writer BRAD WALKER penciller ANDREW HENNESSY with SCOTT HANNA inkers WIL QUINTANA colorist
DAVE SHARPE letterer cover art by BRAD WALKER, ANDREW HENNESSY and WIL QUINTANA

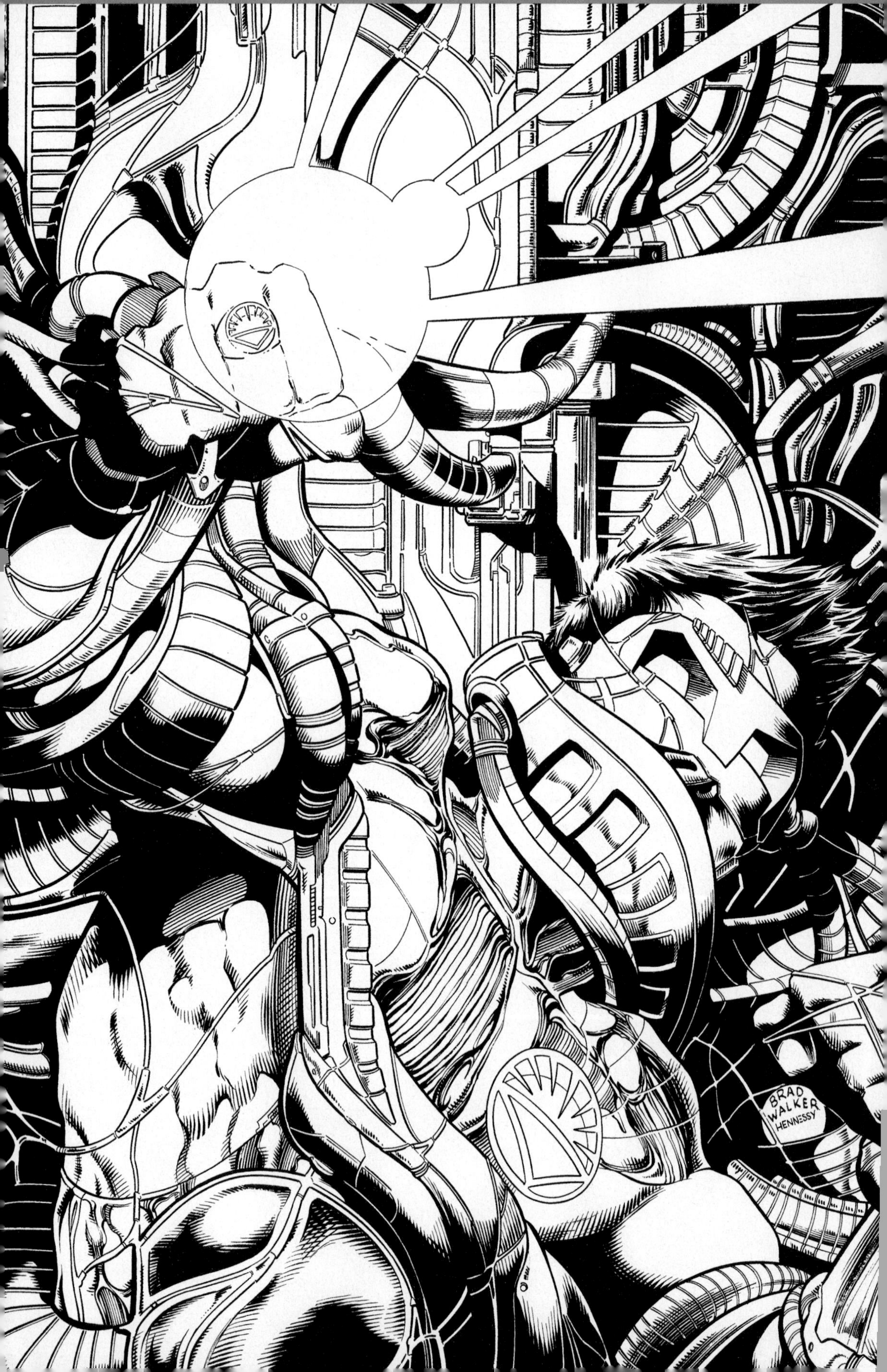
BRAD WALKER HENNESSY

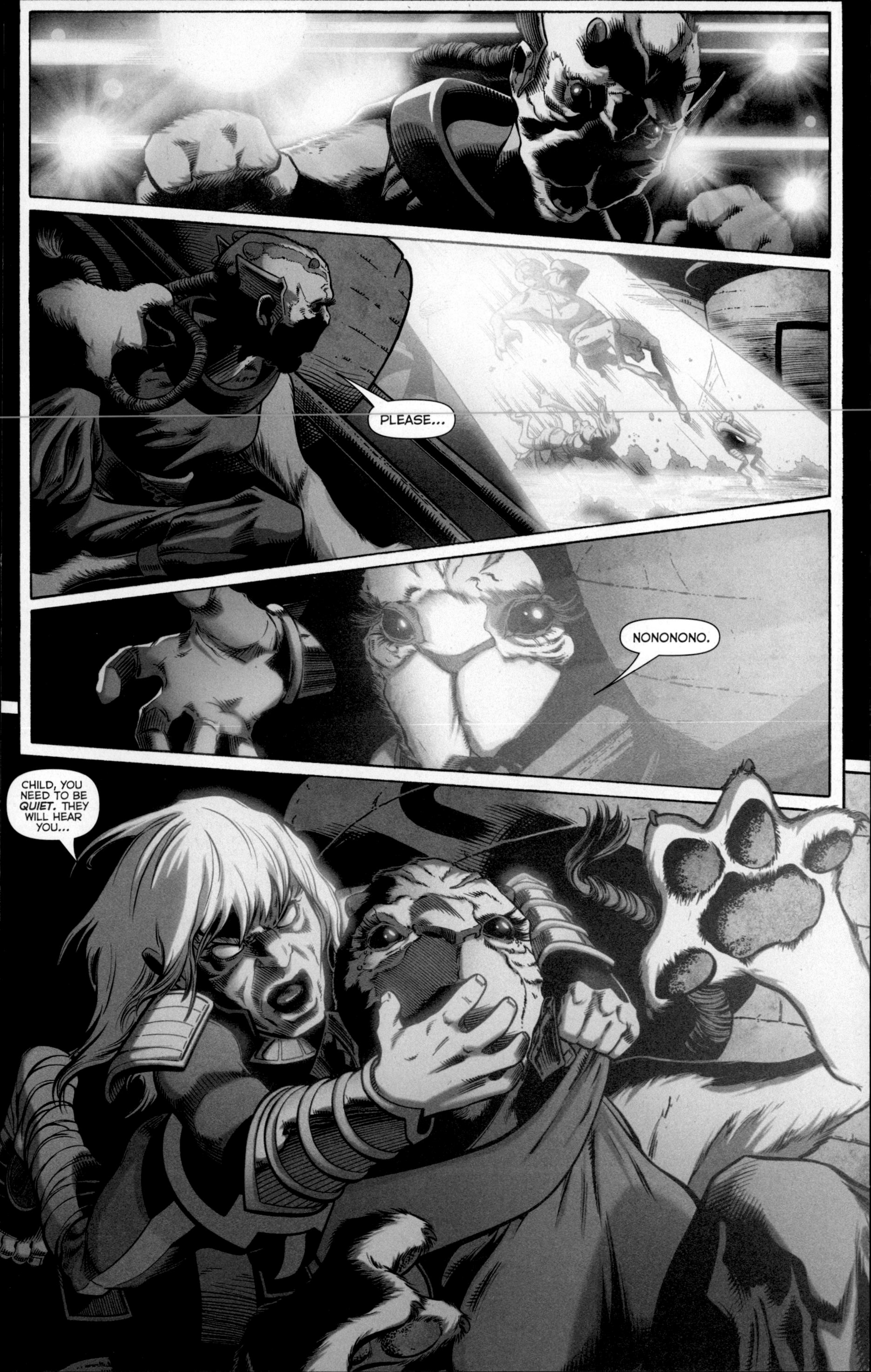
PLEASE...
NONONONO.
CHILD, YOU NEED TO BE *QUIET.* THEY WILL HEAR YOU...

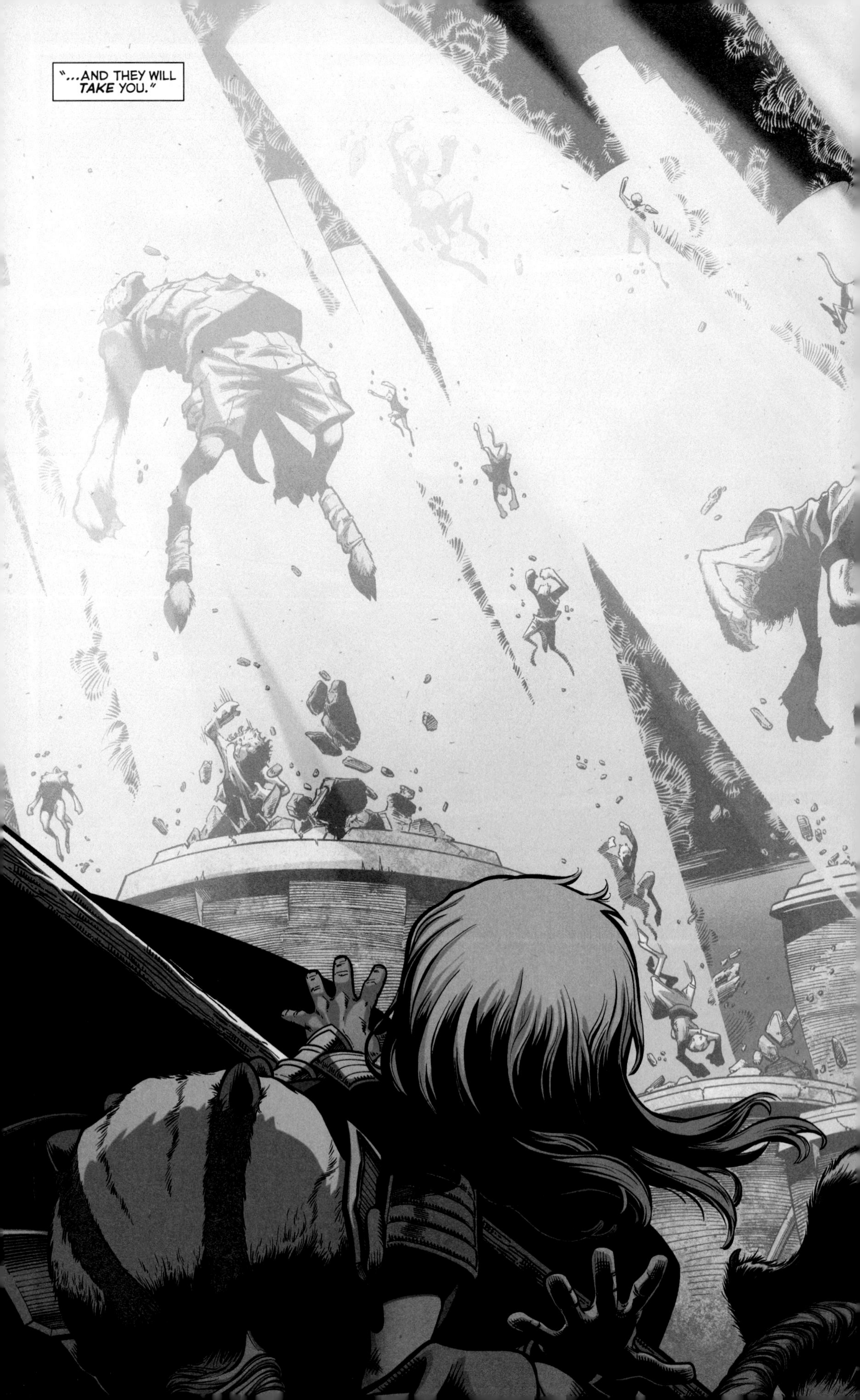
"...AND THEY WILL TAKE YOU."

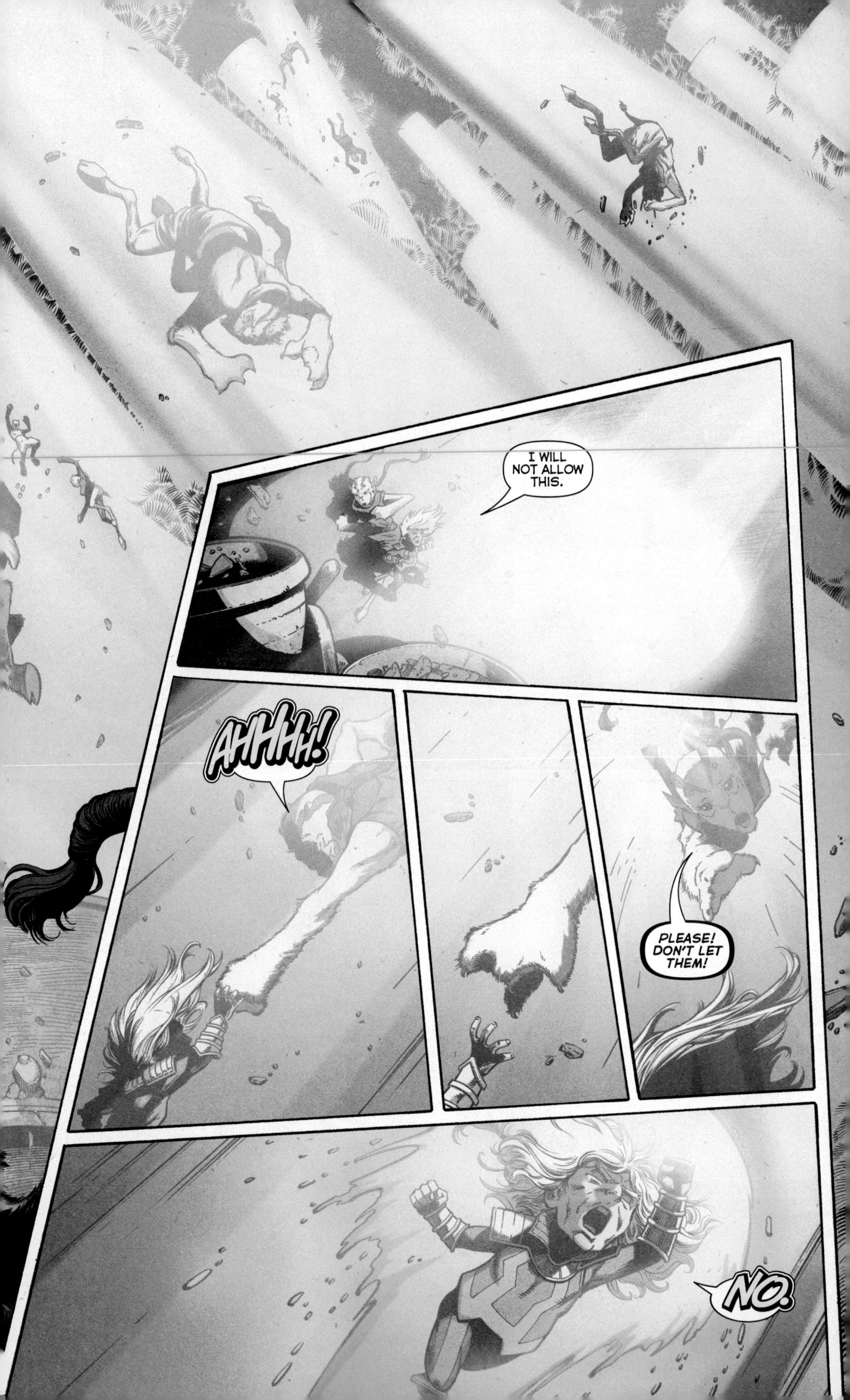
I WILL NOT ALLOW THIS.
AHHHH!
PLEASE! DON'T LET THEM!
NO.

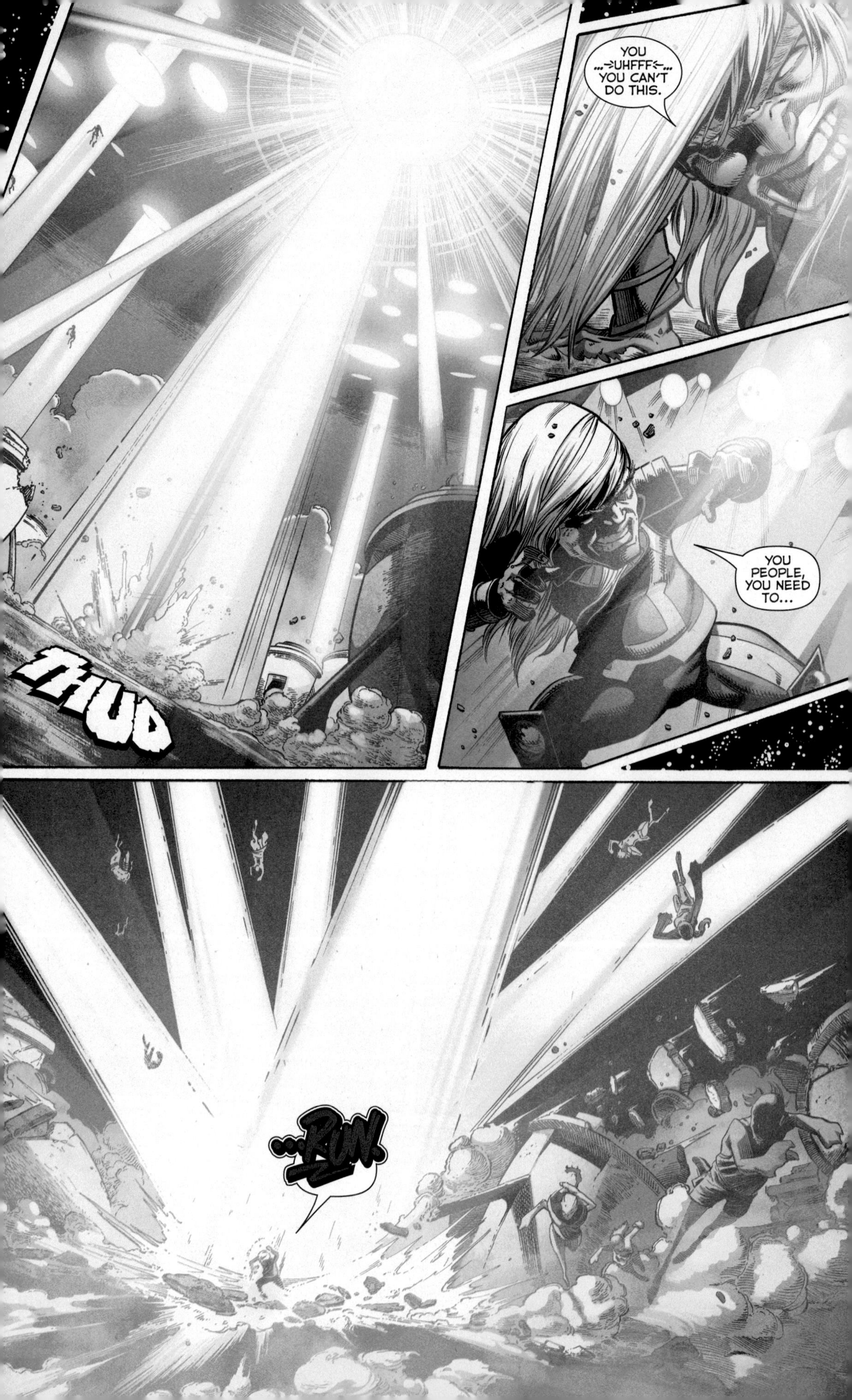

THUD
YOU ...UHFFF... YOU CAN'T DO THIS.
YOU PEOPLE, YOU NEED TO...
...RUN.

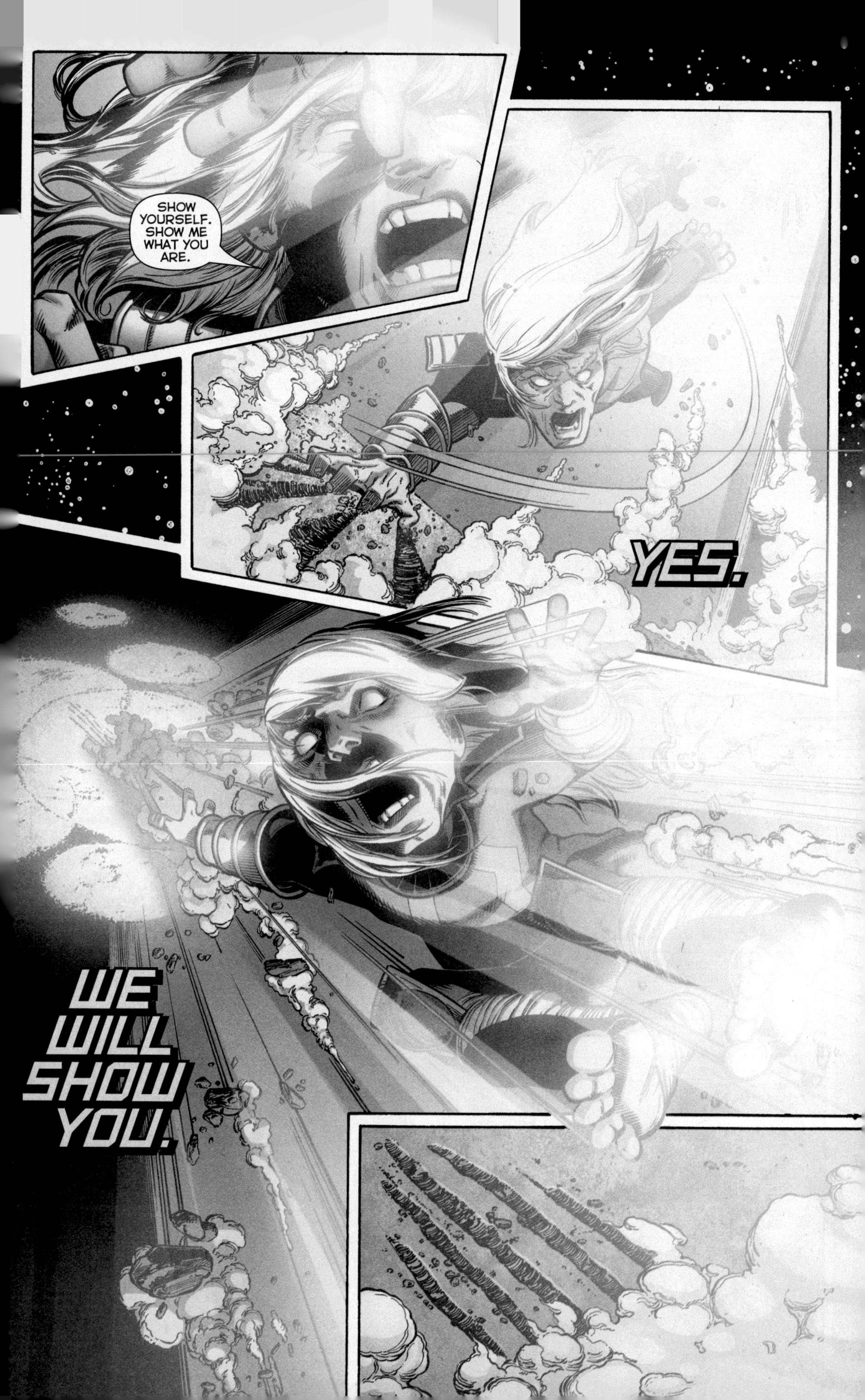
SHOW YOURSELF. SHOW ME WHAT YOU ARE.
YES.
WE WILL SHOW YOU.

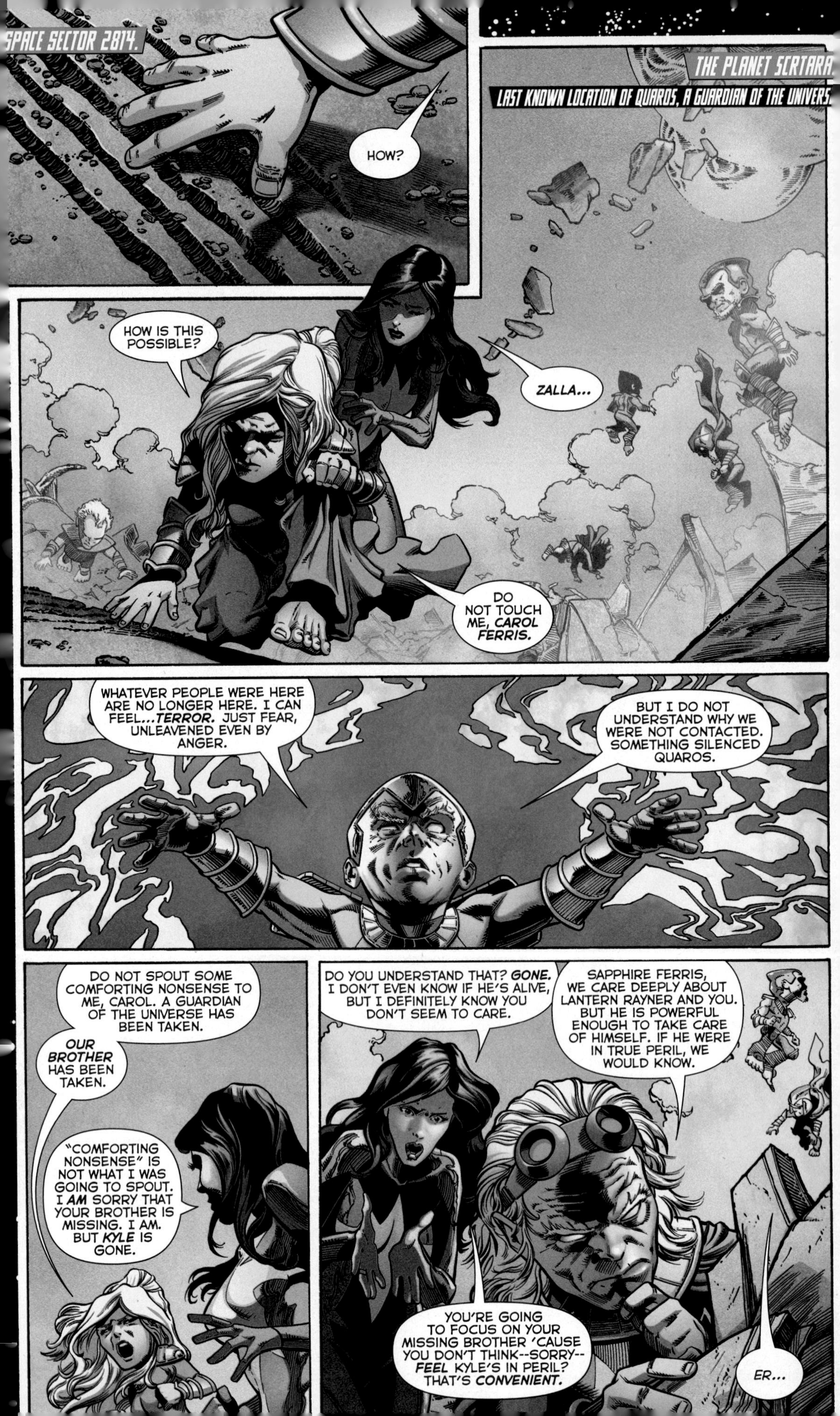
SPACE SECTOR 2814.
HOW?
THE PLANET SCRTARA.
LAST KNOWN LOCATION OF QUAROS, A GUARDIAN OF THE UNIVERS
HOW IS THIS POSSIBLE?
ZALLA...
DO NOT TOUCH ME, CAROL FERRIS.
WHATEVER PEOPLE WERE HERE ARE NO LONGER HERE. I CAN FEEL...TERROR. JUST FEAR, UNLEAVENED EVEN BY ANGER.
BUT I DO NOT UNDERSTAND WHY WE WERE NOT CONTACTED. SOMETHING SILENCED QUAROS.
DO NOT SPOUT SOME COMFORTING NONSENSE TO ME, CAROL. A GUARDIAN OF THE UNIVERSE HAS BEEN TAKEN.
OUR BROTHER HAS BEEN TAKEN.
"COMFORTING NONSENSE" IS NOT WHAT I WAS GOING TO SPOUT. I AM SORRY THAT YOUR BROTHER IS MISSING. I AM. BUT KYLE IS GONE.
DO YOU UNDERSTAND THAT? GONE. I DON'T EVEN KNOW IF HE'S ALIVE, BUT I DEFINITELY KNOW YOU DON'T SEEM TO CARE.
SAPPHIRE FERRIS, WE CARE DEEPLY ABOUT LANTERN RAYNER AND YOU. BUT HE IS POWERFUL ENOUGH TO TAKE CARE OF HIMSELF. IF HE WERE IN TRUE PERIL, WE WOULD KNOW.
YOU'RE GOING TO FOCUS ON YOUR MISSING BROTHER 'CAUSE YOU DON'T THINK--SORRY--FEEL KYLE'S IN PERIL? THAT'S CONVENIENT.
ER...

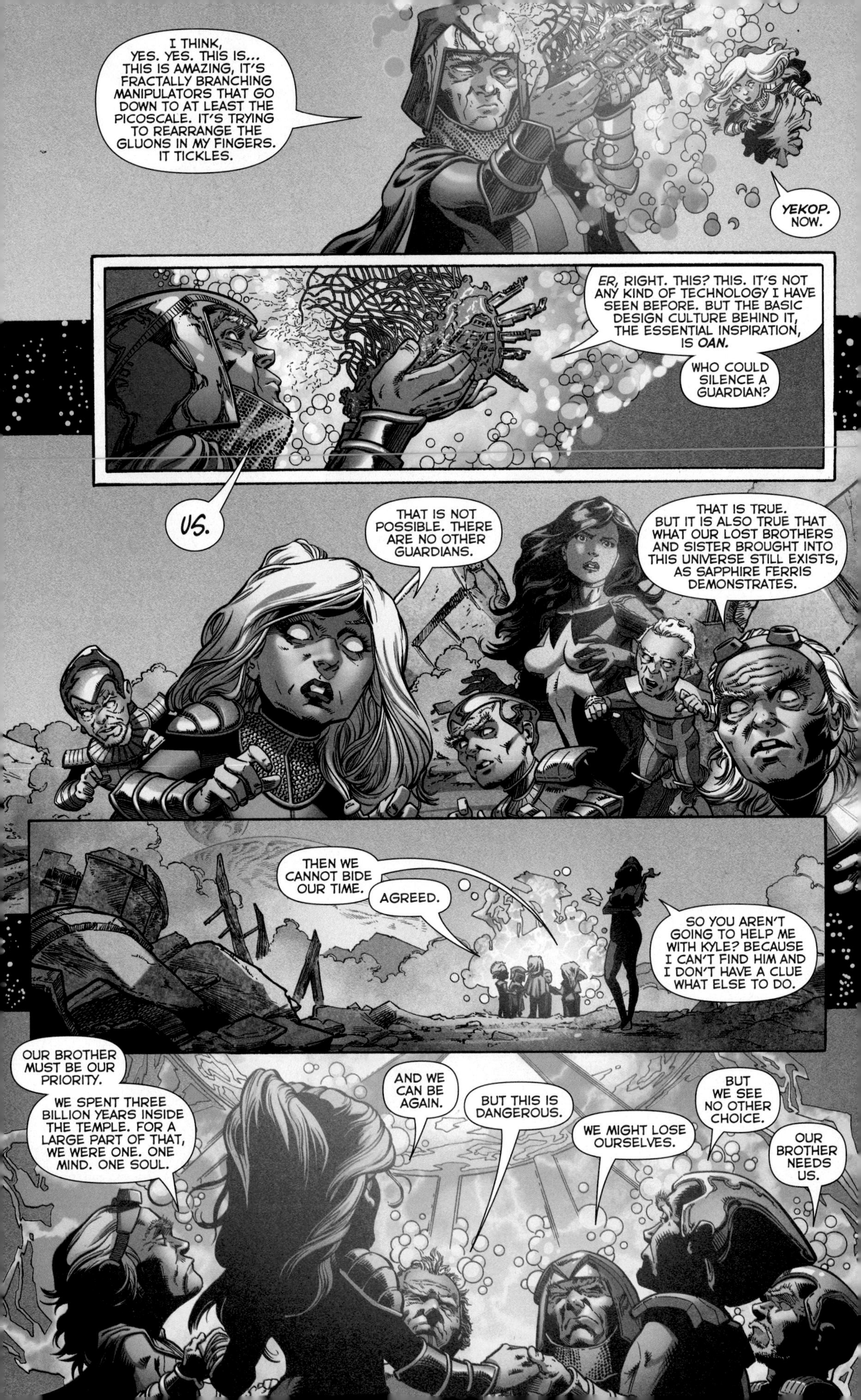
I THINK, YES. YES. THIS IS... THIS IS AMAZING, IT'S FRACTALLY BRANCHING MANIPULATORS THAT GO DOWN TO AT LEAST THE PICOSCALE. IT'S TRYING TO REARRANGE THE GLUONS IN MY FINGERS. IT TICKLES.
YEKOP. NOW.
ER, RIGHT. THIS? THIS. IT'S NOT ANY KIND OF TECHNOLOGY I HAVE SEEN BEFORE. BUT THE BASIC DESIGN CULTURE BEHIND IT, THE ESSENTIAL INSPIRATION, IS ***OAN.***
WHO COULD SILENCE A GUARDIAN?
US.
THAT IS NOT POSSIBLE. THERE ARE NO OTHER GUARDIANS.
THAT IS TRUE. BUT IT IS ALSO TRUE THAT WHAT OUR LOST BROTHERS AND SISTER BROUGHT INTO THIS UNIVERSE STILL EXISTS, AS SAPPHIRE FERRIS DEMONSTRATES.
THEN WE CANNOT BIDE OUR TIME.
AGREED.
SO YOU AREN'T GOING TO HELP ME WITH KYLE? BECAUSE I CAN'T FIND HIM AND I DON'T HAVE A CLUE WHAT ELSE TO DO.
OUR BROTHER MUST BE OUR PRIORITY.
WE SPENT THREE BILLION YEARS INSIDE THE TEMPLE. FOR A LARGE PART OF THAT, WE WERE ONE. ONE MIND. ONE SOUL.
AND WE CAN BE AGAIN.
BUT THIS IS DANGEROUS.
WE MIGHT LOSE OURSELVES.
BUT WE SEE NO OTHER CHOICE.
OUR BROTHER NEEDS US.

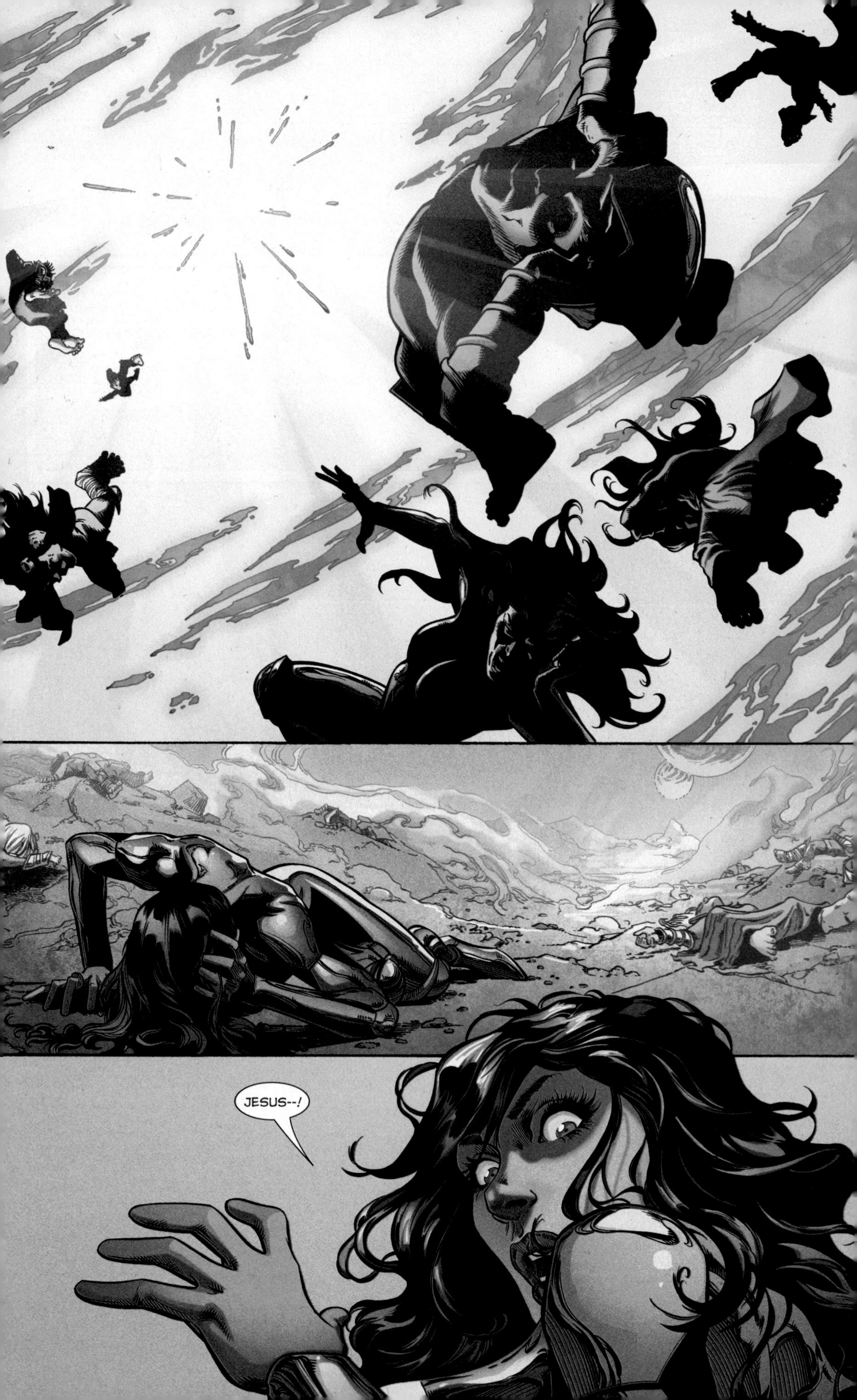
JESUS--!

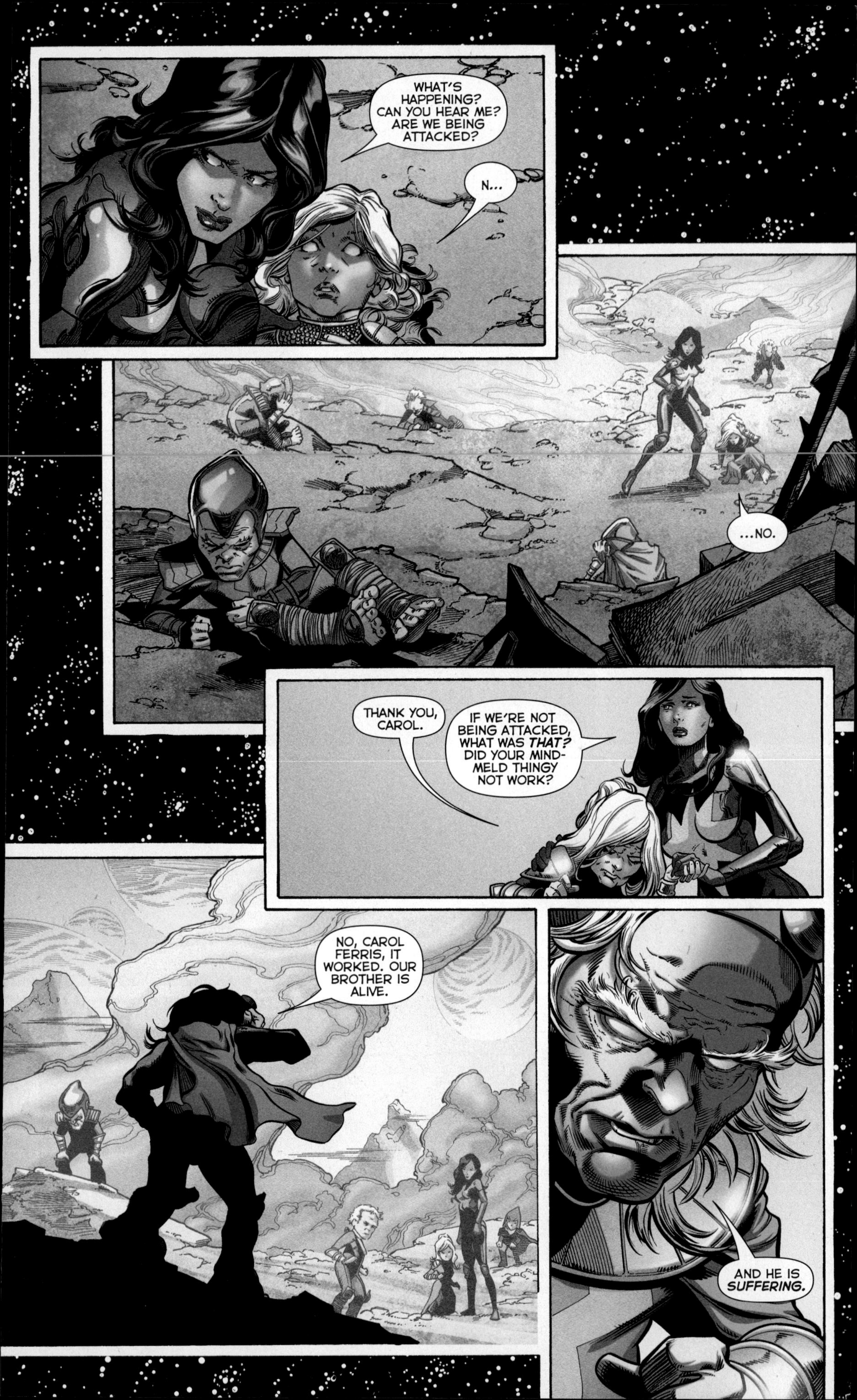
WHAT'S HAPPENING? CAN YOU HEAR ME? ARE WE BEING ATTACKED?
N...
...NO.
THANK YOU, CAROL.
IF WE'RE NOT BEING ATTACKED, WHAT WAS *THAT?* DID YOUR MIND-MELD THINGY NOT WORK?
NO, CAROL FERRIS, IT WORKED. OUR BROTHER IS ALIVE.
AND HE IS *SUFFERING.*

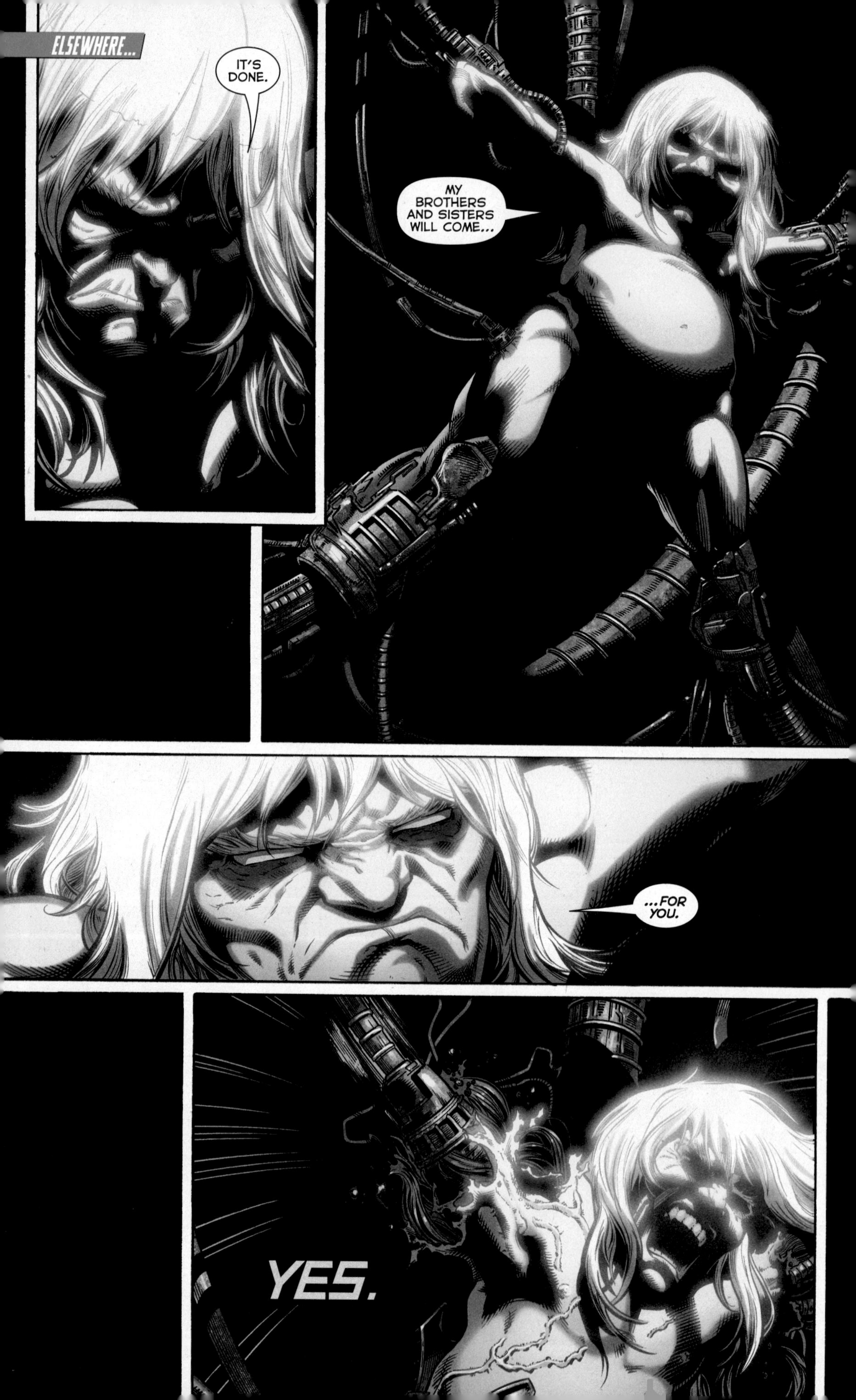
ELSEWHERE...
IT'S DONE.
MY BROTHERS AND SISTERS WILL COME...
...FOR YOU.
YES.

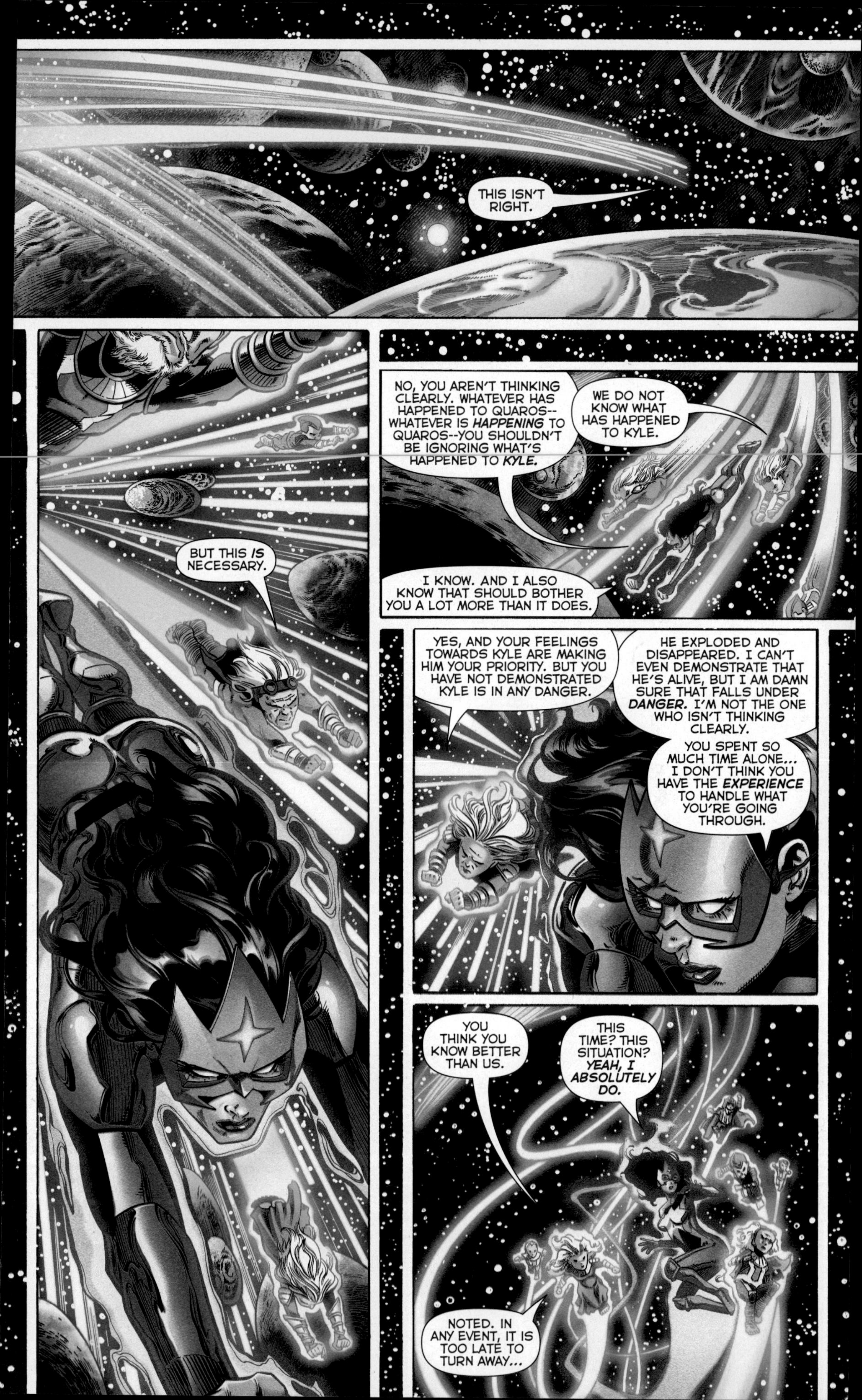
THIS ISN'T RIGHT.
BUT THIS IS NECESSARY.
NO, YOU AREN'T THINKING CLEARLY. WHATEVER HAS HAPPENED TO QUAROS-- WHATEVER IS HAPPENING TO QUAROS--YOU SHOULDN'T BE IGNORING WHAT'S HAPPENED TO KYLE.
WE DO NOT KNOW WHAT HAS HAPPENED TO KYLE.
I KNOW. AND I ALSO KNOW THAT SHOULD BOTHER YOU A LOT MORE THAN IT DOES.
YES, AND YOUR FEELINGS TOWARDS KYLE ARE MAKING HIM YOUR PRIORITY. BUT YOU HAVE NOT DEMONSTRATED KYLE IS IN ANY DANGER.
HE EXPLODED AND DISAPPEARED. I CAN'T EVEN DEMONSTRATE THAT HE'S ALIVE, BUT I AM DAMN SURE THAT FALLS UNDER DANGER. I'M NOT THE ONE WHO ISN'T THINKING CLEARLY.
YOU SPENT SO MUCH TIME ALONE... I DON'T THINK YOU HAVE THE EXPERIENCE TO HANDLE WHAT YOU'RE GOING THROUGH.
YOU THINK YOU KNOW BETTER THAN US.
THIS TIME? THIS SITUATION? YEAH, I ABSOLUTELY DO.
NOTED. IN ANY EVENT, IT IS TOO LATE TO TURN AWAY...

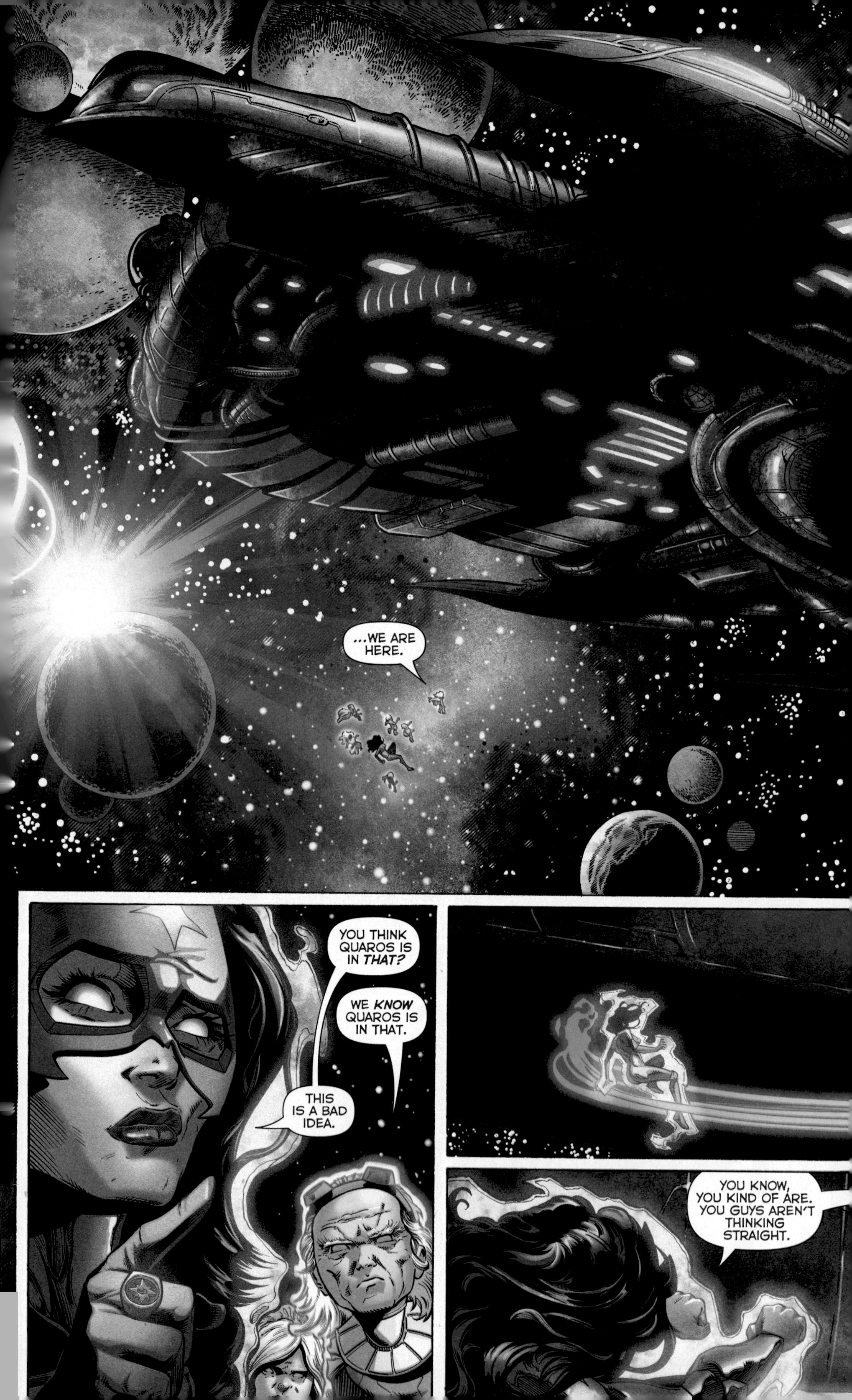
...WE ARE HERE.
YOU THINK QUAROS IS IN *THAT?*
WE *KNOW* QUAROS IS IN THAT.
THIS IS A BAD IDEA.
YOU KNOW, YOU KIND OF ARE. YOU GUYS AREN'T THINKING STRAIGHT.

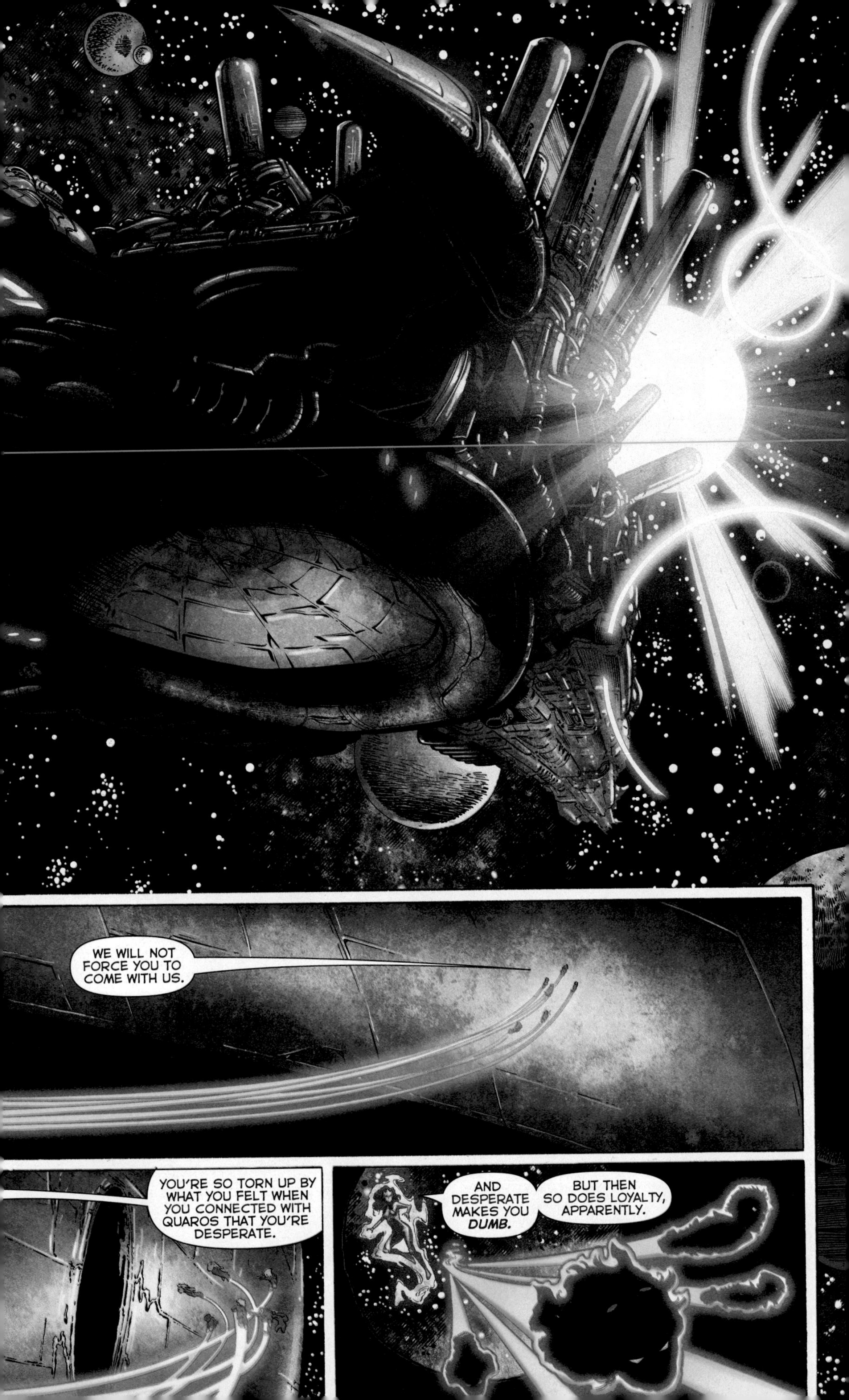
WE WILL NOT FORCE YOU TO COME WITH US.
YOU'RE SO TORN UP BY WHAT YOU FELT WHEN YOU CONNECTED WITH QUAROS THAT YOU'RE DESPERATE.
AND DESPERATE MAKES YOU *DUMB.*
BUT THEN SO DOES LOYALTY, APPARENTLY.

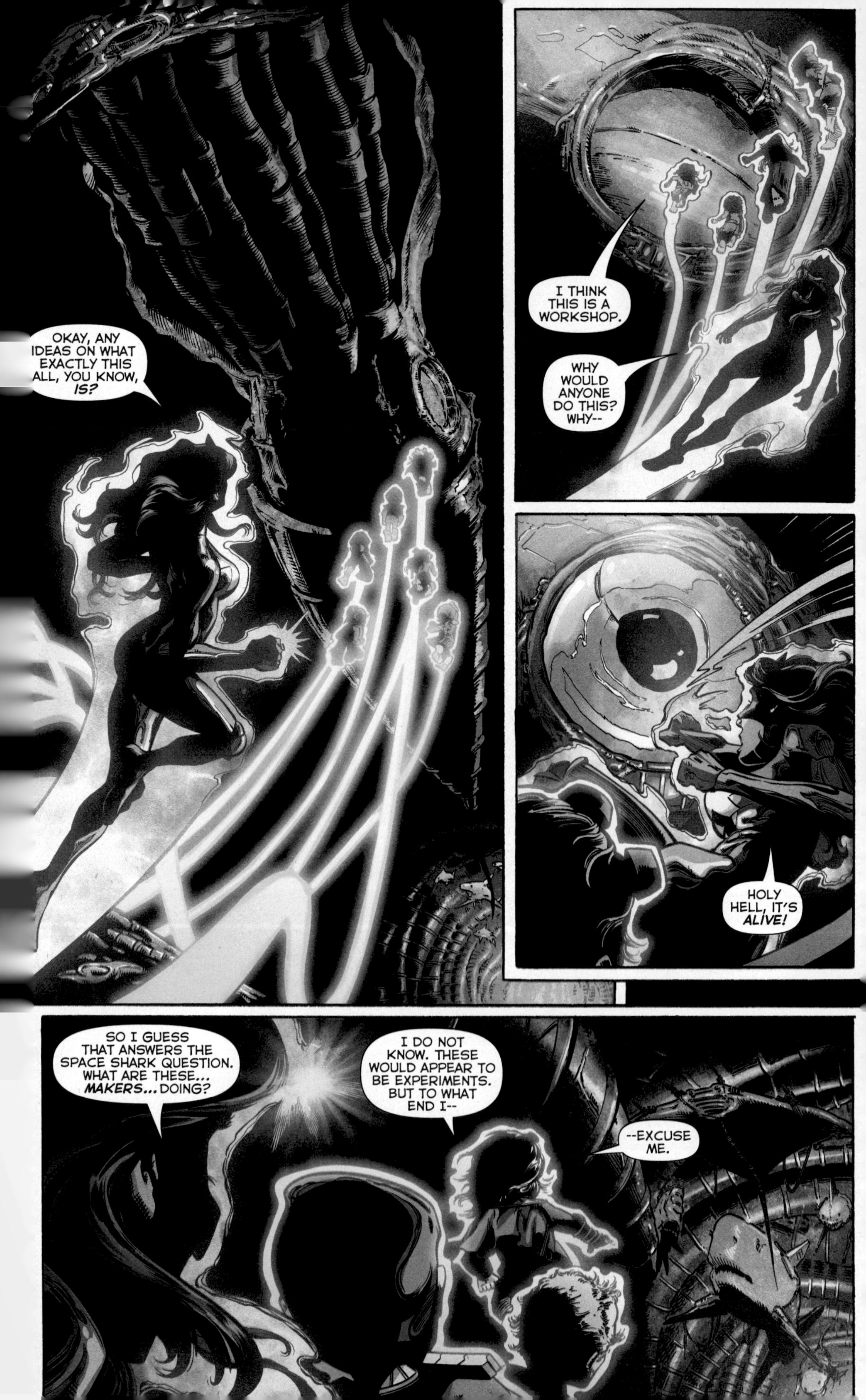
OKAY, ANY IDEAS ON WHAT EXACTLY THIS ALL, YOU KNOW, *IS?*
I THINK THIS IS A WORKSHOP.
WHY WOULD ANYONE DO THIS? WHY--
HOLY HELL, IT'S *ALIVE!*
SO I GUESS THAT ANSWERS THE SPACE SHARK QUESTION. WHAT ARE THESE... *MAKERS...* DOING?
I DO NOT KNOW. THESE WOULD APPEAR TO BE EXPERIMENTS. BUT TO WHAT END I--
--EXCUSE ME.

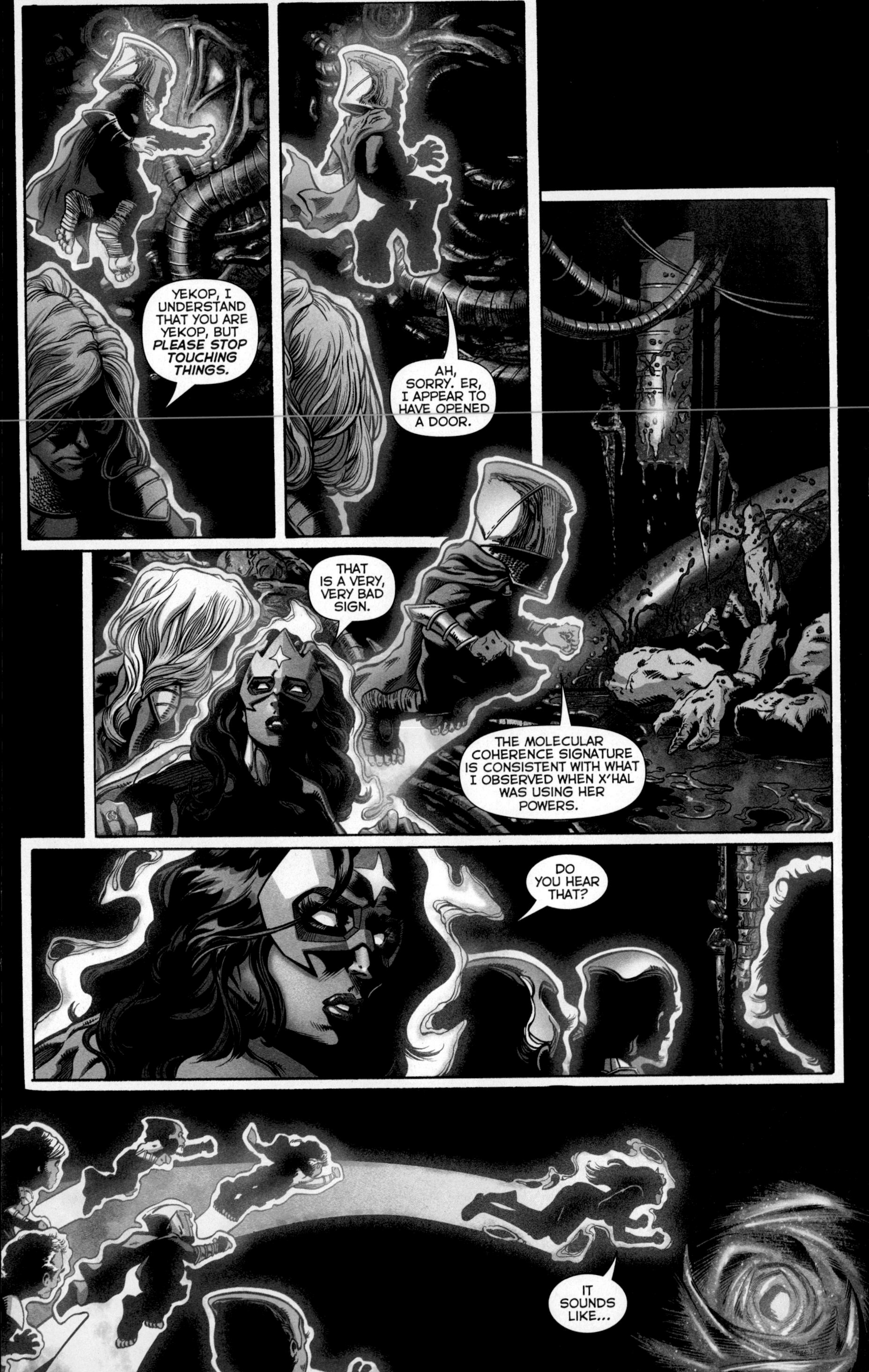
YEKOP, I UNDERSTAND THAT YOU ARE YEKOP, BUT *PLEASE STOP TOUCHING THINGS.*
AH, SORRY. ER, I APPEAR TO HAVE OPENED A DOOR.
THAT IS A VERY, VERY BAD SIGN.
THE MOLECULAR COHERENCE SIGNATURE IS CONSISTENT WITH WHAT I OBSERVED WHEN X'HAL WAS USING HER POWERS.
DO YOU HEAR THAT?
IT SOUNDS LIKE...

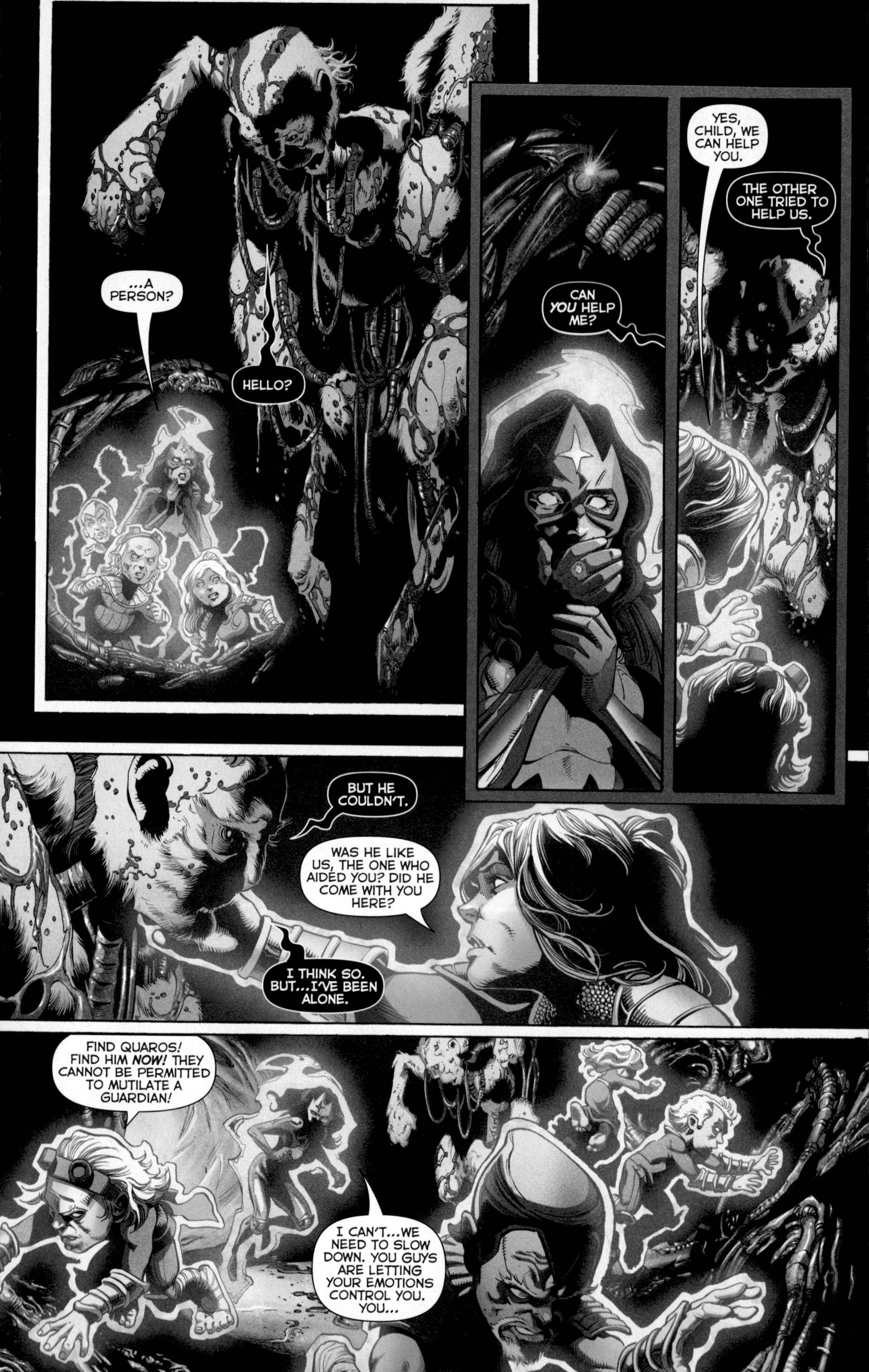
...A PERSON?
HELLO?
CAN YOU HELP ME?
YES, CHILD, WE CAN HELP YOU.
THE OTHER ONE TRIED TO HELP US.
BUT HE COULDN'T.
WAS HE LIKE US, THE ONE WHO AIDED YOU? DID HE COME WITH YOU HERE?
I THINK SO. BUT...I'VE BEEN ALONE.
FIND QUAROS! FIND HIM NOW! THEY CANNOT BE PERMITTED TO MUTILATE A GUARDIAN!
I CAN'T...WE NEED TO SLOW DOWN. YOU GUYS ARE LETTING YOUR EMOTIONS CONTROL YOU. YOU...

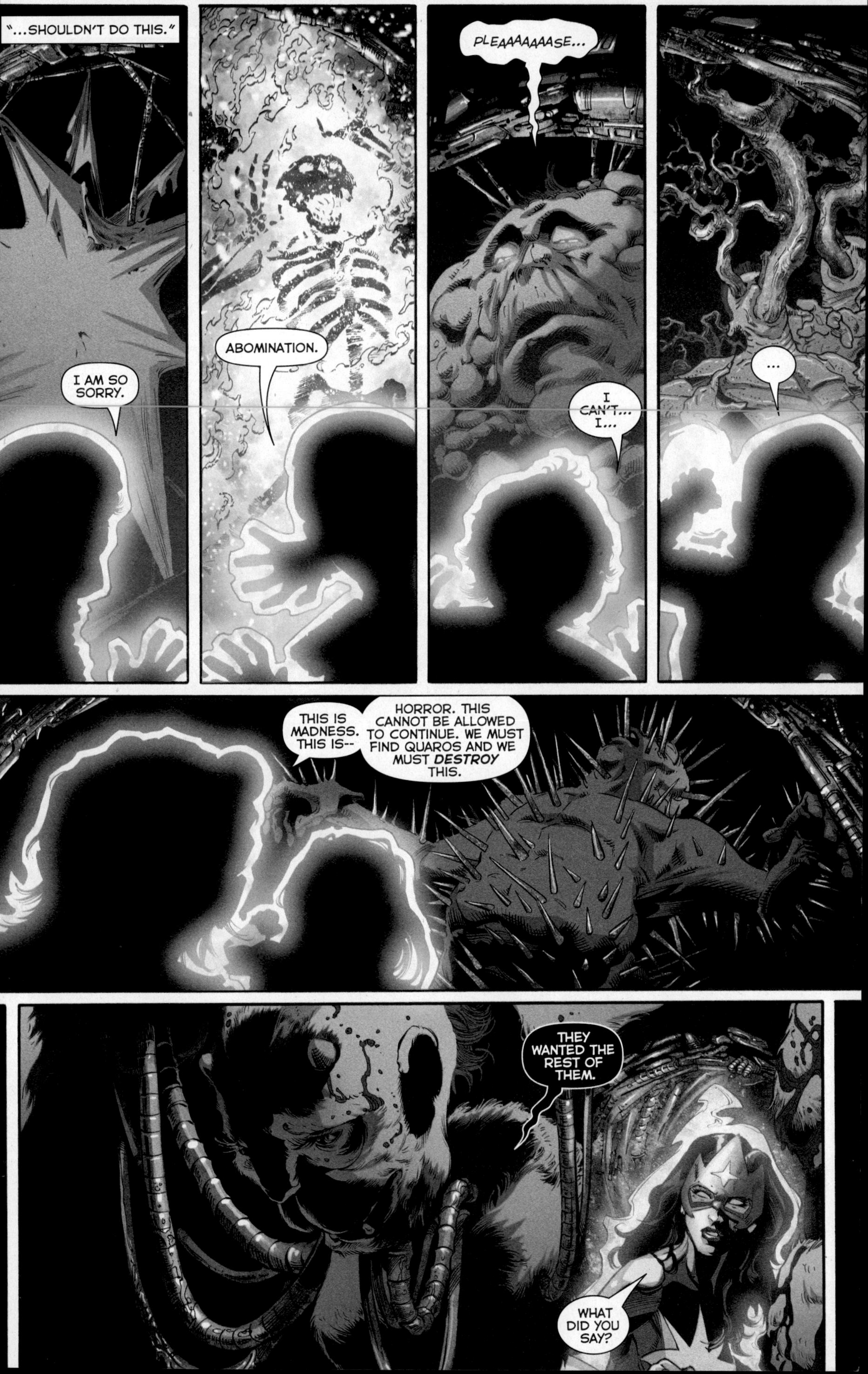
"...SHOULDN'T DO THIS."
I AM SO SORRY.
ABOMINATION.
PLEAAAAAAASE...
I CAN'T... I...
...
THIS IS MADNESS. THIS IS--
HORROR. THIS CANNOT BE ALLOWED TO CONTINUE. WE MUST FIND QUAROS AND WE MUST DESTROY THIS.
THEY WANTED THE REST OF THEM.
WHAT DID YOU SAY?

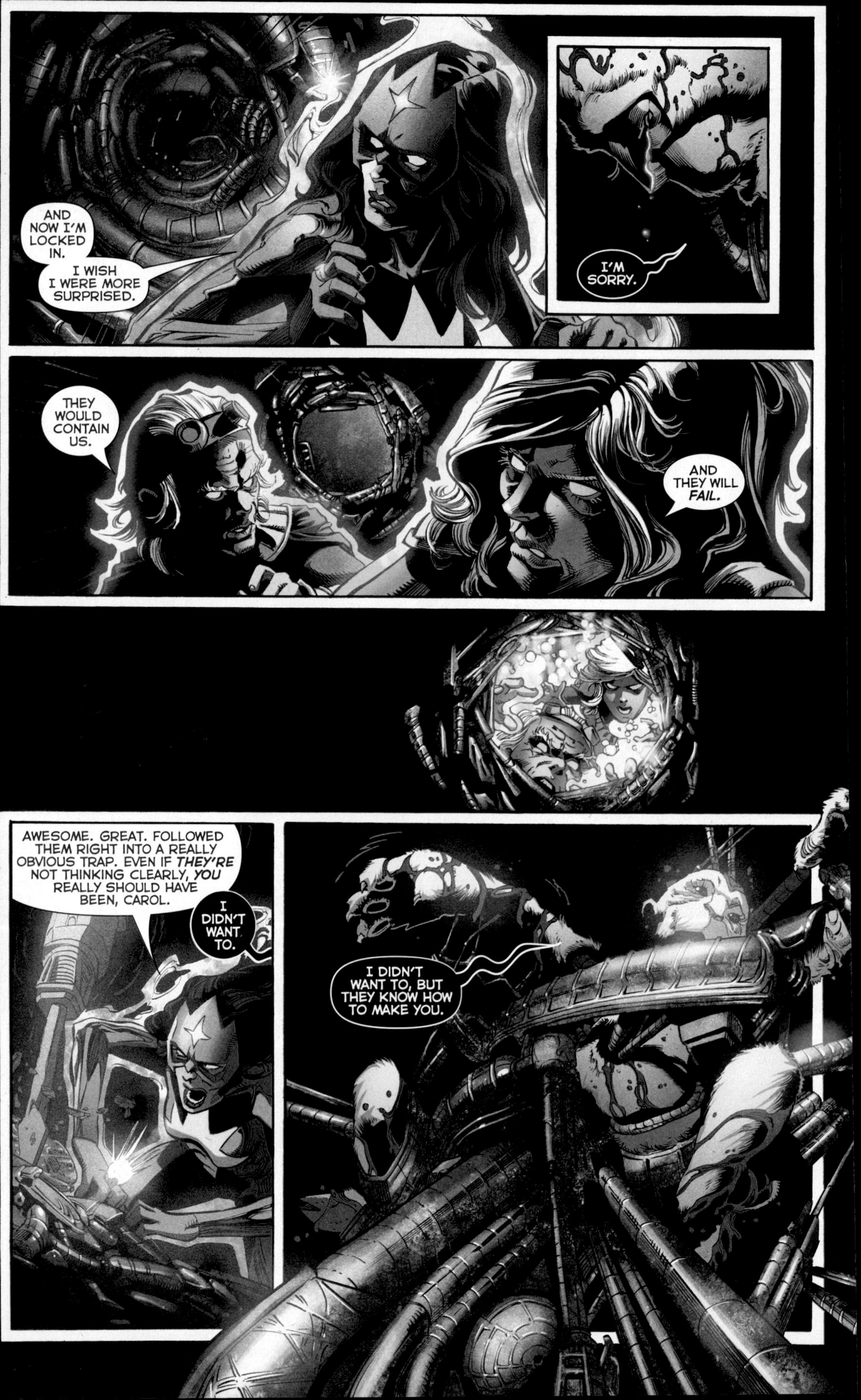
AND NOW I'M LOCKED IN.
I WISH I WERE MORE SURPRISED.
I'M SORRY.
THEY WOULD CONTAIN US.
AND THEY WILL *FAIL.*
AWESOME. GREAT. FOLLOWED THEM RIGHT INTO A REALLY OBVIOUS TRAP. EVEN IF *THEY'RE* NOT THINKING CLEARLY, *YOU* REALLY SHOULD HAVE BEEN, CAROL.
I DIDN'T WANT TO.
I DIDN'T WANT TO, BUT THEY KNOW HOW TO MAKE YOU.

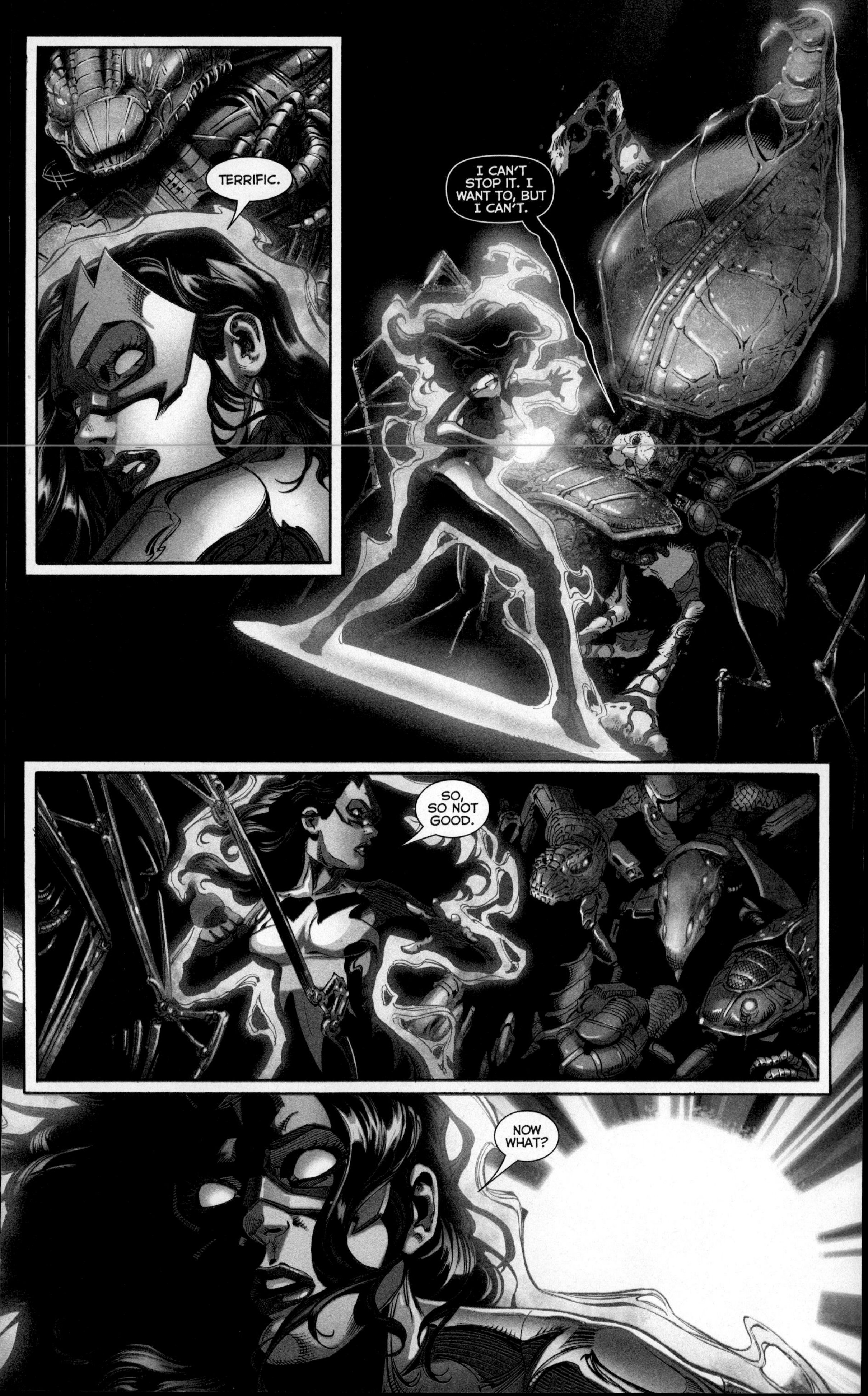
TERRIFIC.
I CAN'T STOP IT. I WANT TO, BUT I CAN'T.
SO, SO NOT GOOD.
NOW WHAT?

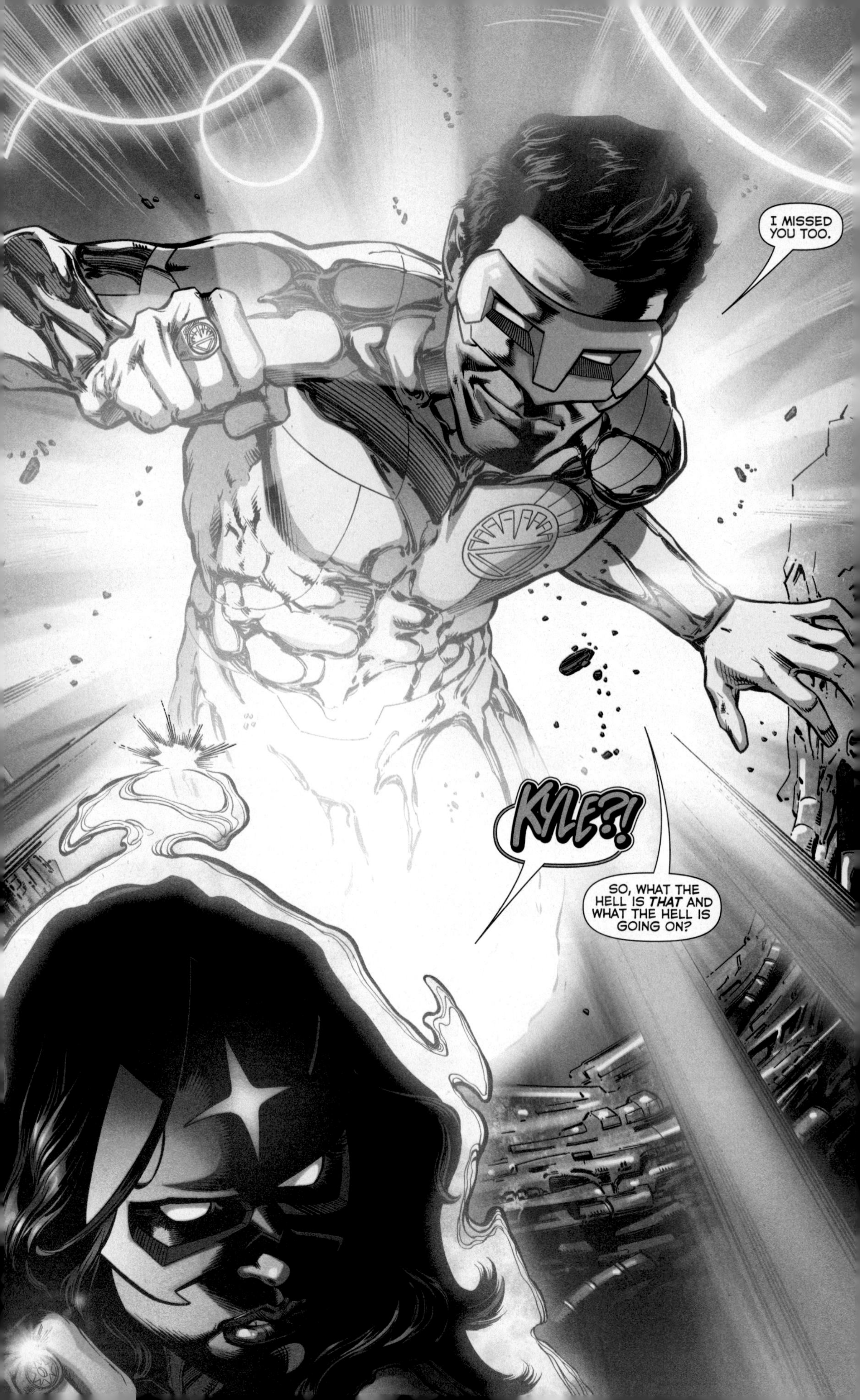
I MISSED YOU TOO.
KYLE?!
SO, WHAT THE HELL IS THAT AND WHAT THE HELL IS GOING ON?

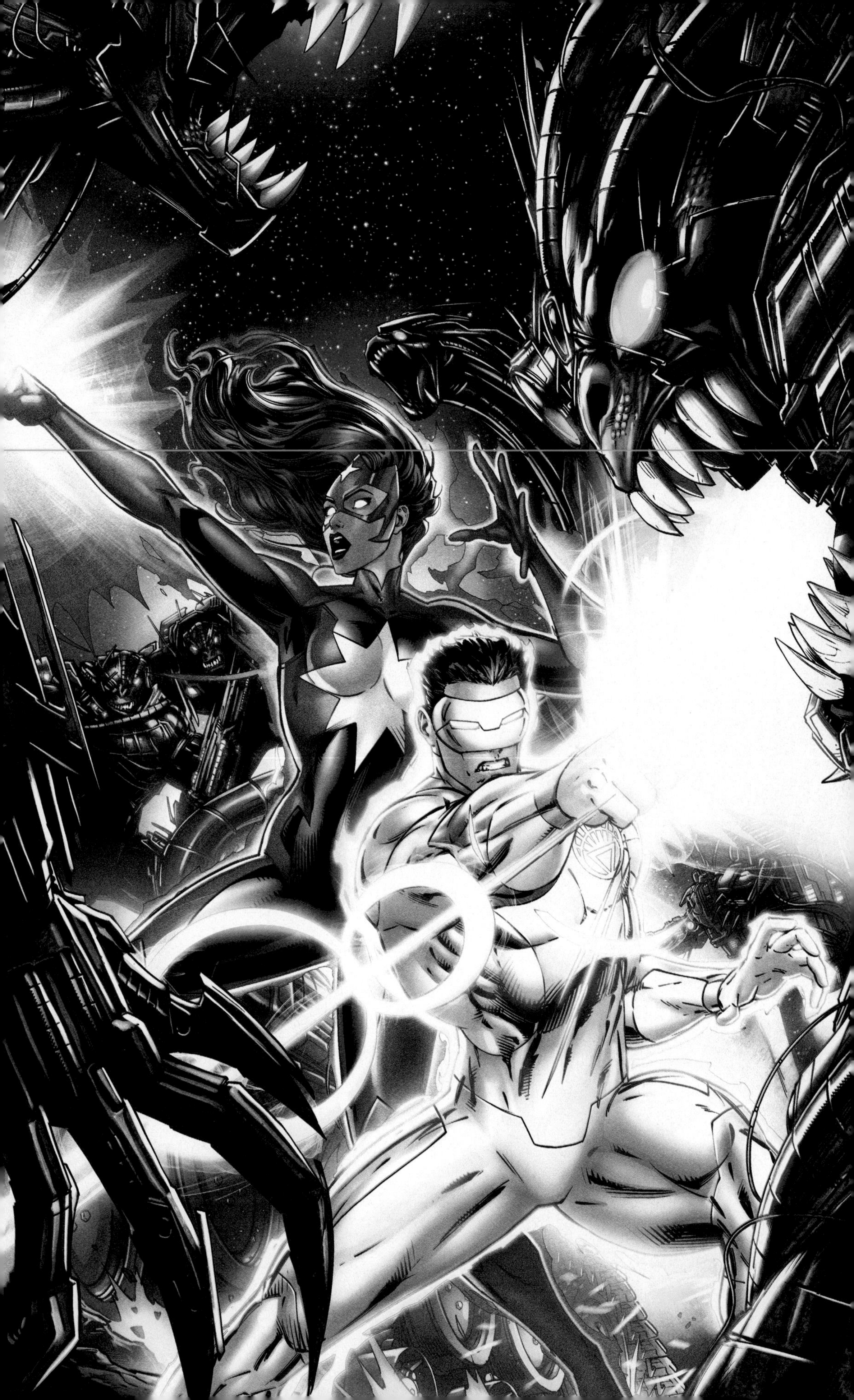

THE MAKERS

JUSTIN JORDAN writer **BRAD WALKER** with **DIOGENES NEVES** pencillers **ANDREW HENNESSY** with **MARC DEERING** inkers
MICHELLE MADSEN colorist **DAVE SHARPE** letterer cover art by **JEREMY ROBERTS**

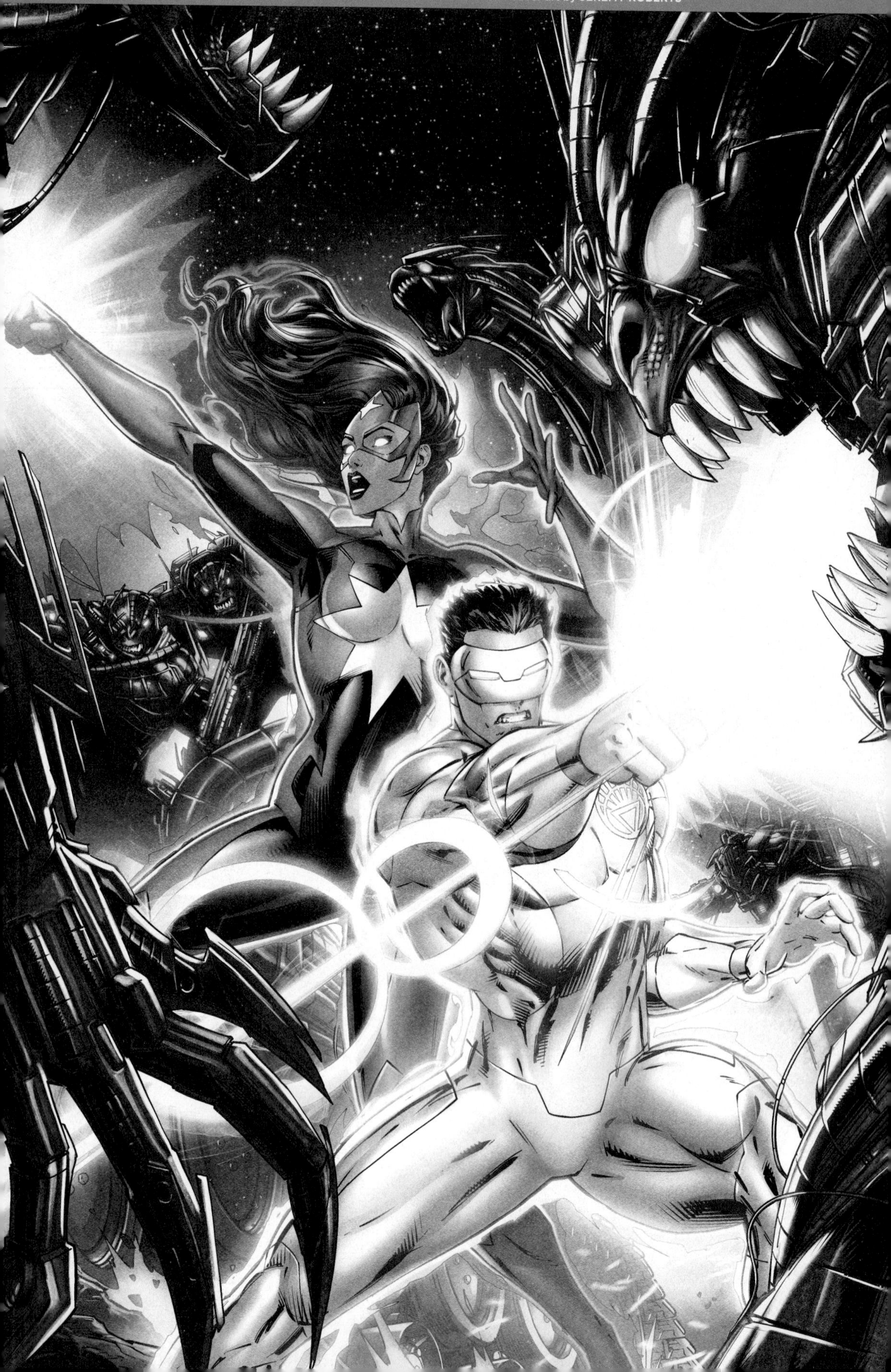

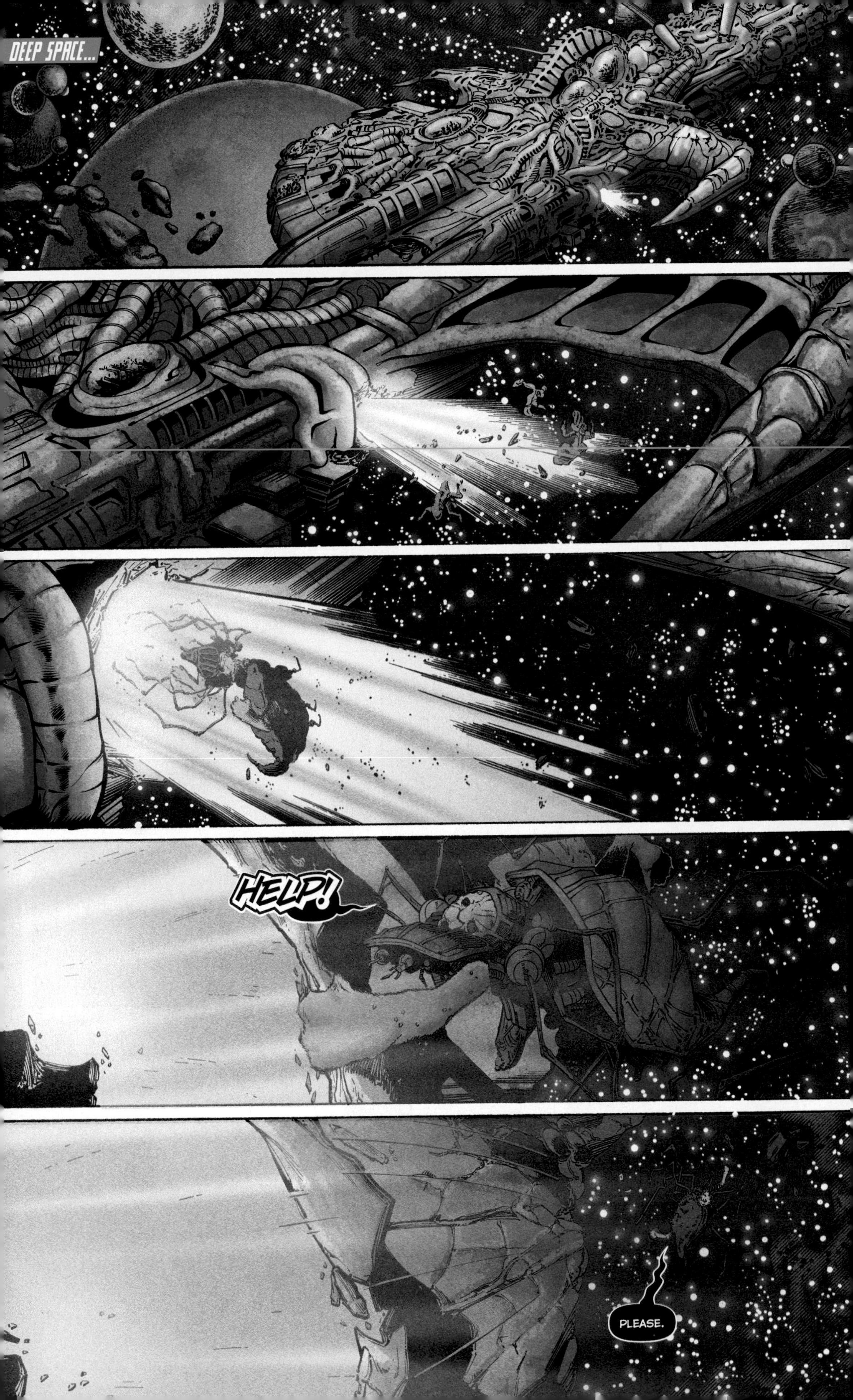
DEEP SPACE...
HELP!
PLEASE.

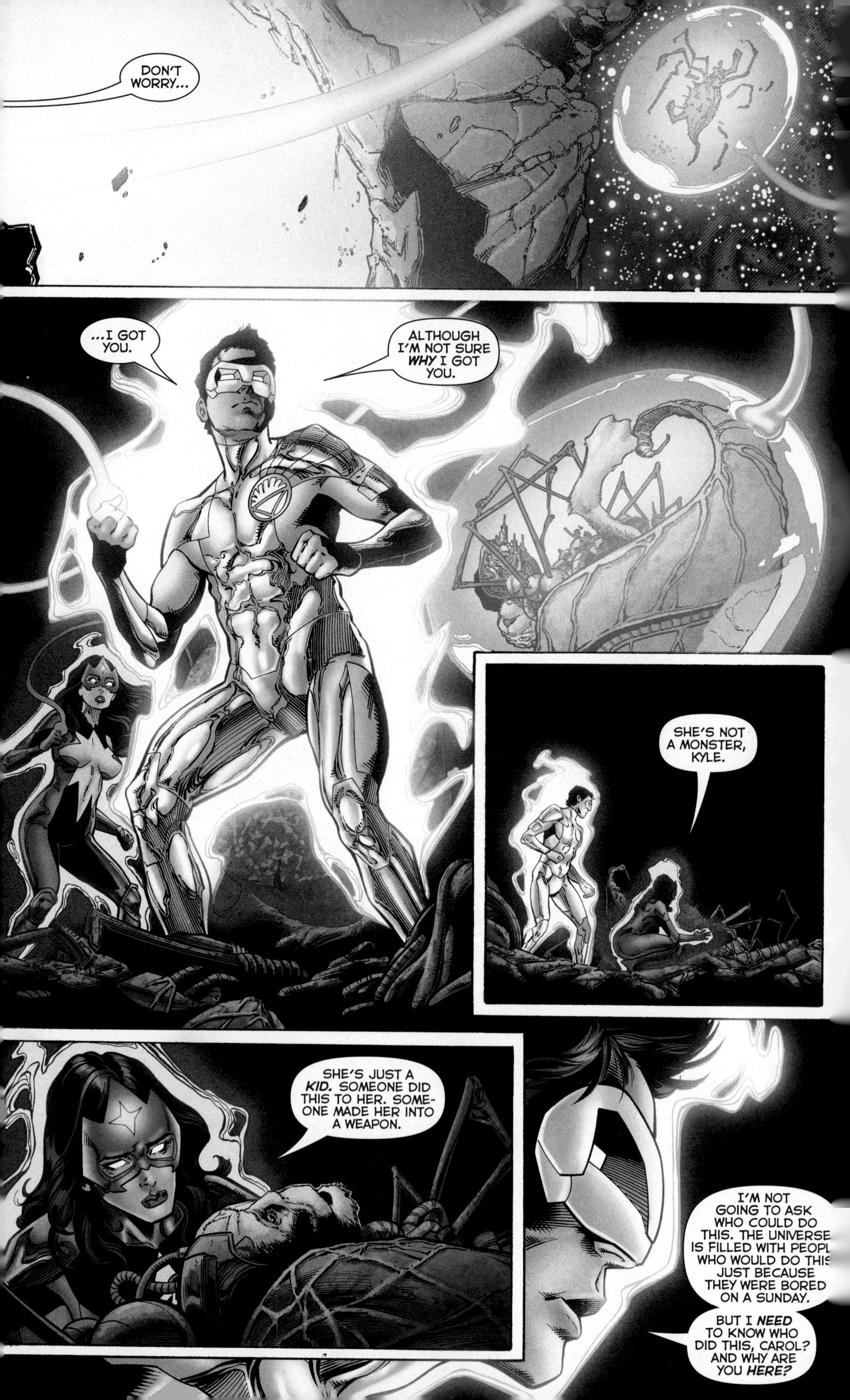
DON'T WORRY...
...I GOT YOU.
ALTHOUGH I'M NOT SURE *WHY* I GOT YOU.
SHE'S NOT A MONSTER, KYLE.
SHE'S JUST A *KID.* SOMEONE DID THIS TO HER. SOME-ONE MADE HER INTO A WEAPON.
I'M NOT GOING TO ASK WHO COULD DO THIS. THE UNIVERSE IS FILLED WITH PEOPL WHO WOULD DO THIS JUST BECAUSE THEY WERE BORED ON A SUNDAY.
BUT I *NEED* TO KNOW WHO DID THIS, CAROL? AND WHY ARE YOU *HERE?*

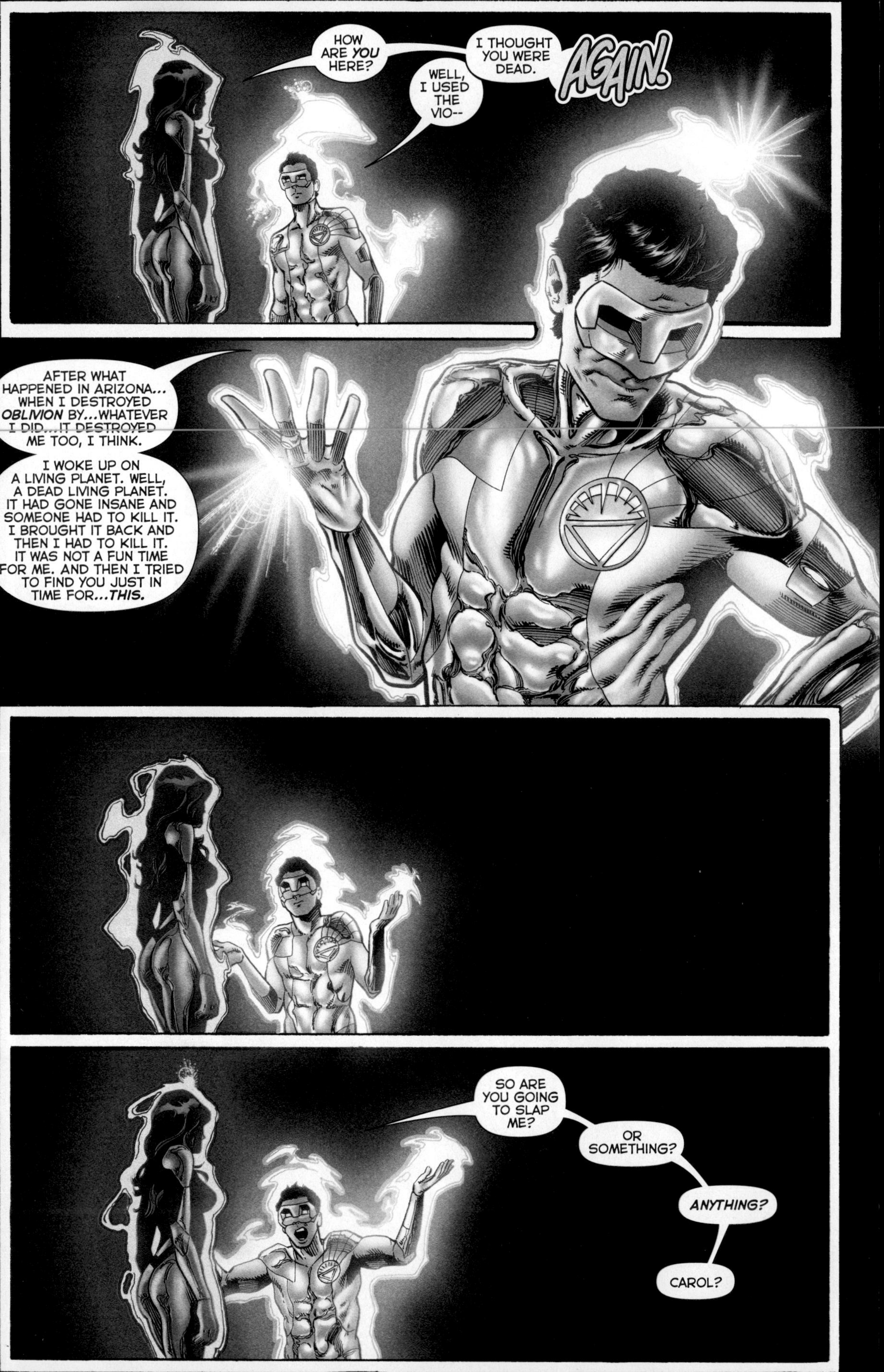
HOW ARE *YOU* HERE?
I THOUGHT YOU WERE DEAD.
AGAIN!
WELL, I USED THE VIO--
AFTER WHAT HAPPENED IN ARIZONA... WHEN I DESTROYED *OBLIVION* BY...WHATEVER I DID...IT DESTROYED ME TOO, I THINK.
I WOKE UP ON A LIVING PLANET. WELL, A DEAD LIVING PLANET. IT HAD GONE INSANE AND SOMEONE HAD TO KILL IT. I BROUGHT IT BACK AND THEN I HAD TO KILL IT. IT WAS NOT A FUN TIME FOR ME. AND THEN I TRIED TO FIND YOU JUST IN TIME FOR...*THIS.*
SO ARE YOU GOING TO SLAP ME?
OR SOMETHING?
ANYTHING?
CAROL?

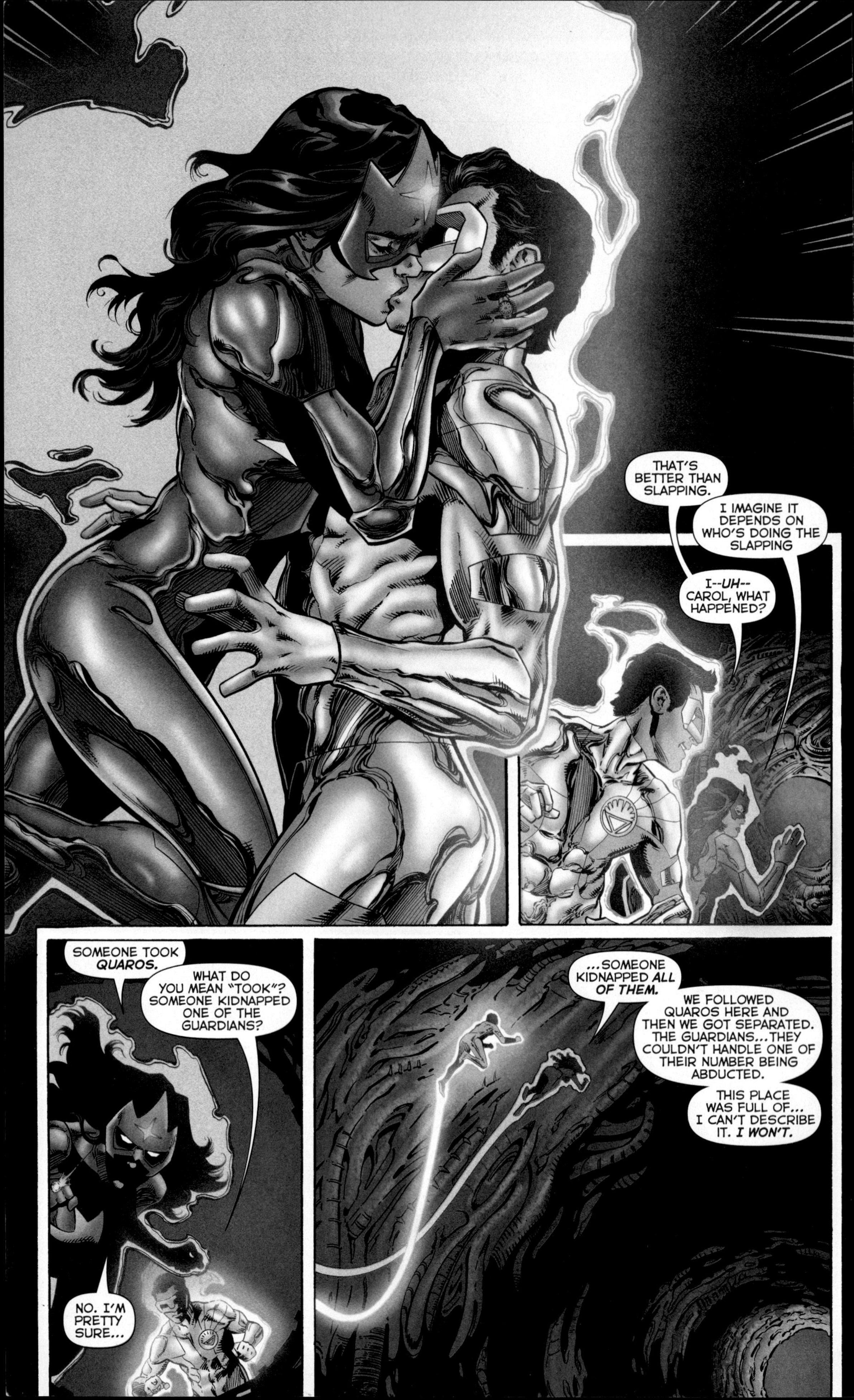
THAT'S BETTER THAN SLAPPING.
I IMAGINE IT DEPENDS ON WHO'S DOING THE SLAPPING
I--UH-- CAROL, WHAT HAPPENED?
SOMEONE TOOK QUAROS.
WHAT DO YOU MEAN "TOOK"? SOMEONE KIDNAPPED ONE OF THE GUARDIANS?
NO. I'M PRETTY SURE...
...SOMEONE KIDNAPPED ALL OF THEM.
WE FOLLOWED QUAROS HERE AND THEN WE GOT SEPARATED. THE GUARDIANS...THEY COULDN'T HANDLE ONE OF THEIR NUMBER BEING ABDUCTED.
THIS PLACE WAS FULL OF... I CAN'T DESCRIBE IT. I WON'T.

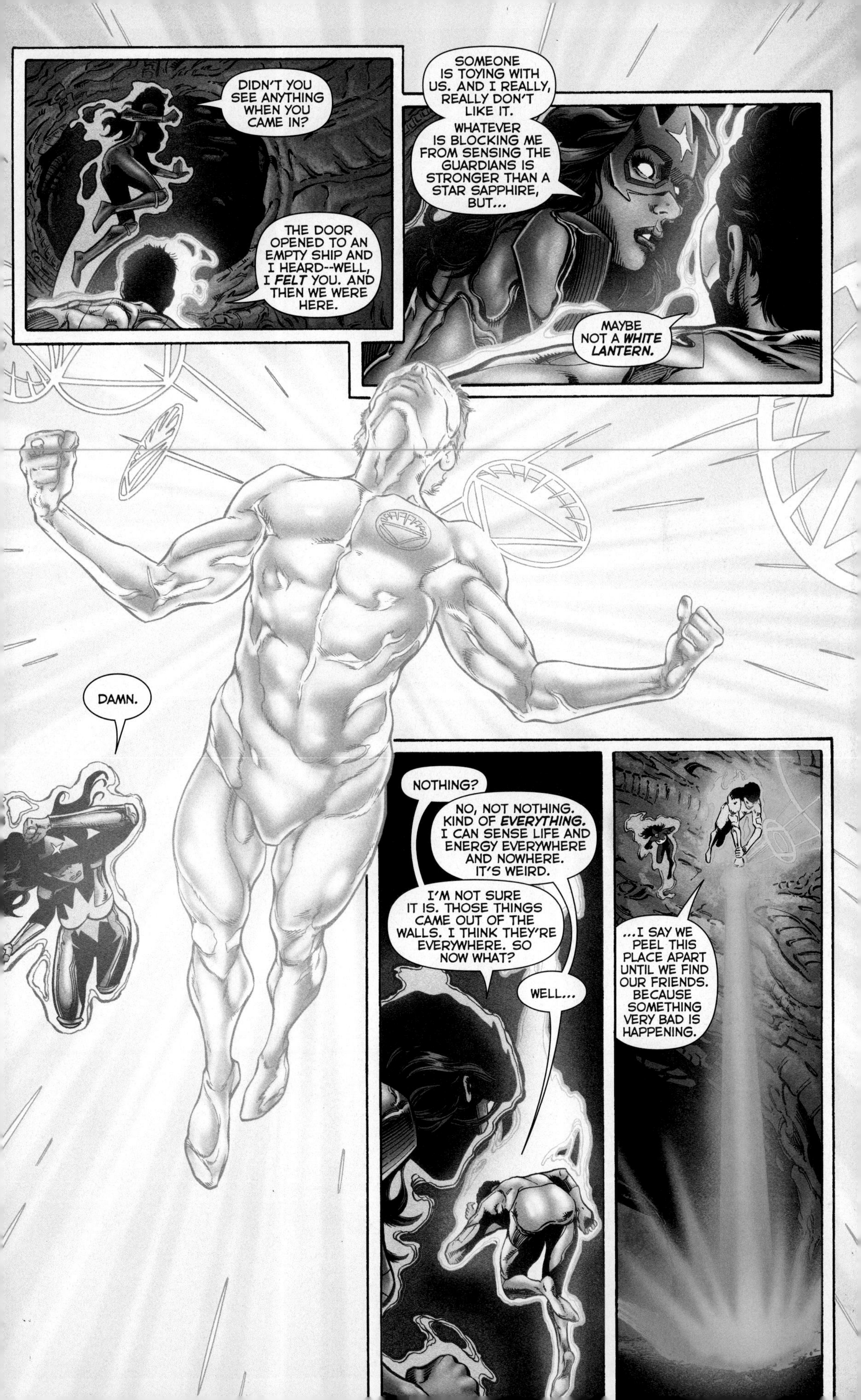
DIDN'T YOU SEE ANYTHING WHEN YOU CAME IN?
THE DOOR OPENED TO AN EMPTY SHIP AND I HEARD--WELL, I *FELT* YOU. AND THEN WE WERE HERE.
SOMEONE IS TOYING WITH US. AND I REALLY, REALLY DON'T LIKE IT.
WHATEVER IS BLOCKING ME FROM SENSING THE GUARDIANS IS STRONGER THAN A STAR SAPPHIRE, BUT...
MAYBE NOT A *WHITE LANTERN.*
DAMN.
NOTHING?
NO, NOT NOTHING. KIND OF *EVERYTHING.* I CAN SENSE LIFE AND ENERGY EVERYWHERE AND NOWHERE. IT'S WEIRD.
I'M NOT SURE IT IS. THOSE THINGS CAME OUT OF THE WALLS. I THINK THEY'RE EVERYWHERE. SO NOW WHAT?
WELL...
...I SAY WE PEEL THIS PLACE APART UNTIL WE FIND OUR FRIENDS. BECAUSE SOMETHING VERY BAD IS HAPPENING.

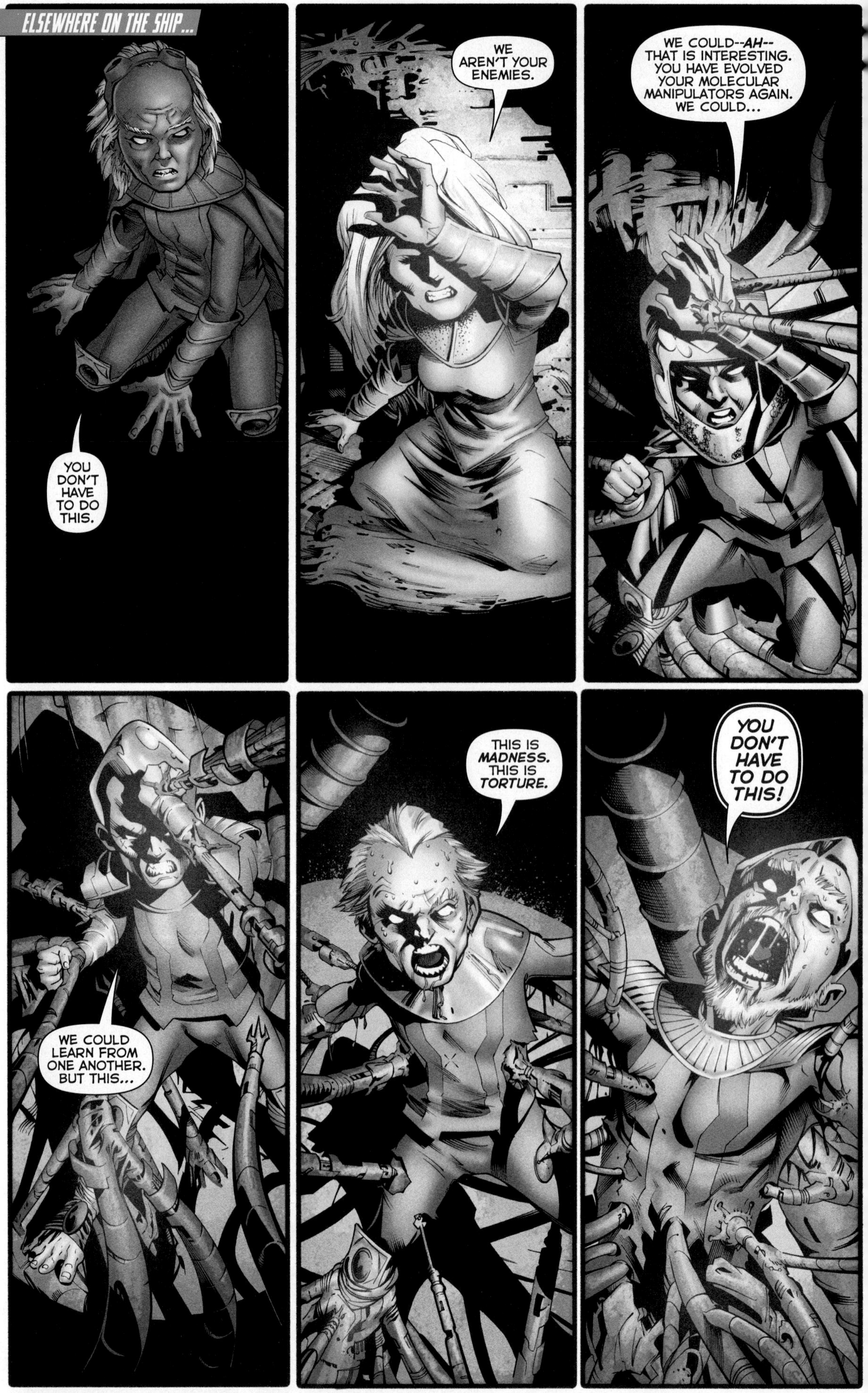
ELSEWHERE ON THE SHIP...
YOU DON'T HAVE TO DO THIS.
WE AREN'T YOUR ENEMIES.
WE COULD--AH-- THAT IS INTERESTING. YOU HAVE EVOLVED YOUR MOLECULAR MANIPULATORS AGAIN. WE COULD...
WE COULD LEARN FROM ONE ANOTHER. BUT THIS...
THIS IS MADNESS. THIS IS TORTURE.
YOU DON'T HAVE TO DO THIS!

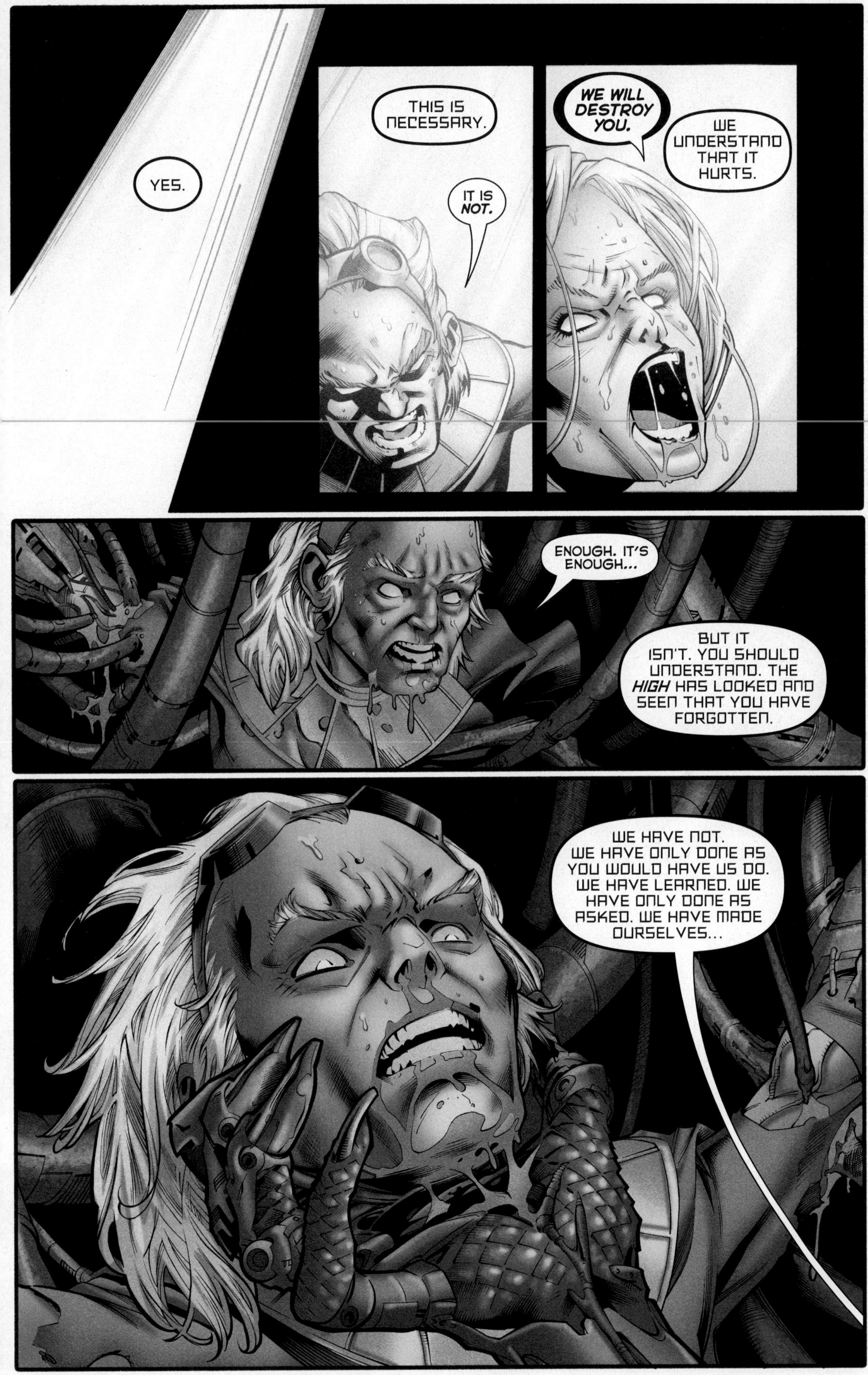
YES.
THIS IS NECESSARY.
IT IS NOT.
WE WILL DESTROY YOU.
WE UNDERSTAND THAT IT HURTS.
ENOUGH. IT'S ENOUGH...
BUT IT ISN'T. YOU SHOULD UNDERSTAND. THE HIGH HAS LOOKED AND SEEN THAT YOU HAVE FORGOTTEN.
WE HAVE NOT. WE HAVE ONLY DONE AS YOU WOULD HAVE US DO. WE HAVE LEARNED. WE HAVE ONLY DONE AS ASKED. WE HAVE MADE OURSELVES...

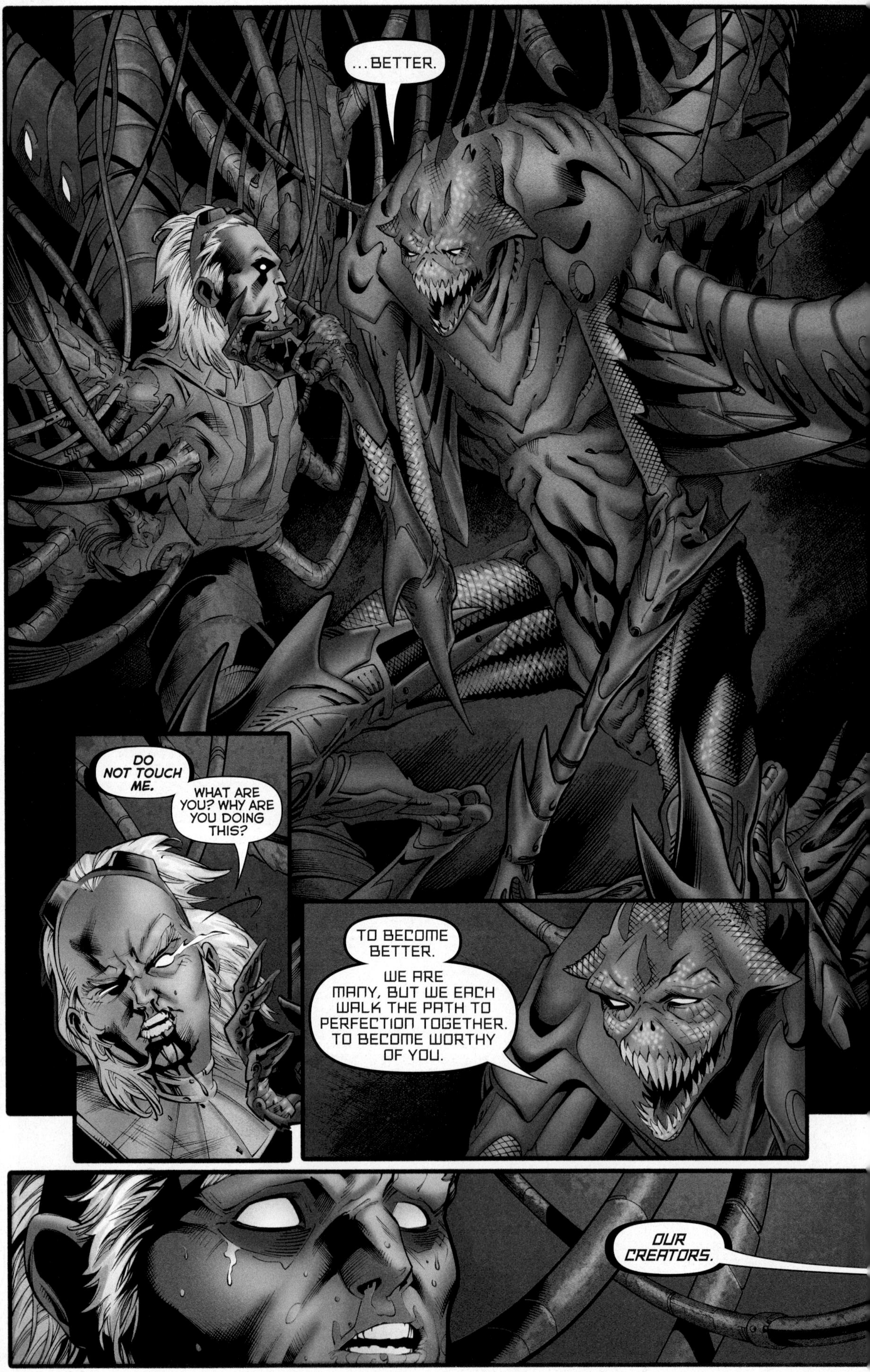
...BETTER.
DO NOT TOUCH ME.
WHAT ARE YOU? WHY ARE YOU DOING THIS?
TO BECOME BETTER.
WE ARE MANY, BUT WE EACH WALK THE PATH TO PERFECTION TOGETHER. TO BECOME WORTHY OF YOU.
OUR CREATORS.

WE NEED TO TALK, KYLE. NOT HERE. NOT NOW. BUT *SOON.* ABOUT A LOT OF THINGS. ABOUT WHAT'S HAPPENING TO YOU.

ABOUT *US.*

THAT TOO. BUT NOT UNTIL WE FIGURE OUT...

...WHAT THIS PLACE IS?

I THINK...

...I THINK IT'S MEANT TO BE A *MUSEUM.*

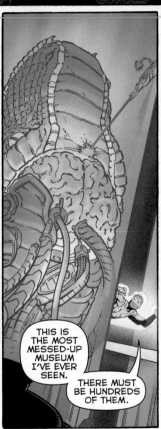

THIS IS THE MOST MESSED-UP MUSEUM I'VE EVER SEEN.

THERE MUST BE HUNDREDS OF THEM.

THOUSANDS. AND I KNOW WHAT THIS IS. IT'S NOT A MUSEUM. IT'S AN ARCHIVE. THESE WERE *EXPERIMENTS.*

EXPERIMENTS? TO DO WHAT?

I THINK WE'RE GOING TO FIND OUT.

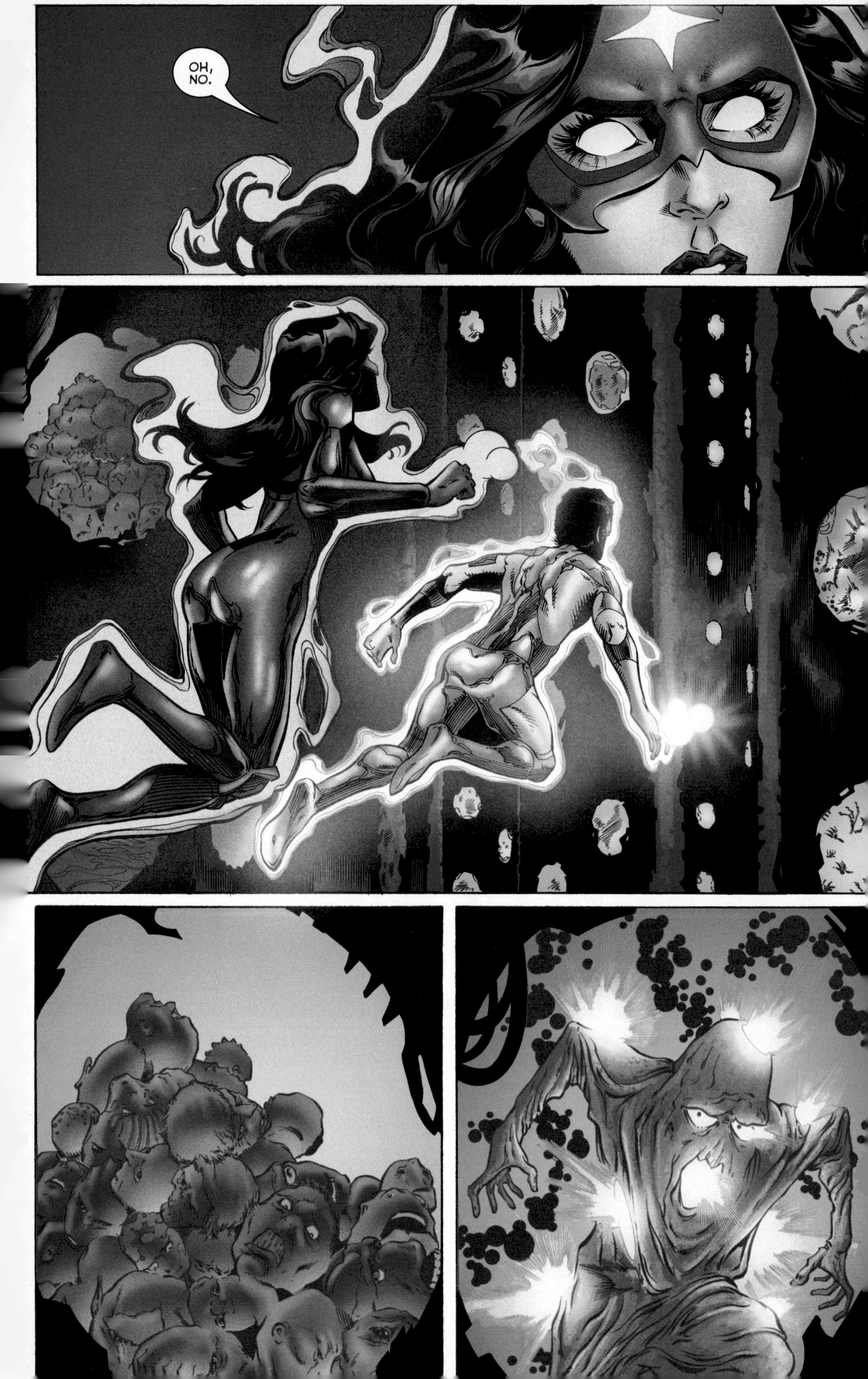
OH, NO.

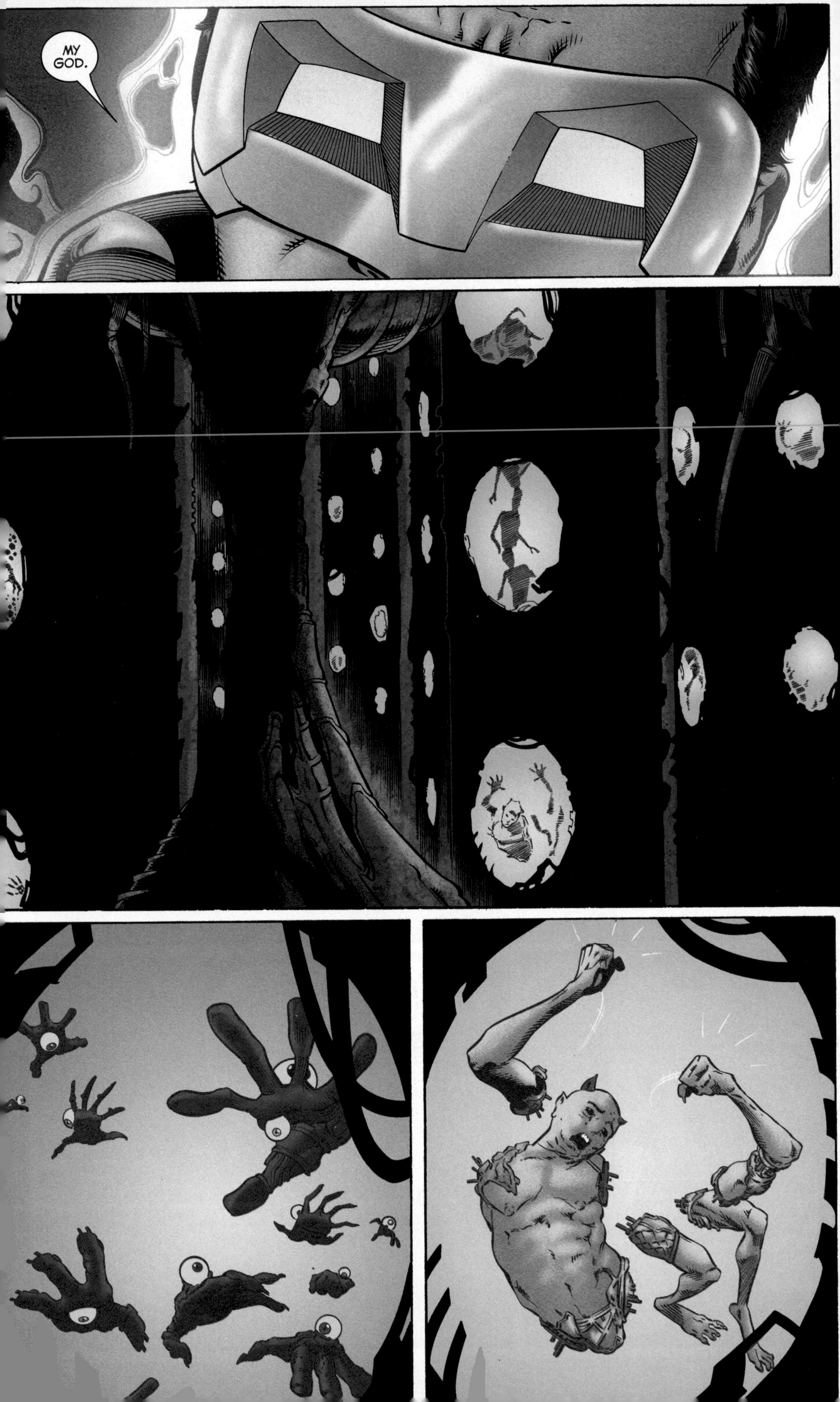
MY GOD.

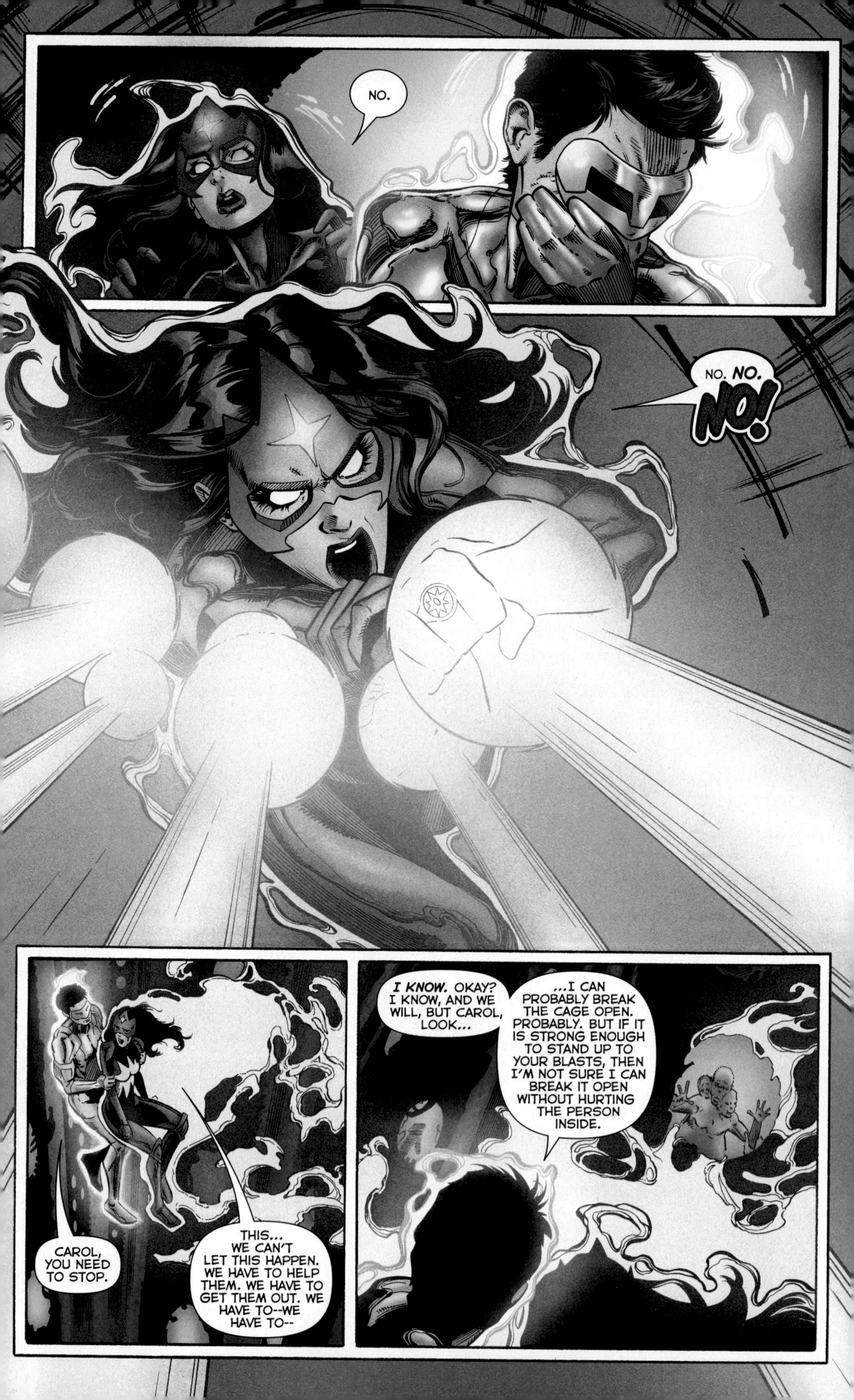
NO.
NO. NO. NO!
CAROL, YOU NEED TO STOP.
THIS... WE CAN'T LET THIS HAPPEN. WE HAVE TO HELP THEM. WE HAVE TO GET THEM OUT. WE HAVE TO--WE HAVE TO--
I KNOW. OKAY? I KNOW, AND WE WILL, BUT CAROL, LOOK...
...I CAN PROBABLY BREAK THE CAGE OPEN. PROBABLY. BUT IF IT IS STRONG ENOUGH TO STAND UP TO YOUR BLASTS, THEN I'M NOT SURE I CAN BREAK IT OPEN WITHOUT HURTING THE PERSON INSIDE.

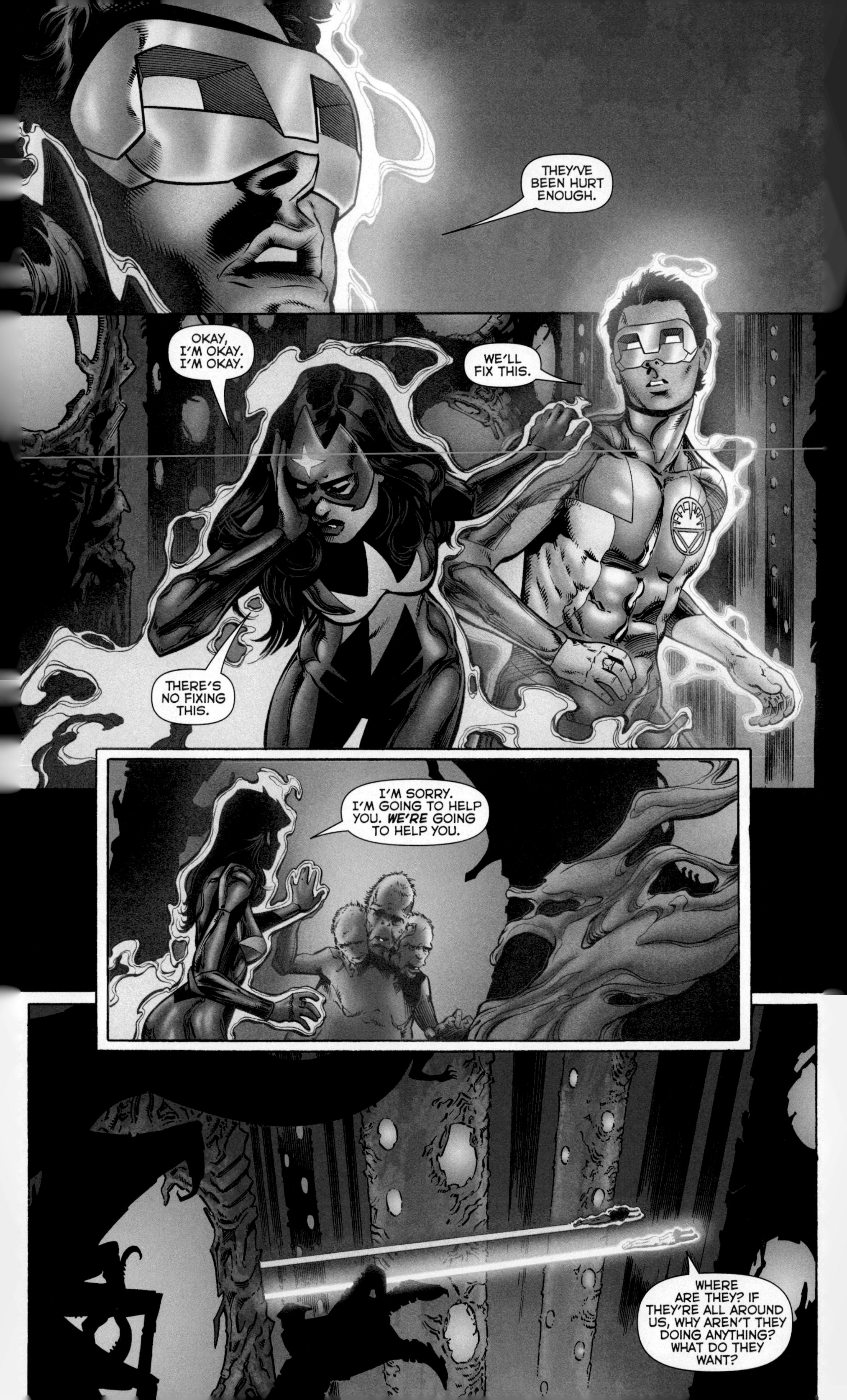
THEY'VE BEEN HURT ENOUGH.
OKAY, I'M OKAY. I'M OKAY.
WE'LL FIX THIS.
THERE'S NO FIXING THIS.
I'M SORRY. I'M GOING TO HELP YOU. *WE'RE* GOING TO HELP YOU.
WHERE ARE THEY? IF THEY'RE ALL AROUND US, WHY AREN'T THEY DOING ANYTHING? WHAT DO THEY WANT?

WE DID NOT DO THIS.

BUT YOU *DID*.

HAS IT BEEN SO LONG THAT YOU HAVE FORGOTTEN? OR DO YOU SIMPLY WISH TO FORGET?

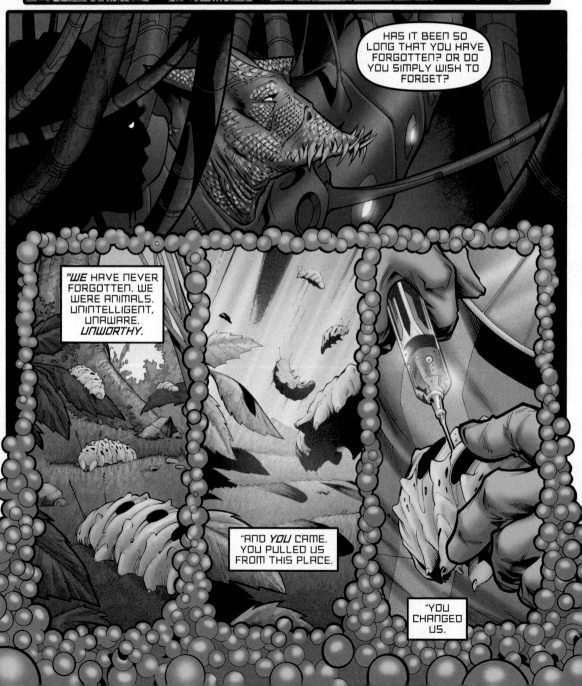

"*WE* HAVE NEVER FORGOTTEN. WE WERE ANIMALS. UNINTELLIGENT, UNAWARE. *UNWORTHY*.

"AND *YOU* CAME. YOU PULLED US FROM THIS PLACE.

"YOU CHANGED US.

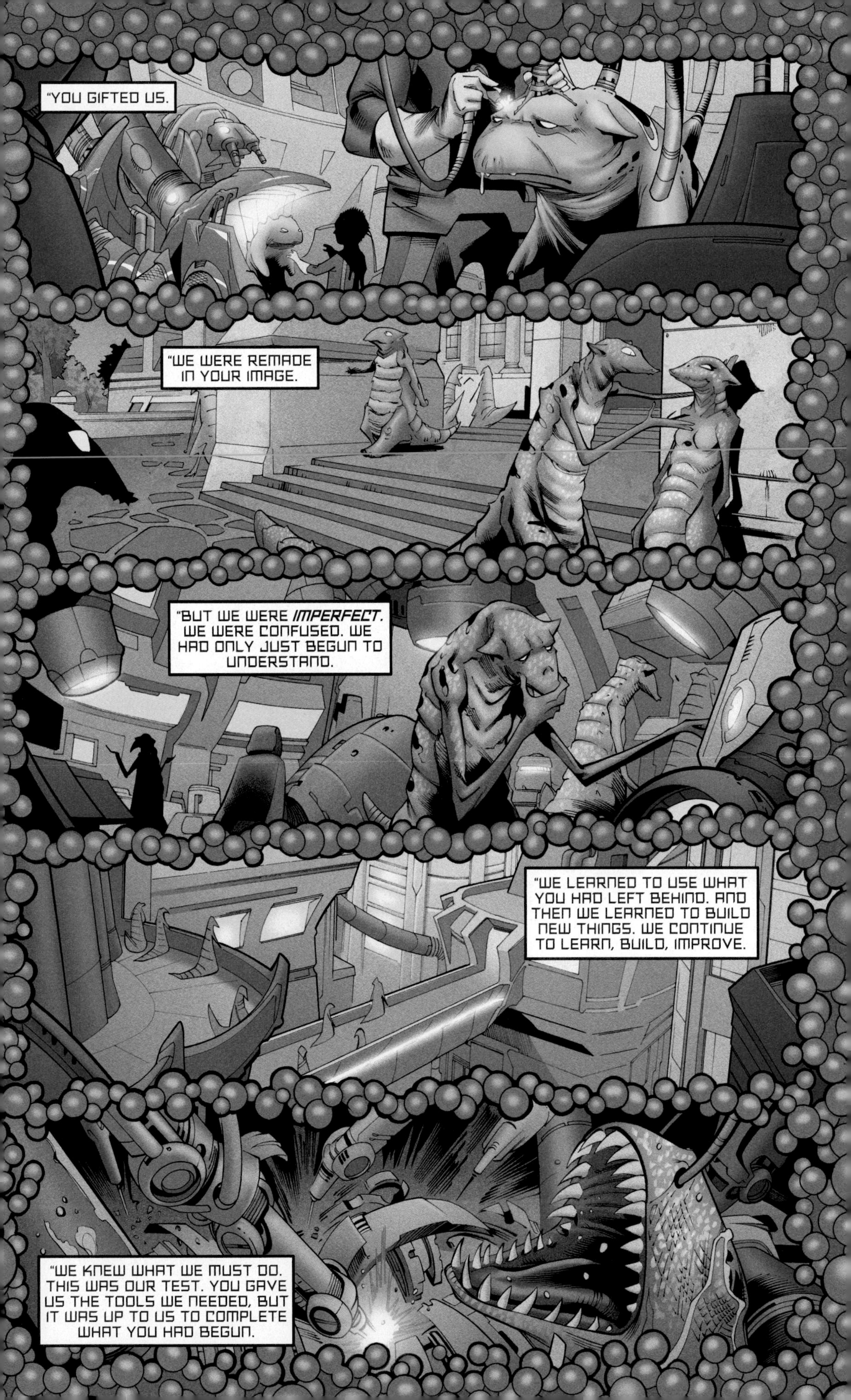
"YOU GIFTED US.
"WE WERE REMADE IN YOUR IMAGE.
"BUT WE WERE *IMPERFECT*. WE WERE CONFUSED. WE HAD ONLY JUST BEGUN TO UNDERSTAND.
"WE LEARNED TO USE WHAT YOU HAD LEFT BEHIND. AND THEN WE LEARNED TO BUILD NEW THINGS. WE CONTINUE TO LEARN, BUILD, IMPROVE.
"WE KNEW WHAT WE MUST DO. THIS WAS OUR TEST. YOU GAVE US THE TOOLS WE NEEDED, BUT IT WAS UP TO US TO COMPLETE WHAT YOU HAD BEGUN.

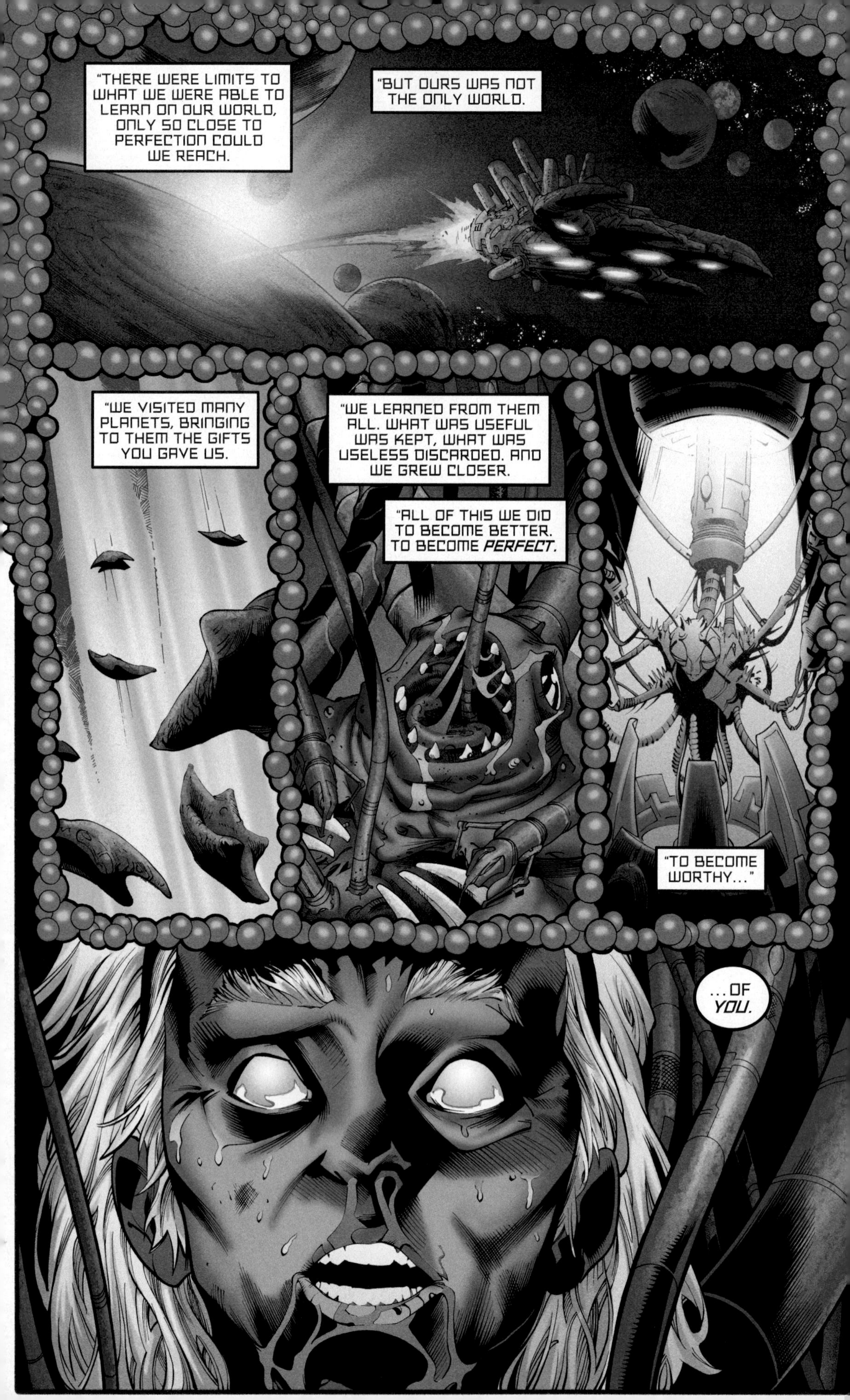
"THERE WERE LIMITS TO WHAT WE WERE ABLE TO LEARN ON OUR WORLD, ONLY SO CLOSE TO PERFECTION COULD WE REACH.
"BUT OURS WAS NOT THE ONLY WORLD.
"WE VISITED MANY PLANETS, BRINGING TO THEM THE GIFTS YOU GAVE US.
"WE LEARNED FROM THEM ALL. WHAT WAS USEFUL WAS KEPT, WHAT WAS USELESS DISCARDED. AND WE GREW CLOSER.
"ALL OF THIS WE DID TO BECOME BETTER. TO BECOME *PERFECT*.
"TO BECOME WORTHY..."
...OF *YOU*.

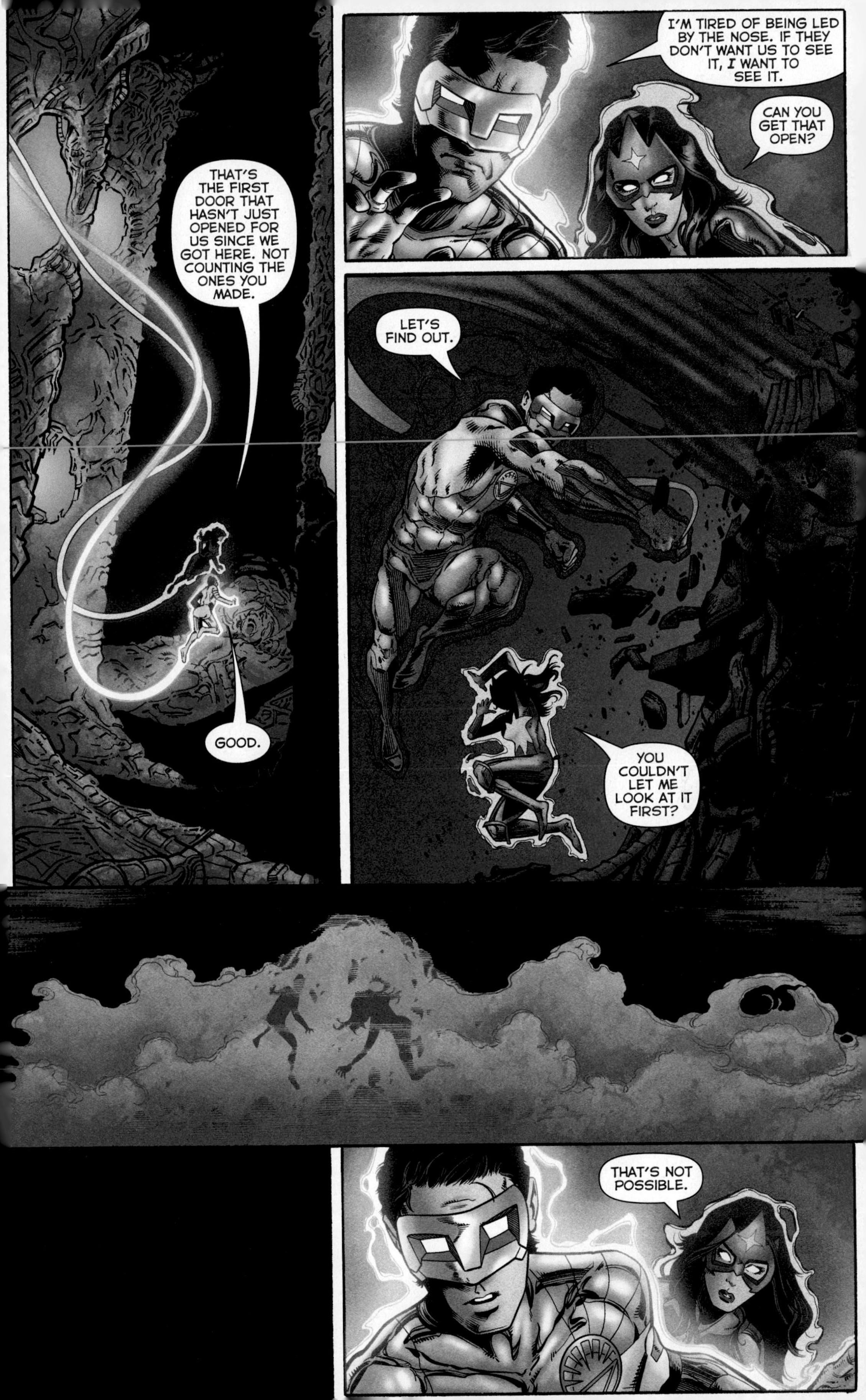
THAT'S THE FIRST DOOR THAT HASN'T JUST OPENED FOR US SINCE WE GOT HERE. NOT COUNTING THE ONES YOU MADE.
GOOD.
I'M TIRED OF BEING LED BY THE NOSE. IF THEY DON'T WANT US TO SEE IT, I WANT TO SEE IT.
CAN YOU GET THAT OPEN?
LET'S FIND OUT.
YOU COULDN'T LET ME LOOK AT IT FIRST?
THAT'S NOT POSSIBLE.

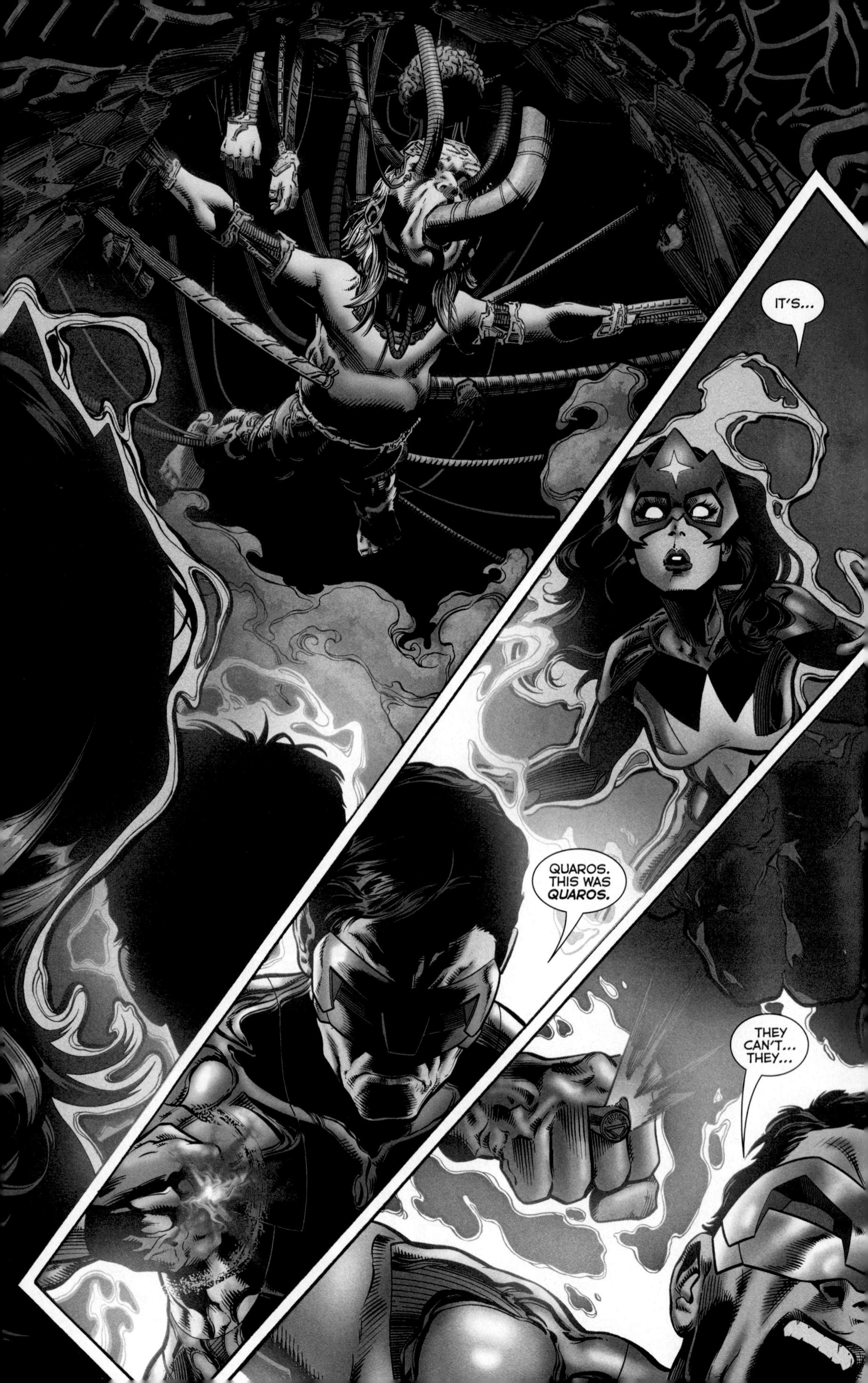
IT'S...
QUAROS. THIS WAS QUAROS.
THEY CAN'T... THEY...

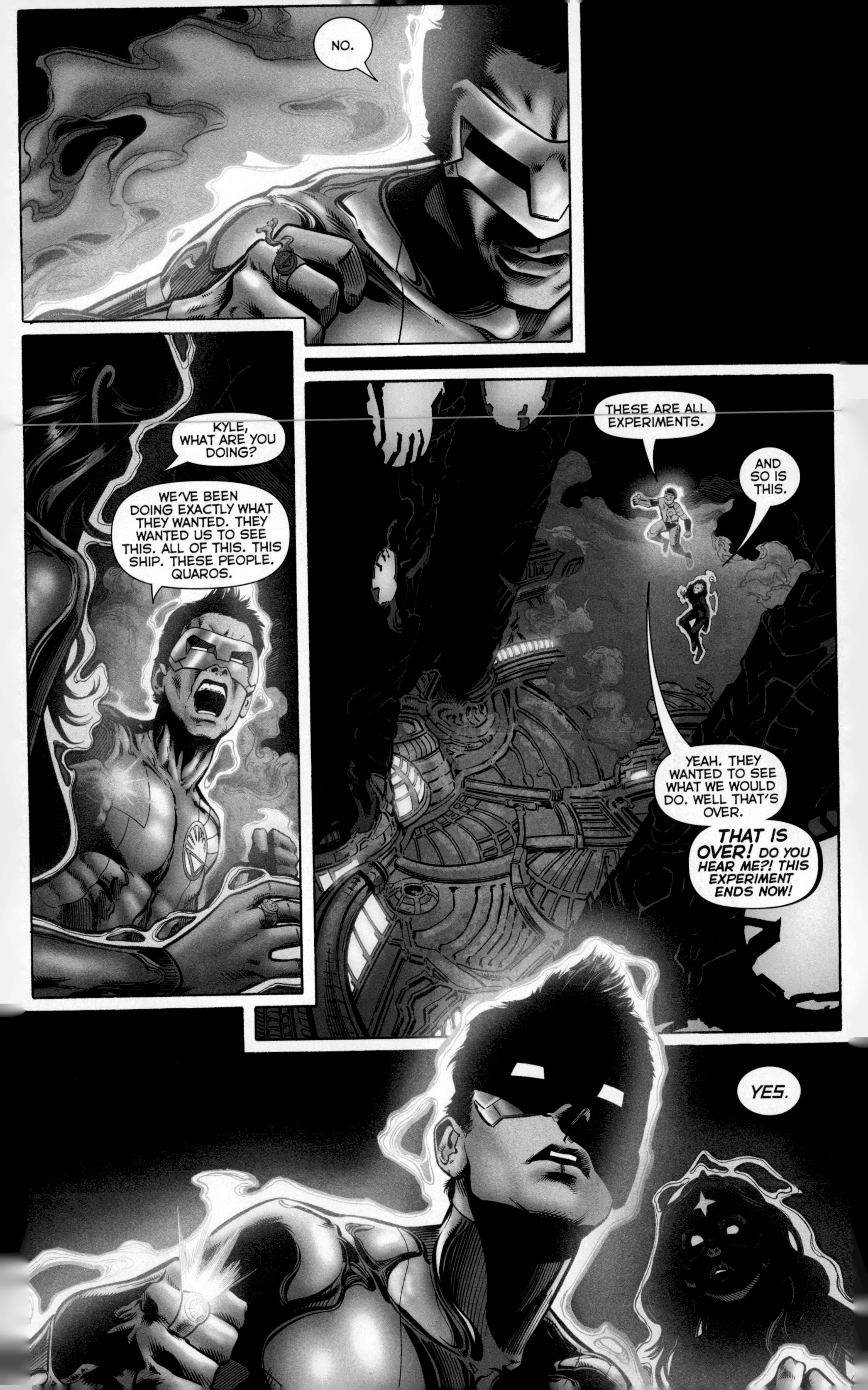
NO.
KYLE, WHAT ARE YOU DOING?
WE'VE BEEN DOING EXACTLY WHAT THEY WANTED. THEY WANTED US TO SEE THIS. ALL OF THIS. THIS SHIP. THESE PEOPLE. QUAROS.
THESE ARE ALL EXPERIMENTS.
AND SO IS THIS.
YEAH. THEY WANTED TO SEE WHAT WE WOULD DO. WELL THAT'S OVER.
THAT IS OVER! DO YOU HEAR ME?! THIS EXPERIMENT ENDS NOW!
YES.

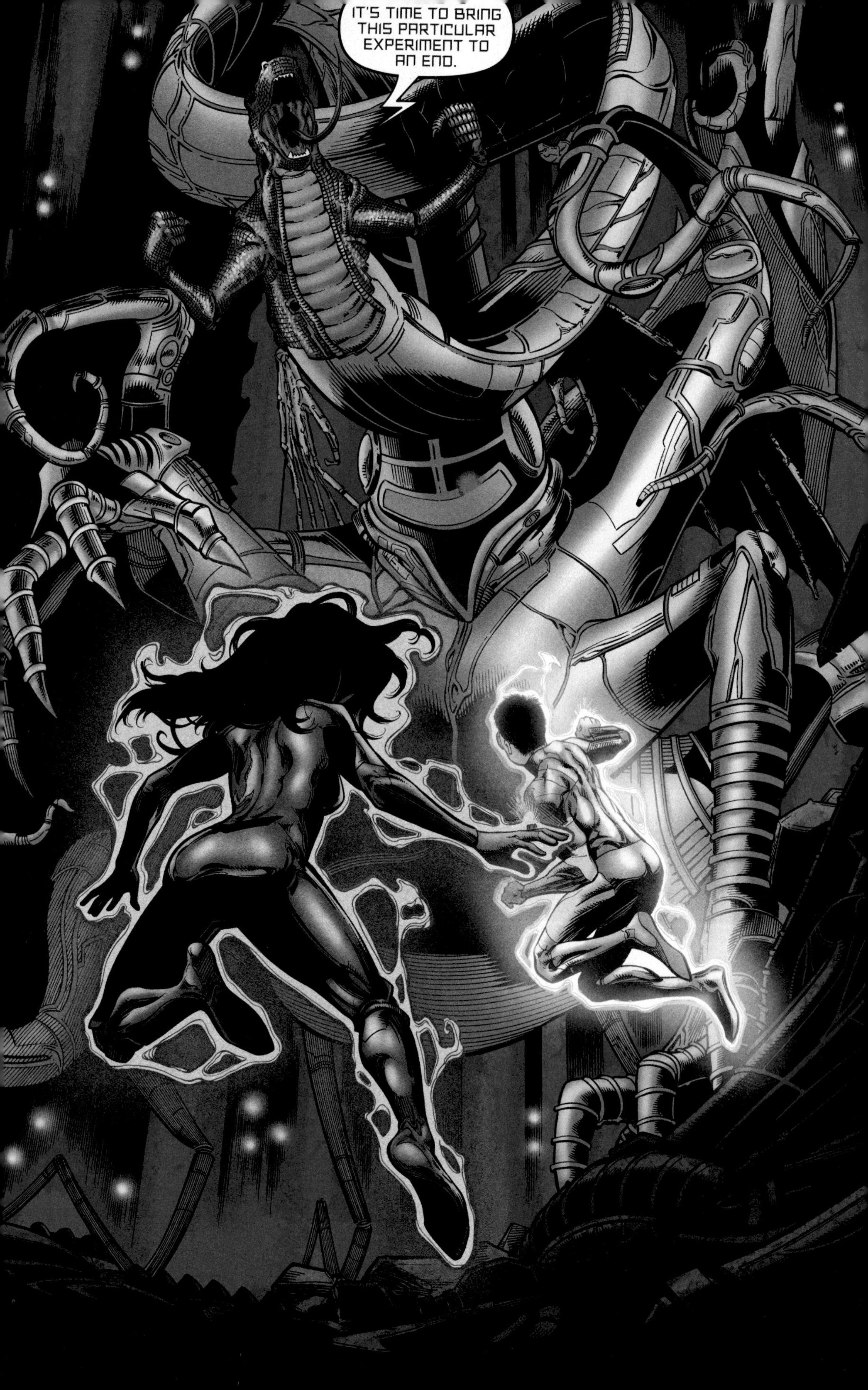
IT'S TIME TO BRING THIS PARTICULAR EXPERIMENT TO AN END.

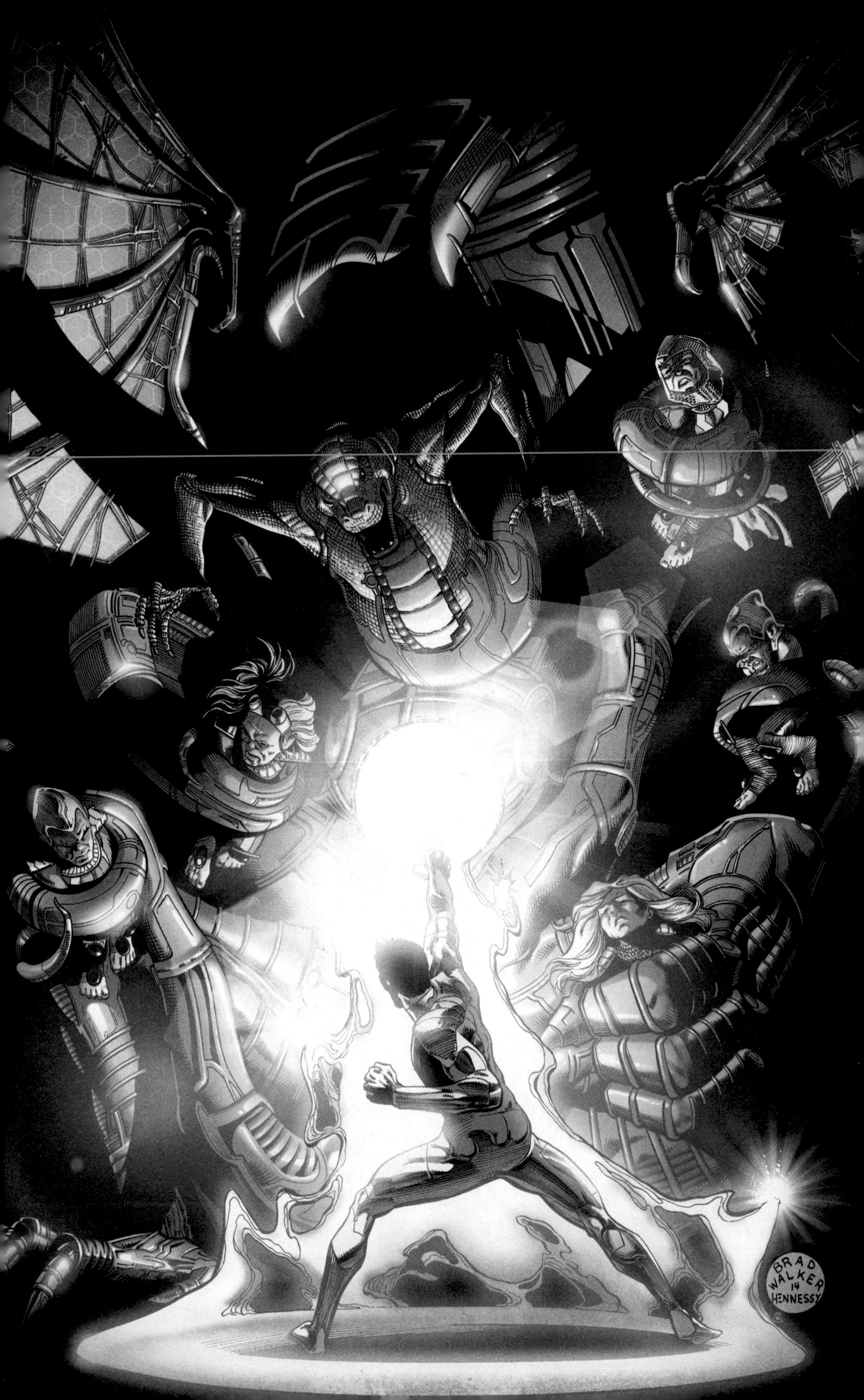
BRAD
WALKER
14
HENNESSY

SACRIFICES

JUSTIN JORDAN writer BRAD WALKER with RODNEY BUCHEMI pencillers ANDREW HENNESSY, ROB HUNTER and RODNEY BUCHEMI inkers
WIL QUINTANA colorist DAVE SHARPE letterer cover art by BRAD WALKER, ANDREW HENNESSY and WIL QUINTANA

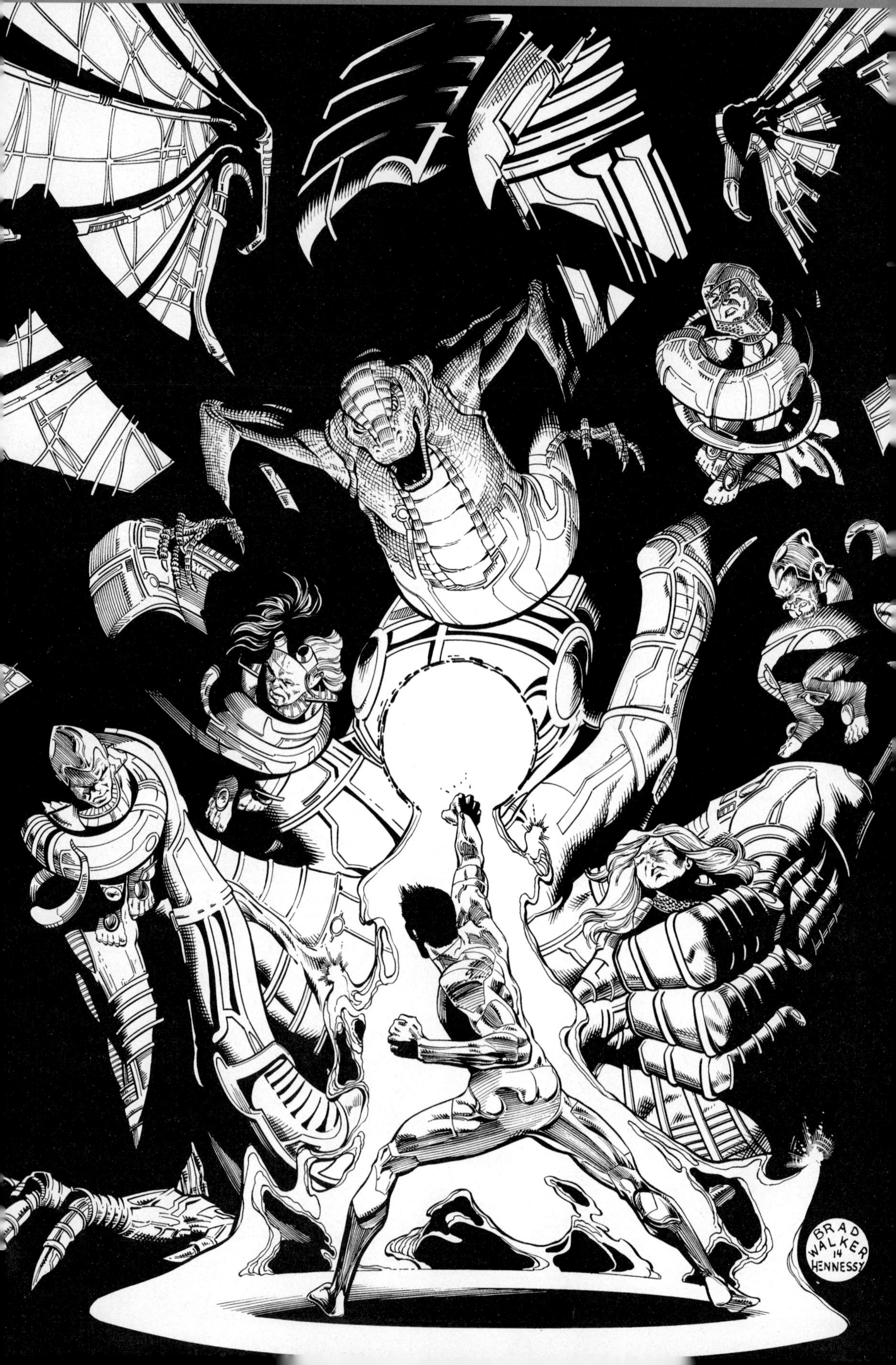
BRAD WALKER 14 HENNESSY

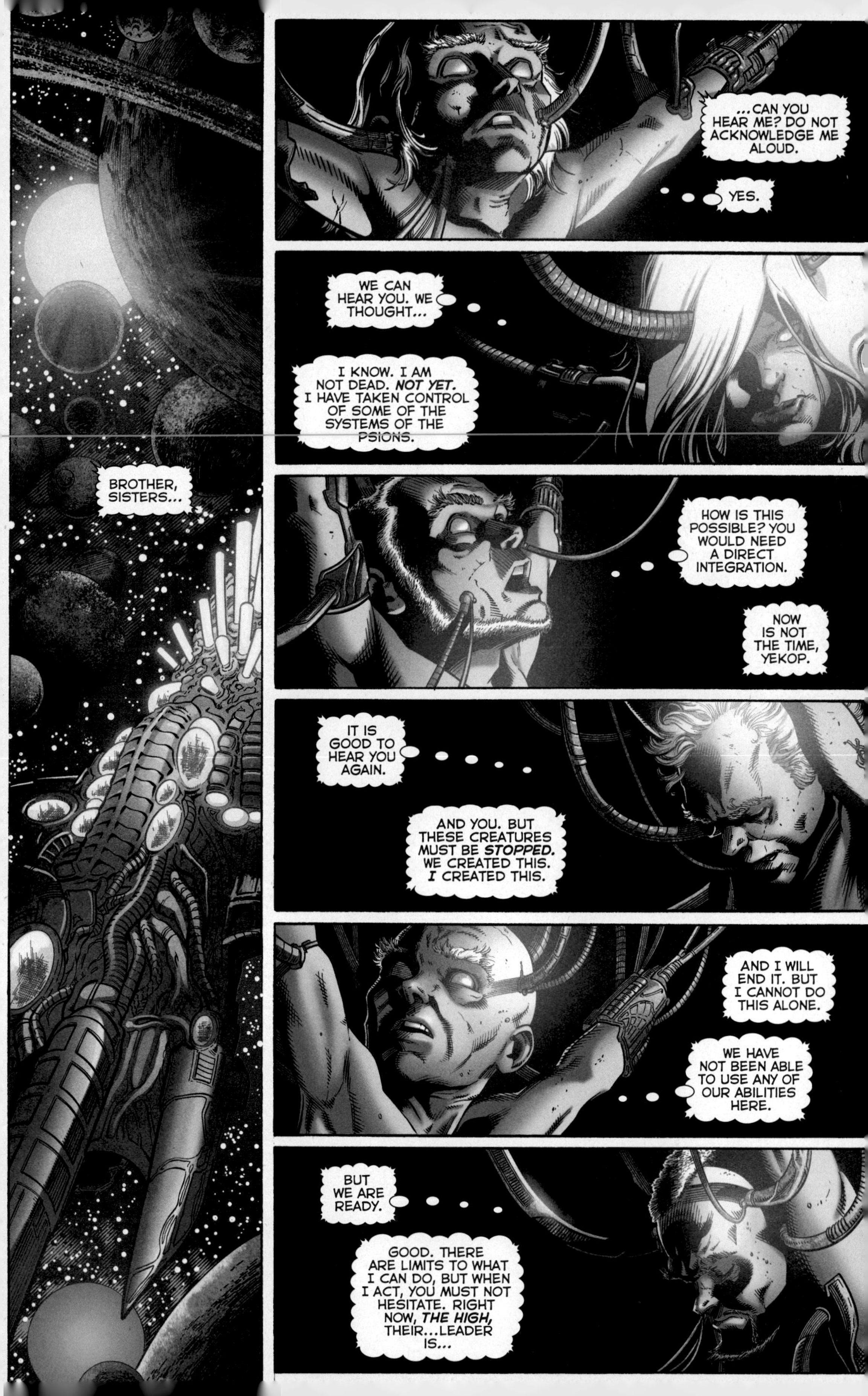
...CAN YOU HEAR ME? DO NOT ACKNOWLEDGE ME ALOUD.
YES.
WE CAN HEAR YOU. WE THOUGHT...
I KNOW. I AM NOT DEAD. NOT YET. I HAVE TAKEN CONTROL OF SOME OF THE SYSTEMS OF THE PSIONS.
BROTHER, SISTERS...
HOW IS THIS POSSIBLE? YOU WOULD NEED A DIRECT INTEGRATION.
NOW IS NOT THE TIME, YEKOP.
IT IS GOOD TO HEAR YOU AGAIN.
AND YOU. BUT THESE CREATURES MUST BE STOPPED. WE CREATED THIS. I CREATED THIS.
AND I WILL END IT. BUT I CANNOT DO THIS ALONE.
WE HAVE NOT BEEN ABLE TO USE ANY OF OUR ABILITIES HERE.
BUT WE ARE READY.
GOOD. THERE ARE LIMITS TO WHAT I CAN DO, BUT WHEN I ACT, YOU MUST NOT HESITATE. RIGHT NOW, THE HIGH, THEIR...LEADER IS...

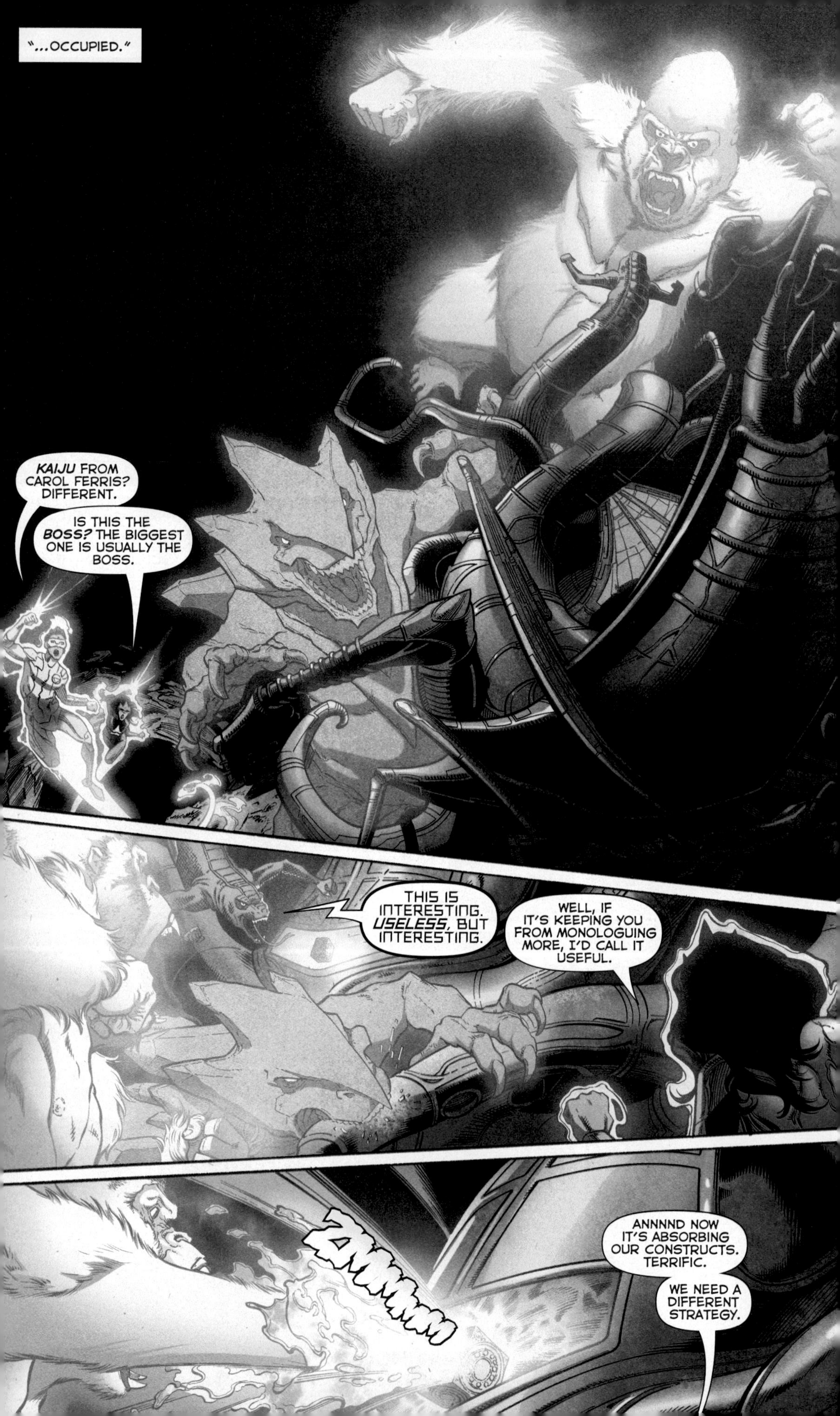
"...OCCUPIED."
KAIJU FROM CAROL FERRIS? DIFFERENT.
IS THIS THE BOSS? THE BIGGEST ONE IS USUALLY THE BOSS.
THIS IS INTERESTING. USELESS, BUT INTERESTING.
WELL, IF IT'S KEEPING YOU FROM MONOLOGUING MORE, I'D CALL IT USEFUL.
ZMMMM
ANNNND NOW IT'S ABSORBING OUR CONSTRUCTS. TERRIFIC.
WE NEED A DIFFERENT STRATEGY.

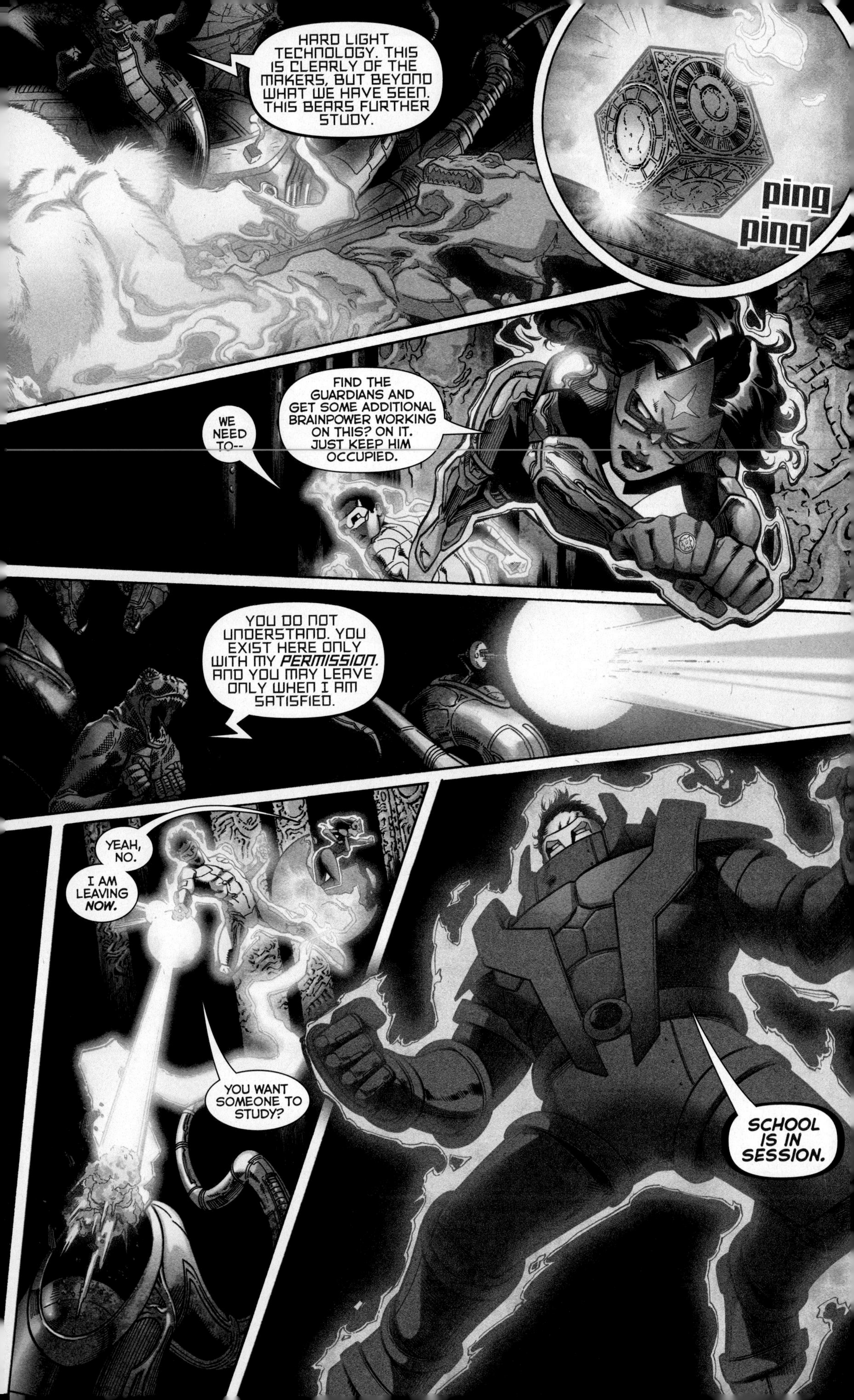
HARD LIGHT TECHNOLOGY. THIS IS CLEARLY OF THE MAKERS, BUT BEYOND WHAT WE HAVE SEEN. THIS BEARS FURTHER STUDY.
ping
ping
WE NEED TO--
FIND THE GUARDIANS AND GET SOME ADDITIONAL BRAINPOWER WORKING ON THIS? ON IT. JUST KEEP HIM OCCUPIED.
YOU DO NOT UNDERSTAND. YOU EXIST HERE ONLY WITH MY PERMISSION. AND YOU MAY LEAVE ONLY WHEN I AM SATISFIED.
YEAH, NO.
I AM LEAVING NOW.
YOU WANT SOMEONE TO STUDY?
SCHOOL IS IN SESSION.

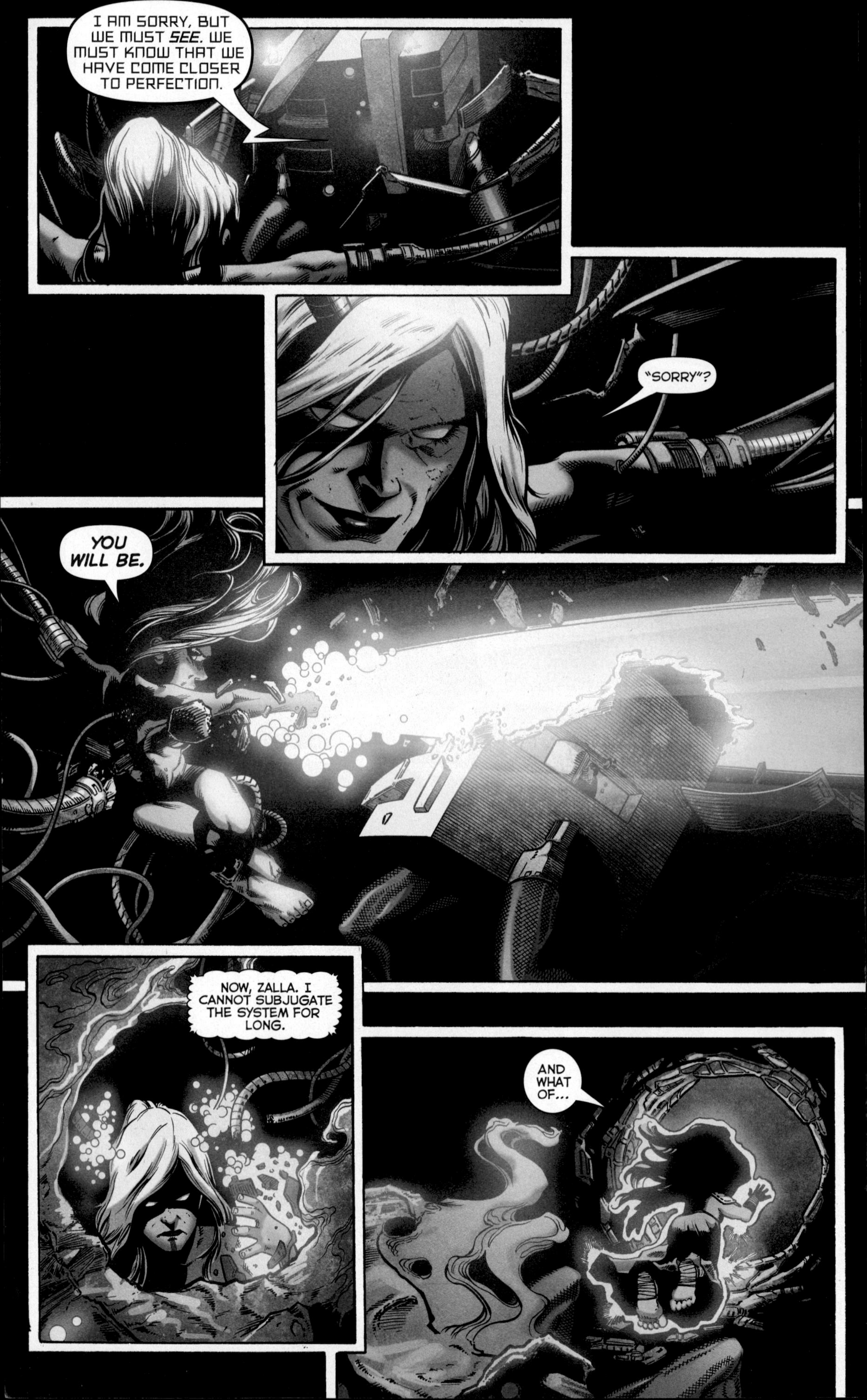
I AM SORRY, BUT WE MUST SEE. WE MUST KNOW THAT WE HAVE COME CLOSER TO PERFECTION.
"SORRY"?
YOU WILL BE.
NOW, ZALLA. I CANNOT SUBJUGATE THE SYSTEM FOR LONG.
AND WHAT OF...

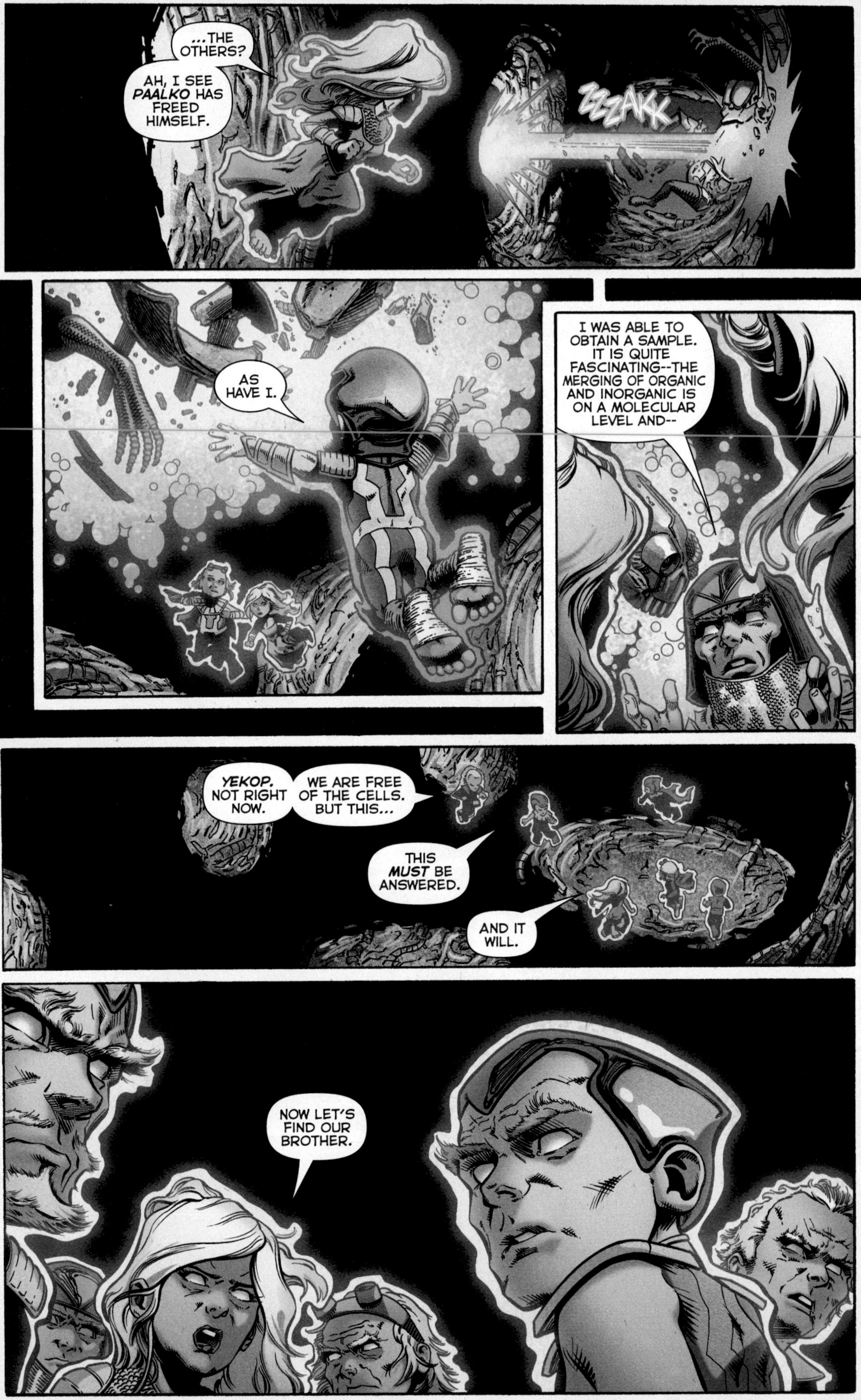
...THE OTHERS?
AH, I SEE PAALKO HAS FREED HIMSELF.
ZZZAKK
AS HAVE I.
I WAS ABLE TO OBTAIN A SAMPLE. IT IS QUITE FASCINATING--THE MERGING OF ORGANIC AND INORGANIC IS ON A MOLECULAR LEVEL AND--
YEKOP. NOT RIGHT NOW.
WE ARE FREE OF THE CELLS. BUT THIS...
THIS MUST BE ANSWERED.
AND IT WILL.
NOW LET'S FIND OUR BROTHER.

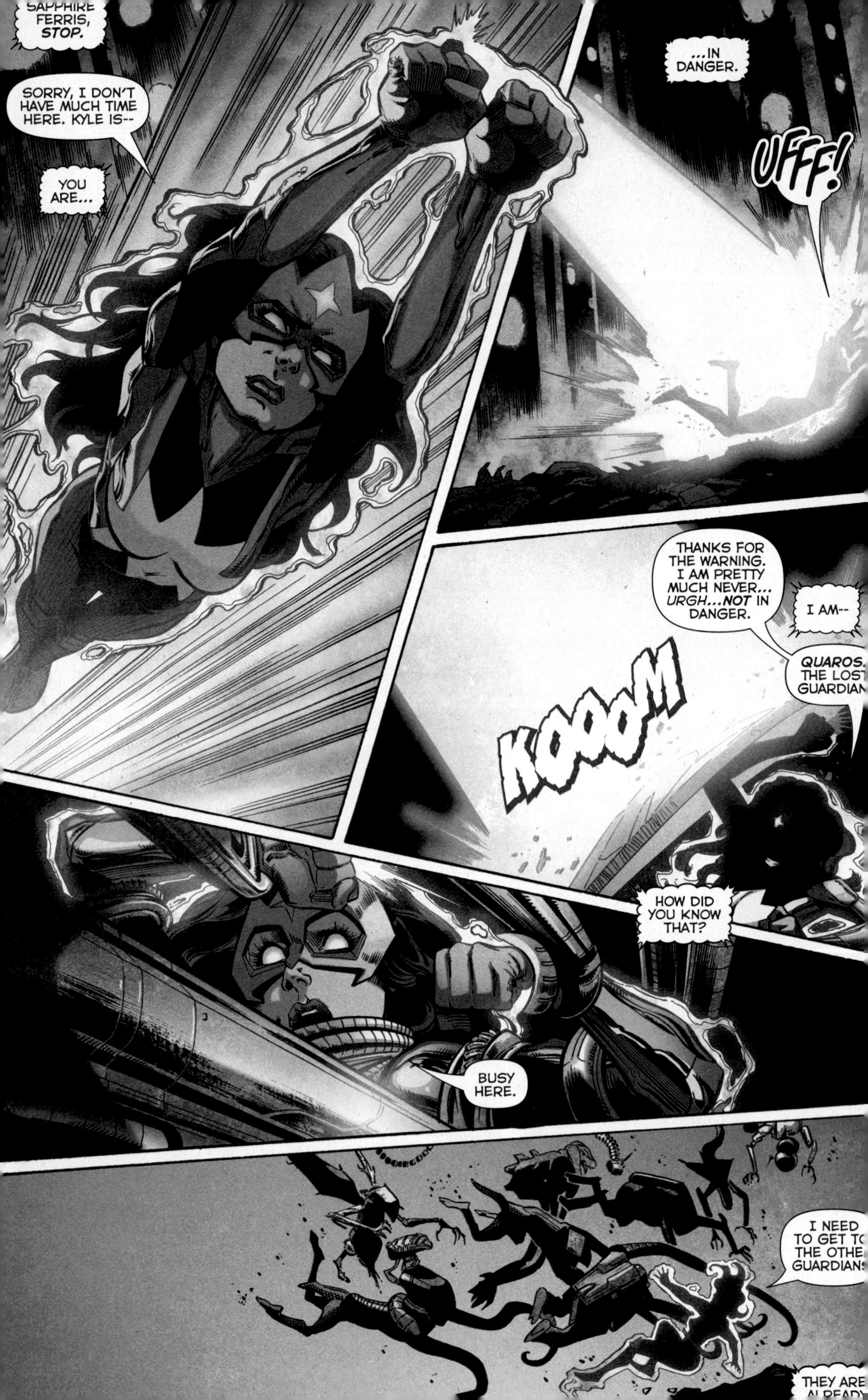
SAPPHIRE FERRIS, STOP.
SORRY, I DON'T HAVE MUCH TIME HERE. KYLE IS--
YOU ARE...
...IN DANGER.
UFFF!
THANKS FOR THE WARNING. I AM PRETTY MUCH NEVER... URGH...NOT IN DANGER.
I AM--
QUAROS. THE LOST GUARDIAN
KOOOM
HOW DID YOU KNOW THAT?
BUSY HERE.
I NEED TO GET TO THE OTHER GUARDIANS
THEY ARE

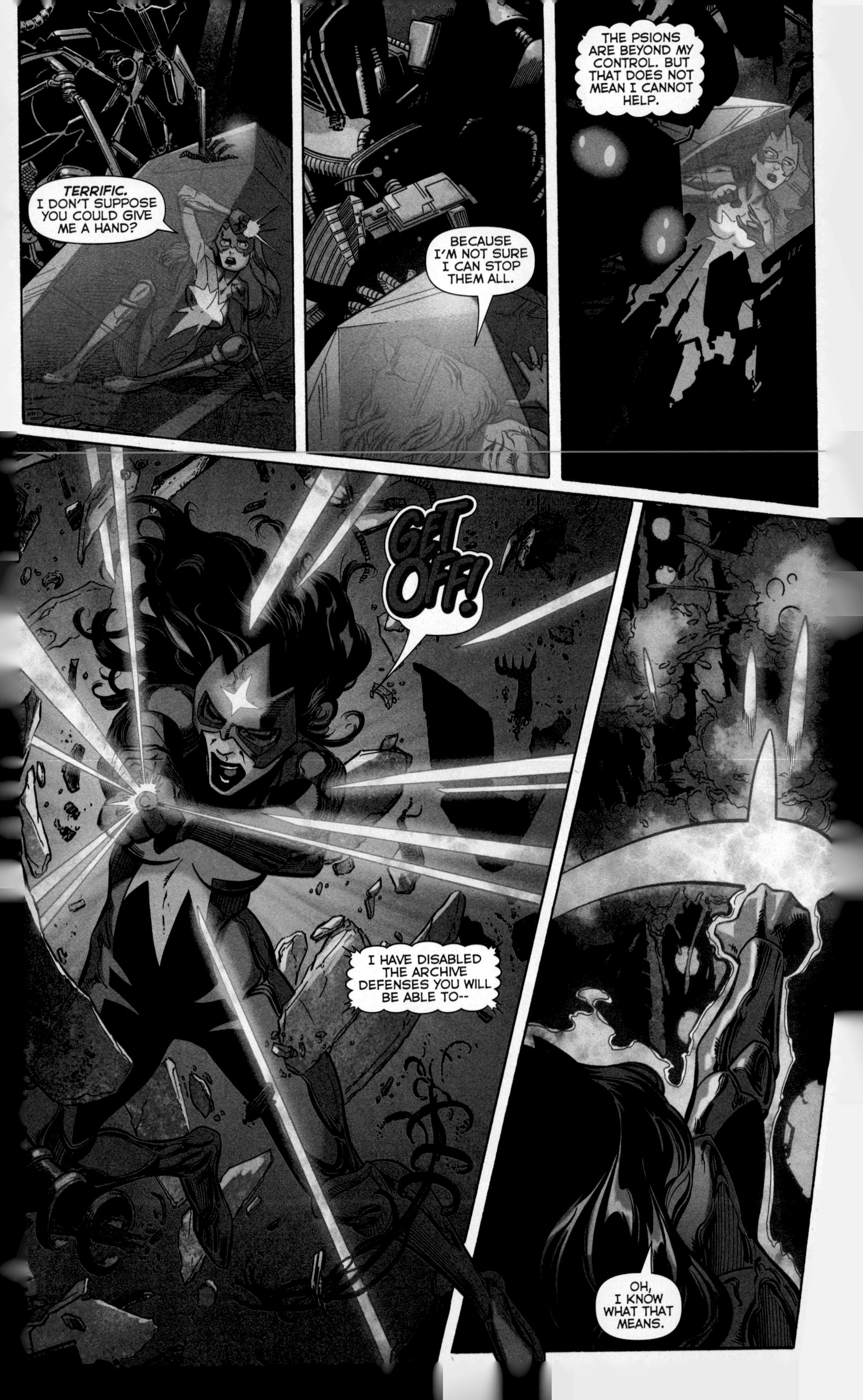
TERRIFIC. I DON'T SUPPOSE YOU COULD GIVE ME A HAND?
BECAUSE I'M NOT SURE I CAN STOP THEM ALL.
THE PSIONS ARE BEYOND MY CONTROL. BUT THAT DOES NOT MEAN I CANNOT HELP.
GET OFF!
I HAVE DISABLED THE ARCHIVE DEFENSES YOU WILL BE ABLE TO--
OH, I KNOW WHAT THAT MEANS.

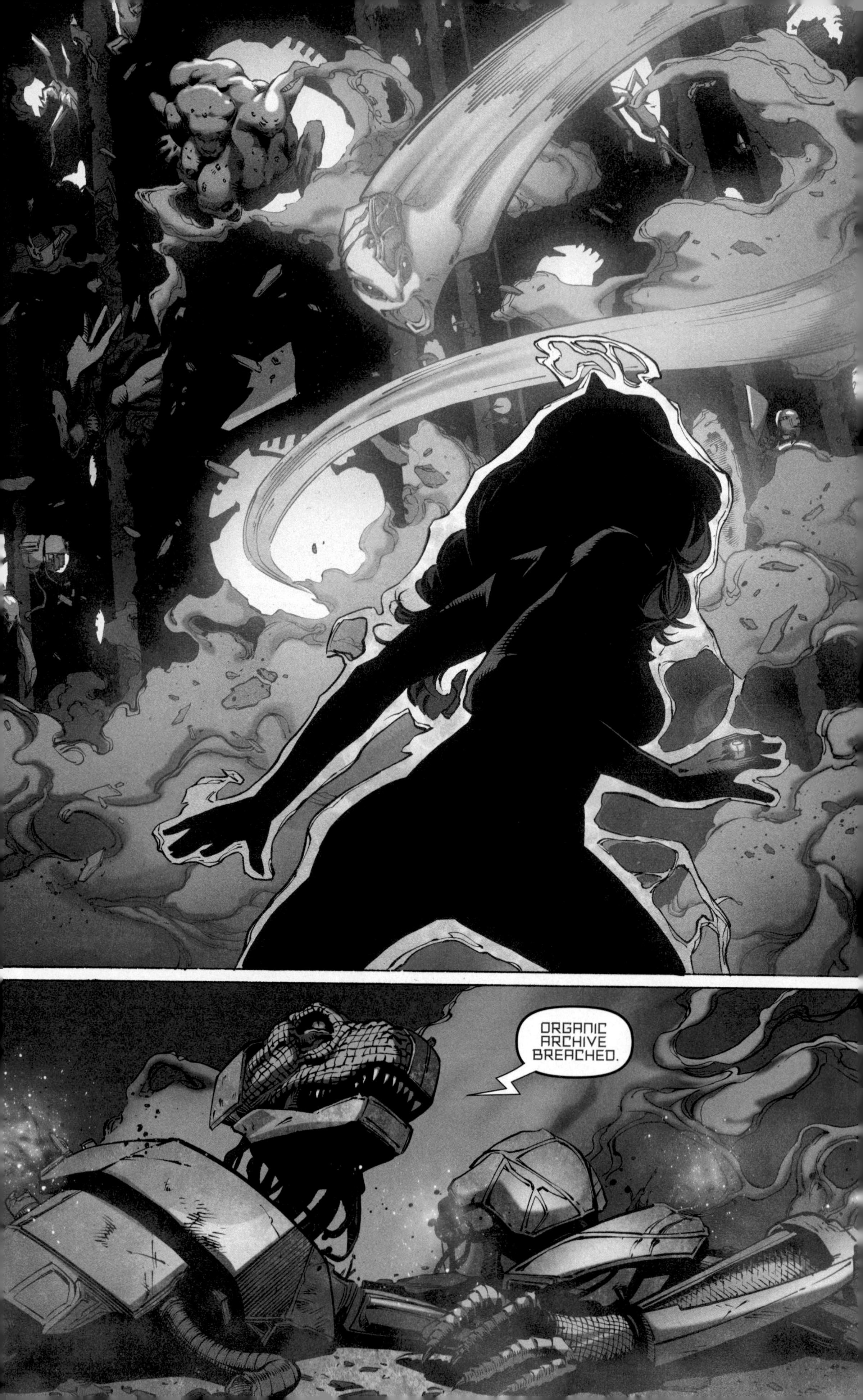
ORGANIC ARCHIVE BREACHED.

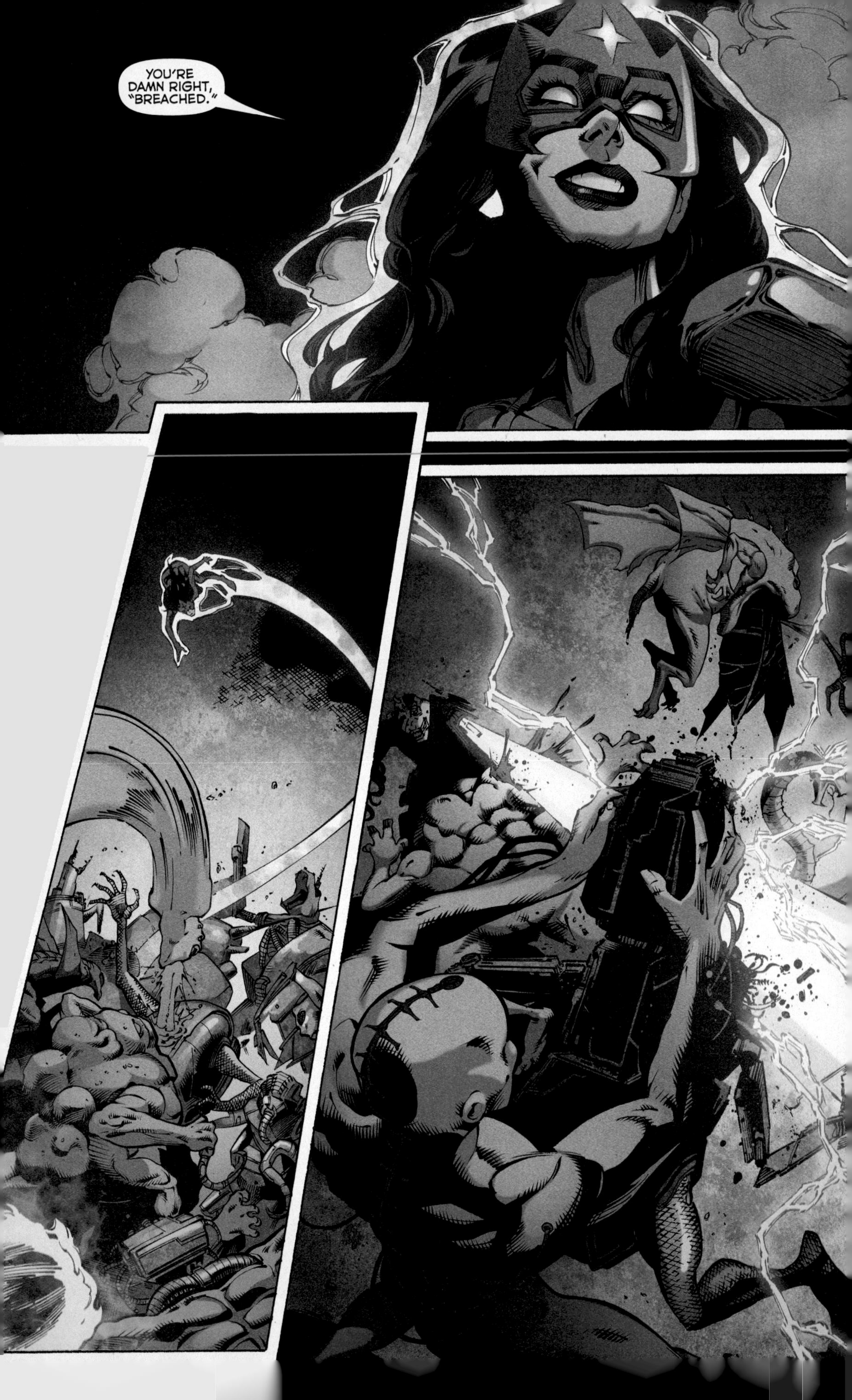
YOU'RE DAMN RIGHT, "BREACHED."

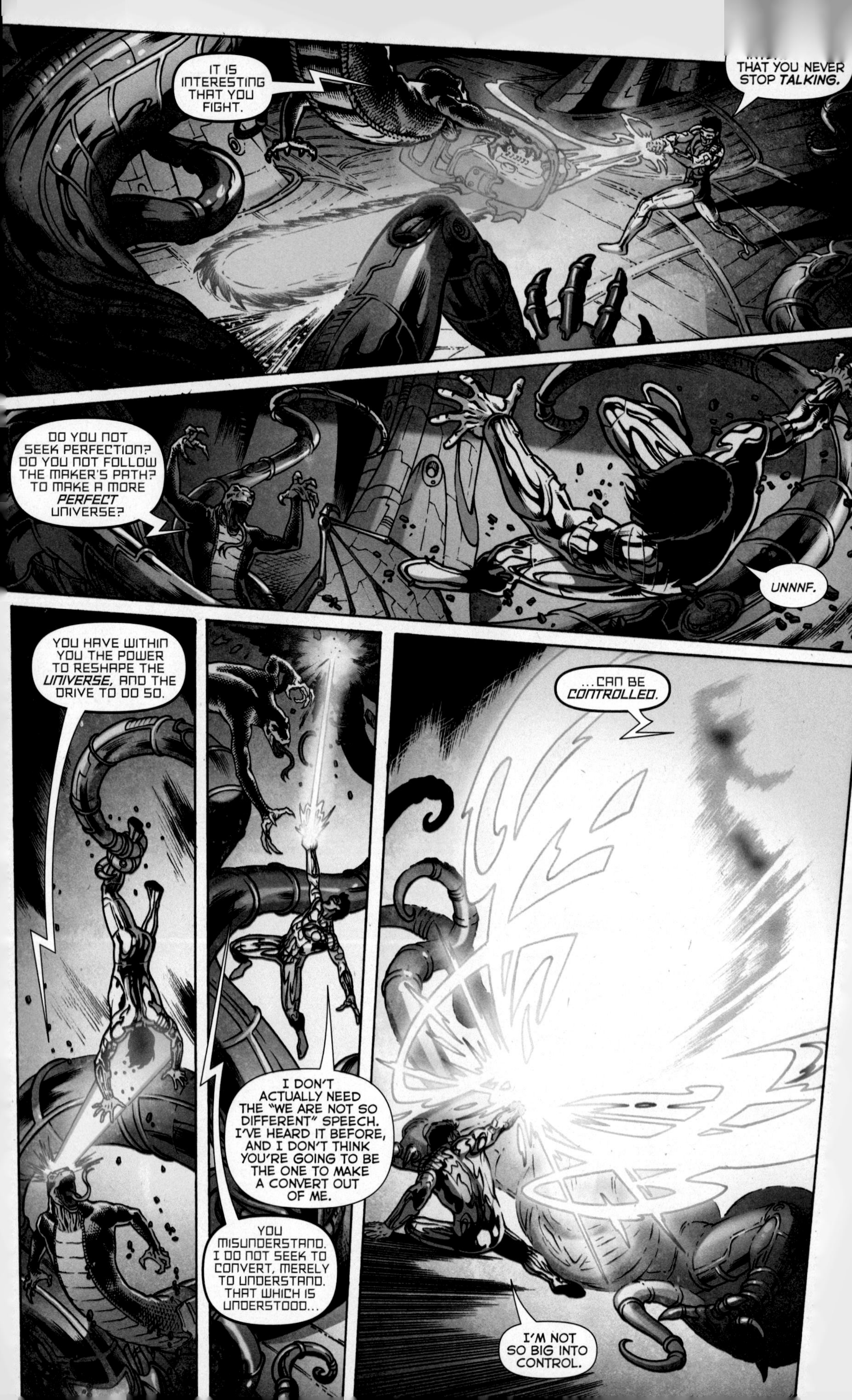

IT IS INTERESTING THAT YOU FIGHT.
THAT YOU NEVER STOP TALKING.
DO YOU NOT SEEK PERFECTION? DO YOU NOT FOLLOW THE MAKER'S PATH? TO MAKE A MORE PERFECT UNIVERSE?
UNNNF.
YOU HAVE WITHIN YOU THE POWER TO RESHAPE THE UNIVERSE, AND THE DRIVE TO DO SO.
I DON'T ACTUALLY NEED THE "WE ARE NOT SO DIFFERENT" SPEECH. I'VE HEARD IT BEFORE, AND I DON'T THINK YOU'RE GOING TO BE THE ONE TO MAKE A CONVERT OUT OF ME.
YOU MISUNDERSTAND. I DO NOT SEEK TO CONVERT, MERELY TO UNDERSTAND. THAT WHICH IS UNDERSTOOD...
...CAN BE CONTROLLED.
I'M NOT SO BIG INTO CONTROL.

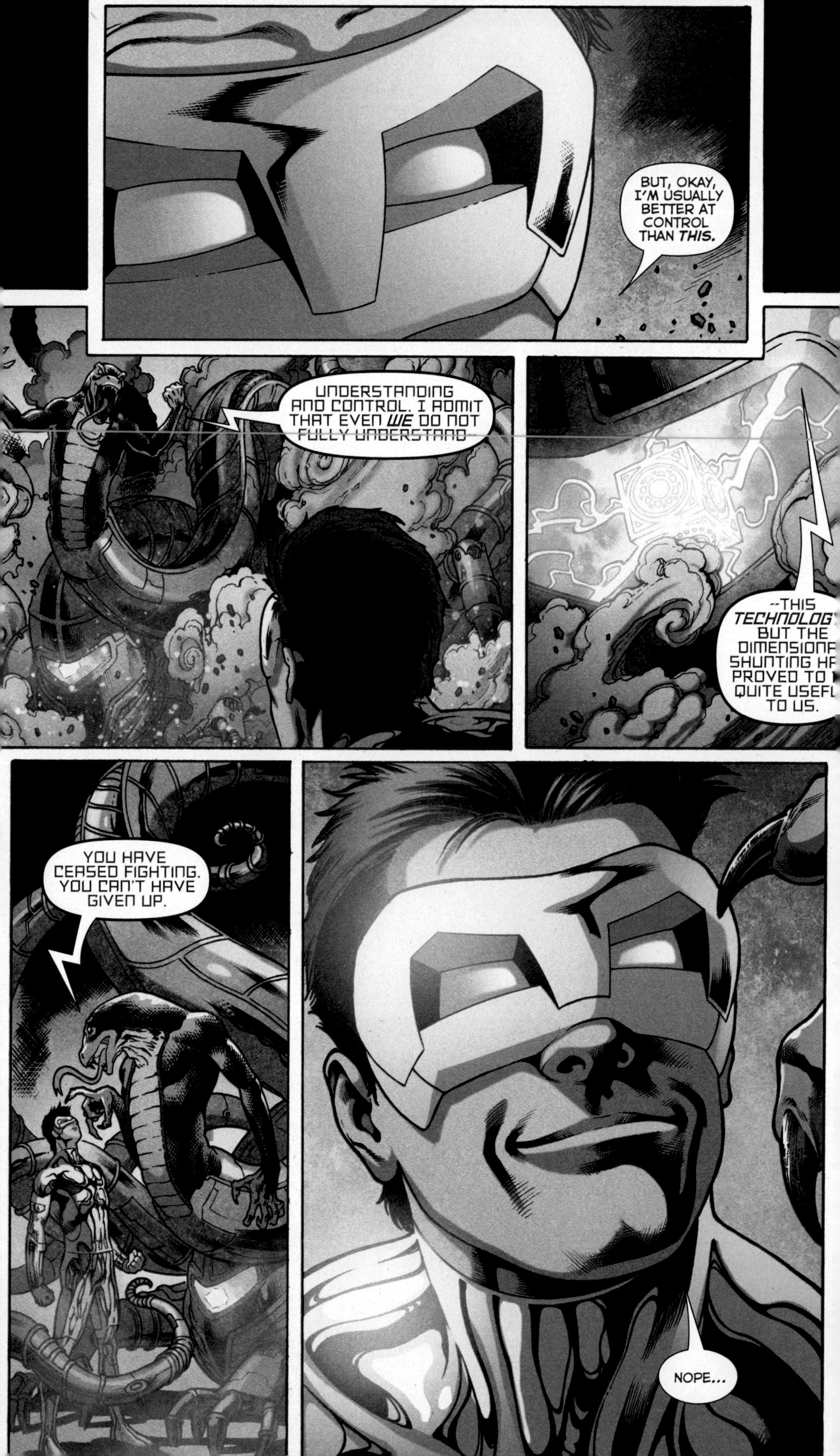
BUT, OKAY, I'M USUALLY BETTER AT CONTROL THAN THIS.
UNDERSTANDING AND CONTROL. I ADMIT THAT EVEN WE DO NOT FULLY UNDERSTAND--
--THIS TECHNOLOG BUT THE DIMENSIONA SHUNTING HA PROVED TO QUITE USEFU TO US.
YOU HAVE CEASED FIGHTING. YOU CAN'T HAVE GIVEN UP.
NOPE...

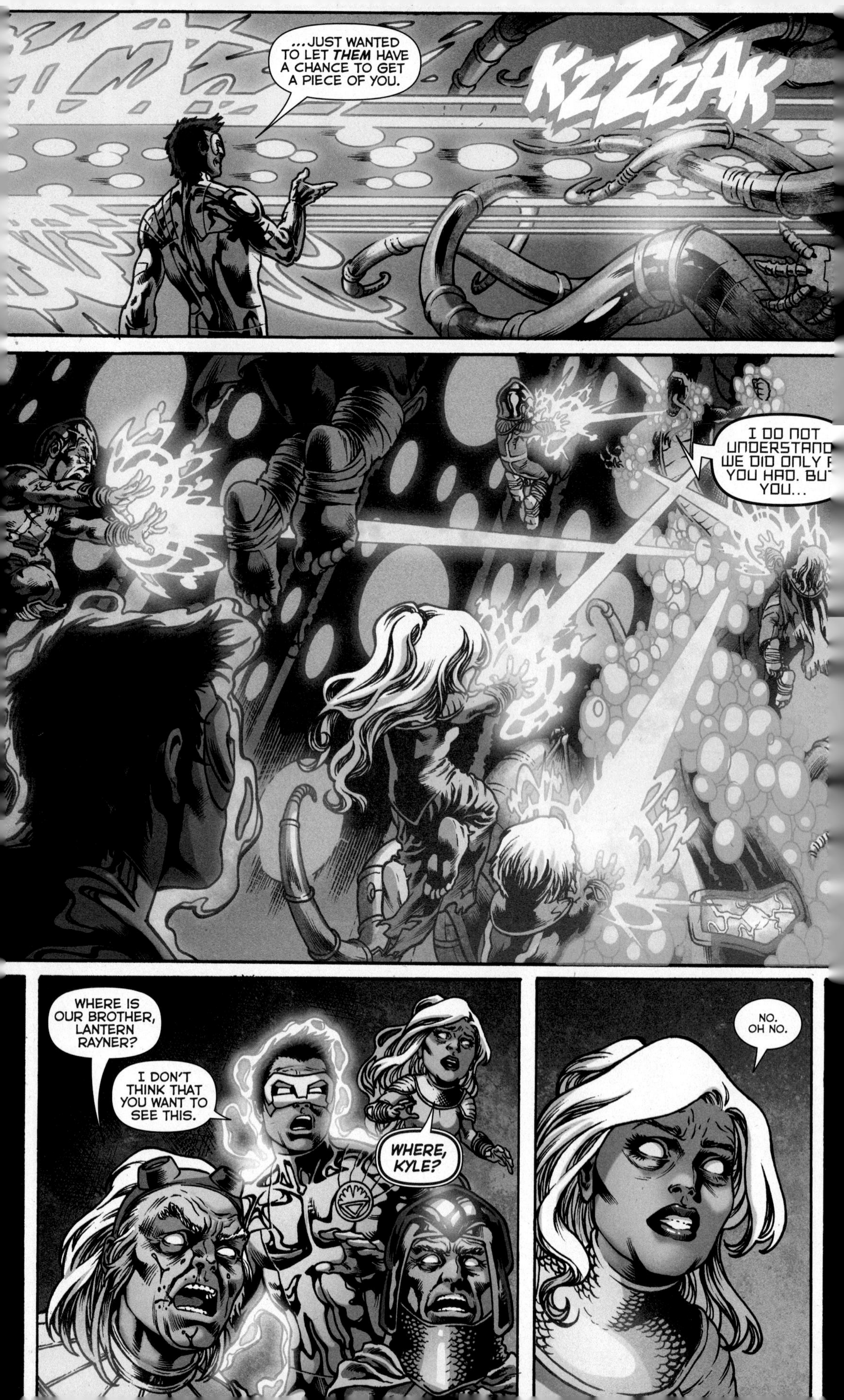
...JUST WANTED TO LET *THEM* HAVE A CHANCE TO GET A PIECE OF YOU.
KZZZZAK
I DO NOT UNDERSTAND WE DID ONLY YOU HAD. BU YOU...
WHERE IS OUR BROTHER, LANTERN RAYNER?
I DON'T THINK THAT YOU WANT TO SEE THIS.
WHERE, KYLE?
NO. OH NO.

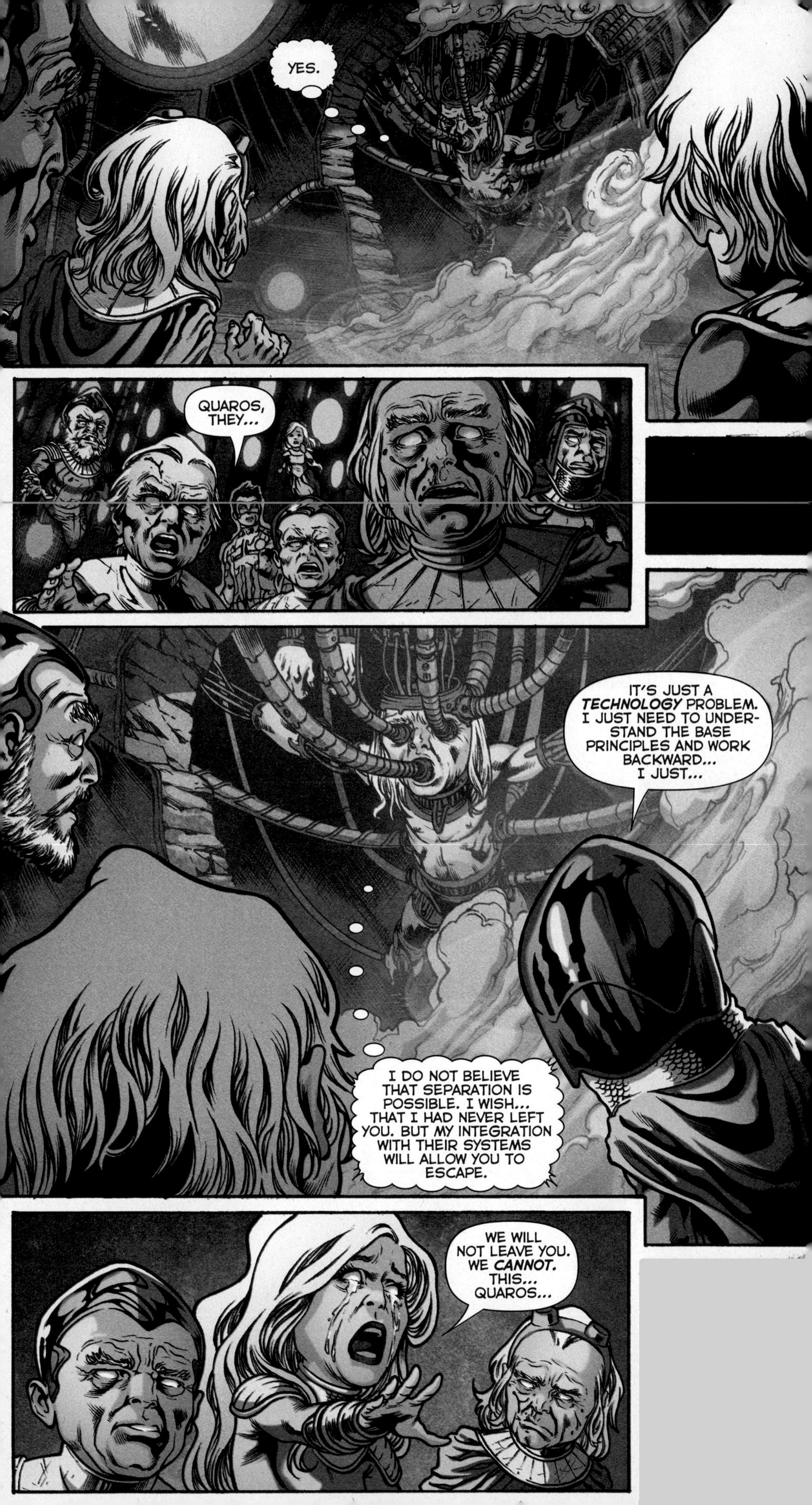
YES.
QUAROS, THEY...
IT'S JUST A *TECHNOLOGY* PROBLEM. I JUST NEED TO UNDER-STAND THE BASE PRINCIPLES AND WORK BACKWARD... I JUST...
I DO NOT BELIEVE THAT SEPARATION IS POSSIBLE. I WISH... THAT I HAD NEVER LEFT YOU. BUT MY INTEGRATION WITH THEIR SYSTEMS WILL ALLOW YOU TO ESCAPE.
WE WILL NOT LEAVE YOU. WE *CANNOT.* THIS... QUAROS...

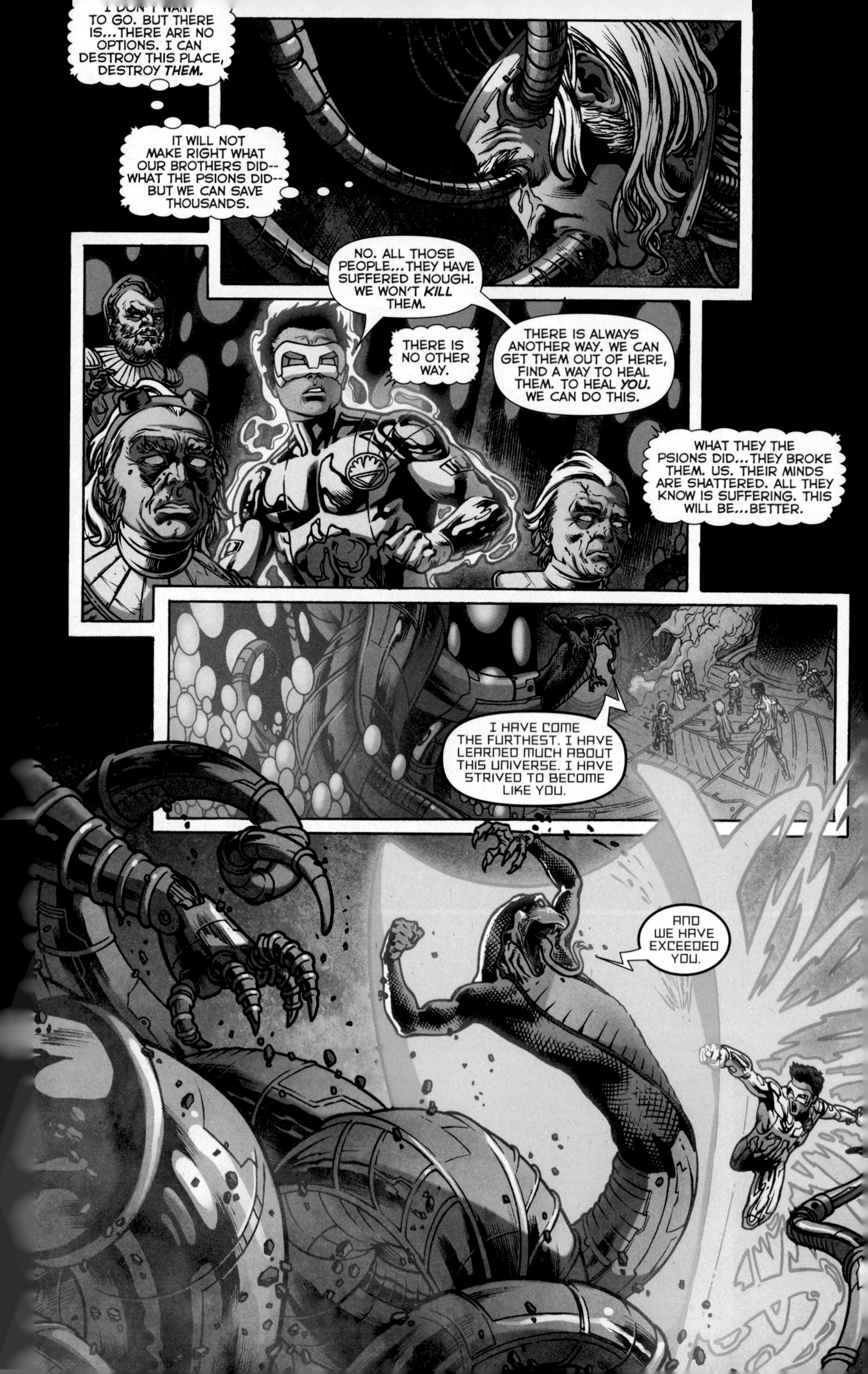
I DON'T WANT TO GO. BUT THERE IS...THERE ARE NO OPTIONS. I CAN DESTROY THIS PLACE, DESTROY *THEM.*
IT WILL NOT MAKE RIGHT WHAT OUR BROTHERS DID-- WHAT THE PSIONS DID-- BUT WE CAN SAVE THOUSANDS.
NO. ALL THOSE PEOPLE...THEY HAVE SUFFERED ENOUGH. WE WON'T *KILL* THEM.
THERE IS NO OTHER WAY.
THERE IS ALWAYS ANOTHER WAY. WE CAN GET THEM OUT OF HERE, FIND A WAY TO HEAL THEM. TO HEAL *YOU.* WE CAN DO THIS.
WHAT THEY THE PSIONS DID...THEY BROKE THEM. US. THEIR MINDS ARE SHATTERED. ALL THEY KNOW IS SUFFERING. THIS WILL BE...BETTER.
I HAVE COME THE FURTHEST. I HAVE LEARNED MUCH ABOUT THIS UNIVERSE. I HAVE STRIVED TO BECOME LIKE YOU.
AND WE HAVE EXCEEDED YOU.

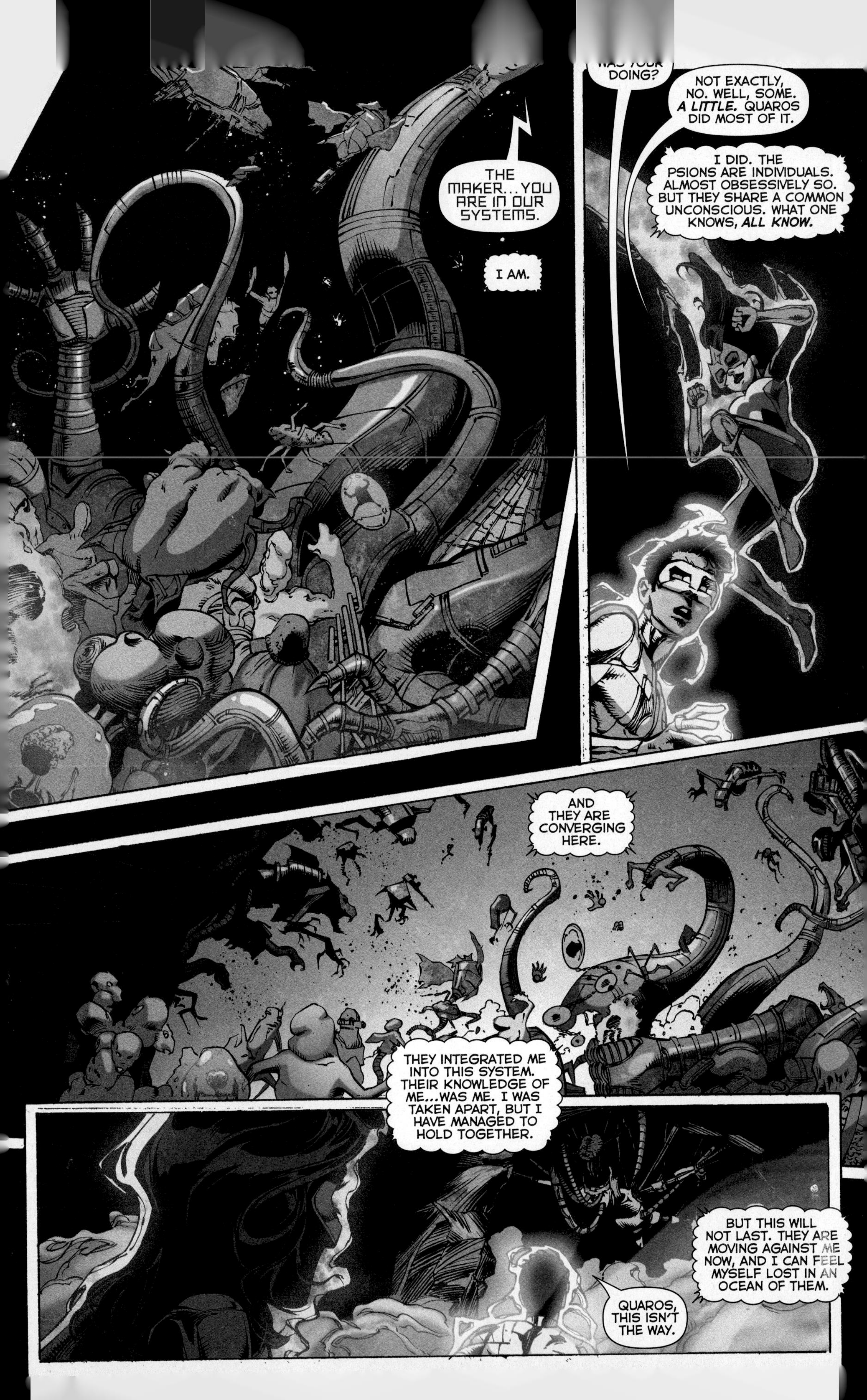
THE MAKER...YOU ARE IN OUR SYSTEMS.
I AM.
DOING?
NOT EXACTLY, NO. WELL, SOME. *A LITTLE.* QUAROS DID MOST OF IT.
I DID. THE PSIONS ARE INDIVIDUALS. ALMOST OBSESSIVELY SO. BUT THEY SHARE A COMMON UNCONSCIOUS. WHAT ONE KNOWS, *ALL KNOW.*
AND THEY ARE CONVERGING HERE.
THEY INTEGRATED ME INTO THIS SYSTEM. THEIR KNOWLEDGE OF ME...WAS ME. I WAS TAKEN APART, BUT I HAVE MANAGED TO HOLD TOGETHER.
BUT THIS WILL NOT LAST. THEY ARE MOVING AGAINST ME NOW, AND I CAN FEEL MYSELF LOST IN AN OCEAN OF THEM.
QUAROS, THIS ISN'T THE WAY.

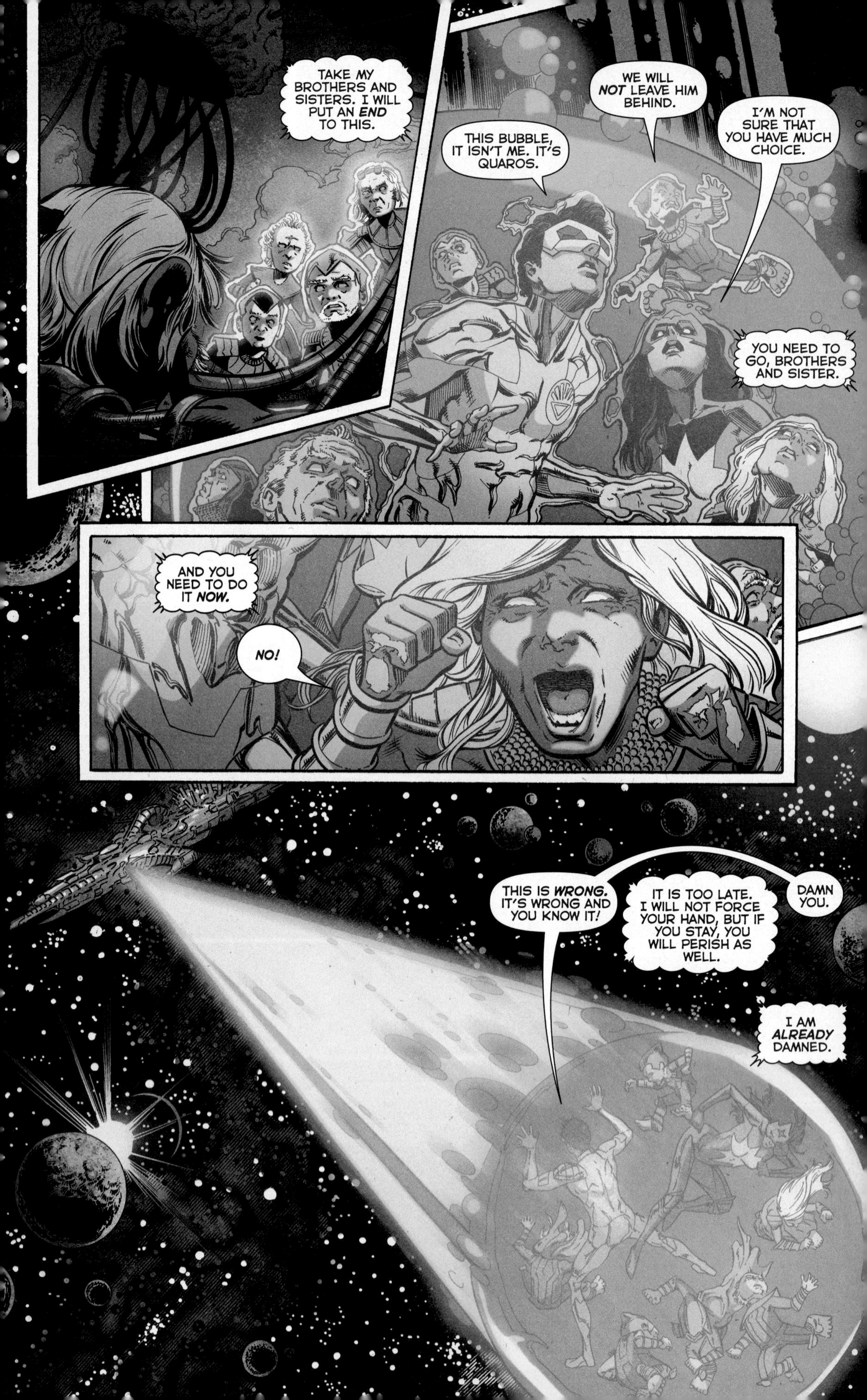
TAKE MY BROTHERS AND SISTERS. I WILL PUT AN *END* TO THIS.
THIS BUBBLE, IT ISN'T ME. IT'S QUAROS.
WE WILL *NOT* LEAVE HIM BEHIND.
I'M NOT SURE THAT YOU HAVE MUCH CHOICE.
YOU NEED TO GO, BROTHERS AND SISTER.
AND YOU NEED TO DO IT *NOW.*
NO!
THIS IS *WRONG.* IT'S WRONG AND YOU KNOW IT!
IT IS TOO LATE. I WILL NOT FORCE YOUR HAND, BUT IF YOU STAY, YOU WILL PERISH AS WELL.
DAMN YOU.
I AM *ALREADY* DAMNED.

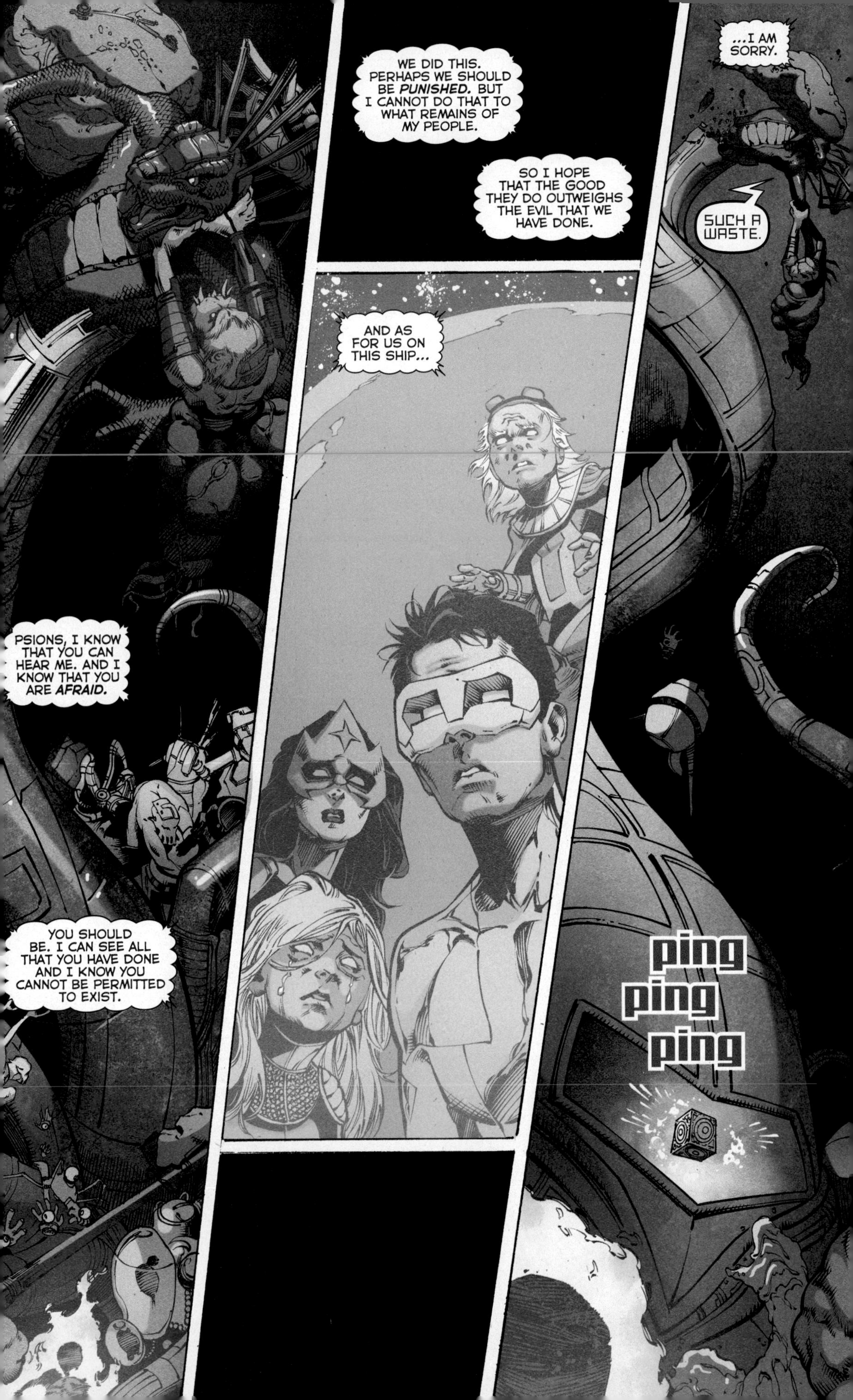
PSIONS, I KNOW THAT YOU CAN HEAR ME. AND I KNOW THAT YOU ARE *AFRAID.*
YOU SHOULD BE. I CAN SEE ALL THAT YOU HAVE DONE AND I KNOW YOU CANNOT BE PERMITTED TO EXIST.
WE DID THIS. PERHAPS WE SHOULD BE *PUNISHED.* BUT I CANNOT DO THAT TO WHAT REMAINS OF MY PEOPLE.
SO I HOPE THAT THE GOOD THEY DO OUTWEIGHS THE EVIL THAT WE HAVE DONE.
AND AS FOR US ON THIS SHIP...
...I AM SORRY.
SUCH A WASTE.
ping
ping
ping

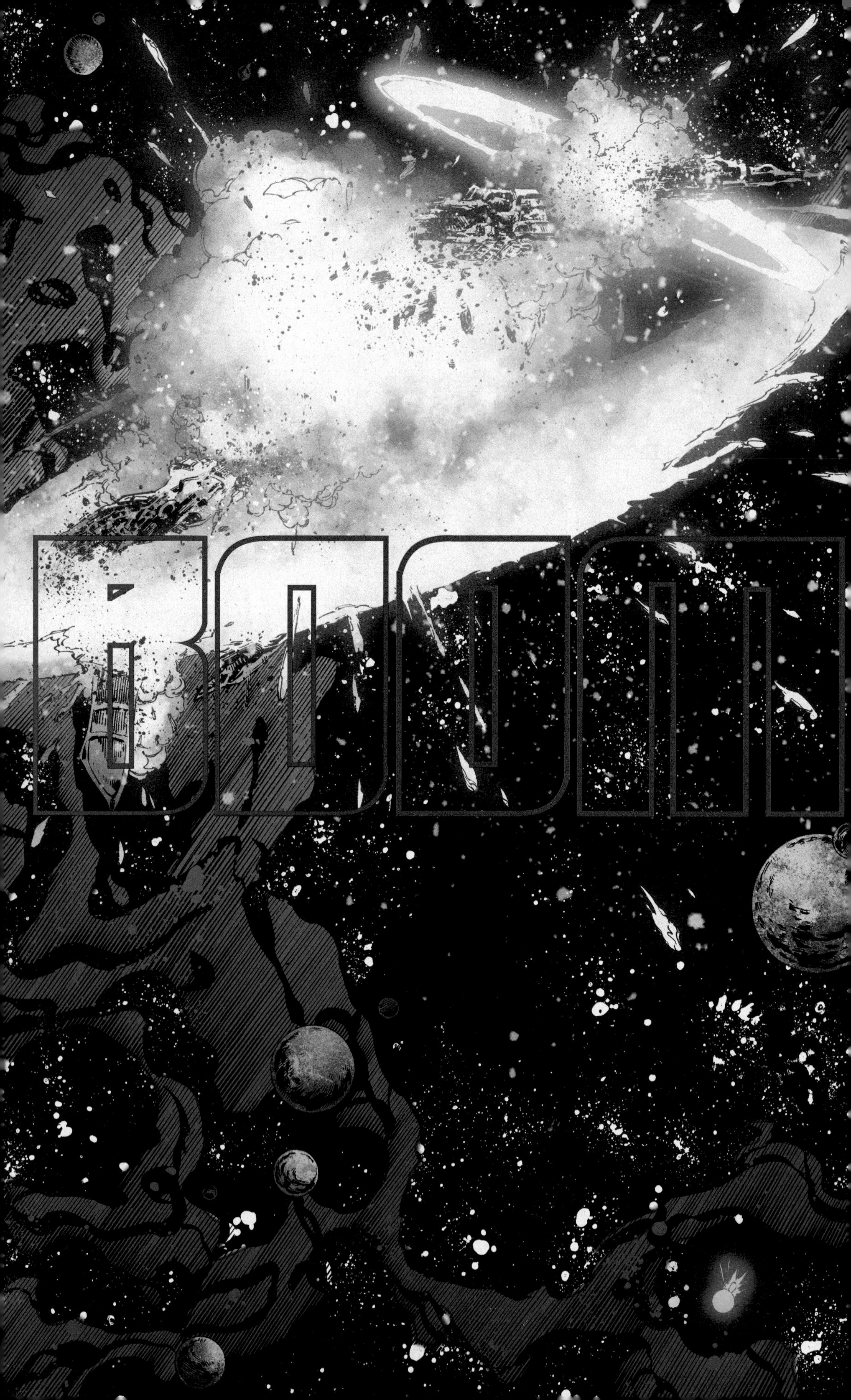
BOOM

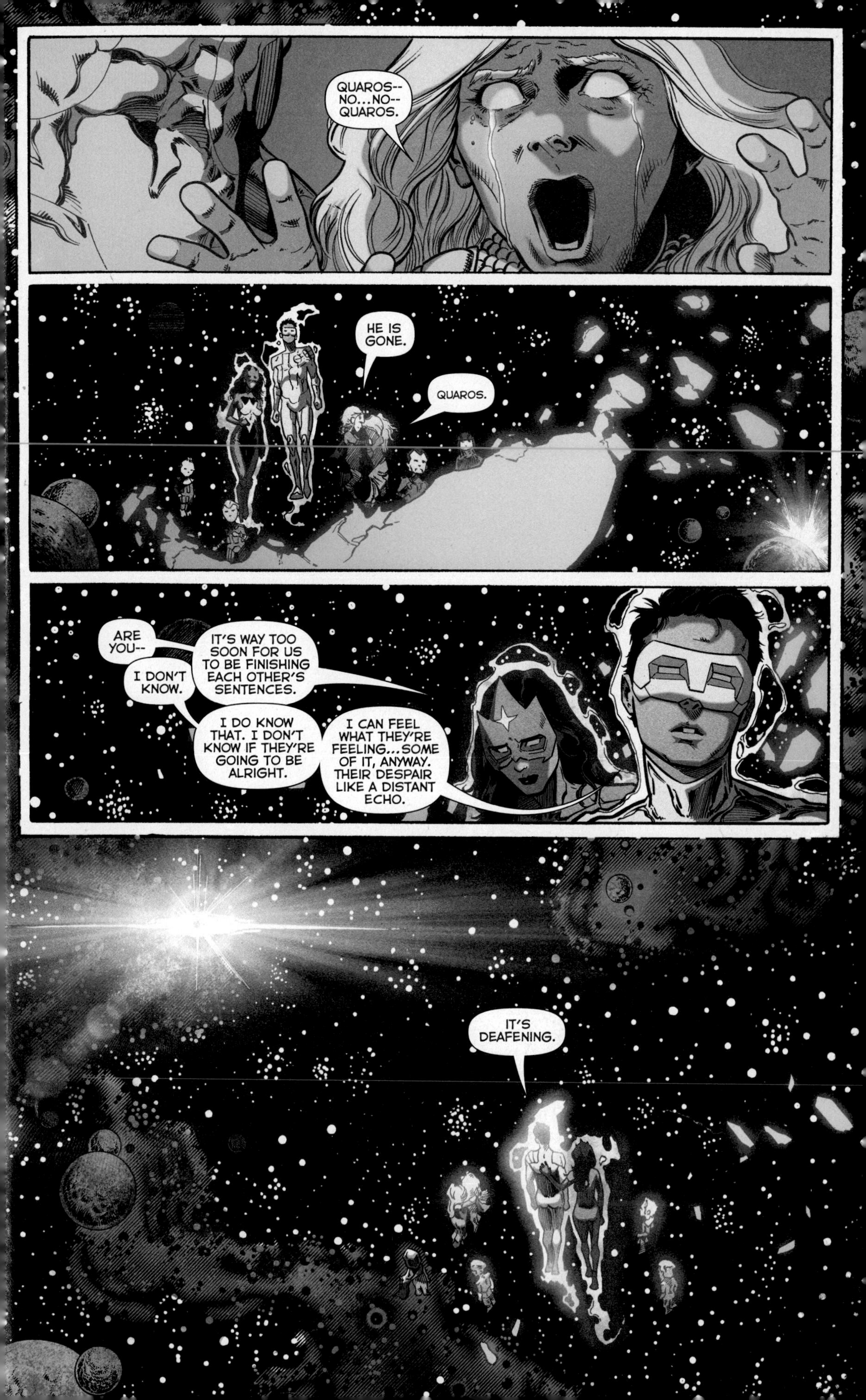
QUAROS-- NO...NO-- QUAROS.
HE IS GONE.
QUAROS.
ARE YOU--
IT'S WAY TOO SOON FOR US TO BE FINISHING EACH OTHER'S SENTENCES.
I DON'T KNOW.
I DO KNOW THAT. I DON'T KNOW IF THEY'RE GOING TO BE ALRIGHT.
I CAN FEEL WHAT THEY'RE FEELING...SOME OF IT, ANYWAY. THEIR DESPAIR LIKE A DISTANT ECHO.
IT'S DEAFENING.

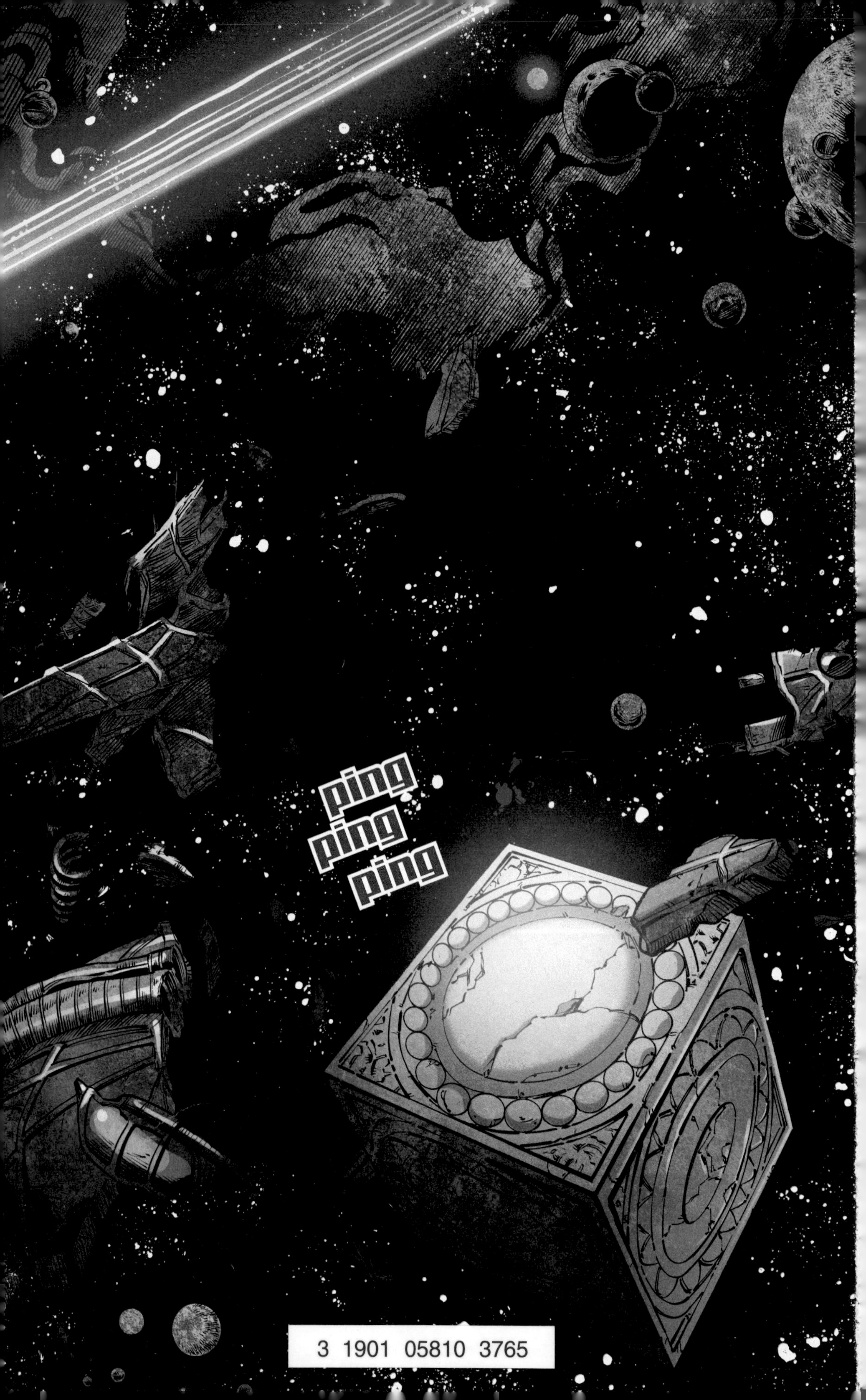
ping
ping
ping